Modern Germany in Transatlantic Perspective

Modern Germany in Transatlantic Perspective

Edited by
Michael Meng and Adam R. Seipp

berghahn
NEW YORK · OXFORD
www.berghahnbooks.com

Published in 2017 by

Berghahn Books

www.berghahnbooks.com

Library of Congress Cataloging-in-Publication Data

Names: Meng, Michael, editor of compilation. | Seipp, Adam R., editor of
compilation. | Jarausch, Konrad Hugo, honoree.
Title: Modern Germany in transatlantic perspective / edited by Michael Meng
and Adam R. Seipp.
Description: New York : Berghahn Books, [2017] | Includes bibliographical
references and index.
Identifiers: LCCN 2017037769 (print) | LCCN 2017041122 (ebook) |
ISBN 9781785337055 (ebook) | ISBN 9781785337048 (hardback : alk. paper)
Subjects: LCSH: Germany—Historiography—20th century. | Germany—
History—20th century. | Jarausch, Konrad Hugo.
Classification: LCC DD232.4 (ebook) | LCC DD232.4 .M64 2018 (print) |
DDC 943.087072—dc23
LC record available at https://lccn.loc.gov/2017037769

British Library Cataloguing in Publication Data

A catalogue record for this book is available from the British Library

ISBN 978-1-78533-704-8 hardback
ISBN 978-1-78533-705-5 ebook

Contents

Tables

Acknowledgments

We would like to thank each of our contributors for writing essays in honor of Konrad Jarausch. Also, we would like to thank Kacie Harris, a graduate student at Clemson University, for formatting the chapters for us, and James Burns and Paul Anderson for locating departmental funds to support her work. At Berghahn, Chris Chappell took a keen interest in the book and guided it through the review and editorial process. Finally, we thank Konrad Jarausch for being an outstanding teacher and mentor to so many students.

Introduction

From Ruination to Renewal
Konrad Jarausch's Europe

Michael Meng and Adam R. Seipp

Few contemporary historians have been more intensely involved in transatlantic conversations about the course of modern German history than Konrad Jarausch. This book honors his decades-long commitment to scholarly exchange across the Atlantic through chapters written by both colleagues who have worked closely with him over the years and by former students who have benefited from his remarkable gift of mentorship, known to his students by his uncanny ability to map out the intellectual interventions of a dissertation project on the spot. As one student recalled to another, Jarausch has the "extraordinary capacity for putting other people's thoughts in order. I would go to his office, find him jetlagged and buried under a stack of mail, lay out what I thought was a brilliant strategy for approaching my next chapter, and he would, off the top of his head, suggest a far more sensible approach."[1]

Jarausch's scholarly career has been shaped by a distinctive combination of breadth and focus. On the one hand, Jarausch seems to be in constant movement, literally and intellectually, in a dynamic interplay of transatlantic exchange about the past. The range of his intellectual interests in nineteenth- and twentieth-century German history and the diversity of the historical methods he has employed to study the past reflects not only a breadth of intellectual interest but also an openness to thinking about the past in fresh and creative ways. One might say that nearly every major debate about modern Germany over the past four decades has triggered some kind of intervention from Jarausch written from a desk in

Chapel Hill, Potsdam, or somewhere between the two. On the other hand, his core contribution to the field lies in the twentieth century and particularly in the post-1945 period. His pioneering work on West, East, and reunited Germany has sought to understand the complex ways in which Germany can be said to have recovered from Nazism during and after the Cold War. Jarausch's scholarship has been animated by the "German problem," as Thomas Mann put it in May 1945, including in regard to his own father's relationship to Nazism.[2]

Like other émigré historians of the postwar era, Jarausch brings to this problem a distinctly transatlantic perspective. One can see traces of this perspective in both his writing and his teaching, but perhaps most notably in his commitment to transatlantic academic exchange. Shuttling across the Atlantic several times per year, Jarausch has worked a great deal to develop and sustain institutional programs that bring North American and European scholars together to discuss the past. The list of his involvement in this area speaks for itself: he has played a central role in the intellectual activity of the Center for European Studies at The University of North Carolina at Chapel Hill; he has been actively involved in the German Studies Association (serving as its president in 1985–86); he has been one of the leading faculty members of the Berlin Program for Advanced German and European Studies at the Free University; and he was codirector of the Zentrum für Zeithistorische Forschung (ZZF) Potsdam from 1998 to 2006. While codirector of the ZZF, Jarausch lived between Chapel Hill in the fall and Berlin in the spring, although he always returned one week each spring during what his colleague, Christopher Browning, called *Konradwoche*, a week packed full of dissertation defenses and student meetings.

Reflecting his transatlantic work and his broad intellectual interests, we have commissioned essays from scholars on both sides of the Atlantic that capture both the wide scope and concentrated focus of Jarausch's work, with a particular emphasis on the post-1945 period, since that period has occupied his attention in a more sustained manner than any other, and it is within that period, we think, that his most distinctive interpretations can be found. The book includes chapters on protest cultures, gender policies in the university historical profession, migration, and German memory debates since 1989. Other chapters deepen Jarausch's contributions to the study of the professions, religion in the modern era, and historiographical approaches to the study of German history. A final two set of essays explore the problem of narrating personal family stories, reflecting Jarausch's own attempt to do so in *Reluctant Accomplice: A Wehrmacht Soldier's Letters from the Eastern Front* (2011). The chapters themselves are grouped into four unifying sections: theory and historiography; memory and professionalization; narratives of German history; and family histories. Together, the essays seek to engage creatively with some of the central themes that have animated Jarausch's thinking with the aim of not only honoring a teacher and colleague but also advancing further the discussion about modern German and European history that he has played an important role in fostering on both sides of the Atlantic.

When we began assembling this volume, we sought to achieve three primary aims. First, we wished to pay tribute to the career of a scholar who is still very active in the field and whose arguments continue to shape and inspire new generations of historians of Germany. This volume is thus not a retrospective on an academic career that has ended but a conversation among scholars from Europe and the United States whose intellectual trajectories have intersected with Jarausch's life and work.

Second, we wanted to bring together a group of authors from a range of academic backgrounds and cohorts. We solicited essays from senior scholars who have worked with Jarausch at some point during his long career, including some of his professional collaborators and others who had worked with him as colleagues. We also solicited essays from his many PhD students, ranging from recent graduates of The University of North Carolina at Chapel Hill back to his days at the University of Missouri. Not only does this volume include contributions from them, but also it features a collaboration between a student and one of his colleagues. Perhaps this collaborative piece speaks to how Jarausch's ideas and mentorship have generated collaboration across generations.

Finally, we commissioned essays that do not summarize Jarausch's intellectual contributions, but reflect on the ways his scholarship has shaped the field of modern German history and continues to do so. This is no small task, since his writing and teaching have touched on many of the major thematic and interpretive developments in the field since the late 1960s. In some ways, the responses we received affirm the current trends in German history. We found it notable, for example, that none of our authors proposed essays on the period before 1914. Aside from that exception, the essays in this volume follow Jarausch's career-long exploration of the political and intellectual history of modern Germany from a transatlantic perspective.

Konrad Jarausch's life story closely reflects the themes our volume addresses. In 2016, a panel at the annual meeting of the German Studies Association in San Diego considered Jarausch's recently published history of twentieth-century Europe. In his comments, Jarausch told the audience that "the history of the twentieth century is in many ways the history of my parents and of me." He was born in August 1941 in Magdeburg, the son of a Protestant theologian and a teacher. His father died of disease on the Eastern Front in early 1942, and the absence of his father shaped his personal and intellectual life, as he has noted when writing about his own trajectory.[3]

Raised by a single mother, Jarausch developed as a young intellectual when a generation of Germans in the Federal Republic began to question the attitudes and politics of their parents and grandparents. Seeking a different kind of education from what was on offer in Germany, he found himself in distant Wyoming, where he excelled as a student and began to develop an appreciation of the United States. This experience made him a keen observer of both the country of his birth and his second home, a mixture of engagement and critical distance that shaped him as a historian.

He completed his PhD at the University of Wisconsin at Madison under Theodore Hamerow, at the same time publishing his MA thesis as his first book.[4] His dissertation on Imperial Chancellor Theobald von Bethmann Hollweg launched his academic career, beginning at the University of Missouri.[5] From there, he initiated a series of interventions in two languages on two continents.

In the 1970s and early 1980s, Jarausch became a pioneer of techniques like quantitative history and the new social history that have become established parts of the historical canon. His scholarship focused on the development of professionals in Germany as a way to understand the formation and durability of German elites. He also moved from Missouri to North Carolina, where he began a new chapter in his academic career.

He developed a talent for translating—in the capacious sense of that word—ideas from German-speaking and English-speaking scholars for the benefit of the other. This is part of what defines Jarausch as a member of the historical profession. He has been involved in building institutions on both sides of the Atlantic that have been fundamental in shaping conversations among historians. There can be few scholars working today whose careers have not at some point intersected with the German Studies Association (of which he was an early member and president), the Friends of the German Historical Institute, the ZZF in Potsdam, or the Center for European Studies at The University of North Carolina at Chapel Hill, just to name a few.

The 1980s and 1990s saw Jarausch engaged in a sustained conversation about the development and demise of the German Democratic Republic, which in turn led to an interest in the intellectual and historiographical challenges of a united German state. When we studied with him at the turn of the millennium, he was wrestling with the problem of "master narratives" in German history and the equally thorny problem of explaining how Germany transitioned from dictatorship, murder, and defeat in 1945 to the liberal-democratic society of today with its attendant strengths and weaknesses. Over the past decade, he has turned his prodigious energy to understanding the history of his own family and the intellectual journey of his father, as well as to bringing many of the threads of his long career together in a general history of twentieth-century Europe.

It is to that general history of Europe in the twentieth century that we should like to begin this volume. In what follows, we consider Jarausch's attempt to analyze and narrate Europe's trajectory from ruination to renewal across the twentieth century.

Europe's "Benign Modernity"

To write an opening essay on Jarausch's work is no easy task given the sheer quantity and breadth of his oeuvre. We might be tempted to offer a grand summation of his work, following his intellectual trajectory from his first to his most recent book; we might produce a history of his histories that traces the continuities and discontinuities of his thought. Such an approach is of course common for volumes such as this one. Yet, Jarausch himself has already offered a developmental narrative of his work: he recently published an extensive overview of his intellectual development, an annotated bibliography of sorts, that we see no reason to supplant with one of our own.[6] Rather, we would like to offer some brief and general reflections on his most recently published book in order to consider his ongoing attempt to understand the "German problem" within a broader history of Europe's tumultuous twentieth century.

More than any other of his recent publications, *Out of Ashes: A New History of Europe in the Twentieth Century,* captures in one single volume his current intellectual concerns and overarching attempt to understanding modern European history. And, inspired by Jarausch's energetic commitment to critical dialogue about the past, our approach here is to engage with the book and write an essay that expands upon some of the themes in it. In so doing, we hope to make a modest historiographical contribution of our own or at the very least raise some questions that historians may find thought provoking; indeed, we can think of no better way to honor Jarausch than by seeking to advance the field of modern German and European history through a spirited reading of his work.

In *Out of Ashes,* Jarausch examines a central problem from four perspectives. First, he seeks to understand the "paradoxical trajectory of European history" during the twentieth century, exploring the continent's movement from extreme violence to relative peace over some one hundred years.[7] He explains this trajectory through the concept of modernity. While mindful of the difficulties that accompany this concept, Jarausch employs it to understand the competing ways that liberalism, fascism, and communism offered profoundly different ways of organizing society.[8] Second, he wishes to understand the particular role that Germany played in the conflict and stability of the twentieth century. To write German history for him is to write European history. The two go hand in hand and cannot be separated from each other.

Third, he spends a substantial amount of attention on the postwar period, especially the period after the collapse of communism by which point he believes that most of Europe had come to embrace a social democratic, liberal vision of modernization centered on the values of peaceful cooperation and social welfare for all. And, finally fourth, Jarausch views a liberal-democratic society centered around the values of peace and egalitarianism as offering the most politically acceptable and progressive approach to "master[ing] the dynamicism of modernity in order to realize its benign potential."[9] The book explicitly advances a normative claim about how European societies ought to govern themselves, uniquely combing historical analysis with a critical engagement with some of the most persistent challenges that the liberal-democratic order faces in the contemporary era. As Jarausch astutely recognizes, the two central values that divide Europeans, to this day, are equality and universalism: there are Europeans who oppose those ideals on the right, nationalists and fascists, while there are Europeans on the left who embrace them, if not in ways that always converge (hence, the split between Social Democrats and Communists over what precisely equality means).

Of these four tasks, the third and fourth tend to receive slightly greater emphasis from Jarausch, since understanding the continent's postwar history appears to him as a striking transformation that deserves to be explained analytically and defended politically. Social democracy deserves to be defended as the most "benign" form of modernity that European history has to offer, and its ascendancy after the war deserves to be explained because, according to Jarausch, it has hitherto not received the attention it deserves from historians and general commentators alike. If most historians have been concerned with understanding how and why Europe collapsed into ruination from 1914 to 1945, Jarausch seeks to understand how and why the continent moved out of ruination from 1945 to the present.

To be sure, Jarausch devotes half his book to the first half of the twentieth century; he pays serious attention to the destructive forces that led to war, genocide, and dictatorship in his attempt to understand the "competing conceptions of modernity" that have animated modern European history.[10] He makes it clear, though, where his emphasis lies. Jarausch's interpretation of the postwar period as a recovery from ruination distinguishes his book from other accounts of Europe's twentieth century.[11]

Indeed, Jarausch sees in the postwar period "the search for potential re-demption," much as he did in one of his other synthetic works, *After Hit-ler: Recivilizing Germans, 1945–1999.* The history he narrates conforms to the basic pattern of a salvation narrative defined by the movement from destruction to renewal.[12] As Jarausch explains in his preface: "This book charts the framework of destructive forces that killed relatives, destroyed homes, threatened livelihoods—in short turned entire worlds upside down. But it also offers an encouraging record of recovery, reconciliation, and emancipation that inspires hope for the future."[13] In short, the dis-tinctiveness of Jarausch's approach to studying twentieth-century German and European history hinges on what he views as Europe's "hopeful re-covery" after 1945.[14] The nature of this recovery, Jarausch claims, lies in the "restoration" of the political commitment and capacity to "master the dynamicism of modernity in order to realize its benign potential" after fascism and communism.[15] This kind of benign modernity did not emerge fully until after the collapse of Soviet communism when, so it seems, most of Europe came to embrace a peaceful and progressive vision of modern-ization after finally "learning the lessons of a murderous past."[16]

The adjective is important here: what does Jarausch mean precisely by benign? Jarausch does not offer a succinct definition. While he briefly dis-cusses his turn to the concept of modernity as the overarching framework for his book, he typically does not lay out in an explicit manner what he means by "benign modernity." Rather, the reader must infer his meaning from the history he tells about Europe's twentieth century.

Jarausch views twentieth-century European history as shaped by com-peting visions of the future offered by liberal democracy, Soviet commu-nism, and fascism. Each of these different political systems attempted to master modernity in different ways: fascism strove to create a new kind of civilization beyond the liberal-democratic order based on a radically violent and exclusive form of nationalism that excluded the proponents of liberal modernity from the national community. Communism was more complicated. While Soviet communism attempted to develop a new kind of society that would transcend the central contradictions of the modern era by abolishing class privileges, creating a planned economy, and ad-vancing technology, it became in reality a highly repressive regime under Stalin and, after his death, effectively turned into a massive bureaucratic machine that proved to be "a reform resistant dead-end."[17] In contrast, liberal democracy has attempted over the twentieth century to offer a po-litical system that allows for the development of individual freedoms, cre-ates an egalitarian society through social welfare programs, and nourishes international ties with other liberal-democratic states to advance a more peaceful and tolerant world.

As Jarausch shows in the first half of the book, this liberal-democratic vision of the future was rejected by both the right and the left as fundamentally erroneous for either its embrace of or definition of equality. Few other issues since the French Revolution have divided European politics more fiercely than equality. Fascism rejected the egalitarian principle of liberal democracy and supplanted it with a worldview that emphasized the centrality of nationalistic and racial struggle. Embracing a politics of violence, fascism promised to rescue the national community from its feared end in the "last man" of liberal modernity.[18] It aimed to preserve struggle as the essence of history against the liberal-democratic striving to end conflict in a peaceful and egalitarian society. In contrast, communism embraced equality as its bedrock principle, but argued that liberal democracy could never produce the egalitarian society it claimed to be creating. Liberal democracy was hobbled by having conceptualized human emancipation in the bourgeois terms of granting and protecting individual rights. Following Marx's radical critique of liberalism, European Communists believed that the kind of emancipation offered by liberal democracy would only continue to perpetuate inequality in a society still profoundly divided by self-interest. The divisions produced by self-interest had to be overcome in a new Communist society that would nourish communal bonds among all members of society and spread the fruits of technological innovation to all.

In the end, these two rivaling critiques of liberal democracy lost supporters in Europe over the course of the twentieth century. Whereas fascism was defeated on the battlefield, communism eventually collapsed after decades of political repression and economic incompetency. In his celebrated essay, the "Power of the Powerless," Václav Havel perceptively identified the repression of the human as a free, creative being as communism's downfall.[19] Added to the repression of the individual was the inability of the Communist system, as Jarausch emphasizes, to provide "the consumer goods that the public really wanted."[20] While other historians have noted this point before, perhaps the irony of communism's defeat by material self-interests has not been fully drawn out: Europeans in the Soviet bloc wanted things, or commodities in Marx's language, that they could own and enjoy.[21] Communism had not only failed to fulfill materialist desires but failed, more deeply, to overcome consumerist desires in the first place. Contrary to Marx's vision of the Communist future, real existing socialism never succeeded in overcoming bourgeois materialism by having failed to change social habits and desires.[22]

With the collapse of Soviet communism in 1989, liberal democracy seemed to stand triumphant, even leading some, such as Francis Fukuyama, to declare insouciantly that history had come to an end with the triumphant victory of liberal democracy. Jarausch certainly does not share this exuberant view of liberal democratic modernity; he is well aware of the many tensions and problems that Europe continues to face. Even so, he tends to see in the post-Communist spread of liberal democracy the arrival of a Europe that seems to have learned, if not all, then at least some of the lessons from its past. In this respect, he affirms Jürgen Habermas's conclusion that Europe—and not least of all Germany—can and has transformed itself in response to the catastrophes of the twentieth century.[23] Indeed, it is in having done so that Jarausch's concept of "benign modernity" comes to play a leading role: "the key lesson of a century of turmoil is therefore the need to master the dynamicism of modernity in order to realize its benign potential."[24]

This brings us back to our question: what is benign modernity? The closest Jarausch comes to stating a clear answer comes in his discussion of the European Economic Community, the institutional framework that would form the basis of the future European Union. In this chapter, it becomes clear that benign modernity represents a consensus of shared political principles that should govern and regulate European society. While these principles certainly existed prior to 1945 (and thus Jarausch often speaks of the "restoration" or "recapturing" of benign modernity), they became accepted as the regulative ideal for European politics and society only after the collapse of Nazism. As Jarausch explains:

> Traumatized by the triple disaster of the world wars, the Great Depression, and the collapse of democracy, the founders of the EEC essentially attempted to recapture the benign aspects of liberal modernity: overcoming the hostility between France and Germany would guarantee continental peace; economic cooperation based on market competition and freed trade would ensue future prosperity; and the establishment of supranational self-governing institutions would cement democracy.[25]

The emergence of such a consensus after 1945—and its expansion into Eastern Europe after the collapse of communism—shapes Jarausch's overall interpretation of postwar European history as one defined by lessons learned after a traumatic past; hence, a great deal hinges on his claim about the ostensibly thorough acceptance of liberal modernity in Europe. If Jarausch is right that democratic principles have found support among Europeans as never before in their history, his interpretation of postwar European history in light of them nevertheless faces two questions: have Europeans lived up to the democratic aspirations they have set for themselves? And has benign modernity in fact become the consensus position in Europe that Jarausch suggests it has?

Jarausch deals with these questions directly in a number of chapters but especially in those on decolonization, revolts against modernity, and global challenges. The postwar history of the collapse of European empire poses a serious challenge to the extent to which Europeans have lived up to the principles of benign modernity, whereas the history of contemporary challenges and protests to liberal modernity raise significant questions about the breadth of that consensus.

In a chapter titled "Disappointing Decolonization," Jarausch sets out to steer between the "anti-imperialist" critique of postcolonialism and the "apologetics" of imperial defenders by illuminating the complex process through which national liberation took place.[26] He notes a central ambivalence to postcolonialism itself. Whereas the desire for national liberation sought to free itself from European domination, it ended up retaining a number of European traditions that remained as a legacy of empire. National liberation only went so far, a development that Jarausch appears to view positively: "the process of decolonization therefore involved a selective rejection *and* retention of the European legacy, which led to the creation of a new hybrid of postcolonial modernity."[27]

While Jarausch's account of decolonization focuses on its causes, challenges, and legacies, it also stresses the violent response of the European powers to national liberation in such places as India, Algeria, Kenya, and Angola, among others. If one must be careful not to reduce decolonization to violence, it is nevertheless of particular importance to Jarausch's argument, since a number of Europeans reacted to (post)colonial violence with a chastened appraisal of Europe's commitment to "benign modernity." Powerful examples that come to mind include Antonio Lobo Antunes's harrowing account of Portugal's bloody conflicts in Africa in *Os Cus de Judas* (1979) or Jean-Paul Sartre's polemic against the hypocrisies of Europe's commitment to universalism in light of imperial violence. Sartre wrote: "Let us quit this Europe which talks incessantly about Man while massacring him wherever it meets him, on every corner of its own streets, in every corner of the world. For centuries … in the name of a supposed 'spiritual adventure,' it has been suffocating almost the whole of humanity."[28]

Such critical voices of European civilization also receive attention in Jarausch's chapter on "revolts against modernity." Discussing the various protest cultures during the 1960s and 1970s on both sides of the Iron Curtain, Jarausch reconstructs the history of intellectual critiques against liberal and Communist modernity. His treatment of these critiques, especially in Western Europe, offers a particularly vivid description of Europeans who rejected the liberal consensus of benign modernity; one such example is the philosopher Herbert Marcuse, one of many brilliant students trained by Martin Heidegger. A German Jew who escaped from Nazi Germany in 1933 and settled in the United States for the rest of his life, Marcuse became one of the most trenchant and creative Marxist voices of the postwar era.

While he was part of the Frankfurt School, Marcuse eschewed the pessimism of his colleagues Max Horkheimer and Theodor W Adorno. Marcuse believed that the possibility of a revolutionary break from liberal capitalism was not only possible but also desperately needed now when the consumerist capitalism of the postindustrial era was turning the human into little more than a consuming being. The benign modernity of the postwar era was hardly benign in Marcuse's view, for it represented the colonization of the life and the mind of the human being by bourgeois society. Even the working class, which could now afford more consumer goods than ever before thanks to global capitalism, had been captured by the bourgeois belief that human freedom existed in ownership and consumption. Yet all hope was not lost for Marcuse. Critical theory could resist bourgeois domination and nourish the possibility of revolutionary change, so Marcuse argued in *An Essay on Liberation* (1969). Written at the height of the student protests, Marcuse believed that far-reaching change might be at bay. "For the world of human freedom cannot be built by the established societies, no matter how much they may streamline and rationalize their dominion," he wrote. "Their class structure, and the perfected controls required to sustain it, generate needs, satisfactions, and values which reproduce the servitude of the human existence."[29] Servitude to materialism might be coming to an end, or so Marcuse hoped.

Critiques of liberal modernity also came from the right but for different reasons. For the right, the problem was not the exploitative nature of capitalism and the goal was not the creation of a more egalitarian community. On the contrary, the problem was "minorities," and the solution was ethno-cultural nationalism. From the 1970s onward, a resurgence of ethno-cultural nationalism unfolded across parts of the European continent. In Western Europe, the context for the rise of nationalism was largely the growing diversification of European societies thanks to labor, asylum, and postcolonial migration since the 1950s.[30] In Eastern Europe, the context was significantly different in places such as Yugoslavia where the death of Tito in 1980 led to a power struggle that ended up favoring the ethno-cultural Serbian nationalist Slobodan Milošević who, when communism collapsed, unleashed horrific violence in Southeastern Europe.

While that kind of violent nationalism has so far proven to be an exception in post-1945 European history, the exclusive imagination of the nation that underpins it has been less than exceptional. Since the 1990s, there has been a significant growth in right-wing nationalistic parties across Europe, with Germany being an exception.[31] Yet the German case is complicated because, while it has not yet seen a nationalistic party successfully appeal to the national electorate, ethno-cultural nationalism has nevertheless shaped discussions about migrants there like everywhere else in Europe.[32] In this sense, very few places in Europe seem immune to right-wing politics and nationalistic arguments against the international democratic order as the recent vote in the United Kingdom to leave the European Union has demonstrated perhaps most surprisingly. Just days after Britain's vote, Marine Le Pen, president of France's National Front party, wrote an op-ed piece for *The New York Times:* "The European Union Has Become a Prison of Peoples." Transnationalism, she explained, was capturing Europeans. "And what about the European Parliament? It's democratic in appearance only, because it's based on a lie: the pretense that there is a homogeneous European people, and that a Polish member of the European Parliament has the legitimacy to make law for the Spanish."[33]

As Jarausch notes, this "ugly nativist backlash" poses one of the most persistent challenges to the moderate politics of benign modernity, since egalitarianism and universalism remain its foundational principles.[34] If ethno-cultural nationalism continues to gain support as it has over the past several years, then the greatest threat to liberal modernity will once again come from the right, not the left.

A Chastened Modernity, A Chastened Germany

Despite the challenges liberal modernity has faced since the 1960s, Jarausch remains impressed by the transformation that Europe—and particularly Germany—has undergone since 1945. Germany today stands as one of the strongest supporters of universalism in the world, a position that has been strengthened in the wake of Britain's vote to exit the European Union and the election of Donald Trump as president of the United States. This transformation is striking in view of the much different Germany that Jarausch left when he came to the United States in 1960 where be discovered his passion for the study of history while studying American studies at the University of Wyoming. He began his career as a professional historian attempting to understand why Germany collapsed into a dictatorship of war and genocide. While his effort to understand German history certainly stimulated a tremendous output of scholarship, it has been neither for him, nor for many of his colleagues on both sides of the Atlantic, merely an academic exercise in deepening historical knowledge. It has also been a deeply political exploration, confirming Theodoro W Adorno's belief that "history is possible only as the philosophy of history."[35] To ask, as Jarausch did in his early work, why nationalistic aggression had triumphed in Germany or why liberalism had failed was also to ask about the political strengths and weaknesses of both in the present.[36] In an interesting way, then, Jarausch contributed to the postwar history that he now analyzes, since he, like others of his generation, critiqued German nationalism by studying its past. By writing history, Jarausch has engaged in what Thomas Mann called "German self-criticism" and, like Mann, he has done so from his perspective as an émigré versed in both North American and European cultures.[37] Underlying this self-critical effort exists an appreciation for the role history plays in human life more broadly. Jarausch believes that societies can learn from their pasts, and here he recasts for the postwar context the old idea that history is to be life's teacher, *historia magistra vitae* in Cicero's words. Tellingly, he ends his book with two sections titled "lessons of history" and "the European alternative."[38]

One lesson stands out as particularly novel, the main lesson told in his book: "The bloody course of the twentieth century taught the Europeans a chastened outlook on modernity—a lesson some overconfident Americans have yet to learn."[39] If not all historians will agree with Jarausch on this point in light of the sheer complexity of contemporary European history that we touched on earlier, the argument in its own right is striking, especially the juxtaposition to the United States. As in his teaching, so too here in this work, more so than in any other, Jarausch brings North America and Europe into conversation with each other.

To speak of differences between the United States and Europe has by now become platitudinous, but Jarausch gestures at something beyond the clichés. He sees an important difference between how the United States and Europe currently comport themselves toward their respective pasts. At least generally speaking, parts of Europe and the United States deal with the lessons of their history in notably different ways at the present moment. Since the 1980s, Europe's catastrophic past has prompted efforts by some Europeans—particularly those on the left—to develop a kind of "postnational" memory culture that critically engages with their nation's history and rejects the glorious myths of the nation that have often underpinned nationalistic violence. In contrast, a public confrontation with the racist violence of the past seems far more hesitant in the United States where patriotic attachments to the nation generally dominate.

Whereas Europe has been chastened by its history, the United States has been less interested in reflecting on the errors of its past. The effect of this divergence seems clear to Jarausch: Europe has sought to learn the lessons of excessive pursuits of ambition and self-interest, whereas the United States has been less inclined to do so.[40] To describe Europe's transformation, Jarausch turns to Goethe's *Faust*. We would like to offer a slightly different take on his point by invoking another commanding writer from the European past, Thucydides. If we look at the issue from the *longue durée*, we might say that Europe tends to act more like Sparta since 1945, while the United States tends to emulate itself more after Athens. Thucydides developed this famous dichotomy in his monumental study of the Peloponnesian War. In the so-called archaeology of book one, he identifies two different kinds of societies or ways of living. Athens represents human ambition and grandeur, while Sparta stands for modesty and simplicity; Sparta recognizes the fragility of human existence, while Athens seeks to overcome human vulnerability through monumental architecture and imperial pursuits. In a very different time period, Jarausch sees in contemporary Europe a place that, by recognizing the sufferings of history, now strives to embrace a more chastened approach to political life in the hope of building a more peaceful century than the one that has just passed. He sees in contemporary Europe a history worth telling for Americans and Europeans alike.

Michael Meng is an associate professor of history at Clemson University. He is the author of *Shattered Spaces: Encountering Jewish Ruins in Postwar Germany and Poland*.

Adam Seipp is a professor of history at Texas A&M University and author of *Strangers in the Wild Place: Refugees, Americans, and a German Town, 1945–1952*.

Notes

1. Elizabeth Heineman, "Crossing the Atlantic Divide with the Carrboro School: An Appreciation of Konrad Jarausch" (Washington, DC, 17 November 2006), 4.
2. Thomas Mann, *Germany and the Germans* (Washington, DC, 1945), 2.
3. Biographical details are taken from Konrad H Jarausch, "Contemporary History as Transatlantic Project: The German Problem, 1960–2010," *Historical Social Research*, no. 24 (2012): 7–49.
4. Konrad H Jarausch, *The Four Power Pact, 1933* (Madison, WI, 1966).
5. Konrad H Jarausch, *The Enigmatic Chancellor: Bethmann Hollweg and the Hubris of Imperial Germany* (New Haven, CT, 1973).

6. Jarausch, "Contemporary History as Transatlantic Project."

7. Konrad H Jarausch, *Out of Ashes: A New History of Europe in the Twentieth-Century* (Princeton, NJ, 2015), vii.

8. "Historians and the Question of Modernity," *The American Historical Review* 116, no. 3 (2011): 631–751.

9. Jarausch, *Out of Ashes,* 16.

10. Ibid., 12.

11. Jarausch himself distinguishes himself chiefly from the accounts written by Mark Mazower and Erich Hobsbawm.

12. See Karl Löwith, *Meaning in History* (Chicago, 1949).

13. Jarausch, *Out of Ashes,* viii.

14. The first half of the book on the period from 1900 to 1945 offers a conventional narrative of Europe's collapse into ruination that one would be hard pressed to identify as distinctive. Jarausch moves from the history of European imperial hegemony to the Great War to fascism to World War II. He ties this history together by exploring the different visions of "modernity" offered by liberalism, Soviet communism, and fascism before then turning to the ascendancy of a social democratic, liberal form of modernity after 1945.

15. Jarausch, *Out of Ashes,* 16.

16. Ibid., 16.

17. Ibid., 449.

18. The "last man" of bourgeois civilization as described by Nietzsche in *Thus Spoke Zarathustra,* trans. Adrian Del Caro, ed. Adian Del Caro and Robert B Pippin (New York, 2006), 9–10.

19. Václav Havel, *Open Letters: Selected Writings, 1965–1990* (New York, 1992), 125–214.

20. Jarausch, *Out of Ashes,* 671.

21. This continuance of commodity fetishism in the Soviet Bloc is not the only irony of Soviet communism. Another important one is the inability of communism to overcome patriarchy. See Donna Harsch, *Revenge of the Domestic: Women, the Family, and Communism in the German Democratic Republic* (Princeton, NJ, 2007); Malgorzata Fidelis, *Women, Communism, and Industrialization in Postwar Poland* (New York, 2010).

22. A compelling study of this problem is Paul Bett's study on everyday consumer life in East Germany, which ultimately attempted to provide what one would be hard pressed not to identify as an essentially bourgeois life for its citizens but failed to do so. The failure of the state began, however, the very moment that it accepted, rather than continuing to resist, the consumerism of late capitalism. See Paul Betts, *Within Walls: Private Life in the German Democratic Republic* (New York, 2010).

23. See Jürgen Habermas, *The New Conservatism: Cultural Criticism and the Historians' Debate,* ed. and trans. Shierry Weber Nicholsen (Cambridge, MA, 1990).

24. Jarausch, *Out of Ashes,* 16.

25. Ibid., 508–9.

26. Ibid., 482.

27. Ibid., 483. See also page 505 where Jarausch reiterates this positive evaluation of decolonization.

28. Jean Pau-Sartre, *Colonialism and Neocolonialism,* trans. Azzedine Haddour, Steve Brewer, and Terry McWilliams (New York, 2001), 76.

29. Herbert Marcuse, *An Essay on Liberation* (Boston, MA, 1969), 6.

30. An impressive overview of this issue can be found in Klaus J Bade, Pieter C Emmer, Leo Lucassen, and Jochen Oltmer, eds, *The Encyclopedia of Migration and Minorities in Europe* (Cambridge, 2011).

31. David Art, *Inside the Radical Right: The Development of Anti-Immigrant Parties in Western Europe* (Cambridge, 2011).

32. Rita Chin et al., *After the Nazi Racial State: Difference and Democracy in Germany and Europe* (Ann Arbor, MI, 2009); Heide Fehrenbach, *Race after Hitler: Black Occupation Children in Postwar Germany and America* (Princeton, NJ, 2005); Sara Lennox, "Divided Feminism: Women, Racism, and German National Identity," *German Studies Review* 18, no. 3 (1995): 481–502; Uta G Poiger, *Jazz, Rock, and Rebels: Cold War Politics and American Culture in Divided Germany* (Berkeley, CA, 2000). On German discourses on integration, migration, and foreigners, see Klaus J Bade, *Ausländer — Aussiedler — Asyl in der Bundesrepublik Deutschland* (Hannover, 1992); Rita Chin, *The Guest Worker Question in Postwar Germany* (New York, 2007); Chin et al., *After the Racial State*; Katherine Pratt Ewing, *Stolen Honor: Stigmatizing Muslim Men in Berlin* (Palo Alto, CA, 2008); Deniz Göktürk, David Gramling, and Anton Kaes, eds, *Germany in Transit: Nation and Migration, 1955–2005* (Berkeley, CA, 2007); Ulrich Herbert, *Geschichte der Ausländerpolitik in Deutschland: Saisonarbeiter, Zwangsarbeiter, Gastarbeiter, Flüchtlinge* (Munich, 2001); Karin Hunn, *"Nächstes Jahr kehren wir zurück ..." Die Geschichte der türkischen "Gastarbeiter" in der Bundesrepublik* (Göttingen, 2005); Leo Lucassen, *The Immigration Threat: The Integration of Old and New Migrants in Western Europe since 1850* (Urbana, IL, 2005); Ruth Mandel, *Cosmopolitan Anxieties: Turkish Challenges to Citizenship and Belonging in Germany* (Durham, NC, 2008); Monika Mattes, *"Gastarbeiterinnen" in der Bundesrepublik: Anwerbepolitik, Migration und Geschlecht in den 50er bis 70er Jahren* (Frankfurt, 2005); Karen Schönwälder, *Einwanderung und ethnische Pluralität. Politische Entscheidungen und öffentliche Debatten in Grossbritannien und der Bundesrepublik von den 1950er bis zu den 1970er Jahren* (Essen, 2001).

33. Marine Le Pen, "After Brexit, the People's Spring Is Inevitable," *The New York Times*, 28 June 2016.

34. Jarausch, *Out of Ashes*, 735.

35. Theodor W Adorno, *History and Freedom: Lectures 1964–1965*, ed. Rolf Tiedemann, trans. Rodney Livingstone (Malden, MA, 2006), 10.

36. On the politics of writing history in the early Federal Republic, see James Sheehan, "Paradigm Lost? The 'Sonderweg' Revisited," in *Transnationale Geschichte: Themen, Tendenzen und Theorien*, ed. Gunilla Budde, Sebastian Conrad, and Oliver Janz (Göttingen, 2006), 150–60. Jarausch's first major monograph, a revision of his dissertation completed at the University of Wisconsin at Madison, intervened in the Fischer controversy through a study of Hollweg. Jarausch, *The Enigmatic Chancellor*.

37. Mann, *Germany and the Germans*, 19.

38. Jarausch, *Out of Ashes*, 787.

39. Ibid., 784.

40. As Jarausch puts it in his preface, Europe after 1945 rejected part one of Goethe's *Faust* for part two.

Bibliography

Adorno, Theodor W. *History and Freedom: Lectures 1964–1965*, edited by Rolf Tiedemann, translated by Rodney Livingstone. Malden, MA: Polity, 2006.

Art, David. *Inside the Radical Right: The Development of Anti-Immigrant Parties in Western Europe.* Cambridge: Cambridge University Press, 2011.

Bade, Klaus J. *Ausländer — Aussiedler — Asyl in der Bundesrepublik Deutschland.* Hannover: Niedersächsische Landeszentrale für politische Bildung, 1992.

Bade, Klaus J, Pieter C Emmer, Leo Lucassen, and Jochen Oltmer, eds. *The Encyclopedia of Migration and Minorities in Europe.* Cambridge: Cambridge University Press, 2011.

Betts, Paul. *Within Walls: Private Life in the German Democratic Republic.* New York: Oxford University Press, 2010.

Chin, Rita. *The Guest Worker Question in Postwar Germany.* New York: Cambridge University Press, 2007.

Chin, Rita, Heide Fehrenbach, Geoff Eley, and Atina Grossman. *After the Nazi Racial State: Difference and Democracy in Germany and Europe.* Ann Arbor: University of Michigan Press, 2009.

Ewing, Katherine Pratt. *Stolen Honor: Stigmatizing Muslim Men in Berlin.* Palo Alto, CA: Stanford University Press, 2008.

Fehrenbach, Heide. *Race after Hitler: Black Occupation Children in Postwar Germany and America.* Princeton, NJ: Princeton University Press, 2005.

Fidelis, Malgorzata. *Women, Communism, and Industrialization in Postwar Poland.* New York: Cambridge University Press, 2010.

Göktürk, Deniz, David Gramling, and Anton Kaes, eds. *Germany in Transit: Nation and Migration, 1955–2005.* Berkeley: University of California Press, 2007.

Habermas, Jürgen. *The New Conservatism: Cultural Criticism and the Historians' Debate.* Edited and translated by Shierry Weber Nicholsen. Cambridge, MA: MIT Press, 1990.

Harsch, Donna. *Revenge of the Domestic: Women, the Family, and Communism in the German Democratic Republic.* Princeton, NJ: Princeton University Press, 2007.

Havel, Václav. *Open Letters: Selected Writings, 1965–1990.* New York: Vintage, 1992.

Heineman, Elizabeth. "Crossing the Atlantic Divide with the Carrboro School: An Appreciation of Konrad Jarausch." Washington, DC: German Historical Institute, 17 November 2006.

Herbert, Ulrich. *Geschichte der Ausländerpolitik in Deutschland: Saisonarbeiter, Zwangsarbeiter, Gastarbeiter, Flüchtlinge.* Munich: Beck, 2001.

"Historians and the Question of Modernity." *The American Historical Review* 116, no. 3 (2011): 631–751.

Hunn, Karin. *"Nächstes Jahr kehren wir zurück ..." Die Geschichte der türkischen "Gastarbeiter" in der Bundesrepublik.* Göttingen: Wallstein, 2005.

Jarausch, Konrad H. "Contemporary History as Transatlantic Project: The German Problem, 1960–2010." *Historical Social Research,* no. 24 (2012): 7–49.

———. *The Enigmatic Chancellor: Bethmann Hollweg and the Hubris of Imperial Germany.* New Haven, CT: Yale University Press, 1973.

———. *The Four Power Pact, 1933.* Madison: State Historical Society of Wisconsin, 1966.

———. *Out of Ashes: A New History of Europe in the Twentieth-Century.* Princeton, NJ: Princeton University Press, 2015.

Lennox, Sara. "Divided Feminism: Women, Racism, and German National Identity." *German Studies Review* 18, no. 3 (1995): 481–502.

Le Pen, Marine. "After Brexit, the People's Spring Is Inevitable." *The New York Times,* 28 June 2016.

Löwith, Karl. *Meaning in History.* Chicago: University of Chicago Press, 1949.

Lucassen, Leo. *The Immigration Threat: The Integration of Old and New Migrants in Western Europe since 1850.* Urbana: University of Illinois, 2005.

Mandel, Ruth. *Cosmopolitan Anxieties: Turkish Challenges to Citizenship and Belonging in Germany.* Durham, NC: Duke University Press, 2008.

Mann, Thomas. *Germany and the Germans.* Washington, DC: The Library of Congress, 1945.

Marcuse, Herbert. *An Essay on Liberation.* Boston, MA: Beacon, 1969.

Mattes, Monika. *"Gastarbeiterinnen" in der Bundesrepublik: Anwerbepolitik, Migration und Geschlecht in den 50er bis 70er Jahren.* Frankfurt: Campus Verlag, 2005.

Nietzsche, Friedrich. *Thus Spoke Zarathustra.* Translated by Adrian Del Caro, edited by Adian Del Caro and Robert B Pippin. New York: Cambridge University Press, 2006.

Pau-Sartre, Jean. *Colonialism and Neocolonialism.* Translated by Azzedine Haddour, Steve Brewer, and Terry McWilliams. New York: Routledge, 2001.

Poiger, Uta G. *Jazz, Rock, and Rebels: Cold War Politics and American Culture in Divided Germany.* Berkeley: University of California Press, 2000.

Schönwälder, Karen. *Einwanderung und ethnische Pluralität. Politische Entscheidungen und öffentliche Debatten in Grossbritannien und der Bundesrepublik von den 1950er bis zu den 1970er Jahren.* Essen: Klartext, 2001.

Sheehan, James. "Paradigm Lost? The 'Sonderweg' Revisited." In *Transnationale Geschichte: Themen, Tendenzen und Theorien,* edited by Gunilla Budde, Sebastian Conrad, and Oliver Janz, 150–60. Göttingen: Vandenhoeck & Ruprecht, 2006.

Part I

Theory and Historiography Questions

Chapter 1

History and Theory
Writing Modern European Histories after the Linguistic Turn

Thomas Pegelow Kaplan

A t a basic level, the study of language is at the center of the academic practice of history. Even the most empirically and positivist-oriented historians tackle issues of language use and the meaning of words in their application of the historical-critical method that evolved with the professionalization of the field in the course of the nineteenth century. Early practitioners of historical methodologies borrowed widely from neighboring fields with an explicit focus on language such as philology. Leopold von Ranke, one of the historical method's most ardent initial advocates, for instance, underwent formal training as a philologist and not as a historian.[1] Reflecting the importance of language, some historians have established the study of linguistic questions as a veritable subfield within the discipline. In postwar West Germany, the project of "conceptual history" (*Begriffsgeschichte*) by scholars such as Reinhart Koselleck and Otto Brunner is one vital example.[2] These historians' impressive multivolume project of "Basic Historical Concepts" (*Geschichtliche Grundbegriffe*) detailed the evolution of key sociopolitical concepts at the cusp of modernity based on the assumption that these concepts had an impact on the transformation of social and political structures.[3] The development of discourse analysis by historians like Régine Robin in 1960s and 1970s France that was informed by quantitative history constitutes another key initiative.[4] Her introduction of discourse analysis integrated linguistic and social-historical approaches without, however, giving up on the ma-

---

Notes for this chapter begin on page 38.

teriality of discourses or implying that language could be fully controlled by individual subjects.[5]

By and large, these approaches remained on the margins of the discipline until the late 1980s, when professional historians in North America and Western Europe, finally, had to confront the profound challenges of the "linguistic turn" that had preoccupied many of their colleagues in the humanities and social sciences for more than two decades. This shift to linguistic and discursive questions was part of a broader "cultural turn." In the academic study of history, this turn underpinned the growing dominance of a new cultural history in an explicit challenge to the previously preeminent practices of social and societal histories.[6] The array of theoretical perspectives bundled under the linguistic-turn label disrupted the conventional premise that language merely reflected an extra-discursive reality. Instead, language and systems of discourse had to be seen as productive and part of the constitution of reality, turning the very process of signification into a subject of analysis.

The ensuing debates unfolded in professional journals such as *Past and Present, History and Theory,* and *German Studies Review,* at academic conferences, and in PhD programs. Often bluntly equated with "poststructuralism" and "postmodernism," the linguistic turn and its initial proponents became the target of often-fierce attacks. Among practitioners of modern European history, many senior scholars, ranging from Hans-Ulrich Wehler to Gertrud Himmelfarb, were dismissive.[7] Some like Thomas Childers cautiously advocated a limited integration of insights and approaches.[8] Still others endorsed and experimented with linguistic-turn approaches as part of a broader rethinking of the study of history. Joan W Scott, for example, explicitly drew on Foucaultian thought on discourse and power/ knowledge to break down the language and production of knowledge of "natural" sexual difference and make the case for multilayered practices of gender history, while Michael Geyer and Konrad Jarausch seized on theorizations of metanarratives to disrupt any "single overarching story" of German history from the nation to Marxist-Leninist approaches in order to recover a "multiplicity of contending continuities."[9]

In their response to theoretical challenges such as the linguistic turn, historians of modern Europe hardly differ from their counterparts in the humanities. As the linguistic turn gave way to new "turns" such as the visual and transnational by the late 1990s, the attention to language subsided. Even after the polemical debates had given way to more nuanced and book-length elaborations on ways to rethink the practices of history, few of the ensuing monographs that grappled with the linguistic turn pushed its implications all too far or modified their source criticism. Even

Joan Scott's subsequent study of French feminism remained strikingly conventional in its analysis of sources.[10]

Reassessing the debates over, implications, and prospects of linguistic and discursive approaches, this essay, first, reflects on the notion of the linguistic turn, which emerged in distinct scholarly contexts and has often been distorted in later discussions. Second, it revisits some of the most pertinent debates of 1980s and 1990s among American and German practitioners of modern European history to demonstrate how scholars have understood the turn's challenges and to what extent they sought to integrate it into their research. Third, the article assesses the state of the field in recent years, i.e. "after" the height of the linguistic turn debates and ponders the practice of modern European history amid a proliferation of new turns. In their quest for novel approaches, historians of modern European, I argue, have left key potentials for a rethinking of their field and its approaches insufficiently explored. At a time, when Lynn Hunt's trenchant 2002 assessment of the "declin[e]" of "theory" in history and the humanities still rings true,[11] it is critical to take stock and ponder, as this essay begins to do in its final section, how rethought theorizations of language and discourse can further enhance the remaking of modern European histories beyond old and new reductionisms.

Defining the Linguistic Turn

"Who is afraid of the linguistic turn?" British historian James Vernon's 1994 tongue-and-cheek question to fellow social historians also brought the issue of what constituted this so-called turn into sharp relief.[12] In their belated reception, many historians of modern Europe readily tied the phenomenon to a number of prominent scholars outside the discipline, ranging from Jacques Derrida to Michel Foucault, which often distorted the theoretical and methodological challenges and, in some quarters, evoked long-established disciplinary defense mechanisms against allegedly unsound "French thought." The oversimplification and not always unintended imprecision, with which the notion has been introduced, makes it all the more necessary to begin this essay with some conceptual remarks about the linguistic turn.

The metaphor of "turn" or "turns," as Doris Bachmann-Medick has rightfully stressed, depicts an "increased incredulity" that prompts the discovery of new areas of study. Moreover, a turn captures the shift from objects of study to approaches and categories of analysis in ways that alter the scholarly understanding of reality.[13] In the reorientation of cultural studies and cultural sciences (*Kulturwissenschaften*) since the 1960s, the linguistic turn has played an especially important role, since the broader "cultural turn" unfolded on the basis of linguistic and discursive approaches. In this sense, the linguistic turn helped trigger the cultural turn, while also responding to much older intellectual challenges and debates about the instability of textual meaning, relativism, and subjectivity.[14]

Closely connected to the philosophy of language, the term "linguistic turn" itself emerged in the work of the Austrian-born American mathematician and philosopher Gustav Bergmann in the 1950s. In turning against positivist and materialist approaches, Bergmann developed an "ideal-language" method that required a reworking of the meaningful sentences of natural language into an artificial language devoid of context. This artificial language could serve, Bergmann argued, as a basis to formulate and solve philosophical problems in their entirety.[15] While Bergmann's terminology received little attention outside his field, it was the widespread reception of American philosopher Richard Rorty's 1967 anthology by the same name that brought the term to prominence. In this anthology, Rorty assembled essays by Anglo-American philosophers of the preceding thirty-five years, including Bergmann, who based their work on linguistic methods and brought about a veritable "philosophical revolution." According to Rorty, these approaches shared the premise that philosophical problems "may be solved (or dissolved) either by reforming language, or by understanding more about the language we presently use."[16] They predominantly prompted a focus "on words alone ... instead of concepts and universals" and in so doing, proceeded to a "dissolution of traditional problems." Rorty consequently characterized the approaches of this linguistic philosophy as having a "merely critical, essential dialectic, function" and wondered about the future prospects of these approaches and the feasibility of a "post-philosophical culture."[17]

Despite its inherent transdisciplinary characteristics, the linguistic turn—like all turns—was in need of "translat[ion]" to the individual disciplines and their methodological apparati.[18] Like Rorty in his take on linguistic philosophers, scholars of literary studies were quick to point out that this "turn" reflected a broader shift to constructivism and cultural reflexivity that began at the onset of the twentieth century and had long been incorporated into literary theory. The translation to the academic practice of history, by contrast, posed more challenges. In its renunciation of positivism and elevation of language to an "instrument of constituting reality," the approaches and traditions associated with the linguistic turn questioned the existence of a unified subject characterized by rational action and intentional meaning cherished not only by neo-historicist scholars. Maximalist readings reduced the subject to a subject position in the form of an intersection of multiple discourses.[19] It also undermined the primacy or even relevance of socioeconomic structures that pervaded the work of social and societal historians.

This rethinking of subjectivity had far-reaching methodological implications, since conventional approaches to the study of historical subjects were grounded in historians' assumed ability to decipher the actions of these subjects by means of a hermeneutical "understanding" (*Verstehen*).[20] Furthermore, as even adherents to pre-poststructuralist approaches such as Hayden White have maintained, historians allegedly engaged in "fictions of factual representation." They questioned and disrupted the discipline's traditional distinction of "subjective" interpretation and "objective" historical source criticism popularized since the works of nineteenth-century scholars such as Johann Gustav Droysen.[21] As White stressed, the "original description (of the facts ...) in a given dominant modality of language use" prefigured and prescribed the formal argument. Put differently, the language of the historians was not the "sufficiently controllable medium" as practitioners in the field had once imagined.[22]

All in all, the notion of a "linguistic turn" is a rather imprecise "umbrella term" that conveys the role of language and discourses in any approach to reality and knowledge. In some fields, scholars, including many practitioners of literary criticism, have sharply rejected the term as too antiquated and vague and opted instead for specific movements and traditions. This said, to equate it with a label such as postmodernism or poststructuralism is misleading at best and ignores a whole array of competing approaches to language. Indeed, the label linguistic term comprises strikingly different theoretical influences, ranging from the structural linguistics of Ferdinand de Saussure and Russian formalism to the deconstruction of Jacques Derrida.[23]

The Linguistic Turn Debated and Practiced

Even if some mainstream Europeanists discussed linguistic theories in journals such as *History and Theory* long before the appearance of Rorty's work,[24] the vast majority of academic historians only began to debate the challenges of linguistic analysis in the late 1980s. American scholars played a key role in popularizing the very term "linguistic turn" among academic historians. The *American Historical Review,* the discipline's premier journal, invited contributions on the topic and published John Toews's 1987 essay on the renewal of intellectual history. In his contribution, the University of Washington in Seattle-based Europeanist argued that the "linguistic turn ... ha[d] enormously enriched our historical understanding of the

complex ways in which meaning is constituted, transmitted and transformed in the heterogeneous, compound, and interrelated worlds we call
culture."[25] Yet, he added that even if these approaches had "dammed" the
"tides of psychological and sociological reductionism," they constituted a
"new form of reductionism," the "reduction of experience to the meanings
that shape it." As some of Rorty's critics, whom Toews's work discusses,
demanded, meanings had to be "judged in terms of their relationship to
the historical reality of social practices."[26]

Some trepidations notwithstanding, a growing number of academic historians, finally, began to explore linguistic approaches, since they offered,
as Toews indicated, powerful tools in the mounting criticism of social history that had dominated the discipline and privileged social and class divisions as the preeminent subjects of historical inquiry. Inherently linked
to the rise of new cultural history, historians drew on linguistic-turn approaches to move beyond reductionisms that had rooted phenomena like
culture in socioeconomic structures and were grounded in functionalist
approaches borrowed from the social sciences.[27] The collapse of communism in Eastern Europe and the end of the Soviet Union as political systems elevating Marxism-Leninism and class analysis also undermined the
practices of social history both in its Marxist and non-Marxist renditions.
The turn to language and culture did not only benefit from this disillusion-
ment. This turn also offered ways to conceptualize and theorize it. Drawing on works that ranged from Hayden White to Jean-François Lyotard,[28]
several Europeanists, including Konrad Jarausch and Lynn Hunt, swiftly
incorporated strands of the broader linguistic turn to make the case for
renarrations of the German past beyond nationalist, Marxist, and structuralist narratives and new readings of the French Revolution and cultural
history, respectively. Collaborating with German colleagues across the Atlantic, Jarausch integrated linguistic-turn approaches as tools to develop
"plural and interdependent" narratives, while also seeking to adapt them
to historical studies.[29] These scholars particularly applied the Lyotardian
concept of "metanarratives" (*grand récits*). In the late French philosopher's
work, the narratives of Enlightenment, historicism, and idealism constituted metanarratives, elevating the rational subject, the hermeneutics of
meaning, and the dialectics of Spirit, respectively. According to Lyotard,
the modern sciences had to legitimate the rules of their language games
by referring to metanarratives as "discourses of legitimation" in order to
distinguish themselves from mere fables. In this sense, "Truth," for example, far from being universal in value, appeared as grounded in "metanarratives" and as a strikingly relational concept.[30] The Lyotard-attested
"collapse" of the *grand récit marxiste* and other metanarratives signaled the
end of their role as apparati of legitimation and the need for alternatives.

Since the Lyotardian theorization of metanarratives and related linguistic-turn approaches undermined concepts of empirically rooted objective
facts, individual agency, and intentional rationality, a considerable number of academic historians from adherents to neo-historicism to practitioners of neo-Marxist social history quickly stepped up their criticism.[31]
On the American academic landscape, historians' debates over the linguistic turn soon went beyond Toews's thoughtful criticism and morphed into
sharp polemics. Among German historians, the contributions of Kenneth
D Barkin, the editor of the influential journal *Central European History*,
were representative of many critics' positions. In a 1995 essay in *German
Studies Review*, Barkin, a specialist in the history of the German Empire,
applied his reading of linguistic approaches to the genre of biographical
studies and concluded that the *Kaiserreich*'s architect and first chancellor
Otto von Bismarck "would become part of the disappearing subject," if
the discipline took the linguist turn. He grounded this claim not only in
these approaches' focus on the everyday and the "Other," but also on their
proponents' rejection of the "linear concept of history and progress" and
"consensual standards of truth."[32] Nonreferential history, as allegedly advocated by adherents of linguistic approaches, made an "appeal to the
records" unfeasible and "knowledge," ultimately, "impossible." Without
offering an all-too detailed examination of linguistic-turn approaches,
Barkin tied them to a number of French scholars from Michel Foucault to
Jacques Derrida and branded U.S. scholars who applied these approaches
to their work as "Francophilic" and wanting "to appear fashionable."[33]

Other American historians took this outright dismissal even further,
seeking to discredit these approaches to history and language along with
their practitioners. They did so by presenting the alleged implications
of these theorizations for the study of the Holocaust, which, by the late
1970s, had been reconfigured, in Jeffrey Alexander's apt words, as a "dominant symbolic representation of evil" that came to serve as the basis of
a "supranational moral universalism."[34] Gertrud Himmelfarb, a prolific
scholar of the history of Victorian England, became a much-cited voice of
this line of criticism. In a book-length essay, Himmelfarb readily dismissed scholars whose work drew on the linguistic turn as engaged in a
rejection of "reality" in favor of "language" and portrayed them as rejecting "morality" in an embrace of "rhetoric and aesthetics."[35] She substan-
tiated this claim in her reading of Hayden White's work and its alleged
position that no historical narrative could "be judged to be more 'true'
to the 'facts' from which one may elicit 'truths.'" If one followed White,
Himmelfarb reasoned, could there remain "any 'limits' on the kind of stories" that could "'responsibly' be told about the Holocaust"? Evoking her
cultural authority as the New York–born daughter of pre–World War I

Russian-Jewish immigrants, she presented White and others as "peril-ously close to the 'revisionists' who deny the reality of the Holocaust." Pushing further, Himmelfarb portrayed Richard Rorty as an "admirer" of Martin Heidegger, the prominent German philosopher who, as the head of University of Freiburg, had joined the Nazi party and voiced his sup-port for Hitler. Meanwhile, Paul de Man, the Belgian-born literary the-orist and deconstructionist, had to be seen as "a Nazi collaborator and anti-Semite."[36] Himmelfarb, thus, sought to delegitimize historians who proposed explorations of the linguistic turn by linking them not only to relativist and nihilist approaches, but also to thinkers directly associated with German fascism and the Holocaust.

All along, most academic historians who voiced their criticism of lin-guistic approaches in the field readily subsumed their opponents under the inherently vague label of "postmodernism." As Himmelfarb con-cluded, these scholars embraced a "postmodernist history" that "may well take the form of fictional history."[37] Not without paradoxes, Himmel-farb and critics like her distinctly criticized historians who experimented with linguistic-turn approaches for their reductionism, while presenting a highly reductionist reading of what these approaches encompassed. As English literature scholar Christoph Reinfandt aptly noted, historians' "apparently widely accepted equation linguistic turn = literary theory = postmodernism" could, however, not hold up to "closer scrutiny."[38] The equation reduced a century-long tradition of a broad array of theoriza-tions and methodologies that were grounded in the shared concern for reflexivity and a focus on language to a maximalist reading of the "post"-theorizations of the 1970s and 1980s. Very few of the academic histori-ans who explored linguistic approaches practiced full-fledged Derridean or Foucaultian-style histories. Even Joan W Scott who went further than most in her rereading of Derrida's work and drew on its insights into how concepts, including that of "woman," had to be seen as "unstable, open to contest and redefinition," explicitly turned away from any "dogmatic ap-plication of any particular philosopher's teachings."[39] It remains striking, nonetheless, that Derrida's philosophy and approaches were often poorly understood. Historians like Himmelfarb construed Derrida's notions of "text" as unrecognizably narrow and his often-cited dictum that there was "nothing outside the text" as simplistic and "a-historical." Yet, Derrida's work on intertextuality explicitly extended beyond verbal and written text. In an interview with Michal Ben-Naftali, Derrida also stressed the importance of "context," for example in using the name Holocaust. As a number of scholars have argued, the Holocaust played a critical role in Derrida's deconstructionist approaches that revealed the complicity of philosophy in totalitarian regimes and its support for the violence of language and exclusion.[40] Still, most historians opted for less "radical" lin-guistic-turn readings.

While supporters of the linguistic turn in Germany initially came from the margins of the discipline and the ranks of junior scholars, in the United States, as Christoph Conrad and Martina Kessel have rightfully stressed, they emerged from the very center of the field.[41] In October 1989, Michael Geyer and Konrad Jarausch, who held two widely recognized chairs in German and European history, convened a conference in Chicago that took on what they—not unlike their critics—termed the "postmodern chal-lenge" and its implication for a rereading of the German past.[42] As Geyer and Jarausch summarized, the conference participants reached a "con-sensus that there [wa]s no unified and autonomous German past beyond the imagination of its makers and consumers." Instead, most participants called for "multiplicity" and ways to "capture the multiple experiences of subjects and objects of history" in conscious rejection of "monumental his-tories with their quest for a totality of sources and synthetic homogeniza-tion of the plotline."[43] While most conference papers engaged the works of Jacques Derrida and Michel Foucault, they hardly advocated Derridean or Foucaultian-style histories. Their authors sought to render the "linguistic turn" as "anything but esoteric," but rather a phenomenon that "shapes the daily practices of every historian."[44] With the simplistic "conflation of signifier (trace, text, artifact, image, commodity) and signified ('reality')" undone, they aimed at swiftly moving beyond criticism and "deconstruc-tion" to present "interacting multiplicity of stories" that problematize ref-erentiality, while taking distinct historical contexts firmly into account.[45]

This "moderate" approach pervaded the Chicago conference contri-bution of Jane Caplan, a British-trained historian of Nazi Germany, who, at the time, was teaching at Bryn Mawr College. Caplan turned her dis-cussions to the Holocaust, which was swiftly emerging as a "privileged site of debate" and test case for linguistic-turn guided work in the field. The author argued that this kind of approach had the potential of mov-ing the study of the Nazi genocide beyond the "intellectually limiting binarism" of "extreme derealization" and "hyperrealism," which had characterized the field of Holocaust Studies by the late 1980s.[46] Caplan, therefore, did not only turn against interpretations that transformed the Holocaust into a "transhistorical event," the true meaning of which could only be grasped by those who survived it. She also rejected competing ap-proaches by leading German and American historians like Martin Broszat and Christopher R Browning who rooted their interpretations in textual sources and analyses that avoided any dehistoricization and substantial theorization.[47] Instead, Caplan advocated a focus on the "texts" of Nazi ideology and the "signifying practices" of fascism for which linguistic approaches could be immensely useful. An obsessive rereading of Heidegger and de Man, by contrast, was unproductive. Furthermore, attesting to the importance of reflexivity in linguistic-turn approaches, Caplan called on historians to learn to be "ultraconscious in [their] choice of language" and link it along with the language of their sources to the "different contexts and conventions of knowledge-production."[48] Postmodernist and other "post"-approaches, Caplan cautioned, had yet to yield full-fledged studies and answers.

The question of how the linguistic turn posed challenges to the representation and study of the Holocaust fully occupied the participants of an influential interdisciplinary conference that Saul Friedländer, a renowned Holocaust scholar and child survivor, convened at UCLA in April 1990. Taking Hayden White's work as a starting point, a group of prominent historians and literature and language scholars began to ponder the implications of the "rejection of the possibility of identifying some stable reality or truth" inherent in White's approaches that postulated the "constant polysemy and self-referentiality of linguistic constructs."[49] As Friedländer stressed, the study of extreme mass murder relied on "a need for 'truth.'" Christopher R Browning eloquently reiterated this position in his conference reflections on reserve police perpetrators by pointing to recent courtroom claims by a neo-Nazi revisionist and his lawyer that "all history [wa]s mere opinion."[50] Ultimately, Friedländer remained much more ambiguous on the implications of the linguistic turn. He argued that it was "precisely the 'Final Solution' which allow[ed] postmodernist thinking to question the validity of any totalizing view of history." There remained an ultimate indeterminacy to these extreme events that Friedländer had already revealed in his earlier calls to study the "mythic memory" and voices of Jewish victims.[51] Consequently, he closed with literary critic Shoshana Felman's admonition that truth did "not kill the possibility of art" and a convergence of the discourses of historians and fiction writers, but "required it for its transmission, for its realization in our consciousness as witnesses."[52]

Some participants like intellectual historian Dominick LaCapra took this unease with traditional Holocaust historiography further. LaCapra argued that this historiography's "conventional techniques" such as "narrowly empirical-analytical inquiry" were insufficient. In confrontations with events like the Holocaust, language often "br[oke] down." Yet, it was the very study of the Holocaust, LaCapra reasoned, that could lead to a remaking of historiography in general. In this undertaking, linguistic-turn approaches had their place, explorations of language remained critical, and nothing less than a conceptualization of new categories of analysis was needed.[53]

Like the Chicago conference attendees, the UCLA conference participants only took the first steps in this direction. The papers and subsequent volumes and special journal editions, meanwhile, also aimed at prompting and providing guidance for new empirically oriented studies that responded to challenges of the linguistic turn. How and to what extent then did these challenges and debates shape empirical research projects?

By the early 1990s, a growing number of historians of modern Europe—both junior and established—were translating their engagements with linguistic-turn and "postmodernist" approaches into the writing and publishing of empirical studies. These scholars also included historians of Nazism and the Holocaust, who grappled with the particularly charged debates over the linguistic turn and postmodernism in their field. Robert Gellately's study on the everyday operations of the Gestapo, Hitler Germany's Secret State Police, is in several ways indicative of the manner in which historians who displayed an openness to "postmodern" approaches tackled the theoretical challenges in their empirical work. First, Gellately offered a rather brief section on conceptual and methodological approaches in the opening pages of the monograph that limited its engagement with postmodern thought to theorizations by Michel Foucault. He evoked the French philosopher's notions of a "disciplined" and "carceral society" as well as his much-discussed conceptualization of power as a "way of acting upon an acting subject" without the exercise of physical force.[54] In so doing, the author began to provide some theoretical underpinning for his argument that the Gestapo, a relatively small police force, acted more on the basis of widespread denunciations from the population rather than systematic large-scale surveillance. In the Reich, this police force also had a "social role" and cannot be reduced to an agency of physical coercion and mass violence.[55] Still, Gellately's borrowing from Foucault's work of a period that marked his transition from structuralist and linguistic approaches to theorization of power/knowledge was highly selective and did not show any concern for how these Foucaultian concepts conflicted with the work's broader epistemological and methodological frameworks. Second, despite these sporadic introductory references to Foucault's genealogy, a theory of practices of power partially devised as a challenge to historical methodology, there is no further engagement with Foucaultian thought past page 22. Indeed, the text chapters are largely based on what LaCapra described as "narrowly empirical-analytical inquiry" with no regard for cultural reflexivity.

Some scholars, by contrast, pushed beyond brief references to "postmodernist" and linguistic approaches. Thomas Childers, a participant of the 1989 Chicago conference, embarked on a study of the "social vocabulary of everyday politics" of the Weimar Republic.[56] He proposed an anal-

ysis of the "actual language of political discourse," therefore, moving linguistic questions both to the center of his methodological apparatus and
the topic of examination. The social vocabulary used by political parties
such as the Nazi movement's employment of the language of "profession"
(*Berufsstand*), Childers reasoned, played a key role in the "formation of
social consciousness and the dynamics of mobilization."[57] Childers's approach challenged both the structuralist readings of West German practitioners of societal history, including proponents of the "special path" (*Sonderweg*) paradigm, and those of their mostly Anglo-American critics who
continued to insist on the differences of articulated ideological positions
and social reality.[58] Like Gellately, Childers, nonetheless, was hardly maximalist in his application of linguistic-turn models. He consistently tied
the analyzed terms and discourses to political parties and their members
and situated them in their distinct social context and "extralinguistic reality."[59] Since the author published a number of intriguing articles, but not
a full-length monograph, the full potential of his approaches, however,
remained unexplored.

Given the space available for this essay, it is not feasible to present a
comprehensive review of the broad array of empirically oriented studies
that explored the linguistic turn for the academic practice of modern European history, including the work of labor and gender historians such as
Judith Walkowitz or discourse analysts such as Philipp Sarasin.[60] And yet,
this essay's brief discussions of empirical research projects already suggest the far-reaching, albeit very uneven impact on the discipline. While
historians of Nazi Germany and the Holocaust remained largely limited
in their application of linguistic-turn models,[61] practitioners in the fields
of cultural and postcolonial studies, the core of the new cultural history of
the 1980s, were among the cohorts of scholars who integrated these models most extensively in their works.

Late Australian historian Greg Dening's study of the late eighteenth-
century mutiny on the British navy ship Bounty is a telling example of this
kind of work. Drawing on ethnographic approaches, Dening explored the
theatrical nature of the events of the mutiny, while self-reflectively com-
posing his work in the form of a play divided by acts and scenes.[62] Dening's
entire study was guided by what Robert F Berkhofer has dubbed practices
of "reflexive contextualization."[63] The study combined narrative sections
that reconstruct the often-conflicting perspectives and languages of loyal
officers, mutineers, and indigenous Tahitians without privileging any of
them with extensive "reflections"—also on the author's strategies and
language use. In the book's analyses, the various power-plays on and beyond the deck of the ship did foreground not only the power of language,
but also the languages of power. The "bad language" of William Bligh,

the Bounty's captain, is a case in point. Dening placed an examination of the captain's language at the center of his study, arguing that its badness rested in the "ambiguous language of [Bligh's] command." The crew, the author reasoned, could not "read in it a right relationship to his authority." Excessive physical violence and abuse were hardly the causes of the mutiny, since Bligh, as Dening showed, punished far fewer of his crew members than other British navy captains. He presented a broad array of sources, including various later textual and cinematic representations of the mutiny. Even if Dening was critical and even dismissive of 1960s feature films on the mutiny, he did not privilege any one representation and voice. Reiterating positions advanced by Hayden White, Dening, instead, celebrated a "presentist" and "relativist" notion of history as "fiction" and the product of human agency.[64]

The "Linguistic Turn" in the Late Twentieth and Early Twenty-First Centuries: Where Are We Now?

Scrutinizing the key historiographical shifts at the turn to the twenty-first century, Georg G Iggers observed that "few" historians in the field of modern European history and beyond had actually taken the linguistic turn.[65] In terms of maximalist models of linguistic-term approaches, including, for example, practices of "reflexive contextualization," Iggers's claim can hardly be disputed. Even the vast majority of proponents of the new cultural history, who consistently displayed the greatest openness to linguistic models, never gave up on the premise of an extra-linguistic reality.[66]

In light of the considerable number of scholars who explored linguistic and discursive models and incorporated them into their work in a selective or minimalist manner, Iggers's claim is, at the same time, also overdrawn. There is a broad array of linguistic-turn approaches that extends far beyond Derridean or Lyotardian theorizations and can hardly be subsumed under any vague and often polemicist label of "postmodernism." They range from early lexicometric and semiotic approaches to non-Foucaultian discourse analysis and works on language and symbolism.[67] No matter what theoretical and methodological approach historians engaged in, language itself became a key topic of study beyond its previous confinement to one of the discipline's small subfields or a general concern as part of the historical-critical method. The array of studies included works by labor historians such as Gareth Stedman Jones and Kathleen Canning and their scrutiny of languages of labor and class. They also encompassed German historians' extensive response to the mid-1990s publication of the diaries by Holocaust survivor and French literature scholar

Victor Klemperer that reflect on the changes in everyday language during
the Nazi period and the belated broad reception of his 1947 study of the
Lingua Tertii Imperii.[68]

As with all historiographical "trends," however, the linguistic turn has
increasingly given way to new developments, including novel "turns"
from the iconic to the spatial and transnational. Several factors account
for this shift. For once, the field of modern European history, the discipline, and academia per se evolve with ever-"new" approaches, which
its practitioners are continually seeking to develop. Once linguistic-turn
approaches had — despite the sharp initial criticism and rejection — moved
from the margins to the center of the field, entered the curricula, and text-
books,[69] they did lose not only their newness, but also more and more of
their innovative impulses. Furthermore, as scholars who took the linguistic
turn applied these approaches in their empirically oriented studies, they
also exposed more of the limitations. Even more moderate linguistic-turn
approaches, for example, still endorsed the primacy of the linguistic over
the pictorial, which had been marginalized by most historians long before
the debates over the challenges of language philosophies.

The emergence of the "pictorial" and related "iconic turn," postulated
by English literature scholar William T Mitchell in 1992 and the art historian Gottfried Boehm in 1994, respectively, in the humanities and social
sciences can also be seen as a direct response to the primacy of linguistic
dimensions.[70] As in the case of the linguistic turn, historians of modern
Europe were hardly at the forefront of these developments. Yet, led by
early modernists,[71] a growing number of modern Europeanists, including
Gerhard Paul in Germany or David Ciarlo in the United States,[72] began
to explore the pictorial by the middle of the twenty-first century's first
decade. Directly drawing on visual culture studies in the United States,
these scholars challenged their discipline's reductionist treatment of images as mostly illustrative, simply "readable," and graspable in a "return
to naïve mimesis." Instead, they followed Mitchell's dictum that images
had to be subjected to a "postlinguisitc, postsemiotic rediscovery" and
analyses that took the "complex interplay between visuality, apparatus,
institutions, discourse, bodies, and figurality" fully into account. Practices of spectatorship, ranging from the gaze to practices of seeing, had
to be seen as equally complex as "forms of reading," and could not be
adequately analyzed by the "model of textuality."[73] While practitioners of
art history and media studies continue to give the most critical impulses,
modern European historians have begun to establish a field of "visual history" that links the exploration of the whole range of visual practices and
visuality of experience and memory to the expanding interdisciplinary
field of visual culture studies.[74]

Proponents of the study of visuality, practices of seeing, and remember-
ing were hardly alone in pointing to the shortcomings of linguistic-turn
readings. The parallel rise of spatial studies, reconceptualized as a veritable "spatial turn" spearheaded by cultural anthropologists and geographers, was also linked to the critique of the primacy of language and
time. Scholars advocating a rethinking of space argued that it should be
regarded as a "social construction," which was subject to change and displayed a distinct materiality. Space did not assume the form of a linguistic or discursive phenomenon.[75] The broad label of a "spatial turn," too,
subsumed a wide range of approaches that proved insightful for various
fields and interdisciplinary initiatives. More recently, scholars of modern
European history, for example, have joined geographers in the Holocaust
Geography Collaborative to make the case for a visualization of spatial
concerns, including the relationships of individual deportees' experiences
of movement through a distinct space, by means of dynamic mapping. In
order to grasp the larger genocidal processes, the location of deportations
or mass shootings, members of this collaborative project argued, was as
critical as their timing.[76]

In their focus on cross-border movements and networks, these recon-
ceptualizations also revealed the inadequacy of nationally oriented concepts of space. Consequently, the spatial turn supported the development
of transnational approaches and was, in turn, supported by them. Modern
Europeanists have drawn extensively on the works by cultural anthropologists and globalization studies scholars such as Arjun Appadurai, who
developed the spatial turn in the realm of transnational territoriality by
focusing on disjunctures in global cultural flows along the lines of, among
others, "ethnoscapes" and "financapes."[77] Among modern German historians, scholars of Imperial Germany and German colonialism were on the
forefront of demonstrating the strength of these spatial and transnational
approaches in the rethinking of their field. They demonstrated that even
during the apparent height of nation building and the corresponding na-
tion-focused historiography in the late nineteenth century, transnational
and globalization processes were already in full play and shaped economic, social, cultural, and political developments in the German lands
and elsewhere on the continent.[78]

While discussions of the linguistic turn have started to disappear from
the pages of journals and conference catalogs, it would be an overstatement to postulate the end of the turn's impact. As Doris Bachmann-Medick
astutely noted, the linguistic turn "pervaded" all subsequent "turns," including the visual and spatial, that largely developed in opposition to it.[79]
Similar to the relations between structuralism and post-structuralism,
the linguistic and successive turns cannot be understood in isolation of

each other and remain inherently connected. While some scholars have envisioned the rethinking of space, for example, as a counterpoint to the primacy of language endorsed by many past proponents of the linguistic turn, spatially oriented models of reception also rely on discursive elements and are shaped by linguistic ties between communities that form the main transnational subjects such as refugees, NGO workers, or students.

The Linguistic Turn: Where to Go?

The recent move away from multifaceted explorations of linguistic-turn approaches has also meant that key potentials for a profound rethinking of the study of modern European histories and the academic discipline as a whole remained un- or not fully explored. This assessment should not be read, however, as a call for a resurrection of labels such as the linguistic turn, which have always lacked precision, or a return to the primacy of linguistic phenomena. Yet, multilayered rereadings of theorizations of language and discourses in sustained conversations and combinations with more recent turns, including the spatial and transnational, hold the promise to increase our comprehension and insights of key areas of study, especially, I would argue, in the often still theory-adverse practices of historians of the Holocaust.

In recent years, spatial and transnational approaches have, finally, made their entry into the fields of Jewish history and Holocaust studies, which, for a long time, were dominated by studies whose authors confined their subjects to national and regional boundaries.[80] As Shulamit Volkov has argued, Jewish history needs to be seen as "inherently transnational." Migration of Jews from Eastern Europe continually remade modern Jewish diaspora communities in Western Europe and helped to establish profound transnational ties and networks.[81] The Holocaust, too, has to be seen as histories of constant and excessively forced border crossings by refugees, deportees, and other persecutes brought about by the Hitler state and its allies. In order to grasp these complex phenomena, it is pivotal to take the emergence of new trans-European speech communities into account that were triggered by these movements and gave rise to novel languages, words, and meanings. Reworked linguistic and discourse analytical approaches would allow to decipher these practices and shed light on survival strategies and transnational webs of communication that played an increasingly important role in the Eastern European ghettos and camps. In his 1986 reflections, Primo Levi memorably dwelled on the "sectorial language" of the "Lager" such as Auschwitz that was dominated by a minimalist German, but also influenced by Yiddish, Polish, and eventually also Hungarian.[82] The ways in which these shifting languages shaped meanings, helped constitute subjects, and interacted with imageries and ways of seeing illustrates the need to rethink linguistic-turn approaches and integrate them in future studies.

In addition, the potentials of exploring intersecting turns, including re-theorizations of language and discourses, also extends to the study of the perpetration of violence by genocidal regimes and their supporters. Peter Burke's perceptive 2004 claim that full-fledged cultural and linguistic histories of violence have yet to be written is hardly outdated.[83] Recent works, including a study by this essay's author,[84] have taken steps in the direction of new linguistic histories of Nazi violence, especially against Jews, that add to the multilayered study of the regime's large-scale physical brutalities. These explorations are based on the premise that before, during, and after the perpetration of genocidal acts, Nazi and other German perpetrators engaged in violence inflicted via language, which was what made the physical violence against racialized minorities possible in the first place. Reassessments of linguistic-turn approaches would demonstrate the need to further move beyond narrow readings that incorporate language in a conceptual grid of top-down manipulation or subsume the phenomenon under conventional categories of ideology that have lost much of their analytical rigor and value. While rethinking language in Nazi Germany and—occupied Europe in a more complex manner that accounts for its strikingly productive, material, and ultimately, violent impact, it is also critical to take its intersections with visual imagery and collective memories into account. "Language" and the ways in which it "wounded" is, as Greg Dening stressed, "notoriously difficult to recapture."[85] Yet, a combination of extensive new sources, some of which belong to archival holdings in Eastern Europe or Southeast Asia still in the process of being made available to researchers, and rethought cultural-turn approaches has the potential of yielding new insights. To proceed in this fashion does not have to amount to a new primacy of language. Forms of linguistic violence intersected and were inherently related to the visuality of violence. Indeed, the many amateur pictures of executions of Jews that Red Army officials took from German POWs on the Eastern front along with letters replete with anti-Semitic diatribes demonstrate the need to systematically analyze the manner in which linguistic and visual violence informed one another.[86]

Finally, a return and reassessment of linguistic approaches could and should not be restricted to a study of specific periods in modern European history. Instead, it should, as scholars such as Jörn Leonhard have explicated, inform a rethinking of the histories of Europe and the transatlantic world that were characterized by a rapid semantic transformation of communicative practices and concepts in the contexts of the far-reaching changes in the politico-societal systems during the twentieth century.[87] This could be also particularly illuminating in explanations of the transition from this century's first half with its wars of annihilation to the second half with its Cold War era bipolar bloc confrontation. For the erosion of ideological constructs and entrenched political practices, language and counter-discursive practices were central. Projects on this scale would go beyond a continuation of the former West German project of "basic historical concepts" that stopped in the mid nineteenth century. Rethought linguistic-turn approaches would need to prove their reach by accounting for the complexities of language use and incorporate synchronic as well as diachronic approaches.

In conclusion, by the second decade of the twenty-first century, historiographical debates have lost much of the polemical nature that they displayed over Marxist, social historical or linguistic-turn challenges. Lynn Hunt's keen observation that the most recent exchanges have "assumed a surprisingly moderate tone" captures much of the discipline.[88] The profound disruptions of established historical narratives as metanarratives also undermined the prospect for the rise—desirable or not—of new grand theories. Instead, the new plurality advocated by many, including modern Europeanists such as Konrad Jarausch and Michael Geyer,[89] has led to a broad range of approaches and topics that strengthened the study of modern European history despite of the often overdrawn criticism that pictured the imminent demise of the field and the rigorous practice of academic history. As part of this plurality, rethought linguistic and discursive readings have a significant role to play in grounding the discipline further in its theoretical underpinnings and in the selection of critical areas of studies, especially in fields once shielded from their impact such as the study of the Holocaust.

Thomas Pegelow Kaplan is the Leon Levine Distinguished Professor of Judaic, Holocaust, and Peace Studies and Director of the Center for Judaic, Holocaust, and Peace Studies at Appalachian State University.

Notes

1. Leopold von Ranke, *The Theory and Practice of History,* ed. Georg G Iggers (New York, 2010); Peter Lambert, "The Professionalization and Institutionalization of

History," in *Writing History: Theory and Practice,* ed. Stefan Berger, Heiko Feldner, and Kevin Passmore (London, 2010), 43.

2. Reinhart Koselleck, *The Practice of Conceptual History: Timing History, Spacing Concepts* (Stanford, CA, 2002).

3. Otto Brunner, Werner Conze, and Reinhart Koselleck, eds, *Geschichtliche Grundbegriffe. Historisches Lexikon zur politisch-sozialen Sprache in Deutschland,* 8 vols. (Stuttgart, 1972–97).

4. Régine Robin, *Histoire et linguistique* (Paris, 1973).

5. Ibid.; Peter Schöttler, "Sozialgeschichtliches Paradigma und historische Diskursanalyse," in *Diskurstheorien und Literaturwissenschaft,* ed. Jürgen Fohrmann and Harro Müller (Frankfurt, 1988), 164–66.

6. Doris Bachmann-Medick, *Cultural Turns: Neuorientierungen in den Kulturwissenschaften* (Reinbek, 2009); Christoph Reinfandt, "Reading Texts after the Linguistic Turn," in *Reading Primary Sources: The Interpretation of Texts from Nineteenth- and Twentieth-Century History,* ed. Miriam Dobson and Benjamin Ziemann (London, 2009), 37–54. On the new cultural history see Lynn Hunt, ed., *The New Cultural History* (Berkeley, CA, 1989).

7. Hans-Ulrich Wehler, "Kommentar," in *Geschichte zwischen Kultur und Gesellschaft: Beiträge zur Theoriedebatte,* ed. Thomas Mergel and Thomas Welskopp (Munich, 1997), 358, 363; Gertrude Himmelfarb, *On Looking into the Abyss: Untimely Thoughts on Culture and Society* (New York, 1994).

8. Thomas Childers, "Political Sociology and the 'Linguistic Turn,'" *Central European History* 22, no. 3/4 (1989): 392–93.

9. Joan W Scott, *Gender and the Politics of History* (New York, 1988); Konrad H Jarausch and Michael Geyer, *Shattered Past: Reconstructing German Histories* (Princeton, NJ, 2003), 103, 17.

10. Joan W Scott, *Only Paradoxes to Offer: French Feminists and the Rights of Man* (Cambridge, 1996).

11. Lynn Hunt, "Where Have All the Theories Gone?," *Perspectives* 40, no. 3 (2002): 5–7.

12. James Vernon, "Who's Afraid of the 'Linguistic Turn'? The Politics of Social History and Its Discontents," *Social History* 19, no. 1 (1994): 81–97.

13. Bachmann-Medick, *Cultural Turns,* 25–26.

14. Ibid., 33; Reinfandt, "Reading Texts," 38.

15. Laird Addis, "The Philosophy of Gustav Bergmann," *Algemeen Nederlands Tijdschrift voor Wijsbegeerte* 63 (1971): 78–98; Gustav Bergmann, *Logic and Reality* (Madison, WI, 1964), 177; Richard Rorty, *The Linguistic Turn: Recent Essays in Philosophical Method* (Chicago, 1967), 9.

16. Rorty, *The Linguistic Turn,* 3.

17. Ibid., 9, 33–34.

18. Bachmann-Medick, *Cultural Turns,* 21.

19. Philipp Sarasin, *Geschichtswissenschaft und Diskursanalyse* (Frankfurt, 2003), 13–18.

20. See also Wilhelm Dilthey, *Hermeneutics and the Study of History,* ed. Rudolf A Makkreel and Frithjof Rodi (Princeton, NJ, 1996), passim.

21. Arthur Alfaix Assis, *What Is History for? Johann Gustav Droysen and the Functions of Historiography* (New York, 2014).

22. Hayden White, "The Fictions of Factual Representation," in *Tropics of Discourse: Essays in Cultural Criticism* (Baltimore, MD, 1978), 128; Sarasin, *Geschichtswissenschaft und Diskursanalyse*, 25.

23. Alun Munslow, *Deconstructing History* (London, 1997), 185; Reinfandt, "Reading Texts," 38.

24. Richard T Vann, "Turning Linguistic: History and Theory in *History and Theory*, 1960–75," in *A New Philosophy of History*, ed. Frank Ankersmit and Hans Kellner (Chicago, 1995), 40–69.

25. John E Toews, "Intellectual History after the Linguistic Turn," *American Historical Review* 92, no. 4 (1987): 906.

26. Ibid.

27. See Hunt, *The New Cultural History*.

28. Hayden White, *Metahistory: The Historical Imagination in Nineteenth-Century Europe* (Baltimore, MD, 1973) and Jean-François Lyotard, *The Postmodern Condition: A Report on Knowledge* (Minneapolis, MN, 1984).

29. Lynn Hunt, "History Beyond Social Theory," in *The States of "Theory*," ed. David Carroll (New York, 1990), 106–8; Konrad H Jarausch, "Die Krise der nationalen Meistererzählungen," in *Die Historische Meistererzählung: Deutungslinien der deutschen Nationalgeschichte nach 1945*, ed. Konrad H Jarausch and Martin Sabrow (Göttingen, 2002), 140.

30. Lyotard, *The Postmodern Condition*, xxiii–xxiv.

31. For an example of a critical account by a Marxist-leaning scholar, see Bryan D Palmer, *Descent into Discourse: The Reification of Language and the Writing of Social History* (Philadelphia, PA, 1990).

32. Kenneth Barkin, "Bismarck in a Postmodern Age," *German Studies Review* 18, no. 2 (1995): 244, 247.

33. Ibid., 246, 249.

34. Jeffrey C Alexander, "On the Social Construction of Moral Universals. The 'Holocaust' from War Crime to Trauma," *European Journal of Social Theory* 5, no. 1 (2002): 5.

35. Himmelfarb, *On Looking into the Abyss*, xi.

36. Ibid., 143–44, xi.

37. Ibid., 146.

38. Reinfandt, "Reading Texts," 37.

39. Scott, *Gender and the Politics of History*, 4–5, 7–8. For an explicit advocate of more "radical" readings of post-approaches, see for example, Munslow, *Deconstructing History*.

40. "An Interview with Professor Jacques Derrida," interview by Michal Ben-Naftali, Shoah Resource Center, 8 January 1998, http://www.yadvashem.org/odot_pdf/Microsoft%20Word%20-%203851.pdf; Dorota Glowacka, "A Date, a Place, a Name: Jacque Derrida's Holocaust Translations," *The New Centennial Review* 7, no. 2 (2007): 113–14.

41. Christoph Conrad and Martina Kessel, eds, *Geschichte schreiben in der Postmoderne. Beiträge zur aktuellen Diskussion* (Stuttgart, 1994), 14.

42. Konrad H Jarausch, "Contemporary History as Transatlantic Project: Autobiographical Reflections on the German Problem, 1960–2010," *Historical Social Research*, Supplement 24 (2012): 32.

43. Konrad Jarausch and Michael Geyer, "The Future of the German Past: Transatlantic Reflections for the 1990s," *Central European History* 22, no. 3/4 (1989): 230–31.

44. Jarausch and Geyer, "The Future of the German Past," 247.

45. Ibid., 245, 248. For the subsequent book-length elaborations on their innovative positions on how to rewrite German histories see Jarausch and Geyer, *Shattered Past*.

46. Jane Caplan, "Postmodernism, Poststructuralism, Deconstruction: Notes for Historians," *Central European History* 22, no. 3/4 (1989): 274, 277.

47. Ibid. See also Martin Broszat and Saul Friedländer, "A Controversy about the Historicization of National Socialism," *New German Critique* 44 (1988): 85–126.

48. Caplan, "Postmodernism, Poststructuralism, Deconstruction," 278.

49. Saul Friedländer, ed., *Probing the Limits of Representation. Nazism and the Final Solution* (Cambridge, MA, 1992), 4–5.

50. Christopher R Browning, "German Memory, Judicial Interrogation, and Historical Reconstruction," in *Probing the Limits of Representation. Nazism and the Final Solution,* ed. Saul Friedländer (Cambridge, MA, 1992), 31.

51. See note 47 above; Friedländer, *Probing the Limits of Representation,* 5.

52. Ibid., 20.

53. Dominick LaCarpa, "Representing the Holocaust: Reflections on the Historians' Debate," in *Probing the Limits of Representation. Nazism and the Final Solution,* ed. Saul Friedländer (Cambridge, MA, 1992), 110–11.

54. Robert Gellately, *The Gestapo and German Society: Enforcing Racial Policy, 1933–1945* (Oxford, 1990), 11.

55. Ibid., 8, 129–58.

56. Thomas Childers, "The Social Language of Politics in Germany: The Sociology of Political Discourses in the Weimar Republic," *American Historical Review* 95, no. 2 (1990): 335.

57. Ibid., 357.

58. Ibid., 335; Childers, "Political Sociology and the 'Linguistic Turn,'" 381–82.

59. Childers, "Political Sociology and the 'Linguistic Turn,'" 393.

60. Judith R Walkowitz, *City of Dreadful Delight: Narratives of Sexual Danger in Late-Victorian London* (Chicago, 1992); Philipp Sarasin, *Reizbare Maschinen: Eine Geschichte des Körpers, 1765–1914* (Frankfurt, 2001).

61. Holocaust studies scholars, not trained as historians, have, by contrast, displayed a far greater openness and made significant contributions. See James E Young, *Writing and Rewriting the Holocaust* (Bloomington, IN, 1988).

62. Greg Dening, *Mr Bligh's Bad Language: Passion, Power, and Theatre on the Bounty* (Cambridge, 1992), 5.

63. Robert F Berkhofer, *Beyond the Great Story: History as Text and Discourse* (Cambridge, 1995), xii, 243–83.

64. Dening, *Mr Bligh's Bad Language,* 366.

65. Georg G Iggers, *Historiography in the Twentieth Century: From Scientific Objectivity to the Postmodern Challenge* (Hanover, NH, 1997), 133.

66. Gabrielle M Spiegel, *Practicing History: New Directions in Historical Writing after the Linguistic Turn* (New York, 2005), 8.

67. For one of the many examples, see Hans-Jürgen Lüsebrink, Rolf Reichardt, and Norbert Schürer, *The Bastille: A History of a Symbol of Despotism and Freedom* (Durham, NC, 1997).

68. Kathleen Canning, *Languages of Labor and Gender. Female Factory Work in Germany, 1850–1914* (Ithaca, NY, 1996); Gareth Stedman Jones, *Languages of Class: Studies in English Working Class History, 1832–1982* (Cambridge, 1983); Victor Klemperer, *I Will Bear Witness: A Diary of the Nazi Years*, 2 vols. (New York, 1998–99); Victor Klemperer, *The Language of the Third Reich. LTI* (London, 2000); Jarausch and Geyer, *Shattered Past*, 149–66.

69. See, for example, Callum G Brown, *Postmodernism for Historians* (Harlow, 2005); Achim Landwehr, *Geschichte des Sagbaren: Einführung in die historische Diskursanalyse* (Tübingen, 2001).

70. WJT Mitchell, *Picture Theory: Essays on Verbal and Visual Representation* (Chicago, 1994), 11; Gottfried Boehm, ed., *Was ist ein Bild?* (Munich, 1994), 11–38.

71. Bernd Roeck, "Visual Turn? Kulturgeschichte und die Bilder," *Geschichte und Gesellschaft* 29 (2003): 294–315.

72. Gerhard Paul, *Bilder des Krieges—Krieg der Bilder. Die Visualisierung des modernen Krieges* (Paderborn, 2004); Gerhard Paul, ed., *Visual History: Ein Studienbuch* (Göttingen, 2006); David Ciarlo, *Advertising Empire: Race and Visual Culture in Imperial Germany* (Cambridge, 2011).

73. Mitchell, *Picture Theory*, 16.

74. See, for example, Gerhard Paul, "Die (Zeit-)Historiker und die Bilder. Plädoyer für eine Visual History," in *Visualität und Geschichte*, ed. Saskia Handro and Bernhard Schönemann (Berlin, 2011), 7–22; Gerhard Paul, ed., *Das Jahrhundert der Bilder. Bildatlas 1949 bis heute* (Göttingen, 2008); Annelie Ramsbrock, Annette Vowinckel, and Malte Zierenberg, eds, *Fotografien im 20. Jahrhundert: Verbreitung und Vermittlung* (Göttingen, 2013).

75. Bachmann-Medick, *Cultural Turns*, 284, 292.

76. Anne Kelly Knowles, Tim Cole, and Alberto Giordano, eds, *Geographies of the Holocaust* (Bloomington, IN, 2014).

77. Arjun Appadurai, "Disjuncture and Difference in the Global Cultural Economy," *Theory, Culture, Society* 7 (1990): 296.

78. Sebastian Conrad, *Globalisation and the Nation in Imperial Germany* (New York, 2010); Sebastian Conrad and Jürgen Osterhammel, eds, *Das Kaiserreich transnational. Deutschland in der Welt 1871–1914* (Göttingen, 2004).

79. Bachmann-Medick, *Cultural Turns*, 33.

80. Cf., for example, Susan Zuccotti, *The Holocaust, the French, and the Jews* (New York, 1993); Randolph Braham, *The Politics of Genocide: The Holocaust in Hungary* (Detroit, 2000). For the more recent works, see, for instance, Norman JW Goda, ed., *Jewish Histories of the Holocaust: New Transnational Approaches* (New York, 2014).

81. Shulamit Volkov, "Jewish History. The Nationalism of Transnationalism," in *Transnationale Geschichte Themen, Tendenzen und Theorien*, ed. Gunilla-Friederike Budde, Sebastian Conrad, and Oliver Janz (Göttingen, 2006), 190, 196.

82. Primo Levi, *The Drowned and the Saved* (New York, 1989), 97–100.

83. Peter Burke, *What Is Cultural History?* (Cambridge, 2004), 108.

84. Thomas Pegelow Kaplan, *The Language of Nazi Genocide. Linguistic Violence and the Struggle of Germans of Jewish Ancestry* (New York, 2009).

85. Dening, *Mr Bligh's Bad Language*, 61.

86. See, for example, Walter Manoschek, *"Es gibt nur eines für das Judentum-Vernichtung": Das Judenbild in deutschen Soldatenbriefen 1939–1944* (Hamburg, 1995); and

Bernd Hüppauf, "Emptying the Gaze: Framing Violence through the Viewfinder," *New German Critique* 72 (1997): 3–44.
87. Jörn Leonhard, "Politisches Sprechen im Zeitalter der Extreme, " in *Zeiträume. Potsdamer Almanach des Zentrums für Zeithistorische Forschung 2010,* ed. Martin Sabrow (Göttingen, 2011), 117–20.
88. Hunt, "Where Have All the Theories Gone," 5–7.
89. Jarausch and Geyer, *Shattered Past,* passim.

Bibliography

Addis, Laird. "The Philosophy of Gustav Bergmann." *Algemeen Nederlands Tijdschrift voor Wijsbegeerte* 63 (1971): 78–98.
Alexander, Jeffrey C. "On the Social Construction of Moral Universals. The 'Holocaust' from War Crime to Trauma." *European Journal of Social Theory* 5, no. 1 (2002): 5–85.
Appadurai, Arjun. "Disjuncture and Difference in the Global Cultural Economy." *Theory, Culture, Society* 7 (1990): 295–310.
Assis, Arthur Alfaix. *What Is History for? Johann Gustav Droysen and the Functions of Historiography.* New York: Berghahn Books, 2014.
Bachmann-Medick, Doris. *Cultural Turns: Neuorientierungen in den Kulturwissenschaften.* Reinbek: Rowohlt, 2009.
Barkin, Kenneth. "Bismarck in a Postmodern Age." *German Studies Review* 18, no. 2 (1995): 241–52.
Bergmann, Gustav. *Logic and Reality.* Madison: The University of Wisconsin Press, 1964.
Berkhofer, Robert F. *Beyond the Great Story: History as Text and Discourse.* Cambridge: The Belknap Press of Harvard University Press, 1995.
Boehm, Gottfried, ed. *Was ist ein Bild?* Munich: Fink, 1994.
Braham, Randolph. *The Politics of Genocide: The Holocaust in Hungary.* Detroit: Wayne State University Press, 2000.
Broszat, Martin, and Saul Friedländer. "A Controversy about the Historicization of National Socialism." *New German Critique* 44 (1988): 85–126.
Brown, Callum G. *Postmodernism for Historians.* Harlow: Pearson Longman, 2005.
Browning, Christopher R. "German Memory, Judicial Interrogation, and Historical Reconstruction." In *Probing the Limits of Representation. Nazism and the Final Solution,* edited by Saul Friedländer, 22–36. Cambridge, MA: Harvard University Press, 1992.
Brunner, Otto, Werner Conze, and Reinhart Koselleck, eds. *Geschichtliche Grundbegriffe. Historisches Lexikon zur politisch-sozialen Sprache in Deutschland,* 8 vols. Stuttgart: Klett, 1972–97.
Burke, Peter. *What Is Cultural History?* Cambridge: Polity Press, 2004.
Canning, Kathleen. *Languages of Labor and Gender. Female Factory Work in Germany, 1850–1914.* Ithaca, NY: Cornell University Press, 1996.
Caplan, Jane. "Postmodernism, Poststructuralism, Deconstruction: Notes for Historians." *Central European History* 22, no. 3/4 (1989): 260–78.
Childers, Thomas. "Political Sociology and the 'Linguistic Turn.'" *Central European History* 22, no. 3/4 (1989): 381–93.

————. "The Social Language of Politics in Germany: The Sociology of Political Discourses in the Weimar Republic." *American Historical Review* 95, no. 2 (1990): 331–58.

Ciarlo, David. *Advertising Empire: Race and Visual Culture in Imperial Germany.* Cambridge, MA: Harvard University Press, 2011.

Conrad, Christoph, and Martina Kessel, eds. *Geschichte schreiben in der Postmoderne. Beiträge zur aktuellen Diskussion.* Stuttgart: Reclam, 1994.

Conrad, Sebastian. *Globalisation and the Nation in Imperial Germany.* New York: Cambridge University Press, 2010.

Conrad, Sebastian, and Jürgen Osterhammel, eds. *Das Kaiserreich transnational. Deutschland in der Welt 1871–1914.* Göttingen: Vandenhoeck & Ruprecht, 2004.

Dening, Greg. *Mr Bligh's Bad Language: Passion, Power, and Theatre on the Bounty.* Cambridge: Cambridge University Press, 1992.

Derrida, Jacques. "An Interview with Professor Jacques Derrida," interview by Michal Ben- Naftali. Shoah Resource Center, 8 January 1998. Retrieved October 12 2015 from http://www.yadvashem.org/odot_pdf/Microsoft%20Word%20-%203851.pdf.

Dilthey, Wilhelm. *Hermeneutics and the Study of History,* edited by Rudolf A Makkreel and Frithjof Rodi. Princeton, NJ: Princeton University Press, 1996.

Friedländer, Saul, ed. *Probing the Limits of Representation. Nazism and the Final Solution.* Cambridge, MA: Harvard University Press, 1992.

Gellately, Robert. *The Gestapo and German Society: Enforcing Racial Policy, 1933–1945.* Oxford: Clarendon Press, 1990.

Glowacka, Dorota. "A Date, a Place, a Name: Jacque Derrida's Holocaust Translations." *The New Centennial Review* 7, no. 2 (2007): 111–39.

Goda, Norman JW, ed. *Jewish Histories of the Holocaust: New Transnational Approaches.* New York: Berghahn Books, 2014.

Himmelfarb, Gertrude. *On Looking into the Abyss: Untimely Thoughts on Culture and Society.* New York: Alfred A Knopf, 1994.

Hunt, Lynn. "History Beyond Social Theory." In *The States of "Theory,"* edited by David Carroll, 95–112. New York: Columbia University Press, 1990.

————. "Where Have All the Theories Gone?" *Perspectives* 40, no. 3 (2002): 5–7.

Hunt, Lynn, ed. *The New Cultural History.* Berkeley: University of California Press, 1989.

Hüppauf, Bernd. "Emptying the Gaze: Framing Violence through the Viewfinder." *New German Critique* 72 (1997): 3–44.

Iggers, Georg G. *Historiography in the Twentieth Century: From Scientific Objectivity to the Postmodern Challenge.* Hanover, NH: Wesleyan University Press, 1997.

Jarausch, Konrad H. "Contemporary History as Transatlantic Project: Autobiographical Reflections on the German Problem, 1960–2010." *Historical Social Research,* Supplement 24 (2012): 7–49.

————. "Die Krise der nationalen Meistererzählungen." In *Die Historische Meistererzählung: Deutungslinien der deutschen Nationalgeschichte nach 1945,* edited by Konrad Jarausch and Martin Sabrow, 140–62. Göttingen: Vandenhoeck & Ruprecht, 2002.

Jarausch, Konrad H, and Michael Geyer. "The Future of the German Past: Transatlantic Reflections for the 1990s." *Central European History* 22, no. 3/4 (1989): 229–59.

————. *Shattered Past: Reconstructing German Histories.* Princeton, NJ: Princeton University Press, 2003.

Jones, Gareth Stedman. *Languages of Class: Studies in English Working Class History, 1832–1982.* Cambridge: Cambridge University Press, 1983.

Kaplan, Thomas Pegelow. *The Language of Nazi Genocide. Linguistic Violence and the Struggle of Germans of Jewish Ancestry.* New York: Cambridge University Press, 2009.

Klemperer, Victor. *I Will Bear Witness: A Diary of the Nazi Years,* 2 vols. New York: The Modern Library, 1998–99.

———. *The Language of the Third Reich. LTI.* London: Athlone, 2000.

Knowles, Anne Kelly, Tim Cole, and Alberto Giordano, eds. *Geographies of the Holocaust.* Bloomington, IN: Indiana University Press, 2014.

Koselleck, Reinhart. *The Practice of Conceptual History: Timing History, Spacing Concepts.* Stanford, CA: Stanford University Press, 2002.

LaCarpa, Dominick. "Representing the Holocaust: Reflections on the Historians' Debate." In *Probing the Limits of Representation. Nazism and the Final Solution,* edited by Saul Friedländer, 108–27. Cambridge, MA: Harvard University Press, 1992.

Lambert, Peter. "The Professionalization and Institutionalization of History." In *Writing History: Theory and Practice,* edited by Stefan Berger, Heiko Feldner, and Kevin Passmore, 40–60. London: Bloomsbury Academic, 2010.

Landwehr, Achim. *Geschichte des Sagbaren: Einführung in die historische Diskursanalyse.* Tübingen: Edition Diskord, 2001.

Leonhard, Jörn. "Politisches Sprechen im Zeitalter der Extreme." In *Zeiträume: Potsdamer Almanach des Zentrums für Zeithistorische Forschung 2010,* edited by Martin Sabrow, 117–20. Göttingen: Wallstein, 2011.

Levi, Primo. *The Drowned and the Saved.* New York: Vintage, 1989.

Lüsebrink, Hans-Jürgen, Rolf Reichardt, and Norbert Schürer. *The Bastille: A History of a Symbol of Despotism and Freedom.* Durham, NC: Duke University Press, 1997.

Lyotard, Jean-François. *The Postmodern Condition: A Report on Knowledge.* Minneapolis, MN: University of Minnesota Press, 1984.

Manoschek, Walter. *"Es gibt nur eines für das Judentum-Vernichtung": Das Judenbild in deutschen Soldatenbriefen 1939–1944.* Hamburg: Hamburger Edition, 1995.

Mitchell, WJT. *Picture Theory: Essays on Verbal and Visual Representation.* Chicago: University of Chicago Press, 1994.

Munslow, Alun. *Deconstructing History.* London: Routledge, 1997.

Palmer, Bryan D. *Descent into Discourse: The Reification of Language and the Writing of Social History.* Philadelphia: Temple University Press, 1990.

Paul, Gerhard. *Bilder des Krieges — Krieg der Bilder. Die Visualisierung des modernen Krieges.* Paderborn: Ferdinand Schöningh Verlag, 2004.

———. "Die (Zeit-)Historiker und die Bilder. Plädoyer für eine Visual History." In *Visualität und Geschichte,* edited by Saskia Handro and Bernhard Schönemann, 7–22. Berlin: LIT Verlag, 2011.

———. *Visual History: Ein Studienbuch.* Göttingen: Vandenhoeck & Ruprecht, 2006.

Paul, Gerhard, ed. *Das Jahrhundert der Bilder. Bildatlas 1949 bis heute.* Göttingen: Vandenhoeck & Ruprecht, 2008.

Ramsbrock, Annelie, Annette Vowinckel, and Malte Zierenberg, eds. *Fotografien im 20. Jahrhundert: Verbreitung und Vermittlung.* Göttingen: Wallstein, 2013.

Ranke, Leopold von. *The Theory and Practice of History,* edited by Georg G Iggers. New York: Routledge, 2010.

Reinfandt, Christoph. "Reading Texts after the Linguistic Turn." In _Reading Primary Sources: The Interpretation of Texts from Nineteenth- and Twentieth-Century History,_ edited by Miriam Dobson and Benjamin Ziemann, 37–54. London: Routledge, 2009.

Robin, Régine. _Histoire et linguistique._ Paris: Colin, 1973.

Roeck, Bernd. "Visual Turn? Kulturgeschichte und die Bilder." In _Geschichte und Gesellschaft_ 29 (2003): 294–315.

Rorty, Richard. _The Linguistic Turn: Recent Essays in Philosophical Method._ Chicago: University of Chicago Press, 1967.

Sarasin, Philipp. _Geschichtswissenschaft und Diskursanalyse._ Frankfurt: Suhrkamp, 2003.

———. _Reizbare Maschinen: Eine Geschichte des Körpers, 1765–1914._ Frankfurt: Suhrkamp, 2001.

Schöttler, Peter. "Sozialgeschichtliches Paradigma und historische Diskursanalyse." In _Diskurstheorien und Literaturwissenschaft,_ edited by Jürgen Fohrmann and Harro Müller, 164–79. Frankfurt: Suhrkamp, 1988.

Scott, Joan W. _Gender and the Politics of History._ New York: Columbia University Press, 1988.

———. _Only Paradoxes to Offer: French Feminists and the Rights of Man._ Cambridge, MA: Oxford University Press, 1996.

Spiegel, Gabrielle M. _Practicing History: New Directions in Historical Writing after the Linguistic Turn._ New York: Routledge, 2005.

Toews, John E. "Intellectual History after the Linguistic Turn." _American Historical Review_ 92, no. 4 (1987): 879–907.

Vann, Richard T. "Turning Linguistic: History and Theory in _History and Theory,_ 1960–75." In _A New Philosophy of History,_ edited by Frank Ankersmit and Hans Kellner, 40–69. Chicago: University of Chicago Press, 1995.

Vernon, James. "Who's Afraid of the 'Linguistic Turn'? The Politics of Social History and Its Discontents." _Social History_ 19, no. 1 (1994): 81–97.

Volkov, Shulamit. "Jewish History. The Nationalism of Transnationalism." In _Transnationale Geschichte: Themen, Tendenzen und Theorien,_ edited by Gunilla-Friederike Budde, Sebastian Conrad, and Oliver Janz, 190–201. Göttingen: Vandenhoeck & Ruprecht, 2006.

Walkowitz, Judith R. _City of Dreadful Delight: Narratives of Sexual Danger in Late-Victorian London._ Chicago: University of Chicago Press, 1992.

Wehler, Hans-Ulrich. "Kommentar." In _Geschichte zwischen Kultur und Gesellschaft: Beiträge zur Theoriedebatte,_ edited by Thomas Mergel and Thomas Welskopp, 351–66. Munich: Beck, 1997.

White, Hayden. "The Fictions of Factual Representation." In _Tropics of Discourse: Essays in Cultural Criticism,_ 121–34. Baltimore, MD: John Hopkins University Press, 1978.

———. _Metahistory: The Historical Imagination in Nineteenth-Century Europe._ Baltimore, MD: Johns Hopkins University Press, 1973.

Young, James E. _Writing and Rewriting the Holocaust._ Bloomington, IN: Indiana University Press, 1988.

Zuccotti, Susan. _The Holocaust, the French, and the Jews._ New York: Basic Books, 1993.

Chapter 2

Paths Forward
In Defense of the History of Disciplines

J. Laurence Hare

The year 2014 should have been especially auspicious for the study of history and disciplinarity. For the American Historical Association (AHA), it was the year of "History and Other Disciplines," a theme that would frame the 129th AHA meeting in New York. The organizers asked its members to reflect on the boundaries of historical study and thereby "share their experiences of encounters with other disciplines."[1] When the conference convened in early January 2015, it featured a number of panels assessing history's ongoing relationship with such neighboring fields as archaeology and geography, or considering the role interdisciplinarity has played in shaping historical methodology, teaching practice, and institution building. Of special note were two panels specifically responding to the organizers' call for discussions of the history of disciplinarity: one on the "history of the human sciences" and another on the "history of history."[2] As the panelists rightly recognized, this sort of research has long been a part of the panoply of historical study. Though practitioners of given disciplines often write their own histories to catalog achievements and critique internal scholarly practices, just as often the task falls to professional historians concerned not only with the origins of disciplines, but also with the relationship between their intrinsic development and the contexts in which they function. Ultimately, as the AHA panels affirmed, such studies aspire broadly to increase our understanding of knowledge and authority in the modern era.

Notes for this chapter begin on page 64.

Thus, it is surprising that 2014 was also the year in which a pair of critical essays cast doubt on current scholarship historicizing the production of knowledge in general and disciplinary practice in particular. One was a highly polemical review of recent literature in the history of medicine published by Richard Horton in the British medical journal *The Lancet*.[3] The other, from historian Suzanne L. Marchand, appeared as a chapter in Darrin M. McMahon and Samuel Moyn's *Rethinking Modern European Intellectual History*. In it, Marchand offered a pessimistic assessment of the history of disciplines, a subfield which studies both the emergence of specific fields of knowledge (i.e. psychology or anthropology) and the underlying processes that have shaped the boundaries of scholarship, particularly in the post-Enlightenment era. She argued that this sort of history, which she identified as a fixed "constellation" of scholarly inquiries, passed its peak in the heyday of poststructuralism and now finds itself on the wane.[4] Though she and Horton dealt with different fields of inquiry, they nevertheless seemed to share some common complaints underlying a dilemma within the histories of medicine and scholarship.

The result was a striking contradiction between the strong presence of the history of human sciences at the AHA conference and the gloomy forecasts about its future from historians like Marchand. As I argue in this essay, this uncertainty is especially relevant in the field of modern German history. After all, Suzanne Marchand is a noted specialist in German intellectual history whose two most significant works to date are penetrating studies of the ways in which humanities and social science scholars forged the powerful cultural currents of philhellenism and Orientalism in Germany. She is a principal American scholar in what is an important element of transatlantic German studies. And she is not alone. Her observation about the decline of a long tradition of historical writing on scholarly disciplines in the United States appears alongside a bevy of new English-language works on the history of the human sciences in Germany. As a historian whose own work on archaeology and museums is among the list of new titles, I was unprepared for such prognostications about the end of a subfield that I see as growing rather than declining.

In this essay, I explain this seeming incongruence by first examining Marchand and Horton's arguments together in order to identify the roots of their respective critical viewpoints and to suggest that they represent less a "moribund" period of decline than the symptoms of an ongoing metamorphosis. I then discuss the ways these trends are at work in German studies, with an emphasis on recent research into the history of human science disciplines. Above all, by privileging the German case in this way, I show how the subfield remains alive and well, and how, even if it has transformed a great deal in the last two decades, it nevertheless holds much potential to contribute unique insights into ongoing historiographical problems within German history.

A History of Scholarship and a Crisis of Disciplinarity

In her account of its decline, Marchand provides a genealogy of the history of disciplines that began as a perennial feature of scholarship from the sixteenth century onward and had coalesced into a sustained intellectual conversation by the mid twentieth century. From there, the subfield reached a high-water mark in the early 1990s, primarily in the United States. Marchand argues that it has since lost momentum because its practitioners have abandoned a set of core theoretical frameworks, most notably those shaped by the historian of science Thomas Kuhn and the French cultural theorist Michel Foucault. Where the former provided a way for scholars to reflect on the prevailing methods and theories within the natural and social sciences, the latter inaugurated a wide-ranging critique of power relationships within scholarly practice that strongly influenced research in the humanities. Over time, however, the heat and light surrounding this discussion of disciplinarity dimmed. Criticisms of Kuhn's paradigmatic model, especially its tendency to oversimplify the operations of normal science, mounted, while Foucault's influence on historical methodology proved limited. The shift was closely tied to history's gradual disengagement from the thornier implications of poststructural theory. As Kevin Passmore has explained, historians drew important lessons from the critical approaches of poststructural theorists but did not follow them into a radical transformation. Rather, they merely "survived poststructuralism."[5] Consequently, Marchand argues that by the turn of the century the enthusiasm for historicizing the humanities and social science disciplines had noticeably ebbed. "There are a number of reasons for this," she concludes, "one of which is simply scholarship's need to change horses after the old ones have carried us as far as they can go."[6]

By limiting the scope of her critique in this way, Marchand makes a convincing case that something has unmistakably changed within the history of disciplines. But she also acknowledges a hint of bias in her own conception of the field, writing, "As I practically grew up in this sub-universe … I probably have an exaggerated view of this constellation's importance."[7] Moreover, she hastens to add that not all scholars who participated in this line of inquiry adhered to Foucauldian or Kuhnian perspectives. Finally, it is worth noting that Marchand's own work does not adhere to the narrow parameters she outlines in her essay. Archaeology and philology featured prominently in her two major monographs, *Down from Olympus: Archaeol-*

ogy and Philhellenism in Germany, 1750–1970 and *German Orientalism in the Age of Empire: Religion, Race, and Scholarship,* but they shared space with many other disciplines and institutions that shaped major strains of German thought across multiple generations. Like the numerous works that she cites as exceptions to the norm in disciplinary history, her own books avoid deep engagement with Kuhnian or Foucauldian theory.[8] Thus, as she readily acknowledges, her judgments about the history of disciplines demand rigorous qualification.

The year 2014 also witnessed a sharp critique within the related field of the history of medicine when Richard Horton, editor-in-chief of *The Lancet,* penned the brief but potent piece, "The Moribund Body of Medical History." As he explained, a field that had once featured probing inquiries into the treatment of disease and provided critical perspectives on otherwise blithe narratives of medical progress has of late given way to more tepid analyses that are "invisible, inaudible, and, as a result, inconsequential." Just as in the case of Marchand and the history of disciplines, Horton hearkens back to the halcyon days of the 1990s, when scholars such as François Delaporte and William Bynum laid bare the power dynamics that informed certain conventional and often triumphalist accounts of medical progress in the nineteenth and twentieth centuries.[9] But now, Horton complains, the field has devolved into "philatelist" chronicles that eschew analysis, leaving him to ask pointedly, "So where are the historians of today to illuminate the past as we struggle with the aggressive commercialization of medicine, failures of professional leadership, notions of free will and death, misuse of medicines, paralysis in public health policy, or catastrophic failures of care?"[10] Perhaps not surprisingly, Horton's polemic has drawn a sharp response from historians, who have complained that Horton omitted important new works and observed that his criticisms hinged on a "whiggish" narrative of progress out of step with contemporary historiography.[11]

Horton adopts a gloomier tone than Marchand, who balances her sense of resignation with the hope that "the history of scholarship has by no means disappeared from intellectual historians' horizons."[12] She even suggests possible "futures" for the subfield as lying with a closer dialogue with the history of science and with a return to "old-fashioned" research in the sociology of knowledge.[13] Yet, while the two essays mentioned here also differ greatly in their focus and depth of coverage, they seem to agree that these fields of study have lost their critical edge. Whether they have deserted their original mission or abandoned their theoretical guideposts, the scholars in these fields seem to be likewise adrift in circumstances that raise larger questions about the state of the field within the larger historiography of knowledge production.

Such similarities speak to a deeper problem connected to contemporary perspectives on the very notion of disciplinarity. One of the legacies of poststructural criticism in the 1980s and 1990s has been a waning confidence in the ability of traditional disciplines to organize adequately the pursuit of knowledge. For example, in a wide-ranging synthesis of literature on the subject, historian and self-avowed Foucauldian Robert Post points to a key paradox within the power relationships most visibly at work in the humanities. Specifically, he claims that the task of maintaining a "disciplining" impulse, which is essential for organizing research, achieving consensus, and assessing results, is inherently at odds with the humanities' purported mission of fostering creative endeavor, especially with respect to their place in challenging conventional thinking. The resulting dilemma creates a crisis of authority, as "creative" scholars working beyond the standards of their discipline become "sage amateurs" rather than true experts, which in turn renders the entire field "internally unstable."[14] At the same time, a number of commentators have observed accelerating trends toward interdisciplinarity.[15] The challenge they pose to the boundaries of established disciplines has increased dramatically, giving rise to a number of new "studies" fields: gender studies, poverty studies, and so on; along with sets of detached research "centers" operating on the edges of conventional university structures. Taken to the extreme, James Chandler has suggested that the lure of interdisciplinary may become so "routinized" that we are left with the "sense that all dynamism in academic intellectual life must *necessarily* occur in the spaces between [disciplines]."[16]

These critiques of the humanities and social sciences parallel discussions underway within the natural sciences, which have wrestled with their own seemingly latent flaws. In perhaps the most radical iteration, science writer John Horgan has suggested that the goals of science, which seek the ultimate answers to questions about the physical universe, are inherently oriented toward an end point. Either they arrive at firm conclusions that satisfy the fundamental questions of the field, or they reach a point where no further empirical discovery is possible. Based on interviews with dozens of leading figures in such fields as biology, neuroscience, and physics, Horgan speculated that we might very soon find ourselves at the "end of science."[17] Many scientists have since rejected Horgan's book as oversimplified and cynical while sympathizing with the anxieties about the range of impasses gripping specific science disciplines.[18]

Tying these critical threads together is an alternative explanation from Paul Forman of the Smithsonian Institution. Where Robert Post and John Horgan follow different paths to envision a waning confidence in disciplinarity and a sense of its looming exhaustion, Forman interprets the crisis as symptomatic of a larger historical rupture. Building on the work of Perry Anderson, who distinguished between "epochal" and "aesthetic" notions of postmodernity,[19] Forman claims that we have entered a distinctly postmodern era whose most tangible hallmark is the shift from the "primacy of science" to the "primacy of technology."[20] Underlying this transformation is a more fundamental reversal in the hierarchical relationship between theory and practice. With the ascendance of the latter, the role of fields as seekers of pure knowledge became effectively obsolete, while the confining "proceduralism" of disciplinary structures, the unmasking of "disinterested" objectivity, and the decline of collegial "solidarity" eroded the foundations of disciplinarity. Just as Post looks to Foucault to explain the tensions within disciplines, so Forman turns to Thomas Kuhn, drawing on his theory of paradigmatic change as a sign that "all truly important and admirable action occurred when a science fell into one its revolutionary phases" outside of the strictures of disciplines. Forman interprets the publication of Kuhn's *Structure of Scientific Revolutions* in 1962 as a bellwether marking the end of a period of decline in traditional fields and the emergence of an "antidisciplinary" attitude in the new postmodern era.[21]

Forman's thesis is intriguing because it directly states what other assessments merely imply, that disciplinarity is historically finite. Yet it is difficult to ignore the many ways in which disciplines remain robust two decades into the twenty-first century and over fifty years after they should have withered into mere vestigial appendages of the postmodern academy. Most scholars still identify themselves as "historians" or "sociologists," or "physicists," and the very fact that we continue to employ the term "interdisciplinary" to describe our more transgressive inquiries nevertheless evinces at least some level of obeisance to the traditional boundaries of knowledge production. To understand its resilience, we might point to the institutional and professional orientation of the academy. Forman argues that the split between theory and practice warrants a clear divide between the notions of "discipline" and "profession," claiming that the former is defined by the "production and curation of a distinctive body of knowledge" while the latter is "oriented primarily to the provision of practical service on the basis of possession ... of a distinctive body of knowledge."[22] But, as James Chandler has explained, "To imagine disciplines as entirely separable from their institutional arrangements is to produce an overly idealized sense of what they are and how they function."[23] In a similar way, the historian James M. Banner Jr. argues that discipline as a "province of inquiry," is distinct from profession as an "arena of action," but that the two overlap in important ways.[24] The transmission of disciplinary knowledge through publishing and teaching is connected to professions, while professional titles represent a form of status signaling acceptance into a disciplinary community. This is why most graduate students train within a defined field, and why most positions in the academic job market seek specialists suited for employment in an academic department usually defined by disciplinary allegiance. In any case, it seems that the notion of discipline as both an organizing principle and collegial community lives on, albeit in a state of dynamic tension.

Understanding these central dilemmas is important because they allow us to frame the related challenges in the history of human sciences. If Forman is correct to say that the intense skepticism of disciplinary practice in the late twentieth century is but a symptom of the inevitable passing of traditional fields of knowledge, then it is easy to understand why commentators such as Marchand and Horton might likewise see their histories in tandem decline, since they would collectively represent another ephemeral sign of the times. However, the persistence of disciplinarity in the twenty-first century and the ongoing influence of professional and institutional practice suggest that we may not have reached such a great caesura in knowledge production. Nevertheless, it is tempting to conclude in the very least that we have experienced the end of a distinct phase in the formation of disciplines lasting from their crystallization in the early nineteenth century to the rise of intense reflexivity within and increasing permeability among fields in the later twentieth century. This is not to suggest that we have "survived disciplinarity" in the same way historians have allegedly "survived poststructuralism." Nor does it necessarily herald the end of disciplinary history. Rather, it warrants, as Marchand and Horton have proposed, an ongoing critical investigation of scholarly fields, and indeed broadens the horizon of study to the practices of interdisciplinarity, institutionalization, and professionalization. It also creates the possibility of researching discrete periods of disciplinarity and deriving not only critical insight into contemporary practice but also a greater sense of the interactions between disciplines and their historical contexts. It thus permits us to explore how national or global events may have altered the institutional setting and thereby informed the production of knowledge within a given field.[25] It facilitates consideration of the fluid boundaries between popular and professional scholarship in the early years of disciplinary formation.[26] And it leads us to ask how disciplinary practices shaped culture, informed policy, and forged identities in the nineteenth and twentieth centuries.

Expanding the domain of inquiry in this way should reassure us generally that the potential future for this brand of intellectual history remains bright. Moreover, it may help us identify the true locus of critique from Marchand and Horton. Rather than accepting the premise that these histories are declining, we can understand the problem differently as a departure from the purported unity that characterized them before the late 1990s. The new scope of study exhibits a much wider diversity of purpose, approach, and method. Consequently, there has been a loss of continuity in subfields whose early mission was to unmask the latent assumptions and orientations of the human sciences. It is this, I think, that informs the recent critiques of the field, along with a creeping concern that the research conversation risks losing its bearings in the future. But it seems clear that its task has become no less pertinent, while the range of possible questions has only grown.

The Human Sciences and Modern German Historiography

The twin challenges of continuity and diversification in research should be readily familiar to students of modern German history. As Konrad Jarausch and Michael Geyer have argued, the ending of the twentieth century, whose terminal point arguably rested atop the ruins of the Berlin Wall, has given scholars of German history an opportunity to reflect on the "overarching narratives of the past that suggest a pattern of historical development for the public as well as the scholar."[27] In part, this exercise has entailed a shift of focus, with scholars seeking what Helmut Walser Smith elegantly describes as new "vanishing points" of German history.[28] At the same time, it has precipitated the gradual unraveling of metanarratives linking the calamities of Germany's twentieth century to developments in previous centuries. Significant among these has been the so-called *Sonderweg* (separate path) thesis, which utilized social science methods, structuralist orientations, and modernization paradigms to produce an account of Germany's modern history at odds with earlier triumphalist narratives of the nation's unification and rise to world power status. By stressing the uneven development between soaring economic, scientific, and technological modernization of the *Kaiserreich* on the one hand, and its lagging political liberalization on the other, the *Sonderweg* provided a fairly comprehensive account of Germany's twentieth century while linking it clearly to developments in the nineteenth. But it faced withering assaults from historians on both sides of the Atlantic who found fault with its methodological neglect of individual agency and experience, its flawed premises about bourgeois culture, or its problematic idealization of modernization.[29] Yet, because this criticism went hand in hand with a growing skepticism of "master narratives," its success in exposing the anomalies of the *Sonderweg* generated no Kuhnian-style paradigmatic revolution in its wake. There was no alternative narrative to offer, and the explanatory power of modernization theory has receded only grudgingly. As a result, our sense of the long-term connections across the nineteenth and twentieth centuries seems uncertain, even as scholars continue to cleave to the *Sonderweg*'s predilection for studying the imperial era.[30]

For this reason, modern German historiography, like disciplinary history, has found itself cast adrift from some of its most prominent theoretical and methodological moorings. But in the same way, this shift has created opportunities to ask new research questions and reexamine older inquiries in revised spatial and chronological frames. Moreover, it allows historians to shift, as Jarausch and Geyer explain, from a "univocal" to a "multivocal" causality to explain developments in the twentieth century.[31] If, for instance, Helmut Walser Smith is right that the *Sonderweg* debate "had the effect of cutting off much of the nineteenth century from the events of the early twentieth," then the diminution of the controversy has created new space for recasting the relationship between the nineteenth and twentieth centuries.[32] At the same time, the widening horizons of research has fostered a reconsideration of space itself.

What I would argue here is that bound up with the historiographic threads are the strands of disciplinary history. Because the dilemmas confronting these fields are so similar, it is perhaps not surprising that the trends in writing the history of human sciences should intersect and inform the changes in modern German historiography. In this vein, the ground for the research of the human sciences published in the twenty-first century was prepared in part by Konrad Jarausch, whose writing on the professions and higher education during the 1980s were based on the premise that grasping the linkages between institutions, politics, and society are essential to understanding the development of a given intellectual climate. Specifically, his *Students, Society, and Politics in Imperial Germany* shifted the study of "academic illiberalism" away from a narrow focus on the "mandarin" intellectual elite and onto a wider range of social factors within the changing structure of higher education in the *Kaiserriech*, including growing enrollments, the changing social backgrounds of students and faculty, and the connections between university curricula and the political socialization of students.[33] A few years later, Jarausch turned his attention to the history of professions, placing the development of lawyers, engineers, and teachers into an equally complex sociological and political matrix but at the same time insisting on a historical analysis that cut across the traditional ruptures of early twentieth-century German history.[34]

Similar themes appeared in the work of Geoffrey Cocks, who tackled the history of psychotherapy during the Third Reich, moving beyond Max Weinreich's revelations about the complicity of academics in the crimes of the Nazi regime to ask more pointed questions about the moral and professional dilemmas in a field that benefitted tremendously from the largesse of the Nazi state.[35] Meanwhile, Woodruff Smith's *Politics and the Sciences of Culture in Germany* sought to reconcile social approaches to the history of human sciences with the cultural turn. In his attempt to account for the sudden and powerful emergence of "cultural science" disciplines in Germany at the end of the nineteenth century, Smith regarded post-structural approaches with skepticism, arguing that Kuhn's concept of paradigmatic change and Foucault's focus on discourse were either overly broad or too "hermeneutic" to explain the process of change he observed within the German academy. Instead, he adopted an approach that preserved Jarausch's concern with social and political variables, arguing that "we cannot postulate a community of scientists separated in their professional work from the outside world."[36]

Taken together, these writings helped create space for later studies to move away from insular approaches to academic knowledge and toward more contextualized assessments of disciplinary formation and efficacy. To a great extent, this new phase of research has been produced by younger scholars rather than solely by seasoned historians or advanced practitioners of the fields under study. Indeed, three of Jarausch's students went on to produce dissertations dealing with the human sciences in nineteenth- and twentieth-century Germany.[37] The disciplinary histories they have written have served principally as a means of answering big questions in German history without falling into the orbit of prevailing master narratives. Thus, from the middle of the 1990s, during the years that Marchand noted as a declining period in traditional disciplinary histories, a new set of works began to appear that typically studied one human science field in order to ask some far-reaching questions about the German past.

The work that immediately stands out at the beginning of this trend is Suzanne Marchand's *Down from Olympus: Archaeology and Philhellenism in Nineteenth-Century Germany,* which appeared in 1996. Though she took her cue from Edith Butler's *The Tyranny of Greece over Germany* (1935), Marchand moved beyond Butler's focus on such seminal intellectual figures as Lessing and Goethe, and looked instead at the ways that more mundane scholars (in this case archaeologists) brought the adoration of ancient Greek art and culture into the German academy, where it became a fixture of educational and scholarly institutions. Along the way, she showed how this effort was inseparable from Germany's political engagement with the Near East and informed German policy into the Third Reich and beyond. In 2009, Marchand followed this work with a second, more ambitious monograph treating the course of Orientalism in Imperial

Germany. Here she picked up where Edward Said had famously left off, and took the opportunity to lift the concept from the sterile realm of discourse and situate it within a concrete "set of *practices* ... bound up with the Central European institutional settings in which the sustained and serious study of the languages, histories, and cultures of Asia took place."[38] With this approach, Marchand explored German Orientalism not through the history of a specific discipline but as a history of interdisciplinarity, where philologists and Biblical scholars crossed paths with historians and ethnographers.

Marchand's work thus made important contributions to the study of German philhellenism and Orientalism, but also set the stage for several new approaches in the history of human sciences. The first of these was Susan A. Crane's *Collecting and Historical Consciousness in Early Nineteenth-Century Germany* (2000), Andrew Zimmerman's *Anthropology and Antihumanism in Imperial Germany* (2001), and H. Glenn Penny's *Ethnology and Ethnographic Museums in Imperial Germany* (2002).[39] Each of these works took on similarly vital themes, including memory, humanism, racism, nationalism, and cosmopolitanism. Moreover, each focused on exploring what Zimmerman referred to as the "profound challenges to the primacy of the university as a location for producing scientific knowledge" during the later nineteenth century.[40] Instead of a conventional account of institutionalization, Crane and Penny examined the intersection of museums and the public, while Zimmerman focused on the interaction between the indigenous peoples of the colonial world and the scholars who developed a science of mankind by studying and exhibiting the artifacts, behaviors, and even the bodies of their subjects. From there, a steady stream of new monographs followed. Andrew Evans charted the ways in which racism became a feature of a formerly liberal German anthropological tradition as a result of mobilization, propaganda, and combat during World War I.[41] Denise Phillips uncovered the transition of natural science from "descriptive label to rallying cry" by tracing the overlapping ties between institutions and "private learned societies" in the late eighteenth and early nineteenth centuries.[42] Finally, Jason Hansen's *Mapping the Germans* and my own *Excavating Nations,* both of which appeared in 2015, considered the thorny connections between varieties of German nationalism and the fields of geography and prehistoric archaeology, respectively.[43]

There are, of course, a number of other studies of the human sciences in Germany appearing in the last two decades that partake in a broader contextualization of disciplinary knowledge by studying, for instance, the connections between German disciplines, politics, and culture, or between emerging fields and gender relations.[44] But the monographs mentioned above share with Marchand's work at least three key characteristics that set them somewhat apart from previous trends in disciplinary history while also bringing them into the orbit of new approaches to German history. The first of these is an attempt to move beyond the limits of post-structuralism. Even as they deal on some level with power dynamics and the discursive ordering of knowledge and thus owe a debt to Foucauldian approaches, these more recent authors place a greater emphasis on the concrete processes of change in practice and representation, as well as on the agency of both the experts and amateurs (and the blurry categories in between) who shaped the boundaries of scholarship in the modern era. The lessons they draw necessarily involve an accounting of the limits of purportedly disinterested learning, but they are not treated in revelatory fashion. Instead, they act as precursors for a new set of arguments about the spread and efficacy of much larger concepts, whether codified in institutional or disciplinary practices, or shaped in associational life and popular culture, or forged through sustained contact with the colonial world. In this way, the ostensible subject of the works–archaeology, geography, etc.—become secondary to the history of philhellenism, nationalism, racism, and so on.

These works stand astride currents in intellectual and cultural history. They are concerned with the creation, transmission, crystallization, and transformation of ideas, and in this way reflect a trend in intellectual history circling back to Lovejoyian approaches.[45] The difference is that the books elide ideas in a narrow sense and focus instead on grander themes or projects that acted as the fertile ground for a range of thought across distinct periods and among distinct groups. In this way, the authors are able to treat the entanglements of ideas, symbols, language, and systems of meaning in a diachronic frame. Just as Konrad Jarausch argued for the power of universities to shape general attitudes about liberalism at the dawn of the twentieth century, so too do these studies link the growth of disciplines with the development of civic and cultural values at home and the collective worldviews that shaped policies abroad. The door, of course, swings both ways, and these histories rightly recognize that cultural assumptions about nation, race, class, or gender also informed scholarship, not only because they colored the perspectives and biases of researchers, but also because they afforded underlying value to the scholarly enterprise.

Another obvious feature is the shared national setting. The books mentioned here are undeniably German histories. Of course, this is not entirely new; a number of earlier studies rooted themselves in national frames, including George Stocking's *After Tylor: British Social Anthropology, 1888–1951* and *Victorian Anthropology,* which confined themselves to the British tradition. Stocking, however, saw himself a historian of anthropology, and many of his other publications extended far beyond British shores to include essays on Boas, Levi-Strauss, Mead, and Malinowski.[46] By contrast, more recent scholarship has emerged from historians whose expertise extends more firmly to national rather than disciplinary histories. It is likely that their interest in the human sciences grew in no small measure due to the rising salience of research into such larger themes as nationalism and racism during the 1990s. Moreover, the emphasis on institutional or associational frameworks, along with the historical training and historiographical engagement of the researcher, made it easier to pursue these questions from the standpoint of a single country. I would argue that this is not an unhealthy development, because it has had the effect of deuniversalizing the history of human sciences, and of seeing these fields as uniquely shaped by regional or national traditions.

At the same time, this trend has gone hand in hand with a growing awareness of the limits of nation as a category of analysis. Here the history of human sciences has been an essential part of respatializing national histories. In the German case, the most obvious contribution has been directed toward studies assessing the nation's relationship with its colonies, which has refashioned an overlooked era of the country's history while aligning its historiography with the more general move toward histories of globalization.[47] This is not, of course, unique to Germany, and we can easily find exemplars in other national settings, among the most recent of which is Alice Conklin's study of social science and empire in France, in which she reveals how anthropologists helped both to make and unmake French imperial culture in the nineteenth and twentieth centuries.[48] Furthermore, this line of inquiry has drawn the attention of world historians like Rainier Buschmann, who investigates the uses of anthropology in German New Guinea in order to understand how specialists, officials, and settlers delineated "ethnographic frontiers," in which local encounters could speak to a more globalized knowledge.[49] Yet the contribution of German specialists has been significant, first because of the powerful historical influence of German social scientists abroad and second because the relatively small size and limited duration of the German colonies highlights the degree of "fantasy" that attached to the history of European colonialism and the complexity of the connections, both real and imagined, between colony and metropole.[50] In this way, for instance, the inseparable ties between anthropology's "worldly" scientific mission and its roots in the homeland explain why, as Penny and Zimmerman showed, anthropologists played a central role in conveying the lessons of empire to the German public.[51] More recently, George Steinmetz has uncovered the ways in which imperial policy informed a set of institutional, financial, and personal circumstances that shaped the relative heteronomy within German sociology and ultimately had a profound influence on research into race and politics.[52]

Despite the intense interest in German colonialism, real or imagined, the respatialization of German history stretches far beyond empire, as does the engagement with the history of human sciences. In *Doctors of Empire*, Hoi-eun Kim brings together the histories of medicine and social science to explore the intellectual ties between Germany and Japan, concerning himself primarily with the spread of German knowledge and culture abroad and with the means by which Germans encountered the other at home. Its title notwithstanding, Kim's book is not another study of colonial relationships or hegemonies; rather, it represents a transnational history preserving the elements of drift and flow evident in German-Japanese exchange and the essential "nodal" elements that comprise the two national cultures. With this approach, Kim aims for a "reciprocal" history that helps explain the modernization of the two countries without falling into overly simplistic or teleological narratives.[53] Meanwhile, Philipp Stelzel's forthcoming study of the community of German historians in the postwar era, *A German Special Path*, offers a different set of horizons, revealing the role of transatlantic ties in reshaping the discipline after the fall of the Third Reich, when historians were forced to negotiate an entrenched set of practices and attitudes to confront and ultimately overturn prevailing nationalist paradigms.[54] To this list, I might add my own work, which has shown how the norms of practices of archaeology functioned in the transnational space of a contested border region and thereby complicated attempts to utilize a growing body of knowledge about the distant past for nation-building projects in Germany and Scandinavia. In this instance, even scholars working in their homeland to lay exclusive claims to border regions depended on cooperation and exchange with colleagues in neighboring countries to access research materials, develop theories, build institutions, and achieve acceptance within the field.[55] As a whole, these examples serve to show how human science histories help push at the edges of national categories but also serve as cautionary reminders, as Stelzel writes, that we "should not define transnational in a normative way."[56]

Alongside the process of respatializing German history has been a series of efforts to reconsider its temporal boundaries. A number of scholars have begun to ask whether the traditional notions of rupture within the country's nineteenth and twentieth centuries, including Germany's unification in 1871, its involvement in the worlds wars, and its reunification after the fall of the Berlin Wall in 1989, might be obscuring some otherwise salient features of the German past while setting others in an overly deterministic light. Studies of the human sciences are important in this regard because they reveal what Glenn Penny has identified as the "affinities" of German culture, which may exhibit a variable political or social valence over time but whose general qualities transcend the vagaries of any given moment.[57] The "affinity" to which Penny referred was the German fascination with Native Americans, but disciplinary histories have yielded similar accounts of Germans' engagement over the last three centuries with the vestiges of the Classical civilization or the Nordic past, or of perennial questions about where the nation's borders properly lay or what it means to be German. These were the sorts of issues that called for expert knowledge, and that drove the development of human science disciplines. Furthermore, the connections between scholarship and culture in this case naturally set the researcher along a different timeline, following not a consensus view on the highpoints of German history but the development of the disciplines under study, defined either through their institutional life or through a more organic assessment of their interaction with a particular theme or issue, whether it be philhellenism or Orientalism, or a border dispute or the "fantasies" of empire.

These developments should not lead us to believe that new considerations of periodization have diminished the historical importance of major moments in German history or hindered the ongoing study of the Nazi past and the Holocaust. Indeed, a number of researchers have followed the lead of Jarausch and Cocks in examining the "conundrum of complicity" of professionals and scholars working with the Nazi regime.[58] An enormous literature has appeared detailing the engagement of engineers, natural scientists, social scientists, mathematicians, and humanities scholars with government offices and Nazi organizations, with much of it stemming from within the given fields.[59] This scholarship has firmly established the relative complicity of professionals across German academia and has detailed the intense pressure that individual practitioners faced from the regime and from opportunistic and ideologically motivated peers. Moreover, by piecing together the complex array of motives driving scholarly collaboration and the range of activities performed under the auspices of the Third Reich, it has also put to rest any notions of a simple moral dichotomy between "good" and "bad" scholarship or of easy distinctions for "Nazi" scholars.

More recently, historians have attended to the ways in which the structure of disciplines and institutions have informed the pressures scholars encountered in Nazi Germany, and how the politicization of "normal" scholarship affected not only their moral choices, but also the outcomes of their research.[60] Thus, the move toward what Kiran Klaus Patel has called a "transnationalization" of Nazism and the Holocaust has led to a reconsideration of how Germans acted as members of international academic communities during these years, while asking how foreign scholars may have accommodated or participated in pursuing the regime's ideological

goals.[61] Meanwhile, the changing periodization evident in recent disciplinary histories has allowed historians to inquire into the knowledge produced within fields closely affiliated with the regime, raising some debate
about the quality of politicized research.[62]

Viewed as a whole, the widening horizons of human science history
have provided important ways, particularly for younger scholars, to contribute to a similarly expanding range of inquiries within German historiography. This research has shed new light on older questions, such
as how and why so many academics allowed their work to be used for
overtly political, ideological, and ultimately criminal ends, and what the
consequences of that sort of collaboration proved to be. And it has en-
hanced new fields of study aimed at creating a more comprehensive pan-
orama of German culture and society, while assessing its formation and
efficacy within the wider world. Certainly, such changes complicate our
view of modern Germany, refusing as they do to reduce its history to a single "vanishing point." To extend the art metaphor, we find our historical
image shifting from realism to cubism, to a scene in which the historian
must confront multiple perspectives at once. Though it may be distorted,
it nevertheless retains a sense of the overall picture, and in many ways the
field may be richer for it.

Conclusion

Given the array of books that have treated the topic over the last twenty
years, it is fair to argue that histories of disciplines have multiplied rather
than diminished. They have found their way into a number of national historiographies while establishing an indispensable presence within studies
of globalization. But it is also undeniable that the subfield is not precisely
what it once was. Even if it remains clearly tied to its development in the
1980s and 1990s, it is no longer quite the self-reflexive, self-critical, and
implicitly presentist pursuit that it was during its purported heyday. What
appears now is a more eclectic set of works joining ongoing trends in the
history of science, technology, and medicine in studying the production
of knowledge with an intense concern for context, treating disciplines
as dynamic groupings bounded historically and intricately connected to
time and place. At the same time, these studies tend to utilize the extant
sources differently, reconstructing the development, practice, and institutionalization of disciplines to illuminate broader themes in cultural and
intellectual history. In these cases, the disciplinary history shares space or
even becomes subordinate to the theme, idea, or movement under study.

It is this set of changes that has allowed the history of the human sciences to converge so nicely with developments in German historiography.

I would suggest that these changes reflect a maturation process in which the early revelations of the history of disciplines have come to serve as the foundation for a more varied set of historical inquiries. They have created the conceptual space necessary to see the human sciences as instruments of policy, generators of social change, and windows into cultural currents. Now historians have been able to move into a more detailed accounting of how they formed, how they operated, and how they changed alongside the societies in which they were embedded. The changes, however, have come at a cost. I suspect that the reason they have drawn such pessimism of late has been due to the decline, not of the subfield itself, but of the sense of community and ongoing dialogue that once characterized it. Indeed, the AHA's decision to emphasize disciplinarity at its 129th meeting in part represented an attempt to inaugurate a new round of conversation among specialists with similar approaches and questions but who are otherwise isolated within national or chronological specialties.

In terms of research, meanwhile, much remains to be done. For German historians, the rich possibilities raised by recent studies of the nineteenth and early twentieth centuries have by no means been exhausted. We would gain much from closer interactions among intellectual historians studying the human sciences and cultural historians and literary scholars approaching the same themes with very different sources and methods.[63] For the later twentieth century, our increasingly firm grasp of the operation of science, social science, and the humanities in Nazi Germany is not yet matched by our understanding of how those same fields reconstituted themselves after the war, and how they thereby shaped society and culture within East and West Germany. Another intriguing approach might evaluate how the continuities within disciplinary practice and production, including a commitment to seeking the truth or a sense of public value, challenge conventional views on the contours of the twentieth century. Just as the study of disciplines in the nineteenth century has lent itself to enlightening narratives of globalization and transnational exchange, so too might concurrent treatment of twentieth-century developments help us better see the historical trends that elided the caesura of war, fascism, genocide, and thereby encompass the entire twentieth century.[64]

It may be the case, as Paul Forman argues, that we have indeed passed through an "age of disciplines." But the work that has followed its supposed moment of eclipse reminds us that the search for knowledge continues to demarcate as well as delineate, and to erect boundaries, whether in scope, method, practice, or authority. As the debates over disciplinarity have shown, the spaces thus bounded—what Suzanne Marchand has called "constellations"—are constantly in flux. For this reason, the work goes on to historicize them. After all, what are constellations but gatherings of stars in constant motion?

J. Laurence Hare is an associate professor of history and Director of International and European Studies at the University of Arkansas.

Notes

1. Jan E. Goldstein, Francesca Trivellato, and Andrew S. Sartori, "'History and Other Disciplines': The Theme of the 129th Annual Meeting," *Perspectives on History* 51, no. 6 (2013), accessed 1 March 2015, http://www.historians.org/publications-and-directories/perspectives-on-history/september-2013/history-and-the-other-disciplines#.
2. Sharon K. Tune and Debbie Ann Doyle, eds, *Program of the 129th Meeting of the American Historical Association* (New York: AHA, 2–5 January 2015).
3. Richard Horton, "The Moribund Body of Medical History," *The Lancet* 384, no. 9940 (2014): 292.
4. Suzanne L. Marchand, "Has the History of Disciplines Had Its Day?," in *Rethinking Modern European Intellectual History,* ed. Darrin M McMahon and Samuel Moyn (Oxford, 2014), 131–52.
5. Erich von Dietze, *Paradigms Explained: Rethinking Thomas Kuhn's Philosophy of Science* (Westport, CT, 2001); Alan Munslow, *Deconstructing History,* 2nd ed. (New York, 2006), 148. Kevin Passmore, "Poststructuralism and History," in *Writing History: Theory and Practice,* 2nd ed., ed. Stefan Berger, Heiko Feldner, and Kevin Passmore (London, 2010), 143.
6. Marchand, "Has the History of Disciplines," 142.
7. Ibid., 132.
8. See Peter Jelavich, "Review of *Down from Olympus: Archaeology and Philhellenism in Germany, 1750–1970,* by Suzanne L. Marchand," *The Art Bulletin* 80 (June 1998): 384.
9. Horton specifically praised, among others, François Delaporte, *The History of Yellow Fever: An Essay on the Birth of Tropical Medicine,* trans. Arthur Goldhammer (Cambridge, MA, 1991); and WF Bynum, *The Science and Practice of Medicine in the Nineteenth Century* (Cambridge, 1994).
10. Horton, "The Moribund Body of Medical History," 292.
11. Pratik Chakrabati, Graham Mooney, and Patricia Skinner, eds, *Social History of Medicine* 27, no. 4 (2014): 629–31; Carsten Timmermann, "Not Moribund at All! An Historian of Medicine's Response to Richard Horton," *The Guardian,* 4 August 2014, accessed 1 March 2015 from http://www.theguardian.com/science/the-h-word/2014/aug/04/not-moribund-historian-medicine-response-richard-horton.
12. Marchand, "Has the History of Disciplines," 146.

13. Ibid., 143, 146.

14. Robert Post, "Debating Disciplinarity," in "The Fate of Disciplines," ed. James Chandler and Arnold I. Davidson, *Critical Inquiry* 35, no. 4 (2009): 749–70.

15. Julie Thompson Klein had already suggested as much in 1990, pointing to a sharp rise in the literature seeking to define and assess the perceived rise of interdisciplinary as a permanent feature of the academic landscape. See Julie Thompson Klein, *Interdisciplinarity: History, Theory, Practice* (Detroit, 1990), esp. 28–39.

16. James Chandler, "Introduction: Doctrines, Disciplines, Discourses, Departments," in "The Fate of Disciplines," ed. James Chandler and Arnold I. Davidson, *Critical Inquiry* 35, no. 4 (2009): 729–46, 739. Emphasis in original.

17. John Horgan, *The End of Science; Facing the Limits of Knowledge in the Twilight of the Scientific Age* (Baltimore, MD, 1996).

18. See among many others Brian Hayes, "Review: The End of Science Writing?," *American Scientist* 84, no. 5 (1996): 495–96; George Cybenko, "Hardly the End of Science," *IEEE Computational Science and Engineering* 4, no. 2 (1997): 1. John Horgan reflected on the controversy in "Looking back at 'The End of Science': More than a Decade of Lively Debate," *Science and Spirit* 19, no. 2 (2008): 40–43.

19. Perry Anderson, *The Origins of Postmodernity* (London, 1998), 5.

20. Paul Forman, "The Primacy of Science in Modernity, of Technology in Postmodernity, and of Ideology in the History of Technology," *History and Technology* 23, no. 1/2 (2007): 1–152. He explains, "In modernity, the cultural rank of science was elevated by … the presupposition of the superiority of theory to practice. … Today … technology is the beneficiary, and science the maleficiary, of our pragmatic-utilitarian subordination of means to ends," 2.

21. Paul Forman, "On the Historical Forms of Knowledge Production and Curation: Modernity Entailed Disciplinarity, Postmodernity Entails Antidisciplinarity," *Osiris* 27, no. 1 (2012): 95.

22. Ibid., 60.

23. Chandler, "Introduction: Doctrines," 734.

24. James M. Banner Jr., *Being a Historian: An Introduction to the Professional World of History* (Cambridge, 2012), 3.

25. David Kaiser takes this very approach when he argues that the Cold War concern with nuclear warfare created a "bust" in physics scholarship that ultimately changed the operation of the field. See Kaiser, "Booms, Busts, and the World of Ideas: Enrollment Pressures and the Challenge of Specialization," *Osiris* 27, no. 1 (2012): 276–302.

26. For a recent example of this sort of inquiry, see Bonnie Effros, *Uncovering the Germanic Past: Merovingian Archaeology in France, 1830–1914* (Oxford, 2012).

27. Konrad H. Jarausch and Michael Geyer, *Shattered Past: Reconstructing German Histories* (Princeton, NJ, 2003), 4.

28. Helmut Walser Smith, *The Continuities of German History: Nation, Religion, and Race across the Long Nineteenth Century* (Cambridge, 2008), 13–38.

29. Konrad H Jarausch, "Towards a Social History of Experience: Postmodern Predicaments in Theory and Interdisciplinarity," *Central European History* 22, no. 3/4 (1989): 427–43; David Blackbourn and Geoff Eley, *The Peculiarities of German History: Bourgeois Society and Politics in Nineteenth-Century Germany* (Oxford, 1984).

30. Helmut Walser Smith, "When the Sonderweg Debate Left Us," *German Studies Review* 31, no. 2 (2008): 225–40, 237.

31. Konrad H. Jarausch and Michael Geyer, "The Future of the German Past? Transatlantic Reflections for the 1990s," *Central European History* 22, nos. 3 and 4 (1989): 229–59.

32. Smith, "When the Sonderweg Debate Left Us," 235.

33. Konrad H. Jarausch, *Students, Society, and Politics in Imperial Germany: The Rise of Academic Illiberalism* (Princeton, NJ, 1982). Jarausch considered the international implications of this research in "Higher Education and Social Change: Some Comparative Perspectives," in *The Transformation of Higher Learning, 1860–1930: Expansion, Diversification, Social Opening, and Professionalization in England, Germany, Russia, and the United States*, ed. Konrad H. Jarausch (Chicago, 1983).

34. Geoffrey Cocks and Konrad H. Jarausch, *German Professions, 1850–1930* (Oxford, 1990).

35. Geoffrey Cocks, *Psychotherapy in the Third Reich: The Göring Institute* (New York, 1985); Max Weinreich, *Hitler's Professors: The Part of Scholarship in Germany's Crimes against the Jewish People* (New York, 1946).

36. Woodruff D. Smith, *Politics and the Sciences of Culture in Germany, 1840–1920* (New York, 1991), 6–7.

37. I include in this list J. Laurence Hare, Philipp Stelzel, and Fabian Link. Link studied with Konrad Jarausch on a fellowship at the University of North Carolina at Chapel Hill before completing a PhD at the University of Basel and publishing *Burgen und Burgenforschung im Nationalsozialismus: Wissenschaft und Weltanschauung, 1933–1945* (Cologne, 2014).

38. Suzanne L. Marchand, *German Orientalism in the Age of Empire: Religion, Race, and Scholarship* (Cambridge, 2009), *xxiii.*

39. Susan A. Crane, *Collecting and Historical Consciousness in Early Nineteenth-Century Germany* (Ithaca, NY, 2000); Andrew Zimmerman, *Anthropology and Antihumanism in Imperial Germany* (Chicago, 2001); H. Glenn Penny, *Objects of Culture: Ethnology and Ethnographic Museums in Imperial Germany* (Chapel Hill, NC, 2002).

40. Zimmerman, *Anthropology and Antihumanism in Imperial Germany*, 239.

41. Andrew D. Evans, *Anthropology at War: World War I and the Science of Race in Germany* (Chicago, 2010).

42. Denise Phillips, *Acolytes of Nature: Defining Natural Science in Germany, 1770–1850* (Chicago, 2012), 9.

43. Jason D. Hansen, *Mapping the Germans: Statistical Science, Cartography, and the Visualization of the German Nation, 1848–1914* (Oxford, 2015); J. Laurence Hare, *Excavating Nations: Archaeology, Museums, and the German-Danish Borderlands* (Toronto, 2015). Also falling into this category is Brent Maner, *Germany's Ancient Pasts: Archaeology and Historical Interpretation since 1750*, which is forthcoming from the University of Chicago Press.

44. See for example David F. Lindenfeld, *The Practical Imagination: The German Sciences of State in the Nineteenth Century* (Chicago, 1997); Ina Lelke, *Die Brüder Grimm in Berlin: zum Verhältnis von Geselligkeit, Arbeitsweise und Diziplingenese im 19. Jahrhundert* (Frankfurt, 2005); Amanda M. Brian, "The Family Science: The Baby Biography in Imperial Germany," *Journal of the History of Childhood and Youth* 4, no. 3 (2011): 404–18; and Egbert Klautke, *The Mind of the Nation: Völkerpsychologie in Germany, 1851–1955* (New York, 2013).

45. Darrin M. McMahon, "The Return of the History of Ideas?," in *Rethinking Modern European Intellectual History*, ed. Darrin McMahon and Samuel Moyn (New York, 2014), 13–31; David A. Hollinger, "American Intellectual History, 1907–2007," in *A Century of American Historiography*, ed. James M. Banner Jr. (Boston, 2010), 21–29.

46. George W. Stocking, *After Tylor: British Social Anthropology, 1888–1951* (Madison, WI, 1995); *Victorian Anthropology* (New York, 1987); *Race, Culture, and Evolution: Essays in the History of Anthropology* (New York, 1968); *Malinowski. Rivers, Benedict, and Others: Essays on Culture and Personality* (Madison, WI, 1986).

47. The most recent word on the emerging globalization paradigm is Lynn Hunt, *Writing History in the Global Era* (New York, 2014). For the German case, Sebastian Conrad and Jürgen Osterhammel discuss colonialism and postcolonialism as an element of globalizing German history in "Einleitung," in *Das Kaiserreich Transnational: Deutschland in der Welt, 1871–1914* (Göttingen, 2004), 7–27; See also Conrad, *Globalization and the Nation in Imperial Germany* (Cambridge, 2010).

48. Alice Conklin, *In the Museum of Man: Race, Anthropology, and Empire in France, 1850–1950* (Ithaca, NY, 2013).

49. Rainer F. Buschmann, *Anthropology's Global Histories: The Ethnographic Frontier in German New Guinea, 1870–1935* (Honolulu, 2008).

50. A great deal of literature has established the "imagined" quality of the Germany's overseas empire, even in the years before its formal establishment. See most notably Susanne Zantop, *Colonial Fantasies: Conquest, Family, and Nation in Precolonial Germany, 1770–1870* (Durham, NC, 1997); Sara Friedrichsmeyer, Sara Lennox, and Susanne Zantop, eds, *The Imperialist Imagination: German Colonialism and Its Legacy* (Ann Arbor, MI, 1998); and more recently, Matthew P. Fitzpatrick, *Liberal Imperialism in Germany: Expansionism and Nationalism* (New York, 2008).

51. H. Glenn Penny and Matti Bunzl, eds, *Worldly Provincialism: German Anthropology in the Age of Empire* (Ann Arbor, MI, 2003).

52. George Steinmetz, "Scientific Autonomy and Empire, 1880–1945: Four German Sociologists," in *German Colonialism in a Global Age,* ed. Bradley Naranch and Geoff Eley (Durham, NC, 2015), 46–73.

53. Hoi-eun Kim, *Doctors of Empire: Medical and Cultural Encounters between Imperial Germany and Meiji Japan* (Toronto, 2014), 9. Michael Geyer also stressed the comparative potential for studying Germany and Japan in "Deutschland und Japan im Zeitalter der Globalisierung. Überlegungen zu einer komparativen Geschichte jenseits des Modernisierungs-Paradigmas," in *Das Kaiserreich Transnational,* ed. Sebastian Conrad and Jürgen Osterhammel (Göttingen, 2004), 49–67. For a strictly European example, see Heather Ellis and Ulrike Kirchberger, eds, *Anglo-German Scholarly Networks in the Long Nineteenth Century* (Leiden, 2014).

54. Philipp Stelzel, "Fritz Fischer and the American Historical Profession: Tracking the Transatlantic Dimension of the Fischer Kontroverse," *Storia della storiografia* 44 (2003): 67–84.

55. Hare, *Excavating Nations.*

56. Philipp Stelzel, "Transnationalism and the History of Historiography: A Transatlantic Perspective," *History Compass* 13, no. 2 (2015): 78–87, 84.

57. H. Glenn Penny, *Kindred by Choice: Germans and American Indians since 1800* (Chapel Hill, NC, 2013), 13–14.

58. Konrad H. Jarausch, "The Conundrum of Complicity: German Professionals and the Final Solution," in *The Law in Nazi Germany: Ideology, Opportunism, and the Perversion of Justice,* ed. Alan Steinweis and Robert D. Rachlin (New York, 2013), 15–36.

59. To name just a few since 2000, see Rüdiger Hohls and Konrad H. Jarausch, eds, *Versäumte Fragen: Deutsche Historiker im Schatten des Nationalsozialismus* (Stuttgart, 2000);

Achim Leube, ed., *Prähistorie und Nationalsozialismus: Die mittel- und osteuropäische Ur- und Frühgeschichtsforschung in den Jahren 1933–1945* (Heidelberg, 2002); Ingo Haar and Michael Fahlbusch, eds, *German Scholars and Ethnic Cleansing, 1919–1945* (New York, 2006); Eric Katz, *Death by Design: Science, Technology, and Engineering in Nazi Germany* (New York, 2006); Taylor Blaine, *Hitler's Engineers: Fritz Todt and Albert Speer: Master Builders of the Third Reich* (Philadelphia, 2010); Sanford L. Segal, *Mathematicians under the Nazis* (Princeton, NJ, 2014); Phillip Ball, *Serving the Reich: The Struggle for the Soul of Physics under Hitler* (Chicago, 2014).

60. Axel Flügel, "Ambivalente Innovation: Anmerkungen zur Volksgeschichte," *Geschichte und Gesellschaft* 26 (2000): 653–71; Riccardo Bavaj, *Die Ambivalenz der Moderne im Nationalsozialismus. Eine Bilanz der Forschung* (Munich, 2003).

61. J. Laurence Hare, "Nazi Archaeology Abroad: German Prehistorians and the International Dynamics of Collaboration," *Patterns of Prejudice* 48, no. 1 (2014): 1–24.

62. I recently had a chance to consider this question with Fabian Link in Link and J. Laurence Hare, "Pseudoscience Reconsidered: SS Research and the Archaeology of Haithabu," in *Revisiting the "Nazi Occult": Histories, Realities, Legacies,* ed. Eric Kurlander and Monica Black (Rochester, NY, 2015), 105–31.

63. For an example, see Chenxi Tang, *The Geographic Imagination of Modernity: Geography, Literature, and Philosophy in German Romanticism* (Stanford, CA, 2008).

64. Jarausch and Geyer suggested reconceptualizing the twentieth century in Germany as a "double reversal" that "conceptualize the century as an unstoppable descent into bloody cataclysm followed by a gradual but ultimately successful return to a greater deal of civility," in *Shattered Past,* 358. Jarausch then followed this with an analysis of postwar Germany drawing on the notion of the second "reversal" in *After Hitler: Recivilizing Germans, 1945–1995* (Oxford, 2006), and then across the twentieth century in *Out of Ashes: A New History of Europe in the Twentieth Century* (Princeton, NJ, 2015).

Bibliography

Anderson, Perry. *The Origins of Postmodernity.* London: Verso, 1998.

Ball, Phillip. *Serving the Reich: The Struggle for the Soul of Physics under Hitler.* Chicago: University of Chicago Press, 2014.

Banner, James M., Jr. *Being a Historian: An Introduction to the Professional World of History.* Cambridge: Cambridge University Press, 2012.

Bavaj, Riccardo. *Die Ambivalenz der Moderne im Nationalsozialismus. Eine Bilanz der Forschung.* Munich: Oldenbourg, 2003.

Blackbourn, David, and Geoff Eley. *The Peculiarities of German History: Bourgeois Society and Politics in Nineteenth-Century Germany.* Oxford: Oxford University Press, 1984.

Blaine, Taylor. *Hitler's Engineers: Fritz Todt and Albert Speer: Master Builders of the Third Reich.* Philadelphia: Casemate, 2010.

Brian, Amanda M. "The Family Science: The Baby Biography in Imperial Germany." *Journal of the History of Childhood and Youth* 4, no. 3 (2011): 404–18.

Buschmann, Rainer F. *Anthropology's Global Histories: The Ethnographic Frontier in German New Guinea, 1870–1935.* Honolulu: University of Hawaii Press, 2008.

Bynum, W. F. *The Science and Practice of Medicine in the Nineteenth Century.* Cambridge: Cambridge University Press, 1994.

Chakrabati, Pratik, Graham Mooney, and Patricia Skinner, eds. *Social History of Medicine* 27, no. 4 (2014): 629–31.

Chandler, James. "Introduction: Doctrines, Disciplines, Discourses, Departments." In "The Fate of Disciplines," edited by James Chandler and Arnold I Davidson. *Critical Inquiry* 35, no. 4 (2009): 729–46.

Cocks, Geoffrey. *Psychotherapy in the Third Reich: The Göring Institute.* New York: Oxford University Press, 1985.

Cocks, Geoffrey, and Konrad H Jarausch, eds. *German Professions, 1850–1930.* Oxford: Oxford University Press, 1990.

Conklin, Alice. *In the Museum of Man: Race, Anthropology, and Empire in France, 1850–1950.* Ithaca, NY: Cornell University Press, 2013.

Conrad, Sebastian. *Globalization and the Nation in Imperial Germany.* Cambridge: Cambridge University Press, 2010.

Conrad, Sebastian, and Jürgen Osterhammel, eds. *Das Kaiserreich Transnational: Deutschland in der Welt, 1871–1914.* Göttingen: Vandenhoek and Ruprecht, 2004.

Crane, Susan A. *Collecting and Historical Consciousness in Early Nineteenth-Century Germany.* Ithaca, NY: Cornell University Press, 2000.

Cybenko, George. "Hardly the End of Science." *IEEE Computational Science and Engineering* 4, no. 2 (1997): 1–1.

Delaporte, François. *The History of Yellow Fever: An Essay on the Birth of Tropical Medicine.* Translated by Arthur Goldhammer. Cambridge, MA: MIT Press, 1991.

Dietze, Erich von. *Paradigms Explained: Rethinking Thomas Kuhn's Philosophy of Science.* Westport, CT: Praeger, 2001.

Effros, Bonnie. *Uncovering the Germanic Past: Merovingian Archaeology in France, 1830–1914.* Oxford: Oxford University Press, 2012.

Ellis, Heather, and Ulrike Kirchberger, eds. *Anglo-German Scholarly Networks in the Long Nineteenth Century.* Leiden: Brill, 2014.

Evans, Andrew D. *Anthropology at War: World War I and the Science of Race in Germany.* Chicago: University of Chicago Press, 2010.

Fitzpatrick, Matthew P. *Liberal Imperialism in Germany: Expansionism and Nationalism.* New York: Berghahn Books, 2008.

Flügel, Axel. "Ambivalente Innovation: Anmerkungen zur Volksgeschichte." *Geschichte und Gesellschaft* 26 (2000): 653–71.

Forman, Paul. "On the Historical Forms of Knowledge Production and Curation: Modernity Entailed Disciplinarity, Postmodernity Entails Antidisciplinarity." *Osiris* 27, no. 1 (2012): 56–97.

———. "The Primacy of Science in Modernity, of Technology in Postmodernity, and of Ideology in the History of Technology." *History and Technology* 23, no. 1/2 (2007): 1–152.

Friedrichsmeyer, Sara, Sara Lennox, and Susanne Zantop, eds. *The Imperialist Imagination: German Colonialism and Its Legacy.* Ann Arbor: University of Michigan Press, 1998.

Geyer, Michael. "Deutschland und Japan im Zeitalter der Globalisierung. Überlegungen zu einer komparativen Geschichte jenseits des Modernisierungs-Paradigmas." In

Das Kaiserreich Transnational, edited by Sebastian Conrad and Jürgen Osterhammel, 49–67. Göttingen: Vandenhoek and Ruprecht, 2004.

Goldstein, Jan E., Francesca Trivellato, and Andrew S. Sartori. "'History and Other Disciplines': The Theme of the 129th Annual Meeting." *Perspectives on History* 51, no. 6 (2013): 57–57.

Haar, Ingo, and Michael Fahlbusch, eds. *German Scholars and Ethnic Cleansing, 1919–1945.* New York: Berghahn Books, 2006.

Hansen, Jason D. *Mapping the Germans: Statistical Science, Cartography, and the Visualization of the German Nation, 1848–1914.* Oxford: Oxford University Press, 2015.

Hare, J. Laurence. *Excavating Nations: Archaeology, Museums, and the German-Danish Borderlands.* Toronto: University of Toronto Press, 2015.

———. "Nazi Archaeology Abroad: German Prehistorians and the International Dynamics of Collaboration." *Patterns of Prejudice* 48, no. 1 (2014): 1–24.

Hayes, Brian. "Review: The End of Science Writing?" *American Scientist* 84, no. 5 (1996): 495–96.

Hohls, Rüdiger, and Konrad H. Jarausch, eds. *Versäumte Fragen: Deutsche Historiker im Schatten des Nationalsozialismus.* Stuttgart: Deutsche Verlags-Anstalt, 2000.

Hollinger, David A. "American Intellectual History, 1907–2007." In *A Century of American Historiography,* edited by James M Banner Jr, 21–29. Boston: Bedford/St. Martin's, 2010.

Horgan, John. *The End of Science; Facing the Limits of Knowledge in the Twilight of the Scientific Age.* Baltimore, MD: Johns Hopkins University Press, 1996.

———. "Looking back at 'The End of Science': More than a Decade of Lively Debate." *Science and Spirit* 19, no. 2 (2008): 40–43.

Horton, Richard. "The Moribund Body of Medical History." *The Lancet* 384, no. 9940 (2014): 292.

Hunt, Lynn. *Writing History in the Global Era.* New York: Norton, 2014.

Jarausch, Konrad H. *After Hitler: Recivilizing Germans, 1945–1995.* Oxford: Oxford University Press, 2006.

———. "The Conundrum of Complicity: German Professionals and the Final Solution." In *The Law in Nazi Germany: Ideology, Opportunism, and the Perversion of Justice,* edited by Alan Steinweis and Robert D Rachlin, 15–36. New York: Berghahn Books, 2013.

———. "Higher Education and Social Change: Some Comparative Perspectives." In *The Transformation of Higher Learning, 1860–1930: Expansion, Diversification, Social Opening, and Professionalization in England, Germany, Russia, and the United States,* edited by Konrad Jarausch, 9–36. Chicago: University of Chicago Press, 1983.

———. *Out of Ashes: A New History of Europe in the Twentieth Century.* Princeton, NJ: Princeton University Press, 2015.

———. *Students, Society, and Politics in Imperial Germany: The Rise of Academic Illiberalism.* Princeton, NJ: Princeton University Press, 1982.

———. "Towards a Social History of Experience: Postmodern Predicaments in Theory and Interdisciplinarity." *Central European History* 22, no. 3/4 (1989): 427–43.

Jarausch, Konrad H., and Michael Geyer. "The Future of the German Past? Transatlantic Reflections for the 1990s." *Central European History* 22, nos. 3 and 4 (1989): 229–59.

———. *Shattered Past: Reconstructing German Histories.* Princeton, NJ: Princeton University Press, 2003.

Jelavich, Peter. "Review of *Down from Olympus: Archaeology and Philhellenism in Germany, 1750–1970*, by Suzanne L Marchand." *The Art Bulletin* 80 (June 1998): 382–84.

Kaiser, David. "Booms, Busts, and the World of Ideas: Enrollment Pressures and the Challenge of Specialization." *Osiris* 27, no. 1 (2012): 276–302.

Katz, Eric. *Death by Design: Science, Technology, and Engineering in Nazi Germany*. New York: Pearson Longman, 2006.

Kim, Hoi-eun. *Doctors of Empire: Medical and Cultural Encounters between Imperial Germany and Meiji Japan*. Toronto: University of Toronto Press, 2014.

Klautke, Egbert. *The Mind of the Nation: Völkerpsychologie in Germany, 1851–1955*. New York: Berghahn Books, 2013.

Klein, Julie Thompson. *Interdisciplinarity: History, Theory, Practice*. Detroit: Wayne State University Press, 1990.

Kurlander, Eric, and Monica Black, eds. *Revisiting the "Nazi Occult:" Histories, Realities, Legacies*. Cambridge: Camden House, 2015.

Lelke, Ina. *Die Brüder Grimm in Berlin: zum Verhältnis von Geselligkeit, Arbeitsweise und Diziplingenese im 19. Jahrhundert*. Frankfurt: Peter Lang, 2005.

Leube, Achim, ed. *Prähistorie und Nationalsozialismus: Die mittel- und osteuropäische Ur- und Frühgeschichtsforschung in den Jahren 1933–1945*. Heidelberg: Synchron, 2002.

Lindenfeld, David F. *The Practical Imagination: The German Sciences of State in the Nineteenth Century*. Chicago: University of Chicago Press, 1997.

Link, Fabian. *Burgen und Burgenforschung im Nationalsozialismus: Wissenschaft und Weltanschauung, 1933–1945*. Cologne: Böhlau, 2014.

Link, Fabian, and J Laurence Hare. "Pseudoscience Reconsidered: SS Research and the Archaeology of Haithabu." In *Revisiting the "Nazi Occult:" Histories, Realities, Legacies*, edited by Eric Kurlander and Monica Black, 105–131. Rochester, NY: Camden House, 2015.

Maner, Brent. *Germany's Ancient Pasts: Archaeology and Historical Interpretation since 1750*. Chicago: University of Chicago Press, forthcoming.

Marchand, Suzanne L. *German Orientalism in the Age of Empire: Religion, Race, and Scholarship*. Cambridge: Cambridge University Press, 2009.

———. "Has the History of Disciplines Had Its Day?" In *Rethinking Modern European Intellectual History*, edited by Darrin M McMahon and Samuel Moyn, 131–52. Oxford: Oxford University Press, 2014.

McMahon, Darrin M. "The Return of the History of Ideas?" In *Rethinking Modern European Intellectual History*, edited by Darrin McMahon and Samuel Moyn, 13–31. New York: Oxford University Press, 2014.

Munslow, Alan. *Deconstructing History*. 2nd ed. New York: Routledge, 2006.

Passmore, Kevin. "Poststructuralism and History." In *Writing History: Theory and Practice*, 2nd ed., edited by Stefan Berger, Heiko Feldner, and Kevin Passmore, 123–46. London: Bloomsbury, 2010.

Penny, H. Glenn. *Kindred by Choice: Germans and American Indians since 1800*. Chapel Hill: University of North Carolina Press, 2013.

———. *Objects of Culture: Ethnology and Ethnographic Museums in Imperial Germany*. Chapel Hill: University of North Carolina Press, 2002.

Penny, H. Glenn, and Matti Bunzl, eds. *Worldly Provincialism: German Anthropology in the Age of Empire*. Ann Arbor: University of Michigan Press, 2003.

Phillips, Denise. *Acolytes of Nature: Defining Natural Science in Germany, 1770–1850.* Chicago: University of Chicago Press, 2012.

Post, Robert. "Debating Disciplinarity." In "The Fate of Disciplines," edited by James Chandler and Arnold I Davidson. *Critical Inquiry* 35, no. 4 (2009): 749–70.

Segal, Sanford L. *Mathematicians under the Nazis.* Princeton, NJ: Princeton University Press, 2014.

Smith, Helmut Walser. *The Continuities of German History: Nation, Religion, and Race across the Long Nineteenth Century.* Cambridge: Cambridge University Press, 2008.

———. "When the Sonderweg Debate Left Us." *German Studies Review* 31, no. 2 (2008): 225–40.

Smith, Woodruff D. *Politics and the Sciences of Culture in Germany, 1840–1920.* New York: Oxford University Press, 1991.

Steinmetz, George. "Scientific Autonomy and Empire, 1880–1945: Four German Sociologists." In *German Colonialism in a Global Age,* edited by Bradley Naranch and Geoff Eley, 46–73. Durham, NC: Duke University Press, 2015.

Stelzel, Philipp. "Fritz Fischer and the American Historical Profession: Tracking the Transatlantic Dimension of the Fischer Kontroverse." *Storia della storiografia* 44 (2003): 67–84.

———. "Transnationalism and the History of Historiography: A Transatlantic Perspective." *History Compass* 13, no. 2 (2015): 78–87.

Stocking, George W. *After Tylor: British Social Anthropology, 1888–1951.* Madison: University of Wisconsin Press, 1995.

———. *Malinowski. Rivers, Benedict, and Others: Essays on Culture and Personality.* Madison: University of Wisconsin Press, 1986.

———. *Race, Culture, and Evolution: Essays in the History of Anthropology.* New York: Free Press, 1968.

———. *Victorian Anthropology.* New York: Free Press, 1987.

Tang, Chenxi. *The Geographic Imagination of Modernity: Geography, Literature, and Philosophy in German Romanticism.* Stanford, CA: Stanford University Press, 2008.

Timmermann, Carsten. "Not Moribund at All! An Historian of Medicine's Response to Richard Horton." *The Guardian,* 4 August 2014. Retrieved 1 March 2015 from http://www.theguardian.com/science/the-h-word/2014/aug/04/not-moribund-historian-medicine-response-richard-horton.

Tune, Sharon K., and Debbie Ann Doyle, eds. *Program of the 129th Meeting of the American Historical Association.* New York: AHA, 2–5 January 2015.

Weinreich, Max. *Hitler's Professors: The Part of Scholarship in Germany's Crimes against the Jewish People.* New York: New York Yiddish Scientific Institute, 1946.

Zantop, Susanne. *Colonial Fantasies: Conquest, Family, and Nation in Precolonial Germany, 1770–1870.* Durham, NC: Duke University Press, 1997.

Zimmerman, Andrew. *Anthropology and Antihumanism in Imperial Germany.* Chicago: University of Chicago Press, 2001.

Chapter 3

Contextualizing the Holocaust
Modernization, Modernity, Colonialism, and Genocide

Christopher R. Browning

In the summer of 1979, I visited the People's Republic of China at a time when that country was fighting a border skirmish with its neighbor to the south, Vietnam. Former allies during the American war in Vietnam, the two countries had become increasingly estranged when a large component of the "boat people" fleeing the victorious Communist regime in Vietnam turned out to be from the diaspora middle class of ethnic Chinese. In my hotel in Beijing, I encountered a political cartoon in an English-language newspaper obviously published with foreign sensibilities in mind. In this cartoon, a boat off shore and overfilled with desperate people is sinking into the sea. On shore, Hitler and a Vietnamese leader stand together observing their plight. Hitler asks, "Why don't you use gas?" The Vietnamese replies, "Because water is cheaper." Clearly, even in as distant a political culture as 1979 China just emerging from the cultural revolution, the passing of Mao, and the rule of the notorious "gang of four," it was understood that the Holocaust—epitomized by its most prominent identifiers, Hitler and mass killing by poison gas—was the ultimate symbol of radical political evil in the modern world. Hence the motive to connect it to one's own suffering and to appropriate it for other agendas.

With its juxtaposition of poisoning by gas vs. drowning in water and its invocation of the Holocaust in a non-European setting, this cartoon also tangentially touched upon two issues that go beyond misappropriation and have been central to historiographic arguments about the wider

---

Notes for this chapter begin on page 87.

context of the Holocaust, namely its relationship to modernization and modernity on the one hand and to European colonialism and overseas genocide on the other. These two contextual debates are the subject of this chapter.[1]

In the 1960s, modernization theory was quite in vogue, both to explain the presumed superiority of Western, industrial, capitalist, democratic, middle-class society as the highest stage of an idealized developmental trajectory and Germany's aberrant history as the product of a flawed development. According to this view, Germany took a wrong turn due to its failed bourgeois-liberal revolution in 1848. Thereafter, the country asymmetrically developed a modern industrial economy and experienced ever greater social tensions, while still dominated by entrenched traditional elites who plunged Europe into the catastrophe of World War I in order to stave off democratization at home through victory and territorial expansion abroad. The incomplete revolution of 1918 left the Weimar Republic helpless against the continued machinations of the old elites who first allied with the Nazis to undermine the fragile German democracy and then hoisted them into power under the illusion that they were restoring a traditional authoritarian regime. In short, Germany followed a "special path" or *Sonderweg* to war and dictatorship rather than the "normal path" to peace and democracy as prescribed in modernization theory.[2] Carrying the *Sonderweg* further, Martin Broszat and Hans Mommsen argued that the disparate and unwieldy coalition upon which Hitler based his dictatorship and the competitive nature of his polycratic regime drove the Nazis—in uncontrolled "forward flight" and "cumulative radicalization"— to emphasize the only policies upon which all elements could agree: territorial expansion, the escalating persecution and exploitation of internal and external enemies, and ultimately genocide.[3] The whole *Sonderweg* approach dovetailed nicely with studies of fascism and Nazism in the 1960s that portrayed the latter as especially archaic, backward looking, and opposed to not only democratization but also economic modernization and cultural modernity—hence the initial compatibility and partnership of Nazism with its Old Right allies.[4]

The image of Hitler and the Nazis as antimodern reactionaries wedded to the return to an imagined agrarian Utopia was openly challenged in the 1980s. Rainer Zitelmann argued instead that Hitler was a modernizing revolutionary, who desired the dismantling of old social barriers and the enhancement of social mobility on the one hand and wholeheartedly embraced modern technology and industrial power on the other. Many other Nazis shared this view, and the modernizing technocratic element was relatively successful, he argues, in shoving aside the archaic elements in the party after 1933.[5] If Zitelmann simply ignored the Holocaust in his modernization argument, Götz Aly did not. Aly argued that the driving force behind the Final Solution was a group of self-consciously modernizing technocrats or "planning intelligentsia" who sought to break the vicious cycle of poverty, low productivity, and overpopulation in German-occupied Eastern Europe. These technocrats advocated the mass murder of Jews as the way to diminish surplus population, consolidate small and backward handicraft production into rationalized modern industry, induce Polish villagers to move into the cities through new economic opportunity, and create a prosperous Polish middle class with a stake in the German New Order. Thus, the Holocaust was not the out-of-control radicalization of a dysfunctional regime, as portrayed by Broszat and Mommsen, but rather a quite conscious and rational albeit inhumane policy for the technocratic and capitalist modernization of the German empire in the east.[6] Aly's description of mid-level German functionaries in Poland as "modernizing technocrats" committed to a consensus model of economic modernization through mass murder has been challenged on empirical grounds.[7] And this theory does not explain the Final Solution as a lethal attack on Jews throughout the German sphere, where no such modernizing agenda existed.

An important change had taken place between the early and late modernization arguments. In the early version, modernization was coded positive, and German development—leading fatefully to Hitler and the Holocaust—was seen as deficient due to its incomplete and flawed modernization. In the later version, as portrayed by Aly, German development, including Hitler and the Holocaust, is an exemplar of modernization, which is coded negative. This negative coding of modernization, maintaining its connection with industrialization, secularization, social mobility, the rise of science and technology, and a rational-instrumental attitude but decisively decoupling it from any notions of democratization and progress, was mirrored in the linguistic turn of the 1980s, when the focus and language shifted from modernization as an idealized trajectory of development to modernity as a set of cultural perceptions and assumptions. What Geoff Eley had deemed a severe crisis in Germany's capitalist economy and class society in the 1920s, Detlev Peukert now termed "the crisis of classical modernity," and the fact that this opened the door to the Nazi dictatorship demonstrated the "pathological" potential of modernity previously misunderstood and wrongly equated with progress.[8] Peukert explicitly connected this "crisis of modernity" to the Holocaust, in that the national/racial community or *Volksgemeinschaft* of the Nazis—their essential Utopian answer to the ills of modern society—was formed and made credible only by boundary-drawing that excluded both the nonconforming and the "guilty," i.e. the Jew, Bolshevik, and exploiting Capitalist merged into one. Moreover, the regime's need to sustain its central Utopian myth had destructive consequences. "The more the Nazis' unmasking of racial enemies failed to deliver the promised concord of the *Volksgemeinschaft* and the solution of society's real problems and contradictions, the more radical and ruthless had to be the destructive pressures exerted against the 'community aliens.'" For Peukert, this process of boundary-drawing that lay at the core of Nazi racial policy traced back not to traditional anti-Semitism of earlier centuries but rather to the modern academic-medical-welfare practice of selection and separation on the basis of distinguishing between value and nonvalue, or in short-hand "the spirit of science." Nazi racialism, he concluded, was an example of the seductive power of the "pathology" of progress and modernity, and the Holocaust was one possible, though not inevitable, result.[9]

Others outside of Germany (and thus without the need to deal with that country's particular burden) paralleled Peukert in proclaiming the Holocaust as a manifestation of modernity and hence a warning of modernity's negative and pathological potentialities. Predating and anticipating Peukert, Richard Rubenstein had argued that the Holocaust was "a thoroughly modern exercise in total domination that could only have been carried out by an advanced political community" and should be regarded "as the expression of some of the most profound tendencies of Western civilization in the twentieth century."[10] These tendencies included the pervasive secularization of culture, dehumanizing bureaucratic domination, economic rationalization, and the deluge of stateless, superfluous peoples. Zygmunt Baumann, as the title of his book *Modernity and the Holocaust* implies, rejected the teleological myth of Western civilization as a progressive triumph and characterized the Holocaust as a modern phenomenon in which bureaucratic culture based on obedience to authority, organized routine, and rational calculation—not rage, passion, spontaneity—neutralized moral inhibition and shaped the ethos within which the Holocaust could be implemented. Only the engineering attitude derived from scientific empowerment, in which government envisaged itself as "rational management" aiming at social therapy through "applied science" (thus echoing Peukert) made the idea of exterminatory anti-Semitism even conceivable in the first place. For Baumann, the Holocaust was the modern idea of exterminatory anti-Semitism married to modern bureaucracy.[11]

Edward Ross Dickenson has argued that the analytical shift from modernization focused on social structure to what he calls "discursive modernity" characterized by instrumental rationality, scientism, and a belief in the capacity to renovate or remake society signaled the emergence of a new "biopolitical" master narrative of German history. In this regard, Germany both shared in wider developments in the modern world but also exhibited a "particular variant of biopolitics." In place of the fear of democratization and revolution on the part of the old elites that dominated the previous master narrative, in this approach broad sectors of German society shared a fear of the degeneration of the *Volkskörper* (national/racial body). "Germany," he concludes, "appears here not as a nation having trouble modernizing but as a nation of troubling modernity."[12]

But Dickenson argues for a nonteleological perspective, noting that the anti-Semitic "race hygiene" branch of German eugenics and biopolitics was a fringe group until co-opted and empowered by the Nazis in 1933 for their shared beliefs in mass sterilization, eugenic abortion, and mass killing (euphemistically dubbed euthanasia) of those deemed "life unworthy of life."[13] And the "euthanasia" program, Henry Friedlander and others have argued, was central to the origins of the Final Solution.[14] But Dickenson is quite emphatic about cause and effect: "Eugenics did not 'pave the way' for the murder of millions of Jews. Ethnic racism—and particularly anti-Semitism—did." And again, "Modernity and science were not responsible for the crimes of the Nazis. The Nazis were."[15]

How have these two phases or generations of analyzing German history and National Socialism through the respective lenses of modernization and modernity helped to contextualize and enrich our understanding of the Holocaust? Basically, they have attempted answers to two key questions about the Holocaust, namely "why the Germans?" and "why in the 20th century?" They have helped explain some of the circumstances under which Germany failed to develop a viable democracy but have been less helpful in explaining why the Nazis were the ultimate beneficiaries of this failure. They have shown how the modern setting of the twentieth century not only did not hinder but in some ways facilitated the implementation of the Final Solution, but not why modern means and sensibilities were harnessed to the purpose of Judeocide. In short, they have been least helpful in dealing with a third key question, "Why the Jews?" As one participant at the conference where Detlev Peukert presented his essay on the Holocaust and "the spirit of science" remarked, he had portrayed a "*judenrein* Holocaust." I return to this issue later, but first, how does a second major historiographical effort at wider contextualization, focusing on imperialism, colonization, and genocide, fare in regard to these key questions?[16]

Parallel to interpretations focused on modernization, one of those emphasizing the colonial context implies a kind of German *Sonderweg* by drawing a direct line from the genocide of the Hereros and Nama in German Southwest Africa back to German behavior on the European continent. Isabell Hull notes that "imperialism *was* war" and insists on the continuity of institutional culture in the German military as key to waging wars of "absolute destruction" first in Southwest Africa and then in

World War I. But she draws an indirect rather than direct connection to the subsequent Nazi *Vernichtungskrieg* and the Holocaust. National Social-ism reified practices of violence that had become "severed" from the old Imperial military culture and "harnessed" them for "ideological ends of even greater mass destruction and death."[17] Others have made the direct connection, none more emphatically than Jürgen Zimmerer, who posed the question in his book title *Von Windhuk nach Auschwitz?* and answered that question affirmatively with a chapter entitled "The Birth of the Ost-land Out of the Spirit of Colonialism."[18] He argues that both the ideologi-cal justifications (racial binary of superior, cultured European and inferior, primitive native) and methods of rule (forced labor and eviction from the land on the one hand; war of destruction characterized by scorched earth, massacre, extermination by neglect in camps for prisoners, and ultimately genocide on the other) were similar. Indeed, for German Southwest Africa "a system of total control and mobilization was planned that was prob-ably unique in the history of colonialism," thus making it "the paradig-matic case linking colonialism and National Socialism."[19] Moreover, the widespread dissemination and positive reception of colonial and racial thinking in Germany allowed Germans to perceive of their behavior in Eastern Europe as "normal" rather than criminal. Only from the modern Western perspective that has forgotten its own nineteenth-century over-seas behavior, not the nineteenth-century colonial or the pre-1945 German perspective, was Nazi behavior taboo-breaking and unprecedented.

Zimmerer focuses on German Southwest Africa in part to refute what he considers his own country's naïve view of a benevolent German colo-nial past on the one hand and rejection of continuity between the Imperial and Nazi eras in German history on the other.[20] Concerning the broader relationship between colonialism, genocide, National Socialism, and the Holocaust, he takes a relatively qualified view. Accepting the definition of the Lemkin-inspired UN convention, with "intent" at its core, Zimmer-man argues that "colonial genocide" is "not a fundamentally different category" from Nazi genocide. The same notions of race and space were at the heart of each. But given the low level of state development on the colonial frontier, individual cases of colonial genocide are much harder to identify than is the case for Nazi genocide, and most of the loss of life in the colonies came from disease and enslavement, not intended destruc-tion. Zimmerer is not looking for equivalence but rather what he calls the "archeology of genocide." He sees himself excavating the origins of geno-cidal thinking, with German Southwest Africa standing as a connecting point between "genocidal moments" on the colonial frontier and the "un-precedented" extent of "planned murder" in the "largest colonial war in history" of National Socialism.[21]

Concerning other colonial settler genocides that have been seen as either precursors of or parallel to the Holocaust, the fate of the indigenous populations of the Western hemisphere in general and North America in particular has been the subject of both heated polemics and careful study. Carroll Peter Kakel has attempted the most systematic comparison of the American "wild West" and the German "wild East" to make the argument for "the Holocaust as colonial genocide."[22] Kakel emphasizes the "disquieting underlying patterns of empirical similarity"[23] between the two: relentless territorial expansion by the nation-state combined with settler colonialism; assumptions of racial superiority; genocidal warfare; and the resulting destruction of "indigenous peoples," whether native Americans or "Slavs and Jews" in Eastern Europe. The differences between the two colonial genocides Kakel traces to situational factors (such as the vastly denser indigenous population of Eastern Europe that required conquest by a much more concerted military effort, which ultimately failed), temporal factors (as the most recent variant of colonial genocide, only the Nazi version radicalized into "industrial" as well as colonial genocide), and ideological factors (the American version gave primacy to space, while the Nazi version was equally devoted to race and space).

But Kakel does more than pose similarities and differences. He argues that the former significantly outweigh the latter, and moreover that "the general patterns, logics, and pathologies" of the Nazi colonial project "*derived* (italics mine) from the USA settlement model." In my opinion, a few scattered Hitler quotes do not provide sufficient evidence for such an assertion of derivation. For instance, in all the planning documents for the Lublin Reservation and Madagascar Plan, I never saw one specific reference to Indian Reservations in the American West—a seemingly inescapable reference if Nazi planning was as derivative as Kakel asserts. Kakel acknowledges several "singular aspects of the Nazi Judeocide" or Shoah—the totality of intent to kill all Jews and the method of gassing—but this does not lead him to ask the question "why the Jews." On the contrary, applying the term "Holocaust" to the Nazi mass killing of all noncombatants, he consistently subsumes the Jews into the broader indigenous population of Eastern Europe. And faced with the Nazi murder of German and other West European Jews outside the Nazi East, he simply asserts that this is best understood as the "internal application of an essentially imperial logic" or as "internal colonialism."[24] Certainly, there are many ways in which the origins of the Final Solution are intertwined or interconnected with the Nazi conquest of Eastern Europe and plans for colonization and demographic revolution, as many historians (myself included) have argued, but Kakel's formulation hinders rather than facil-

itates careful examination of the particularities and priority of the Final
Solution and Jewish victimization within Nazi mass killing.

At the opposite end of the spectrum from scholars who focus on particular colonial settler genocides, such as German Southwest Africa or
the American West, are scholars who indict all colonialism as genocidal.
Explicitly critical of Zimmerer, for instance, is Dominik Schaller, who argues that "whenever colonizers aim at imposing" a different way of life
on "dominated populations" by violence, colonialism is "inherently genocidal." He insists "that not only are genocides always colonial, but colonial
rule and colonialism as such are constantly genocidal."[25] As Thomas Kühne
has noted, such blanket generalizations provide an easy equation between
nineteenth-century European and twentieth-century Nazi colonialism, but
only by ignoring the important variations and differences among and between them. Whatever its undoubted brutalities, nineteenth-century European colonialism also involved ameliorating notions of westernizing,
developing, educating, and Christianizing. Hitler may have occasionally
cited British rule in India as his model, but there is a world of difference
between Himmler's statement that Poles did not need to learn to count past
five on the one hand and Gandhi receiving legally training at the Inner Temple and Nehru being educated at Harrow and Trinity College, Cambridge,
on the other.[26] It was precisely these ameliorating tendencies, according to
Vejas Liulevicius, that disappeared from German rule in Eastern Europe in
the course of World War I and the postwar depredations of the *Freikorps.*[27]

Taking the middle ground between Zimmerer and Schaller are a group
of scholars, typified by A Dirk Moses,[28] who are impatient with the highly
polarized debate that pits the Holocaust and colonial genocide against one
another in a "zero-sum" game, in which both definition and assessment
of similarities and differences are ultimately political rather than historical judgments. Thus, he gives political labels to the two competing conceptions of genocide. The first he dubs the "liberal" conception, which
stresses state agency and intention and for which the Holocaust is paradigmatic. The second is the "post-liberal" conception, in which structural
determinants and social forces (usually understood as manifestations of
Western intrusion) not only drive a "genocidal process" or create "genocidal relations" but also make intention difficult to conceptualize and
agency difficult to locate. The first stresses genocidal intent while the later
stresses genocidal outcome in terms of the destruction or permanent crip-
pling of human groups.

I think Moses makes an important distinction here, but I would prefer
the descriptive terms of "systematic" and "systemic" genocide rather than
"liberal" and "post-liberal" conceptions of genocide derived from the political labeling of their respective proponents.[29] I think we need to liberate

ourselves somewhat from the Holocaust-derived Lemkin/UN Convention paradigm, where the "intent" or "aim" of annihilating a group is paramount rather than co-equal with a result-oriented concept. I would suggest "systematic" genocide for the reigning Holocaust-derived paradigm, where identifiable actors—usually the state—plan and implement measures to destroy entire groups as such, regardless of how successful. I would suggest "systemic" genocide for the successful or near successful destruction of groups not achieved through an identifiable planning agency (a crime of commission) but rather produced through the encounter and conflict between such inherently unequal groups that without the alteration or reversal of obvious trend lines (a crime of omission) the gradual destruction and disappearance of the weaker is quite predictable. Here not just government programs of mass killing but the introduction of new diseases, ceaseless encroachment and seizure of land, displacement, and destruction of traditional economies—pursued incrementally over a long period of time by generations of actors against generations of victims—can have catastrophic results without clear intent. The Australian aborigines and native Americans experienced far greater genocidal consequences than world Jewry, both in terms of percentage of population loss and entire tribes, cultures, and languages rendered forever extinct. Though different in dynamic and implementation, both should be considered forms of genocide in my opinion, if the controlling issue is the destruction of an entire group as such.

Despite his two labels, Moses does not go so far as to embrace two categories of genocide. But he does suggest several ways of changing "the rules" of the "zero-sum game" that pits his "liberal" and "post-liberal" conceptions of genocide against one another. One is to take a broader view of intent by invoking the legal concept of "foreseeability." The destructive outcome of settler colonization was perfectly foreseeable, he argues, but actual people (not anonymous structures and forces) accepted the "doom" of indigenous populations as "inevitable" and made policy decisions that insured precisely that outcome as a self-fulfilling prophecy. Second, invoking Hannah Arendt's *Origins of Totalitarianism*, though not uncritically, Moses conceives of a "unified process" in what he calls the "racial century" (1850–1945), in which the competitive violence unleashed by European modernity and nation-state system moved from the periphery to the core, from imperialism overseas to the European civil war, and culminated in National Socialism and the Holocaust. Hitler sought to achieve *consciously* in Europe in the twentieth century what other Western nations had accomplished *haphazardly* (italics mine) overseas in the nineteenth century.

What insight does the colonial context bring to understanding the Holocaust, if any? Virtually all recent scholarship agrees that the Nazi regime was engaged in a vast campaign of territorial conquest and colonization, with the goal of carrying out a racial revolution to remake the demographic map of Eastern Europe as outlined in the *Generalplan Ost*. And I think that Moses is correct that many features of this plan revealed the Nazi leadership's desire to achieve systematically and quickly what unsystematic settler colonization had achieved gradually and incrementally in North American in the previous century, with the same consequences for the Slavic inhabitants as for the Native Americans.

In contrast to some of his colleagues, however, Moses is ready to concede that, unlike the Nazi genocidal policies toward the Slavs, the Holocaust cannot be explained "in terms of imperial and colonial logics."[30] But he does argue that the Holocaust can and should be situated "in processes that are universal in imperial and colonial situations," and indeed "*needs to be understood* (italics mine) ... in terms of subaltern genocide" because it is "best explained in terms of the subaltern's racist nationalism." In addition to the fact that the *Ostjuden* were "treated in the customary colonial manner" for the "colonial other"—namely starvation, forced labor, eviction, incarceration, and decimation—the Nazis also conceived of the Jews as the dominators of Germany and a security threat to Germany from which Germans needed to be freed through the equivalent of a genocidal war of national liberation.

The problem with this approach, as Moses admits, is that this notion of the Jewish domination and threat was "a fantastical belief." Nothing in Moses' psychological parallel to subaltern rage against very real suffering explains why in a powerful modern nation and indeed across an entire continent people could be mobilized to perpetrate genocide by a paranoid fantasy. We are back to the same unanswered question, why the Jews? What was the nature of the "fantastical belief" about Jews, and how did it shape Nazi policy?

The answer, I would argue, begins with distinguishing the Final Solution from the *Generalplan Ost* and the Holocaust from colonial genocide. In 1939 and 1940, the fate of Jews and Poles were intertwined in various schemes of ethnic cleansing and demographic engineering. And the same German occupation personnel dealt with both. For instance, on its 1940 tour of duty in the Warthegau, Police Battalion 101 both guarded the Lodz ghetto and expelled 37,000 Poles into the General Government. Preparations for the war of destruction in the spring of 1941 envisaged lethal treatment of both Jews and Slavs. But in the summer of 1941, solving the Nazis' self-imposed "Jewish question" through mass murder gained an autonomy and priority vis-à-vis other demographic measures. While the *Generalplan Ost* remained in the planning stages in 1941–43, the Final Solution was implemented with devastating speed, and Jews from all over

Europe were murdered, not just those in the East. While the last version of *Generalplan Ost* was still on the drawing boards in the spring of 1943, over three-quarters of all Holocaust victims were already dead. Jews from the furthest corners of the German empire not central to Nazi dreams of a colonial settlement in the East—Norway to the northwest, France to the southwest, Greece to the southeast—were being deported and murdered. The racial/colonial *Generalplan Ost* and the racial/anti-Semitic Final Solution certainly overlapped in many ways, but they did not fully coincide either geographically or temporally.

Ultimately, the Jews of Europe were not murdered because their land was coveted, or they were deemed a primitive and doomed population standing in the way of progress.[31] Rather, they were murdered because Hitler and the anti-Semitic ideologues of the Nazi leadership considered them a dire threat to Germany's long-term capacity to fulfill their dreams of German acquisition of *Lebensraum* and hegemony, and seeming victory in the east offered the opportunity for solving their fantasized Jewish problem through total destruction after previous attempted solutions through expulsion had proved impractical. Whether as the contaminators of Aryan blood, the carriers of subversive ideas that undermined German willingness to fight, or as a worldwide conspiracy that militarily blocked Germany's expansion through pulling the strings of both the Communist regime in the Soviet Union and the Democratic regimes of Britain and the United States, the Jews were perceived as a mortal threat to Germany's very existence—a problem that elicited ever more radical solutions and culminated in a genocidal program to murder every last Jew—man, women, and child—who fell into the German grasp. This fantastical anti-Semitism—what other scholars have tried to capture by the terms "redemptive anti-Semitism" (Saul Friedländer), "chimeric anti-Semitism" (Gavin Langmuir), or "mystical anti-Semitism" (Dan Stone)—posited "the Jew" as a prior existential threat to Germany. Solving the Nazis' imagined "Jewish problem" was a precondition for fulfilling their colonial aspirations in the East, which derived from the broader racial interpretation of history that offered the stark alternatives of expansionary victory against rival races to obtain *Lebensraum* or inevitable contraction and demise.[32]

How did such "a fantastical belief" become the ideological keystone of a political movement controlling the most powerful nation-state in Europe? I would suggest that neither the contextualization of modernity in Europe nor colonization outside Europe that focus on the nineteenth century alone will answer this question sufficiently. I would suggest that we must return to the experience of modernization and its impact on the position and perception of Jews in European society over a much longer

period of time that is not restricted to the modern era in order to understand the historical construction of chimeric anti-Semitism.

In the first millennium of the adversarial relationship between Christians and Jews, the conflict was primarily theological. By the last century
of that millennium, the beleaguered people of Western Europe lived in
a society characterized by sparse population, subsistence agriculture, il-
literacy, and recurrent invasion. Over the next three centuries, however,
Europe experienced what I would call its first great modernization. Population exploded, cities grew up, wealth multiplied as trade supplemented
agriculture and money replaced barter, centralizing monarchies began the
long process of taming feudal anarchy, universities were invented, literacy spread, at least part of the classical tradition was recovered (throwing
doubt on accepted religious certainties), and the borders of Christendom
expanded. As in any great transformation, there was also much disloca-
tion and anxiety. For all that was new and unsettling, the Jewish minority
provided an apt symbol, and theological anti-Judaism was superseded
by what Gavin Langmuir called "xenophobic anti-Semitism"—a widely
held negative stereotype made up of various assertions that did not describe the real Jewish minority but rather symbolized various threats and
menaces that the Christian majority could not and did not want to understand.[33] Generally banned from land ownership, guild membership, and
the military profession, the Jews became a ghettoized urban, commercial,
and nonmilitary minority now branded not only as unbelievers but also
as clannish cowards, parasites, and usurers. Religiously driven anti-Semitism took on economic, social, and political dimensions. This soil of xenophobic anti-Semitism was fertile for the planting and luxuriant growth
of fantastical and demented accusations, such as ritual murder and well-
poisoning, that Langmuir dubs "chimeric anti-Semitism," and this increasingly inextricable mix of xenophobic and chimeric anti-Semitism became
deeply embedded in European culture by the end of the Middle Ages.

The Dual Revolution that began in the late eighteenth century seemed
a great boon to Europe's Jews. The Liberal-Democratic Revolution proclaimed freedom of conscience and equality before the law, and emancipated Jews from centuries of legal discrimination. The Industrial Revolution opened up unprecedented economic opportunities for a mobile,
educated, entrepreneurial, adaptable minority eager to leave the past behind. But ultimately, Europe's second great "modernization crisis" was
fraught with even greater danger for the Jews than the first. Once again
the "social losers"—traditional elites and small-scale producers in particular—could find in the Jews a convenient symbol for their anguish and
envy over Jewish success. In a secular and scientific age, race rather than

religion now provided the purported explanation for Jewish behavior, and the negative anti-Semitic stereotype was easily updated with new layers of accusations, both xenophobic and chimeric. The Jew was the "xenophobic" symbol of all that threatened the old order—both liberalism and Bolshevism, rapacious capitalism and proletarian revolution, internationalism and national disloyalty, cultural experimentation and contempt for tradition—as well as the "chimeric" accusations of blood poisoning and world conspiracy. If in the late nineteenth century anti-Semitism was still a "cultural code" among conservatives "inseparable from their anti-modernism,"[34] the sequence of disasters that struck European society in the first decades of the twentieth century—World War I, the humiliation of defeat and collapse of empires, revolution, inflation, and the Great Depression—threatened total implosion and opened the door for the rapid emergence of the new political movement of fascism that promised rescue and regeneration and demonstrated the ability—at least in Italy and Germany—to construct a broad and socially diverse coalition of discontent and hope. This European crisis was more than a "crisis of modernity," and neither fascism nor Nazism is best understood as either modern or antimodern—a binary form of categorization more important to 1960s social scientists than to the fascists themselves.

In Germany, these developments took on a particular cast and intensity. As Götz Aly implies in the title of his most recent book on the "prehistory of the Holocaust," *Why the Germans? Why the Jews?*, these two questions were inseparable.[35] The sluggish German response to modernization early in the nineteenth century—in contrast to rapid and successful Jewish adaptation—spurred tremendous envy and sense of inferiority, while the reaction to the Napoleonic occupation led to bitter rejection of essential aspects of liberalism. The especially compressed and volatile burst of modernization in Germany at the last decades of the nineteenth century intensified this envy of Jewish success. In effect, Germany was the European land of greatest Jewish assimilation, economic prosperity, and cultural achievement, and simultaneously home to a strident anti-Semitic reaction unmitigated by entrenched liberal values.

While single-issue anti-Semitic parties initially failed to find wider political traction in Germany in the nineteenth century, a cult of redemptive/chimeric/mystical anti-Semitism took root and then grew explosively during the sequence of disasters—total war, defeat, revolution, inflation, and Great Depression—that struck Germany so severely. Among both the *déclassé* war veterans like Hitler and the slightly younger university students dubbed the "uncompromising generation" by Michael Wildt,[36] not only "xenophobic" but also "chimeric" anti-Semitism became the core of their ideology. The Nazi attempt to carry out a demographic revolution and create a colonial empire in twentieth-century Europe formed the crucial context for how the Holocaust came about and how the Nazis could harness so many to that genocidal enterprise. But obsessively held "fantastical" beliefs—not the systemic tendencies of imperial expansion and colonial settlement or the "pathologies" of modernity—drove the Nazi genocide of the Jews at the leadership level of the regime.

But anti-Semitism also had another function in the Third Reich. It played a crucial role as the "glue" holding Hitler, various strands of National Socialism, the traditional German conservatives, and broad sections of disaffected German society together. For the archaic and restorationist elements of the party, as well as the conservative allies, anti-Semitism functioned as the code for all manifestations of hated modernization and change. For the modernists, anti-Semitism facilitated and mirrored Hitler's own selective and ambivalent attitude that accepted: German *national* socialism but not international, subversive, "Jewish" socialism; that accepted managed and planned German capitalism subordinate to the state but not exploitive, egoistic "Jewish" capitalism putting profit above nation; that accepted modern politics of mass mobilization but not "Jewish" participatory democracy; that accepted social mobility and careers open to talent unhindered by old social barriers within the German *Volk* but not "Jewish" egalitarianism defending the rights of the weak against the strong and vitiating the recruitment of a new elite through the process of struggle for survival decreed by nature.[37]

In short, the centrality of anti-Semitism to National Socialism derived not only from Hitler's personal obsession or even as a means to mobilize a minority of "redemptive" anti-Semites and party radicals who shared that obsession. Anti-Semitism was also a cohering factor meaning different things to different people but nonetheless providing common ground. It allowed Hitler and the "chimeric" anti-Semites, the modernizing Nazis, the archaic Nazis, the traditional conservative allies, other disaffected and distraught Germans, and ultimately collaborators throughout Europe to speak the same words though not the same language, to take the same political train in a common political direction without agreeing beforehand at which stop they would all get off. As we know now, the train—ultimately driven by the chimeric anti-Semites though carrying many others—did not stop until it reached "Auschwitz."

Christopher R. Browning is the Frank Porter Graham Professor Emeritus of History at the University of North Carolina at Chapel Hill.

Notes

Parts of this essay originally appeared in Christopher R. Browning, "Contestualizzare la Shoah," *Passato e Presente* XXX, no. 86 (Maggio–Augosto 2012), 15–27.

1. For the most sophisticated, complete, and current discussion of the first debate, see: Dan Stone, *Histories of the Holocaust* (New York, 2010), 113–59; and Mark Roseman, "National Socialism and Modernisation," in *Fascist Italy and Nazi Germany: Comparisons and Contrasts*, ed. Richard Bessel (Cambridge, 1996), 197-229 and "National Socialism and the End of Modernity," *The American Historical Review* 116, no. 3 (2011), 688–701. It should also be noted that already in the early 1950s, Hannah Arendt had examined the connection of both nineteenth-century European imperialism and the corrosive impact of modernization on European society, producing superfluous people, as fundamental to the "origins of totalitarianism" and especially the Nazi variant. Hannah Arendt, *The Origins of Totalitarianism* (New York, 1951). For a more recent attempt at "synthesis," Enzo Traverso, *The Origins of Nazi Violence* (New York, 2003).

2. For the classic formulation of this Sonderweg thesis: Hans-Ulrich Wehler, *The German Empire* (Dover, NH, 1985). This interpretation was vulnerable on several fronts. Barrington Moore noted that there was nothing "special" about this trajectory, as "conservative modernization from above" elsewhere also produced authoritarian and expansionist regimes (such as in Japan). Barrington Moore Jr., *Social Origins of Dictatorship and Democracy: Lords and Peasants in the Making of the Modern World* (Boston, 1966). Geoff Eley and David Blackbourn questioned the whole notion of a failed bourgeois-liberal revolution and asserted that a bourgeois-liberal transformation had come about in a gradual though pervasive manner despite the apparent failure of 1848. Eley in particular went further, arguing that the Nazi rise to power was not the product of desperate precapitalist elites but the outcome of a particularly severe crisis in Germany's modern capitalist society in the 1920s. David Blackbourn and Geoff Eley, *The Peculiarities of German History* (Oxford, 1984); Geoff Eley, "What Produces Fascism: Pre-Industrial Traditions or a Crisis of the Capitalist State," in *From Unification to Nazism: Reinterpreting the German Past* (Boston, 1986), 254–82.

3. Martin Broszat, "Soziale Motivation und Führer-Bindung im Nationalsozialismus," *Vierteljahrshefte für Zeitgeschichte* 18, no. 4 (1970), 392–404; Hans Mommsen, "Die Realisierung des Utopischen: Die Endlösung der Judenfrage' im 'Dritten Reich,'" *Geschichte und Gesellschaft* 9, no. 3 (1983): 381–420.

4. For example, Henry Turner, "Fascism and Modernization," in *Reappraisals of Fascism,* ed. Henry Turner (New York, 1975) 117-39; and John Weiss, *The Fascist Tradition* (New York, 1967). Insofar as the Nazi regime furthered modernization, it was out of the necessity to fight for antimodern goals with modern means and was an *unintended* consequence of waging total industrial war in the twentieth century; Ralf Dahrendorf, *Society and Democracy in Germany* (New York, 1967), and David Schoenbaum, *Hitler's Social Revolution* (New York, 1966).

5. Rainer Zitelmann, *Hitler: Selbstverständnis eines Revolutionärs* (Hamburg, 1987).

6. Götz Aly, "The Economics of the Final Solution: A Case Study from the General Government," *Simon Wiesenthal Center Annual* V (1988): 3–48; Götz Aly and Susanne Heim, *Vordenker der Vernichtung: Auschwitz und die deutsche Pläne fur die europaische Ordnung* (Hamburg, 1991). Also emphasizing the compatibility between National Socialism,

modernization, and the Holocaust, though with much greater emphasis on ideology: Michael Thad Allen, *The Business of Genocide: The SS, Slave Labor, and the Concentration Camps* (Chapel Hill, NC, 2002).

7. Christopher R. Browning, "German Technocrats, Jewish Labor, and the Final Solution: A Reply to Götz Aly and Susannne Heim," in *The Path to Genocide: Essays on Launching the Final Solution* (New York, 1992), 59–76.

8. Detlev Peukert, *The Weimar Republic: The Crisis of Classical Modernity* (New York, 1992).

9. Detlev Peukert, *Inside Nazi Germany: Conformity, Opposition, and Racism in Everyday Life* (New Haven, CT, 1987), 34–45; and "The Genesis of 'the Final Solution' from the Spirit of Science," in *Reevaluating the Third Reich,* ed. Thomas Childers and Jane Caplan (New York, 1993), 234–52. For an insightful early analysis of the views of Zitelmann, Aly, and Peukert, see: Norbert Frei, "Wie modern war der Nationalsozialismus," *Geschichte und Gesellschaft* 19 (1993), 367–87. The American historian Ronald Smelser posed the same question in: "How Modern Were the Nazis," *German Studies Review* XIII, no. 2 (1990): 285–302.

10. Richard Rubenstein, *The Cunning of History* (New York, 1975), 4, 21. Rubenstein openly acknowledges his debt to Hannah Arendt.

11. Zygmunt Baumann, *Modernity and the Holocaust* (Ithaca, NY, 1989), esp. 11–13, 17, 90. George Kren and Leon Rappoport, *The Holocaust and the Crisis of Human Behavior* (New York, 1980) also portrayed the Shoah as quintessentially modern.

12. Edward Ross Dickinson, "Biopolitics, Fascism, Democracy: Some Reflections on Our Discourse about 'Modernity,'" *Central European History* 37, no. 1 (2004): 1–48.

13. For the historical background: Paul Weindling, *Health, Race and German Politics between National Unification and Nazism 1870–1945* (Cambridge, 1989).

14. Henry Friedlander, *The Origins of Nazi Genocide: From Euthanasia to the Final Solution* (Chapel Hill, NC, 1995).

15. Dickinson, "Biopolitics, Fascism, Democracy," 19 and 21.

16. Two impressive historiographical reviews of this issue, to which I am much indebted, are: Thomas Kühne, "Colonialism and the Holocaust: Continuities, Causations, and Complexities," *Journal of Genocide Research* 15, no. 3 (2013): 339–62; and Stone, *Histories of the Holocaust,* 203–44. See also the recent scholarly forum on the Holocaust and genocide in *Dapim: Studies on the Holocaust* 27, no. 1 (2013): 40–73, with contributions by Roberta Perched and Mark Roseman, Jürgen Zimmerer, Shelly Baranowski, and Doris Bergen.

17. Isabell Hull, *Absolute Destruction* (Ithaca, NY, 2005), especially 332–33. For a recent study of the course of German imperialism from 1871 to 1945, with greater focus on the later years and stressing differences more than similarities: Shelley Baranowski, *Nazi Empire: German Colonialism and Imperialism from Bismarck to Hitler* (New York, 2011).

18. Jürgen Zimmerer, *Von Windhuk nach Auschwitz: Beiträge zum Verhältnis von Kolonialismus und Holocaust* (Berlin, 2011), and "The Birth of the Ostland Out of the Spirit of Colonialism: A Postcolonial Perspective on the Nazi Policy of Conquest and Extermination," *Patterns of Prejudice* 39, no. 2 (2005): 197–219. Another chapter in the book with a title in the same vein is: "Von Windhuk nach Warschau. Die rassische Privilegiengesellschaft in Deutsch-Südwestafrika—-ein Modell mit Zukunft?," in *Von Windhuk nach Auschwitz: Beiträge zum Verhältnis von Kolonialismus und Holocaust* (Berlin, 2011). For colonial and Nazi racial legislation, see: Annegret Ehmann, "From Colonial Racism to Nazi Population Policy: The Role of the So-Called Mischlinge," in *The Holocaust and History: The*

Known, the Unknown, the Disputed, and the Reexamined, ed. Michael Berenbaum and Abraham Peck (Bloomington, IN, 1998), 115–33.

19. Zimmerer, "The Birth of the Ostland," 207.

20. Jürgen Zimmerer, "Colonial Genocide: The Herero and Nama War (1904–8) in German South West Africa and Its Significance," in *The Historiography of Genocide,* ed. Dan Stone (New York, 2008), 323–43.

21. Jürgen Zimmerer, "Colonialism and the Holocaust: Towards an Archeology of Genocide," in *Genocide and Settler Society: Frontier Violence and Stolen Indigenous Children in Australian History,* ed. A Dirk Moses (New York, 2004), 49–76.

22. Carroll Peter Kakel, *The American West and the Nazi East: A Comparative and Interpretive Perspective* (New York, 2011), and *The Holocaust as Colonial Genocide: Hitler's "Indian Wars" in the "Wild East"* (New York, 2013).

23. Kakel, *The American West and the Nazi East,* 213.

24. Ibid., 213–17; Kakel, *The Holocaust as Colonial Genocide,* vii, 4, 65–74. In his recent book examining the same two cases, Edward Westermann argues for a fundamental difference between an American "intentional policy of subjugation" involving many specific acts of atrocity and massacre and a Nazi "intentional policy of annihilation." Edward B. Westermann, *Hitler's Ostkrieg and the Indian Wars: Comparing Genocide and Conquest* (Norman: University of Oklahoma, 2016), p. 251.

25. Dominik Schaller, "From Conquest to Genocide: Colonial Rule in German Southwest Africa and German East Africa," in *Empire, Colony, Genocide: Conquest, Occupation, and Subaltern Resistance in World History,* ed. A. Dirk Moses (New York, 2008), 288–324, esp. 316–17. He is following in the footsteps of nonhistorian, anticolonial activists like Aimé Césaire, Fritz Fanon, and Jean-Paul Sartre.

26. Kuhne, "Colonialism and the Holocaust," 343–46.

27. Vejas Liulevicius, *War Land on the Eastern Front: Culture, National Identity, and Occupation in World War I* (Cambridge, 2000).

28. I am relying upon two key articles among a host of publications: A. Dirk Moses, "Conceptual Blockages and Definitional Dilemmas in the 'Racial Century': Genocides of Indigenous Peoples and the Holocaust," in *Colonialism and Genocide,* ed. A. Dirk Moses and Dan Stone (London, 2007), 149–80; and "The Holocaust and Genocide," in *The Historiography of the Holocaust,* ed. Dan Stone (New York, 2005), 533–53.

29. Thomas Kühne offers yet a third set of terms: "specific" and "general intent," with the latter designating what an actor could and should have known about the impact of his actions, even if he did not want it. Kühne, "Colonialism and the Holocaust," 343.

30. A. Dirk Moses, "Empire, Colony, Genocide: Keywords and the Philosophy of History," in *Empire, Colony, Genocide: Conquest, Occupation, and Subaltern Resistance in World History* (New York, 2008), 3–54, especially 34–40.

31. Thomas Kühne also concludes: "The continuities suggested under the colonial paradigm operate on such a high level of abstraction and generalization that parallels and similarities are obvious but of not much value for identifying historically specific settings," and "Explaining the Holocaust, i.e. the murder of the Jews, in terms of colonialism and imperialism rather than anti-Semitism and racist nationalism has not led to convincing results." Kühne, "Colonialism and the Holocaust," 352, 356. Likewise Dan Stone concludes: "whilst the idea of the Nazi occupation of eastern Europe as a colonial project is relatively easy to accept, the question of what this has to do with the Holocaust is less obvious." *Histories of the Holocaust* (New York, 2010), 227.

32. In a sense, then, Kakel's assertion that the Nazi genocide of the Jews was "ultimately caused by Nazi colonial ambitions" is not so much incorrect as insufficiently explained, because that would require a "partitioning" of the final solution from other Nazi mass killing that he opposes in principle. Kakel, *The Holocaust as Colonial Genocide*, 72, 78.

33. Gavin Langmuir, "Prolegomena to Any Present Analysis of Hostility against the Jews," in *The Nazi Holocaust*, vol. 2, ed. Michael Marrus (Westport, CT, 1989), 133–71, and "From Anti-Judaism to Anti-Semitism," in *History, Religion, and Anti-Semitism* (Berkeley, CA, 1990), 275–305.

34. Shulamit Volkov, "Anti-Semitism as a Cultural Code," *Leo Baeck Institute Yearbook* 23 (1978): 25–46.

35. Götz Aly, *Why the Germans? Why the Jews? Envy, Race Hatred, and the Prehistory of the Holocaust* (New York, 2014). This book stands in contrast to Aly's previous books, in which he emphasized economic and material factors and downplayed the importance of ideology in general and anti-Semitism in particular. Others before Aly have also emphasized the catalytic impact of Jewish success (Albert Lindemann) and the antimodernism of the anti-Semitic movement in nineteenth-century Germany (Peter Pulzer).

36. Michael Wildt, *The Uncompromising Generation: The Nazi Leadership of the Reich Security Main Office* (Madison, WI, 2009).

37. For National Socialism's selective relationship to modernization: Jeffrey Herf, *Reactionary Modernism: Technology, Culture, and Politics in Weimar and the Third Reich* (Cambridge, 1984).

Bibliography

Allen, Michael Thad. *The Business of Genocide: The SS, Slave Labor, and the Concentration Camps.* Chapel Hill: University of North Carolina Press, 2002.

Aly, Götz. "The Economics of the Final Solution: A Case Study from the General Government." *Simon Wiesenthal Center Annual* V (1988): 3–48.

———. *Why the Germans? Why the Jews? Envy, Race Hatred, and the Prehistory of the Holocaust.* New York: Metropolitan Books, 2014.

Aly, Götz, and Susanne Heim. *Vordenker der Vernichtung: Auschwitz und die deutsche Pläne fur die europaische Ordnung.* Hamburg: Hoffmann und Campe, 1991.

Arendt, Hannah. *The Origins of Totalitarianism.* New York: Harcourt Brace, 1951.

Baranowski, Shelley. *Nazi Empire: German Colonialism and Imperialism from Bismarck to Hitler.* New York: Cambridge University Press, 2011.

Baumann, Zygmunt. *Modernity and the Holocaust.* Ithaca, NY: Cornell University Press, 1989.

Blackbourn, David, and Geoff Eley. *The Peculiarities of German History.* Oxford: Oxford University Press, 1984.

Broszat, Martin. "Soziale Motivation und Führer-Bindung im Nationalsozialismus." *Vierteljahrshefte für Zeitgeschichte* 18, no. 4 (1970): 392–404.

Browning, Christopher R. "German Technocrats, Jewish Labor, and the Final Solution: A Reply to Götz Aly and Susannne Heim." In *The Path to Genocide: Essays on Launching the Final Solution,* 59–76. New York: Cambridge University Press, 1992.

Dahrendorf, Ralf. *Society and Democracy in Germany.* New York: Doubleday, 1967.

Dapim: Studies on the Holocaust 27, no. 1 (2013): 40–73.

Dickinson, Edward Ross. "Biopolitics, Fascism, Democracy: Some Reflections on Our Discourse about 'Modernity.'" *Central European History* 37, no. 1 (2004): 1–48.

Ehmann, Annegret. "From Colonial Racism to Nazi Population Policy: The Role of the So-Called Mischlinge." In *The Holocaust and History: The Known, the Unknown, the Disputed, and the Reexamined*, edited by Michael Berenbaum and Abraham Peck, 115–33. Bloomington: Indiana University Press, 1998.

Eley, Geoff. "What Produces Fascism: Pre-Industrial Traditions or a Crisis of the Capitalist State." In *From Unification to Nazism: Reinterpreting the German Past*, 254–82. Boston: Allen and Unwin, 1986.

Frei, Norbert. "Wie modern war der Nationalsozialismus." *Geschichte und Gesellschaft* 19 (1993): 367–87.

Friedlander, Henry. *The Origins of Nazi Genocide: From Euthanasia to the Final Solution.* Chapel Hill: University of North Carolina Press, 1995.

Herf, Jeffrey. *Reactionary Modernism: Technology, Culture, and Politics in Weimar and the Third Reich.* Cambridge: Harvard University Press, 1984.

Hull, Isabell. *Absolute Destruction.* Ithaca, NY: Cornell University Press, 2005.

Kakel, Carroll Peter. *The American West and the Nazi East: A Comparative and Interpretive Perspective.* New York: Palgrave Macmillan, 2011.

———. *The Holocaust as Colonial Genocide: Hitler's "Indian Wars" in the "Wild East."* New York: Palgrave Pivot, 2013.

Kren, George, and Leon Rappoport. *The Holocaust and the Crisis of Human Behavior.* New York: Holmes & Meier, 1980.

Kühne, Thomas. "Colonialism and the Holocaust: Continuities, Causations, and Complexities." *Journal of Genocide Research* 15, no. 3 (2013): 339–62.

Langmuir, Gavin. "From Anti-Judaism to Anti-Semitism." In *History, Religion, and Anti-Semitism*, 275–305. Berkeley: University of California Press, 1990.

———. "Prolegomena to Any Present Analysis of Hostility against the Jews." In *The Nazi Holocaust*, vol. 2, edited by Michael Marrus, 133–71. Westport, CT: Meckler, 1989.

Liulevicius, Vejas. *War Land on the Eastern Front: Culture, National Identity, and Occupation in World War I.* Cambridge: Cambridge University Press, 2000.

Mommsen, Hans. "Die Realisierung des Utopischen: Die Endlösung der Judenfrage' im 'Dritten Reich.'" *Geschichte und Gesellschaft* 9, no. 3 (1983): 381–420.

Moore, Barrington, Jr. *Social Origins of Dictatorship and Democracy: Lords and Peasants in the Making of the Modern World.* Boston: Beacon Press, 1966.

Moses, A. Dirk. "Conceptual Blockages and Definitional Dilemmas in the 'Racial Century': Genocides of Indigenous Peoples and the Holocaust." In *Colonialism and Genocide*, edited by A. Dirk Moses and Dan Stone, 149–80. London: Routledge, 2007.

———. "Empire, Colony, Genocide: Keywords and the Philosophy of History." In *Empire, Colony, Genocide: Conquest, Occupation, and Subaltern Resistance in World History*, edited by A. Dirk Moses, 3–54. New York: Berghahn Books, 2008.

———. "The Holocaust and Genocide." In *The Historiography of the Holocaust*, edited by Dan Stone, 533–53. New York: Palgrave Macmillan, 2005.

Peukert, Detlev. "The Genesis of 'the Final Solution' from the Spirit of Science." In *Reevaluating the Third Reich*, edited by Thomas Childers and Jane Caplan, 234–52. New York: Holmes & Meier, 1993.

————. *Inside Nazi Germany: Conformity, Opposition, and Racism in Everyday Life*. New Haven, CT: Yale University Press, 1987.

————. *The Weimar Republic: The Crisis of Classical Modernity*. New York: Hill and Wang, 1992.

Roseman, Mark. "National Socialism and the End of Modernity." *The American Historical Review* 116, no. 3 (2011): 688–701.

————. "National Socialism and Modernisation." In *Fascist Italy and Nazi Germany: Comparisons and Contrasts*, edited by Richard Bessel. Cambridge: Cambridge University Press, 1996.

Rubenstein, Richard. *The Cunning of History*. New York: Harper & Row, 1975.

Schaller, Dominik. "From Conquest to Genocide: Colonial Rule in German Southwest Africa and German East Africa." In *Empire, Colony, Genocide: Conquest, Occupation, and Subaltern Resistance in World History*, edited by A Dirk Moses, 288–324. New York: Berghahn Books, 2008.

Schoenbaum, David. *Hitler's Social Revolution*. New York: Doubleday, 1966.

Smelser, Ronald. "How Modern Were the Nazis." *German Studies Review* XIII, no. 2 (1990): 285–302.

Stone, Dan. *Histories of the Holocaust*. New York: Oxford University Press, 2010.

Traverso, Enzo. *The Origins of Nazi Violence*. New York: The New Press, 2003.

Turner, Henry. "Fascism and Modernization." In *Reappraisals of Fascism*, edited by Henry Turner. 117–39. New York: New Viewpoints, 1975.

Volkov, Shulamit. "Anti-Semitism as a Cultural Code." *Leo Baeck Institute Yearbook* 23 (1978): 25–46.

Wehler, Hans-Ulrich. *The German Empire*. Dover, NH: Leamington Spa, 1985.

Weindling, Paul. *Health, Race and German Politics between National Unification and Nazism 1870–1945*. Cambridge: Cambridge University Press, 1989.

Weiss, John. *The Fascist Tradition*. New York: Harper & Row, 1967.

Wildt, Michael. *The Uncompromising Generation: The Nazi Leadership of the Reich Security Main Office*. Madison: University of Wisconsin Press, 2009.

Zimmerer, Jürgen. "The Birth of the Ostland Out of the Spirit of Colonialism: A Postcolonial Perspective on the Nazi Policy of Conquest and Extermination." *Patterns of Prejudice* 39, no. 2 (2005): 197–219.

————. "Colonial Genocide: The Herero and Nama War (1904–8) in German South West Africa and Its Significance." In *The Historiography of Genocide*, edited by Dan Stone, 323–43. New York: Palgrave Macmillan, 2008.

————. "Colonialism and the Holocaust: Towards an Archeology of Genocide." In *Genocide and Settler Society: Frontier Violence and Stolen Indigenous Children in Australian History*, edited by A. Dirk Moses, 49–76. New York: Berghahn Books, 2004.

————. *Von Windhuk nach Auschwitz: Beiträge zum Verhältnis von Kolonialismus und Holocaust*. Berlin: Lit, 2011.

————. "Von Windhuk nach Warschau. Die rassische Privilegiengesellschaft in Deutsch-Südwestafrika—-ein Modell mit Zukunft?" In *Von Windhuk nach Auschwitz: Beiträge zum Verhältnis von Kolonialismus und Holocaust*. Berlin: Lit, 2011.

Zitelmann, Rainer. *Hitler: Selbstverständnis eines Revolutionärs*. Hamburg: Berg, 1987.

Part II

Memory, Professionalization, and Professions

Chapter 4

Gender and Academic Culture
Women in the Historical Profession in Germany
and the United States since 1945

Karen Hagemann and Sarah Summers

> During my job interview, one of the professors asked me, "How do you envision reconciling a professorship and your family responsibilities? You have two children after all." Neither the female professors present nor the women's affairs liaison protested against this question. A few minutes later, another committee member inquired, "Your research and publications are impressive. You are often invited to give lectures and conference papers. How do you intend to combine these extensive activities with your administrative and teaching duties in the department?" Not a single member of the search committee seemed to see any contradiction between the two questions.[1]

This story was told by a historian recently interviewed about her experiences on the German academic job market. A plethora of national and international studies on the situation of women in research and teaching reports similar stories and confirms continuing discrimination in the academic system in spite of all the progress made in past decades.[2] This applies not just to Germany, which in the European context still has a relatively low proportion of female professors, especially among the highest rank, the so-called C4/W3 professorships, which correspond to tenured full professorships in other countries.[3] It is also true of many other countries in Europe and the United States. The report *She Figures 2012: Gender in Research and Innovation* published by the European Commission in 2013 notes that of the twenty-seven member states in the European Union, women held on average only 20 percent of all full professorships. The pro-

Notes for this chapter begin on page 113.

portion in Germany was 15 percent, greatly surpassed by Scandinavian countries such as Finland (24 percent) and Sweden (20 percent) on the one hand, and Eastern European countries such as Romania (36 percent) and Latvia (32 percent) on the other.[4] In the United States, according to a survey by the American Association of University Professors, the proportion of women among full professors was 23 percent in 2012.[5]

The vast majority of international studies indicate that despite very different national structures in higher education, similar mechanisms of discrimination appear to be at work. This is likely the case for the historical profession in Germany and the United States as well, in spite of very different university systems. More precise information does not exist, however, since discipline-specific comparisons are extremely rare due to the considerable methodological difficulties involved.[6] This contribution ventures an attempt to offer a comparative analysis of the integration of women into the historical profession in Germany and the United States. The comparison seeks to reveal the interplay among various factors that have hindered or promoted women's integration into the discipline. These include the institutional structures in higher education, its historical traditions and overall academic culture, the degree of professionalization and social prestige of a career in the discipline, disciplinary culture, and the political and social conditions.[7] Our essay focuses mostly on developments since the end of World War II, but as both the structural and the cultural barriers to women's equal integration have a long "path dependency," the analysis needs to begin earlier. The concept of "path dependency" used here stresses the processual nature of policies and the institutions that implement and sustain them. Path dependency explains why and how systems, structures, and cultures become "cemented" after their introduction, which is what makes change so difficult. Universities and disciplines are among the systems that display a high degree of path dependency. For that reason, we can only explain the mechanisms of discrimination in these systems historically. At the same time, by looking at the time frames in which change became possible, the concept of path dependency also helps to determine more precisely the factors that modified these mechanisms.[8]

The First Female Students, Doctoral Candidates, and Professors, 1900–45

In 1905, the newspaper *Berliner Lokalanzeiger* reported on "Women's university education in America": "In the 'New World,' anyone can convince himself that everything ... is splendidly set up for the education of women, in both school and university."[9] More than one hundred years ago, German middle-class women with educational aspirations were already looking to America. While in most states of the German Empire, women still fought for access to university studies in 1905, the diversified American system of higher education, with its large number of private and public institutions, already accommodated female students since the early nineteenth century. Alongside two-year junior colleges (from which the present-day community college system emerged) and teachers' colleges, there were four-year liberal arts colleges leading to a bachelor of arts (BA) degree and universities at which students could earn a BA, a master of arts (MA), or a PhD.[10] The women's colleges, which offered female students academic training at a BA level and gave women with doctoral degrees the opportunity to teach as professors, were especially important for women's education. Around 1900, there were already several hundred women's colleges in the United States.[11]

The majority of young women who studied history in the United States finished with a BA and aspired to become schoolteachers. Only 3 percent of the 1,688 institutions of higher learning that existed in the 1930s offered a PhD program in history.[12] Between 1893 and 1920, 81 women attained such a degree, a figure that rose to 121 between 1920 and 1930 and to 122 between 1931 and 1935 alone. These 344 women represented an average of 16 percent of all doctoral candidates in the discipline.[13] This corresponded to the proportion of female members who belonged to the American Historical Association (AHA), which fluctuated around 15–20 percent between 1895 and 1940. These first female holders of a PhD in history were still very far from equal integration into the field at the university level. Their main workplaces remained the women's colleges, teachers' colleges, academic libraries, and high schools. In the journal of the AHA, the *American Historical Review* (AHR), the proportion of articles published by women between 1914 and 1940 remained marginal at just 4 percent, and their proposals for the program of the annual AHA conventions were rarely accepted.[14] Historian Jacqueline Goggin summarized the experiences of this first generation of female historians 1992 in the *AHR*: "Male historians served as the gatekeepers for the profession, not only by defining history as a male enterprise but also by writing history that dealt mainly with men and male institutions, while purporting to deal with society. They determined what constituted history in all its various subfields and specializations."[15]

From a comparative perspective, however, conditions in the United States up to the end of World War II appear relatively advanced, since women after all represented 16 percent of full professors in 1930 and the first woman—the medievalist Nellie Neilson—was elected president of the AHA in 1943.[16] This was the result of intense lobbying by her female colleagues, who beginning in 1930, joined forces to form the Lakeville Conference. In 1936, members changed its name to the current Berkshire Conference of Women Historians. The aim was to integrate women into the historical profession on a more equal footing with men.[17]

Germany, in contrast, was one of the last European countries that admitted women to university studies. Until the turn of the twentieth century, authorities allowed women to study and attain doctorates at German universities only in exceptional cases. Baden was the first state in the German Empire to afford women full access to university studies in 1899. Bavaria followed in 1903, Württemberg in 1904, Saxony in 1906, and Prussia only in 1908. In the same year, Prussia forbade women to *habilitate*, that is, to write a second major scholarly work and to take part in the associated academic examination process, which was the central prerequisite for gaining permission to teach in a university discipline (*venia legendi*). In this way, the Prussian minister of culture sought to prevent "women from being admitted to an academic career," which he believed "is consistent neither with the present structure nor the interests of the universities."[18] University teaching in particular should remain a "male preserve."[19] Since only scholars who had completed the *Habilitation* process could be appointed to a professorship and were permitted to teach as *Privatdozenten* (private lecturers without a permanent position and any payment) and nontenured professors, the ban on *Habilitation* for women seemed the most effective means of ensuring this exclusion.[20] Long after the revocation of the ban of the *Habilitation* in 1920, male resistance to women in academic teaching persisted. A study published in 1960 that surveyed 138 male university instructors found that 40 percent "fundamentally" and another 40 percent "to some extent" opposed women teaching in higher education.[21]

Apart from the misogynistic climate, additional factors also impeded the integration of women into German universities: the largely state-run organization of higher education, more extensive professionalization in occupations requiring an academic degree, and the concurrent significance of university education for the formation of the elite. The German university system was controlled by the state, far less diversified, and much more difficult to access. The universities educated a small social elite of largely Protestant young men from the "better classes," who enjoyed extraordinary social status after completing their studies. A strict university entrance process via the *Abitur* examination (taken in the final year of academic preparatory secondary school, the *Gymnasium*) and state-controlled academic courses of study regulated access to many privileged positions and professions in the state and economy.[22] The educational reforms, and the students' and women's movements of the late 1960s and beyond, only gradually opened up this extremely socially segregated structure and culture of German higher education.

Subsequently, the proportion of female students at German universities grew only slowly: the figure was 4 percent in 1909/10, rising to 19 percent in 1931/32. During the Nazi period, it fell again to 14 percent, in history to 16 percent, because of policies aimed at restricting studies for women. During the Second World War, however, more women were admitted to university again, mainly in order to replace conscripted men in the fields of teaching and health care. The proportion of women among all students rose overall to 49 percent in 1943/44 and in history already 51 percent in 1941.[23] Few women earned doctorates; in history, a total of 414 between 1908 and 1933, most of them after 1918. This number was a good deal higher than during the same period in the United States, but because of the larger total number of PhDs granted in Germany (a reflection of the higher degree of professionalization), the proportion of women was lower. In Germany, most women with doctorates in history taught in secondary schools (*Gymnasien*).[24] Even fewer women cleared the hurdle of *Habilitation* in Germany before 1945. In the Weimar Republic, only two female historians gained their *Habilitation*, and two more followed during the Third Reich. This meant that women at German universities, unlike their counterparts in the United States, were largely excluded from teaching history in the university setting up until 1945.[25]

Setbacks and Advancements, 1945–80

The situation for women in the American historical profession changed dramatically after World War II—but not for the better. As part of the politics of postwar demobilization and the climate of the Cold War, which was marked by dichotomous gender and family images—in the communist East the dual earner family and in the democratic West the male breadwinner-female homemaker family—[26] women were increasingly pushed out of the profession: significantly fewer women completed their doctoral studies. Their proportion of PhD candidates fell to 11 percent in 1969 and only returned to the prewar level of 16 percent in the decade that followed. The proportion of women with full professorships also fell dramatically—to 6 percent in 1960—and stagnated at this level until 1980. In total, 906 women (14 percent) were members of the full-time teaching staff in 330 history departments in this year (see Table 4.1).[27] Several factors contributed to this development. More generally, as the 1970 *Report of the American Historical Association Committee on the Status of Women* noted, an attitude became widespread in American higher education that rejected the promotion of female PhDs with the argument "that women prefer to marry and devote themselves to domestic life."[28] Even women's colleges increasingly hired male professors. On the one hand, the growth of coeducation starting in the 1950s fostered this trend, since women were not considered suitable to teach male students. Accordingly, the decline in the proportion of women among full professors in history departments at coeducational colleges was especially strong, falling from 16 percent in 1959–60 to less than 1 percent ten years later.[29] On the other hand, the general spread of the tenure process at American colleges and universities from the 1930s and 1940s onward also contributed to the decline in female history professors. The reason given for introducing this system was to ensure academic freedom for instructors in a market-dependent system. At the same time, however, the advent of tenure further standardized the quality criteria for professorships and thus tailored them more to the male model and its research mainstream. In the years that followed, it became more difficult for women to gain appointments to full professorships.

Despite this setback in the first three postwar decades, the situation of the young women who, encouraged by the new women's movement, flocked to American colleges and universities for undergraduate and graduate study from the late 1960s on was much better than that of their German sisters. They could call upon a long tradition of women as university students,

Table 4.1. Faculty of the History Departments at U.S. Colleges and Universities, 1980–2007[30]

Year [a]	Number of History Departments	Fulltime teaching staff in History Departments						
		Overall fulltime teaching staff			Assistant Professors	Associate Professors	Full Professors
		Total	Women				
			T	%	Proportion of women in %		
1980	330	6,469	906	14	N/A[b]	N/A[b]	6
1987/88	444 (1985)	8,082	1,374	17	N/A[b]	N/A[b]	8
1993/94	595 (1990)	10,718	3,001	28	44 (1992)	24 (1992)	12 (1992)
2003	671 (2005)	15,487	4,646	30	33	36	17
2007	N/A[b]	N/A[b]	N/A[b]	35	N/A[b]	N/A[b]	N/A[b]

Notes:
a. For many years no data exist, because no annual figures are published for the individual disciplines, but only for groups of disciplines, i.e. the Humanities.
b. No data available.

researchers, and instructors, and a larger number of female professors to serve as role models, who supported their attempts to open up the historical profession in a dual sense: while aiming to integrate more women as students, scholars, and teachers, they also sought to transform *his*tory into *her*story.[31] The fact that the Berkshire Conference had already existed for decades as a lobbying organization, and that the introduction in 1973 of the "Big Berks" every three years significantly expanded its influence, was also helpful. In addition, in 1969 American women historians began organizing in the Coordinating Council for Women in History (CCWH) whose declared aim was and is "to educate men and women on the status of women in the historical profession and to promote research and interpretation in areas of women's history."[32] The CCWH pushed through the compilation of the 1970 *Report of the American Historical Association Committee on the Status of Women,* and that same year also saw to the establishment of a Standing Committee on Women Historians within the AHA, and the adoption of an extensive AHA program of action for the advancement of women.[33] The CCWH also lobbied for the election of the early modern historian Natalie Zemon Davis in 1987 as the first female president of the AHA in many years, followed by ten women colleagues thus far.[34]

A further important factor that promoted the greater integration of women into the discipline was the growing market dependency of American higher education, where students at both private and public institutions pay tuition fees, which have risen drastically over the past forty years.[35] In the United States, the openness to hiring more female professors and the introduction and expansion of courses first in women's history and later in gender history were therefore not least reactions to student wishes and demands. College and university administrators reached the conclusion that given the rising number of female students, hiring more female professors and opening the curriculum to women's history would ultimately mean higher enrollment figures and thus financial advantages.[36]

In West Germany, too, with the return of young soldiers after 1945, the economic hardships of the postwar period, and the perceived "crisis of the family," the Christian-conservative dominated federal government pushed in the context of the Cold War for family and labor policies that fostered the dominance of the male-breadwinnder-female-homemaker family. As a result, the proportion of female students dropped significantly in the first postwar decade. Until 1951/52 it fell in average to 16 percent; but increased slowly during the 1950s and reached in 1959 again 26 percent. Two-fifths of all female students were concentrated in the humanities, much as in the United States. It was only in the context of educational reforms at the national and federal state level in the 1960s, which sought to create more "equal chances in society," that the percentage of women at universities began to increase in the Federal Republic of Germany (FRG).[37] This also applied to history as a discipline. In the early 1970s, women made up 38 percent of all students and 21 percent of all doctoral candidates in history (see Table 4.2). Most were preparing to become teachers. In 1975, 88 percent of the 2,602 degree examinations in history were for a teaching degree (*Lehramtsprüfung*), only 9 percent for doctorates and 3 percent for a master's degree.[38] This general trend was even more pronounced among women, as is indicated by their extremely different representation in the two professional organizations: at the end of the 1970s, women made

Table 4.2. Students, PhDs, and Habilitations in History, a Comparison of the Federal Republic of Germany and the United States, 1982–2012[40]

Year	USA		FRG		USA		FRG			
	Bachelor of Arts in History		History Students		Granted PhDs		Completed			
							Dissertations		Habilitations	
	Total	%	Total	%	Total	%	Total	%	Total	%
1972	---	---	11,974 (1972/73)	38	---	13 (1970)	217 (1973)	21	---	---
1982	---	36 (1980)	16,715 (1982/83)	45	---	25	231	29	36	4
1987	18,207	37	19,598 (1987/88)	43	517 (1988)	37	252	31	33	6
1992	27,774 (1993)	38	23,203 (1992/93)	42	690 (1993)	35	365	33	46	17
1997	25,726 (1998)	39	27,428 (1997/98)	42	954	38	454	39	60	23
2002	26,001	41	25,890 (2002/03)	43	1,030	40	453	38	93	34
2007	34,446	41	38,484 (2007/08)	46	969 (2008)	42	419	40	49	31
2011	35,121	40	43,419 (2011/12)	46	1,006	45	407	41	43	32
2012	N/A[b]	41	44,221 (2012/13)	46	N/A[b]	45	466	44	48	33

Notes:
a. Data for East and West Germany have been combined since the WS (winter semester) of 1992/93. The figures for Germany reflect enrolment/degrees for the winter semester, while those for the USA refer to academic years.
b. No data available

up 30 to 40 percent of members of the German history teachers' association (Verband der Geschichtslehrer Deutschlands), but only 9 percent of members of the German historian's federation (Verband der Historiker Deutschlands, VHD).[39]

The number of women attaining a *Habilitation* in history increased very slowly in comparison to that of female students and doctoral candidates. Only thirteen women habilitated between 1945 and 1970.[41] In 1960 there were only fifteen women teaching history at German universities, four of them with the status of *Privatdozentin*. Women made up 5 percent of academic staff in history departments, compared with 19 percent in the United States.[42] The first habilitated female historian was appointed to a professorship in the FRG in 1964.[43] By 1977, the number had risen to sixteen, or 4 percent of history professors. It is striking that, just as in the United States, the majority of female historians appointed to a professorship in the FRG did not work in the fields of modern and contemporary German history that were most important for the creation of the national "master narratives." Rather, they worked in fields considered "marginal," such as ancient and medieval history, the history of Eastern or Western Europe, non-European history, or developing fields such as early modern or social history, which appear to have been more open to women.[44]

Compared with their counterparts in the United States, women in West Germany encountered far greater problems gaining acceptance in the historical profession after 1945. One indicator is the practice of the VHD. In its venerable journal, the *Historische Zeitschrift*, the proportion of articles by women remains very low even today. Between 1950 and 1990, women wrote no more than 2 to 3 percent of the contributions; in the 1990s, the proportion rose to 4 percent; in 2013, it was 12 percent, in striking contrast to the *AHR*, where it was 38 percent in the same year.[45] Rarer still are articles on women's and gender history, which was and is also a clearly underrepresented subject at the national VHD congress, the *Deutscher Historikertag*, which takes place every two years.[46]

From the perspective of the mainly young feminist historians whose numbers were growing rapidly in the FRG as well in the 1980s, and who promoted the development of women's and soon also gender history, thereby contributing significantly to innovation in the discipline of history more broadly, the situation in American history departments looked comparatively more positive.[47] But this impression arose above all based on three factors: the much larger absolute number of female full professors; the tenure-track system that promised earlier job security; and last but not least the earlier and faster evolution of women's history in the United States, which on both sides of the Atlantic emerged from the new women's movement. In 1975, only 1 percent of history faculty primarily taught in the field of women's and gender history; in 2007, the figure was 9 percent. This made the field the most strongly represented in U.S. history departments, after social history.[48] In Germany even today, there are only five history professorships partly dedicated to women's and gender history, which represent 1 percent of the 721 professorships in history at 108 universities. Overall, some twenty-five to thirty professors (4 percent) are considered experts in this research field.[49]

The impression of a far better situation in the United States was also heightened by the much earlier and higher degree of organization of women historians in the United States. The Working Group on Women's History (Arbeitskreis Historische Frauenforschung, AKHF) in the FRG was only founded in 1990,[50] joining the International Federation of Research in Women's History (IFRWH) established in 1987.[51] The central aims of the AKHF include intensifying scholarly exchange among all those working in women's and gender history, supporting them with a network, and establishing women's and gender history in the academic and cultural landscape of the Federal Republic, both within and outside the universities on a lasting basis. In the very first year, nearly 300 mainly female historians from East and West Germany joined the network, which speaks to the broad interest at the time of its founding.[52] In 2015 the working group, which became an association in 2007 and renamed itself the Working Group on Women's and Gender History (Arbeitskreis Historische Frauen- und Geschlechterforschung, AKHFG), had about 277 members, seventeen of them men and fifty-seven male and female professors.[53]

Those who looked to the United States usually overlooked that the proportion of women among both full-time teaching staff and full professors in history departments in the early 1980s, at 14 and 6 percent, respectively, was not that much higher than in the FRG (see Tables 4.1 and 4.3). This situation changed very quickly, however. While in the United States, women were increasingly appointed to history professorships from the 1980s on, initially mainly to assistant and associate professorships, in Germany this development only began after 2000. In both countries, from the 1980s on, women's and gender studies had awakened awareness of the gender gap at universities and its structural and cultural causes. But unlike in the United States, where the interplay between lobbying by organized women historians, AHA policies aimed at greater equality, and the academic market already initiated rapid change in the 1980s, the slow transformation in Germany, which had reunified in 1990, was a result of the increased intensity of the intervention by federal and state governments into the gender equality policies at universities and nonuniversity research institutes. Beginning in 1996, the gender mainstreaming agenda of the European Union intensified the pressure exerted by such policies.[54]

Table 4.3. Full-Time Teaching Staff in History at Universities in the Federal Republic of Germany, 1982–2012[55]

Year	Total (T)	Women (W)		Total Professorships b) (C4/W3, C3/W2 and C2/W1)				Tenured Full Professorships (C4, C3)						Temporary Professorships (C2/WI)					
								C4			C3			C2 permanent			C2/W1 temporary		
		T	%	T	Proportion of all instructors %	Total of women[c]	%	T	W	%	T	W	%	T	W	%	T	W	%
1982	1,400	197	14	575	41	27	5	310	13	4	160	7	4	83	4	5	13	1	8
1992	1,917	397	21	694	36	44	6	419	16	4	151	15	10	84	9	11	21	3	14
2002	2,192	604	28	662	30	85	13	399	36	9	213	41	19	36	3	8	14	5	36
2012	2,954	1,136	39	721	24	196	27	N/A[c]			N/A[c]			—	—	—	89	—	—

Notes:

a. Universities including teachers' colleges and theological seminaries.

b. W salary groups were introduced with the advent of a new salary grade for university teachers in 2005.

c. There are no data differentiated by status.

Growing Integration since the 1980s

More detailed statistics are available for a comparative view of developments since the 1980s. Gender-specific data has been gathered in the FRG
since the 1970s and in the United States since the 1980s. This makes it possible to better examine the degree of women's integration on all levels and
to make the proportion of women among students the point of departure
for an analysis of the "leaky pipeline." A comparison of students is difficult, however, because the American National Center for Education only
counts students who completed a BA in history, while the German Federal Statistical Office (Statistisches Bundesamt) counts all students who
are enrolled in a history program.[56] In addition, all figures on the German
development have to keep in mind reunification, which, however, had remarkably little overall effect on the proportion of women among history
students, and doctoral and habilitation candidates (see Table 4.2).

In the FRG and the United States alike, while the number of history
students rose markedly from the 1980s, the proportion of women among
them increased only slightly in both countries. The total number of students enrolled in history grew from 19,598 in the winter semester of 1987–
88 in the old FRG to 23,203 in the winter semester of 1992–93 in reunified
Germany, and reached 43,419 in the winter semester of 2011–12. In the
United States, in the same period, the number of students earning a BA in
history rose from 18,207 in 1987 to 35,121 in 2011, and was thus consistently
lower than the figures in the FRG. The proportion of women among history students, however, increased only slightly in both countries over these
twenty-five years: from 43 to 46 percent in the FRG and from 37 to 40 percent in the United States.[57] In contrast to the 1970s, in the two decades that
followed many more students finished their historical studies with a master's or doctoral degree. The significance of the German state examination
for teachers fell dramatically, which primarily reflects the poor job opportunities for those pursuing teaching degrees during those two decades in
Germany. In 2000, of all examinations in history, 18 percent were for PhDs,
32 percent for teaching degrees, and 50 percent for master's degrees.[58]

Developments in the number of completed doctoral degrees reflect the
academic job market in the Federal Republic. In the field of history, the
number rose from 252 in 1987 to 365 in 1992. In 2011, the figure was 407.
Unlike among students, the proportion of women rose sharply, but only
toward the end of the 1990s. It increased from 31 percent in 1987 to 33 percent in 1992, and reached 41 percent in 2011 and 44 percent in 2012. This
means that the difference between the proportion of women among students and among doctoral candidates in history has virtually disappeared
in Germany over the past two decades. Compared with the average of Ger-

man universities, the discipline of history has caught up. According to data collected by the Joint Science Conference (Gemeinsame Wissenschaftskonferenz, GWK), women made up 50 percent of all new student enrollments in 2010, 52 percent of all completed degrees, and 44 percent of doctorates awarded.[59] The increase in the total number of history PhDs granted in the United States was greater still. Here the number grew from 517 to 1,006 between 1988 and 2011. The proportion of women grew at a rate similar to that in the Federal Republic, from 37 to 45 percent.[60] The proportion of women among granted history PhDs therefore exceeded that for BAs.

The number of women with completed *Habilitationen* in history and their proportion of the total rose especially sharply in the FRG from the late 1980s, growing from 33 in 1987 to 93 in 2002. During this period, the proportion of women among those gaining *Habilitationen* rose from 6 to 34 percent. Since then, the number of completed *Habilitationen* has declined strongly again, though, which must be interpreted primarily as a response to the unfavorable academic employment market. The figure was 43 in 2011 and the proportion of women was 32 percent, and thus a good deal higher than the average for all disciplines of 25 percent.[61] Since 2000, however, women have never represented more than about one-third of all completed habilitations.[62]

It has only been since the late 1990s that the proportion of women among doctoral candidates and later also *Habilitation* candidates in Germany has reached the proportion among students, which indicates growing equality on the lower levels of the hierarchy in the field of history. But how should we interpret this development? Here, too, a comparative perspective is useful. From an international perspective, the *habilitation* process, as the prerequisite for a permanent position in the academic system, is a wholly obsolete German peculiarity, which keeps younger scholars, during the already precarious phase when they might start a family, in an unnecessarily prolonged period of economic uncertainty. In this interpretation, the *Habilitation* stabilizes the hierarchies of the academic system and contributions to its ossification. Moreover, the German historical profession today, as was the case ten or twenty years ago, produces far more highly qualified young academics than can be hired, which the most recent (2012) study of the *Situation of Young Scholars in the Historical Profession* published by the VHD also points out.[63] This increases the insecurity, dependence, and also hierarchies, despite a variety of temporary funding opportunities for individual projects that foundations such as the German Research Foundation or the Volkswagen Foundation offer to doctoral and habilitation candidates, as well as positions for junior scholars in large-scale research projects (collaborative research centers, clusters of excellence, research training groups).[64] The introduction of the Excellence

Initiative, the federal and state program initiated in 2005–6 to promote excellent scholarship and research at German universities, has not improved this situation.[65]

The massive overproduction of doctorates and habilitations in the German historical profession, as in the German academic system more generally, appears inefficient from the American perspective. In the United States, one factor that influences the national ranking of (history) departments is the success in the placement of new PhDs in academic positions. This, alongside the limited means to finance graduate students as teaching assistants (TAs), helps to regulate the growth. After completing the dissertation, the most successful career path is the integration into the academic labor market through a tenure-track assistant professorship. After an agreed upon number of years in such a position, most research universities expect that the dissertation will have been published in expanded form as a monograph, leading to tenure and the position of associate professor. The publication of a second monograph is usually the prerequisite for promotion to full professor.

The very different career paths must be taken into account when comparing the number of history instructors, which in both countries—like the proportion of women among teaching staff—has risen considerably since the 1980s. In the FRG, the number of people "teaching history full-time in higher education," which encompasses all status groups from "instructors with special tasks" (*Lehrkräften mit besonderen Aufgaben*) and *wissenschaftliche Mitarbeiter* (generally PhD candidates working on a research project) to C4/W3 professors (tenured full professors), more than doubled between 1982 and 2012, from 1,400 to 2,954 (see Table 4.3). This substantial rise was accompanied by a decline in the proportion of professors among university teaching staff from 41 to 24 percent; at the same time, the proportion of women increased from 14 to 39 percent.[66] The feminization of university teaching thus clearly went hand in hand with a decline in the percentage of professors among academic staff and the increasingly precarious nature of the available positions, i.e. more temporary and part-time positions. In 2012, 70 percent of teaching staff in history at German universities were working as temporary *wissenschaftliche Mitarbeiter*, 5 percent were "instructors with special tasks," and 2 percent were lecturers (*Dozenten*) and assistants. At 42 percent, the proportion of women was especially high among *wissenschaftliche Mitarbeiter*. Of overall academic staff (4,879), only 61 percent had full-time positions. Of the 1,925 part-time staff, 55 percent were instructors paid by the course (*Lehrbeauftragte*), honorary professors and *Privatdozenten* (proportion of women, 32 percent), and 44 percent *wissenschaftliche Hilfskräfte* (student assistants) and (student) tutors (proportion of women, 53 percent).[67]

The trend toward increasingly precarious employment for a growing number of research and teaching staff at universities and a simultaneous growth in the proportion of female personnel on all levels, but above all on the lower echelons, is also evident in the United States. We have no figures specifically for history departments, however. According to data collected by the U.S. Department of Education, 76 percent of the instructional workforce at all two- and four-year institutions of higher education were in temporary positions and often also worked part-time—as adjunct faculty members, full-time nontenure-track members, or TAs. A 2012 study by the Coalition on the Academic Workforce describes in detail their miserable working conditions and shamefully low pay.[68] In Germany, too, protest has been growing against the increasingly precarious conditions facing younger scholars.[69] In both countries, neoliberal policies have responded to the growing need for teaching staff occasioned by the increasing number of students by using more and more cheap young personnel in temporary positions and paying instructors by the course.

At the same time, however, there was a clear rise in the proportion of women among professors of history (see Tables 4.1 and 4.3). In the Federal Republic, the number of female history professors rose from 27 to 196 between 1982 and 2012, while the proportion grew from 5 to 27 percent in the same period.[70] On average, women held 20 percent of professorships at German universities.[71] These figures conceal the substantial differences in the development of the various salary grades, however. Official statistics lump together the old C4/C3 and the new W3/W2 full professorships that were introduced with the University Instructors' Salary Scale of 2005, as well as the generally temporary C2/W1 positions (untenured time limited professorships), including the junior professorships introduced in 2002 with the fifth amendment to the German Higher Education Framework Act. Of the last-mentioned group, only very few were able to transfer to permanent positions, contrary to the promises made. This innovation did not succeed in replacing *Habilitation* as a key prerequisite for a W3/W2 full professorship, as was originally hoped.[72] Figures differentiated by discipline, status group, and gender, exist only for the period up to 2002. They show that between 1982 and 2002, the proportion of women in C4 professorships had risen only from 4 to 9 percent, but in C3 professorships from 4 to 19 percent and C2 positions from 8 to 36 percent. The higher the academic position, the fewer women were found there.[73] The trend toward a relatively large increase in the proportion of women in the lower salary grades probably continues today.

German reunification did little to alter this trend. In 1989, women represented 35 percent of all history teaching staff in the German Democratic Republic (GDR), with 13 percent of lecturers (*Dozenten*) and 5 percent of professors. Because of the economically necessary integration of women into paid employment, an extensive network of all-day care for children of all ages, and a generous leave policy, the proportion of women teaching at East German universities, especially in the lower echelons, was significantly higher than in the FRG.[74] When East German institutions were taken over by the West, however, conditions quickly adapted to those in the Federal Republic, where motherhood and an academic career were and often still are considered irreconcilable. One consequence of this anti-child and anti-mother climate was that in 2005, 49 percent of all female academics over thirty-five in Germany had no children.[75]

There are no comparable figures for the United States, since here annual developments are only documented for large disciplinary groups. The 2005 AHA survey on *The Status of Women in the Historical Profession* and later publications point to similar trends as in the Federal Republic, however.[76] In 1980, women represented 14 percent of full-time teaching staff in history departments, but only 6 percent of full professors. In 1988, their proportion of teaching staff rose to 17 percent, and was just slightly behind the figure of women who had completed a doctorate. The proportion of women among full professors, however, had only risen to 8 percent. The greatest increase was at the entry-level of American academic careers, the assistant professorship. In 2003, the figure here was 33 percent. That same year, 36 percent of associate professors were women, but only 17 percent of full professors. There have been no data since then. Overall, the proportion of women among full-time teaching staff in the United States is now 45 percent.[77] A key difference between the American and German systems is the tenure-track, which helps women at American universities at least to rise to the level of associate professor. The strong rise in this group of professors since the 1990s suggests this trend. At the same time, however, it is remarkable that after a wave of hiring of female assistant professors in the 1990s, their proportion fell markedly after 2000. In 1992, women still made up 45 percent of assistant professors, compared to 33 percent in 2003. This downward trend will mean that in the future, fewer women will be able to rise to the ranks of associate and full professor.[78] Women's opportunities in the American historical profession, although they remain better than those in Germany, are still far from being equal. The 2005 AHA report accordingly concluded:

> In addition to the studies of history and other disciplines that testify to the perspective of significant gender differences in nearly every aspect of academic employment, and find that women are disproportionately underrepresented at all levels of the academic hierarchy, several recent reports ... found that even those women at the very top of the hierarchy felt marginalized in their depart-

ments, discouraged and unsatisfied in their professional lives, and most strikingly, that their dissatisfaction and sense of exclusion increased as they rose though the ranks. ... Gender discrimination ... can take many forms and many of these are not simple to recognize. ... [It consists in] a pattern of powerful but unrecognized assumptions and attitudes that work systematically against women faculty even in the light of obvious good will.[79]

The different forms of structural and cultural discrimination discussed in the report and other AHA publications certainly have their counterparts in the German historical profession.[80] The VHD has not, however, felt compelled to commission a similar study. It would quickly dispense with the common preconception among male historians that women are given equal or even preferential treatment in appointments to professorships in history. The statistics say something very different.

Such a study would also confirm that, contrary to the widespread assumption, which is also reflected in policy on the federal and state level, it is neither a lack of qualified women, who require preparation especially for higher positions, nor the difficulty of combining family and academic employment that disadvantages women, but above all the culture of academia more generally and that of a discipline in particular. Robert B. Townsend, then the deputy director of the AHA, reached a similar conclusion for the U.S. historical profession in 2010. In a contribution on the situation of women historians in the AHA journal *Perspectives on History*, he wrote, "The data suggest ... that at the root of gender disparities ... could be the structure and culture of history departments."[81] The long-held notions of what constitutes a qualified scholar/historian appear to be particularly influential. They also determine the academic habitus of professions. Quality and qualification continue to be measured by male standards. All studies show that in order to be recognized as equally qualified, women still have to do a good deal more than men.[82] Moreover, their achievements tend to be attributed to "diligence" and rarely to "brilliance." A study recently published in the journal *Science* shows "that across the academic spectrum, women are underrepresented in fields whose practitioners believe that raw, innate talent is the main requirement for success, because women are stereotyped as not possessing such talent."[83]

In most disciplines, there is a particular suspicion of women who successfully combine motherhood and an academic career, and who therefore do *not* confirm the preconception that the two are incompatible because research and teaching demand a (male) scholar's complete and undivided attention and time. The literature speaks here of a "motherhood penalty" and demonstrates that mothers are subject to even higher expectations than childless women: "Mothers were judged as significantly less competent and committed than women without children ... Mothers were also held to harsher performance and punctuality standards."[84] At the same time, there is a clear "fatherhood bonus." Fathers surpass not just women with equal qualifications and productivity, but also childless men: "Compared to men without children, highly successful fathers are perceived as significantly less hostile, as more likeable and warmer. Parenthood enhances the perceived interpersonal qualities."[85]

Particularly in Germany, many women who aspire to an academic career draw the personal conclusion that it is better to forego having children. As recent studies show, the increasingly precarious academic job market has led to a diminished willingness to have children among younger scholars of both sexes. More than 80 percent of both male and female scholars with temporary contracts are childless. Those with permanent positions — above all men — frequently have one, two, or more children. Accordingly, 66 percent of male professors, but only 38 percent of female professors, are parents. Although there are no comparable figures for the United States, there are many indications that the situation is similar. In his above cited contribution in *Perspectives on History* from 2010, Robert B. Townsend concludes, "there is ample evidence of the costs to many female associate professors — they are significantly more likely than their male counterparts to be single, divorced."[86] In general, however, the tenure system makes life planning easier and allows scholars to start families at an earlier age than in Germany. The social and culture frameworks also differ: because of economic conditions in the United States, the dual-income family has been necessary for many years and thus enjoys greater social acceptance. This also affects the climate in many history departments. This does not, however, mean that it is not still difficult above all for women to combine a family with an academic career.[87]

Conclusion: Gender, Profession, and Academic Culture

The comparison of women's integration into the historical profession in Germany and the United States reveals a marked path dependency. The complex interplay among a whole series of factors promoted or hindered the equal inclusion of women. The institutional structures of the scholarly landscape and with them also the conditions and opportunities for an academic career were and remain very different in the United States and Germany, which strongly affected the professional prospects, career paths, and working conditions of historians both male and female. The four decisive factors favoring the integration of women in the United States were the greater breadth and market dependency of the higher education system, the long tradition of women's colleges, the development of the tenure process since the 1930s and 1940s, the much earlier and higher degree of organization of women historians, and the AHA's systematic policy of promoting equal opportunities since the 1970s. The growing integration of women into the discipline went hand in hand with the establishment of women's and gender history as a research approach. This change would have been inconceivable without the new women's movement and its struggle for gender equality.

The highly professionalized state-controlled German higher education system with its relatively small number of history institutes or departments exerted a far higher degree of segregation based on social origin and gender. A gradual opening began only in the period of educational reform in the 1960s, which showed results first among students and doctoral candidates up to the 1980s, among habilitation candidates from the 1990s, and among professorships only in the new millennium. This development was encouraged from the 1980s by an intensification of gender policies on the part of the federal and state governments and in the 1990s by the European Union.[88] Even today, however, these policies have not succeeded in removing the main obstacle to women's equal integration into the historical profession and academia more generally: the traditions deeply inscribed in an academic culture made and still dominated by men.

Karen Hagemann is the James G. Kenan Distinguished Professor of History and Adjunct Professor of the Curriculum in Peace, War, and Defense at the University of North Carolina at Chapel Hill.

Sarah Summers is an instructor of history at Wilfrid Laurier University.

Notes

We would like to thank Pamela Selwyn for the translation from German into English. For more details on the German development see, Karen Hagemann, "Gleichberechtigt? Frauen in der bundesdeutschen Geschichtswissenschaft," *Zeithistorische Forschungen*, no. 1 (2016): 108–35.

1. Anonymized interview, 7 July 2014; see also Bundesministerium für Bildung und Forschung, *Familienfreundlichkeit an deutschen Hochschulen: Schritt für Schritt* (Bonn, 2013).

2. For example see Birgit Riegraf et al., eds, *Gender Change in Academia: Re-Mapping the Fields of Work, Knowledge, and Politics from a Gender Perspective* (Wiesbaden, 2010); Sabine Grenz et al., eds, *Gender Equality Programmes in Higher Education: International Perspectives* (Wiesbaden, 2008); and Annette Zimmer et al., *Frauen an Hochschulen: Winners among Losers: Zur Feminisierung der deutschen Universität* (Opladen, 2007).

3. The brief names of the postions in the pay system of the German universities, like C4/ W3 full professorships, can not be translated. We have to use them, but try to explain them by contextualizing them.

4. See European Commission, *She Figures 2012: Gender in Research and Innovation — Statistics and Indicators* (Luxembourg, 2013), 39–145 and 90.

5. American Association of University Professors, "Distribution of Faculty, by Rank, Gender, Category, and Affiliation, 2011–2012 (Percent)" (Washington, DC, 2012), Retrieved 1 March http://www.aaup.org/NR/rdonlyres/889956C2-6DBE-48A1-B64A-BB69 DAF4C6C6/0/Tab12.pdf.

6. One main problem is the comparability of institutions and data. As an example of a comparison, see Levke Harders, "Disziplin(ierung) und Geschlecht in den Geisteswissenschaften in den USA und Deutschland," in *Das Geschlecht der Wissenschaften: Zur Geschichte von Akademikerinnen im 19. und 20. Jahrhundert,* ed. Ulrike Auga (Frankfurt/ Main, 2010), 259–80.

7. Ilse Costas, "Diskurse und gesellschaftliche Strukturen im Spanungsfeld von Geschlecht, Macht und Wissenschaft: Ein Erklärungsmodell für den Zugang von Frauen zu akademischen Karrieren im internationalen Vergleich," in *Frau Macht Wissenschaft: Wissenschaftlerinnen gestern und heute,* ed. Immacolata Amodeo (Königstein/Taunus, 2003), 157–83, 160.

8. See Paul Pierson, "Increasing Returns, Path Dependency, and the Study of Politics," *American Political Science Review* 94, no. 2 (2000): 251–67; and Kathleen Thelen, "How Institutions Evolve: Insights from Comparative Historical Analysis," in *Comparative Historical Analysis in the Social Sciences,* ed. James Mahoney and Dietrich Rueschemeer (New York, 2002), 208–40.

9. Quoted in Harders, "Disziplin(ierung)," 259.

10. Ibid., 260.

11. See Helen Lefkowitz Horowitz, *Alma Mater: Design and Experience in the Women's Colleges from Their Nineteenth-Century Beginnings to the 1930s* (Amherst, MA, 1993); and Irene Harwarth et al., *Women's Colleges in the United States: History, Issues, & Challenges* (Washington, DC, 1997).

12. Jacqueline Goggin, "Challenging Sexual Discrimination in the Historical Profession: Women Historians and the American Historical Association, 1890–1940," *American Historical Review* 97, no. 3 (1992): 769–802, 771; see also William B Hesseltine and Louis Kaplan, "Doctors of Philosophy of History: A Statistical Study," *American Historical Review* 47, no. 4 (1942): 765–800.

13. Goggin, "Challenging Sexual Discrimination," 771.

14. Ibid., 781; see also American Historical Association, "1970 Report of the American Historical Association Committee on the Status of Women" (Washington, DC, 1970), http:// www.historians.org/about-aha-and-membership/aha-history-and-archives/archives/ report-of-the-aha-committee-on-the-status-of-women; also Arthur S. Link, "The American Historical Association, 1884–1984: Retrospect and Prospect," *American Historical Review* 90, no. 1 (1985): 1–17; and Robert B. Townsend, *History's Babel: Scholarship, Professionalization, and the Historical Enterprise in the United States, 1880–1940* (Chicago, 2013).

15. Goggin, "Challenging Sexual Discrimination," 780.

16. Ibid., 802 and 795–802.

17. Ibid., 794; see also Julie Des Jardins, *Women and the Historical Enterprise in America: Gender, Race, and the Politics of Memory, 1880–1945* (Chapel Hill, NC, 2003), 219–25.

18. Quoted in Annette Vogt, "Wissenschaftlerinnen an deutschen Universtäten (1900–1945): Von der Ausnahme zur Normalität," in *Examen, Titel, Promotion: Akademisches und staatliches Qualifikationswesen vom 13. bis 21. Jahrhundert,* ed. Rainer C. Schwinges (Basel, 2007), 707–30, 714.

19. Edith Glaser, "'Sind Frauen studierfähig' Vorurteile gegen das Frauenstudium," in *Geschichte der Mädchen,* vol. 2, ed. Kleinau and Opitz (Frankfurt/Main: 1996), 299–324, 300.

20. See Hiltrud Häntzschel, "Zur Geschichte der Habilitation von Frauen in Deutschland," in *"Bedrohlich gescheit": Ein Jahrhundert Frauen und Wissenschaft in Bayern,* ed. Hiltrud Häntzschel and Hadumod Bußmann (Munich, 1997), 84–104; and Sylvia Paletschek, "Verschärfte Risikopassage: Ein historischer Blick auf Nutzen und Nachteil der deutschen Privatdozentur," *Forschung und Lehre,* no. 11 (2004): 598–600.

21. See Sylvia Paletschek, "Berufung und Geschlecht: Berufungswandel an bundesrepublikanischen Universitäten im 20. Jahrhundert," in *Professorinnen und Professoren gewinnen: Zur Geschichte des Berufungswesens an den Universitäten Mitteleuropas,* ed. Christian Hesse and Rainer C. Schwinges (Basel, 2012), 307–52, 312.

22. Costas, "Diskurse und gesellschaftliche Strukturen," 166–70; Rainer C. Schwinges, ed., *Examen, Titel, Promotionen: Akademisches und staatliches Qualifikationswesen vom 12. bis zum 21. Jahrhundert* (Basel, 2007); and Volker Müller-Benedict, ed., *Akademische Karrieren in Preußen und Deutschland 1850–1940,* vol. 6: *Datenhandbuch zur deutschen Bildungsgeschichte* (Göttingen, 2008), esp. 24–70.

23. See Heike Anke Berger, *Deutsche Historikerinnen: 1920–1970: Geschichte zwischen Wissenschaft und Politik* (Frankfurt/Main, 2007), 49–50; Claudia Huerkamp, "Geschlechtsspezifischer Numerus Clausus—Verordnung und Realität," in *Geschichte der Frauen- und Mädchenbildung,* vol. 2: *Vom Vormärz bis zur Gegenwart,* ed. Elke Kleinau and Claudia Opitz (Frankfurt/Main, 1996), 325–41, 331; and Claudia Huerkamp, *Bildungsbürgerinnen: Frauen im Studium und in akademischen Berufen 1900–1945* (Göttingen, 1996), 80–91. On female students, see also Patricia M. Mazon, *Gender and the Modern Research University: The Admission to German Higher Education, 1865–1914* (Stanford, CA, 2003).

24. Peter Lundgreen, "Promotionen und Professionen," in *Examen, Titel, Promotionen: Akademisches und staatliches Qualifikationswesen vom 12. bis zum 21. Jahrhundert,* ed. Rainer C. Schwinges (Basel, 2007), 353–369, 365; and Hesseltine and Kaplan, "Doctors of Philosophy," 778–84.

25. See Berger, *Deutsche Historikerinnen,* 56–57.

26. For a comparative perspective, see Karen Hagemann and Sonya Michel, eds., *Gender and the Long Postwar: Reconsiderations of the United States and the Two Germanys, 1945–1989* (Baltimore, MD, 2014).

27. See Goggin, "Challenging Sexual Discrimination," 802; and Lynn Hunt, "Has the Battle Been Won? The Feminization of History," *Perspectives on History* (May 1998).

28. American Historical Association, "1970 Report."

29. Ibid.

30. See Elizabeth Lunbeck, *The Status of Women in the Historical Profession* (Washington, DC, 2005), 1–6; Hunt, "Has the Battle Been Won?"; Carla Hesse, "Report on the Status and Hiring of Women and Minority Historian in Academia," prepared by the AHA's Committee on Women Historians (Washington, DC, 2014); Linda Kerber, "The Equitable Workplace: Not for Women Only," *Perspectives on History* (February 2006); and Robert B. Townsend, "What the Data Reveal about Women Historians," *Perspectives on History* (May 2010).

31. On the early development, see Phyllis Stock-Morton, "Finding Our Own Ways: Different Paths to Women's History in the United States," in *Writing Women's History: International Perspectives*, ed. Karen Offen et al. (Basingstoke, 1991), 50–78.

32. "Berkshire Conference of Women Historians," http://berksconference.org/about/history/; "Coordinating Council for Women in History," http://theccwh.org/about-the-ccwh/history/45th-anniversary/; and Eileen Boris and Nupur Chaudhuri, eds, *Voices of Women Historians: The Personal, the Professional, the Political* (Bloomington, IN, 1999), xiii.

33. See American Historical Association, "1970 Report."

34. See Goggin, "Challenging Sexual Discrimination," 802; and Hunt, "Has the Battle Been Won?"

35. See "Average Undergraduate Tuition and Fees and Room and Board Rates Charged for Full-Time Students in Degree-Granting Institutions, by Level and Control of Institution: 1969–70 through 2011–12," http://nces.ed.gov/programs/digest/d12/tables/dt12_381.asp.

36. See Marilyn J. Boxer, *When Women Ask the Questions: Creating Women's Studies in America* (Baltimore, MD, 1998); and Karen Hagemann and Jean H Quataert, "Comparing Historiographies and Academic Cultures in Germany and the United States through the Lens of Gender," in *Gendering Modern German History: Rewriting Historiography*, ed. Karen Hagemann and Jean H. Quataert (New York, 2007), 1–39, 11–18.

37. See Karin Kleinen, "Frauenstudium in der Nachkriegszeit (1945–1950): Die Diskussion in der britischen Besatzungszone," *Jahrbuch für Historische Bildungsforschung* 2 (1993): 281–300, 283–84; and Sigrid Metz-Göckel, "Die 'deutsche Bildungskatastrophe' und die Frau als Bildungsreserve," in *Geschichte der Frauen- und Mädchenbildung*, vol. 2: *Vom Vormärz bis zur Gegenwart*, ed. Elke Kleinau and Claudia Opitz (Frankfurt/Main, 1996), 373–85, 380–81.

38. Lundgreen, "Promotionen und Professionen," 365.

39. Hans-Jürgen Puhle, "Warum gibt es so wenige Historikerinnen? Zur Situation der Frauen in der Geschichtswissenschaft," *Geschichte und Gesellschaft* 7, no. 3/4 (1981): 364–93, 371. Since 2004, the VHD has been called the "Verband der Historiker und Historikerinnen Deutschlands," that is, its name now explicitly acknowledges the membership of both men and women; see the statutes of 25 September 2004, http://www.historikerverband.de/de/verband/satzung.html.

40. The figures on students, doctoral dissertations, and habilitations in the FRG for 1972 to 2012 were kindly provided by the Federal Office of Statistics (Statistisches Bundesamt). For PhDs from 2003–2011 and habilitations from 2002–2011, see also Hans-Joachim Lincke and Sylvia Paletschek, "Situation des wissenschaftlichen Nachwuchses im Fach Geschichte: Berufsaussichten und Karrierestadien von Historikern und Historikerinnen an deutschen Universitäten. Ergebnisse einer Erhebung im Jahr 2002," in *Jahrbuch der Historischen Forschung in der Bundesrepublik Deutschland 2002*, ed. Hans-Martin Hinz et al. (Munich, 2003); Hans Andreas Eckert et al., *Die Situation des wissenschaftlichen Nachwuchs in der Geschichtswissenschaft*, ed. VHD (Frankfurt/Main: 2012), 6. For 2012, see Statistisches Bundesamt, *Bildung und Kultur: Personal an Hochschulen 2012, Fachserie 11*, series 4.2 and 44 (Wiesbaden, 2012). On the United States, see National Center for Education Statistics, "Digest of Education Statistics, 1994–2012"; National Science Foundation, "Doctorate Recipients from US Institutions, 1994–2012"; and also Lunbeck, *The Status of Women.*

41. Berger, *Deutsche Historikerinnen*, 56–7; see also Sylvia Paletschek, "Ermtrude und ihre Schwestern: Die ersten habilitierten Historikerinnen in Deutschland," in *Politische Gesellschaftsgeschichte im 19. und 20. Jahrhundert*, ed. Henning Albrecht et al. (Hamburg, 2006), 175–87; and Paletschek, "Berufung und Geschlecht," 306–14.

42. Puhle, "Warum gibt es so wenige Historikerinnen?," 390; and Ann Taylor Allen, "The March through the Institutions: Women's Studies in the United States and West and East Germany, 1980–1995," *Signs* 22, no. 1 (1996): 152–80, 154–56.

43. See Paletschek, "Ermtrude und ihre Schwestern," 181.

44. See Berger, *Deutsche Historikerinnen*, 56–64; Goggin, "Challenging Sexual Discrimination"; and more generally on the practices of inclusion and exclusion in the historiography of the discipline: Bonnie G. Smith, *The Gender of History: Men, Women, and Historical Practice* (Cambridge, MA, 1998); and Angelika Epple and Angelika Schaser, eds, *Gendering Historiography: Beyond National Canons* (Frankfurt/Main, 2009).

45. Paletschek, "Ermtrude und ihre Schwestern," 184; see also Dagmar Feist, "Zeitschriften zur Historischen Frauenforschung," *Geschichte und Gesellschaft* 22, no. 1 (1996): 97–117.

46. See "Resolution an den Verband," AKHFG (Berlin, May 2005): http://www.akgeschlech tergeschichte.de/aktuelles/stellungnahmen-seit-2002/resolution-an-den-verband.html.

47. Karin Hausen, "Women's History in den Vereinigten Staaten," *Geschichte und Gesellschaft* 7, no. 3/4 (1981): 347–63; Ute Frevert, Heide Wunder, and Christina Vanja, "Historical Research on Women in the Federal Republic," in *Writing Women's History*, ed. Karen Offen et al. (Bloomington, IN, 1991), 291–332; Hagemann and Quataert, "Comparing," 11–18; and Claudia Opitz-Belakhal, *Geschlechter-Geschichte* (Frankfurt/Main, 2010).

48. Robert B. Townsend, "What's in a Label? Changing Patterns of Faculty Specialization since 1975," *Perspectives on History* (March 2010).

49. See "Professuren mit einer Teil- oder Voll-Denomination für Frauen- und Geschlechter-forschung / Gender Studies an deutschsprachigen Hochschulen," Datenbank der Zentraleinrichtung zur Förderung von Frauen- und Geschlechterforschung an der Freien Universität Berlin (ZEFG) und des Kompetenzzentrums Frauen in Wissenschaft und Forschung (CEWS)—ein Arbeitsbereich des Leibniz-Instituts für Sozialwissenschaften (GESIS), http://www.zefg.fu-berlin.de/Datenbanken/Genderprofessuren/index.html. The figure of twenty-five to thirty is an estimate by the AKHFG.

50. Karen Hagemann, "Der Arbeitskreis historische Frauenforschung," *Metis* 2, no. 1 (1993): 87–92.

51. For further information on the International Federation of Research, see http://www .historians.ie/women/; and Ida Bloom, "Forward," in *Writing Women's History: International Perspectives*, ed. Karen Offen et al. (Basingstoke, 1991).

52. Hagemann, "Der Arbeitskreis."

53. Information by AKHFG from 29 December 2015. See also http://www.akgeschlechter geschichte.de/fileadmin/user_upload/2011-11-03_flyer_akhfg.pdf.

54. See Andrea Löther and Brigitte Mühlenbruch, "Gleichstellungspolitik in den Hochschulsonderprogrammen und im Hochschul- und Wissenschaftsprogram," in *Erfolg und Wirksamkeit von Gleichstellungsmaßnahmen an Hochschulen*, ed. Andrea Löther (Bielefeld, 2004), 22–37; Quirin J. Bauer and Susanne Gruber, "Balancing and Optimising Gender Mainstreaming at German Universities," in *Gender Equality Programmes in Higher Education: International Perspectives*, ed. Sabine Grenz et al. (Wiesbaden, 2008), 119–35; and Karin Zimmermann, "Gender Knowledge Under Construction: The Case

of the European Union's Science and Research Policy," in *Gender Change in Academia: Re-Mapping the Fields of Work, Knowledge, and Politics from a Gender Perspective,* ed. Brigit Riegraf et al. (Wiesbaden, 2010), 173–88.

55. The figures for the years 1972 to 2002 were kindly supplied by the Statistisches Bundesamt. For 2002–12, see Statistisches Bundesamt, *Bildung und Kultur. Personal an Hochschulen, Fachserie 11, Reihe 4.4* (Wiesbaden, 2003–11); and Statistisches Bundesamt, *Bildung und Kultur. Personal an Hochschulen 2012, Fachserie 11, Reihe 4.4* (Wiesbaden, 2013), 95.

56. As well as first-semester students enrolled to study history; the comparison showed that the proportion of women was virtually identical.

57. On the sources, see Table 4.1.

58. Lundgreen, "Promotionen und Professionen," 365.

59. Gemeinsame Wissenschaftskonferenz (GWK), *Chancengleichheit in Wissenschaft und Forschung. 16. Fortschreibung des Datenmaterials (2010/2011) zu Frauen in Hochschulen und außerschulischen Forschungseinrichtungen* (Bonn, 2012), 6–7.

60. On the sources, see Table 4.1.

61. Ibid.; and GWK, *Chancengleichheit,* 6.

62. See Eckert et al., *Die Situation des wissenschaftlichen,* 9.

63. Ibid., 14–16; and Lincke and Paletschek, "Situation des wissenschaftlichen Nachwuchses," 45–56, 40–52; for more detailed statistics, see http://hsozkult.geschichte.hu-berlin.de/daten/2002/lincke_paletschek_2002.pdf.

64. The work for 11 percent of all PhDs and 12 percent of all habilitations is done in the context of a large-scale research project; see Eckert et al., *Die Situation des wissenschaftlichen,* 14–16.

65. On the Excellence Initiative, see http://www.bmbf.de/en/1321.php; on its gender policy, see also Stephanie Zuber, "Women in Cutting-Edge Research—Gender Equality and the German Excellence Initiative," in *Gender Change in Academia: Re-Mapping the Fields of Work, Knowledge, and Politics from a Gender Perspective,* ed. Birgit Riegraf et al. (Wiesbaden, 2010), 189–202.

66. On the sources, see Table 4.2.

67. Statistisches Bundesamt, *Bildung und Kultur* (2013), 95; and Eckert et al., *Die Situation des wissenschaftlichen,* 15.

68. Coalition on the Academic Workforce, "A Portrait of Part-Time Faculty Members," 2012, 1, http://www.academicworkforce.org/survey.html.

69. Lidia Guzy et al., eds, *Wohin mit uns?: Wissenschaftlerinnen und Wissenschaftler der Zukunft* (Frankfurt/Main, 2009).

70. On the sources, see Table 4.2.

71. GWK, *Chancengleichheit,* 6–7.

72. See the critique by Karin Hausen, "Juniorprofessuren als Allheilmittel? Ein zorniger Blick zurück auf das vermeintliche Vorwärts," *feministische studien* 20, no. 1 (2002): 87–92.

73. See Table 4.2; and Christine Färber und Ulrike Spangenberg, *Wie werden Professuren besetzt?: Chancengleichheit in Berufungsverfahren* (Frankfurt/Main, 2008).

74. See Anke Burkhardt and Ruth Heidi Stein, "Frauen an ostdeutschen Hochschulen vor und nach der Wende," in *Geschichte der Mädchen,* vol. 2, ed. Elke Kleinau and Claudia Opitz (Frankfurt/Main, 1996), 497–516.

75. Allen, "The March through the Institutions," 159–64; and Nicole Auferkorte-Michaelis, "Junge Elternschaft und Wissenschaftskarriere: Wie kinderfreundlich sind Wissenschaft und Universitäten?" *Zeitschrift für Frauenforschung und Geschlechterstudien* 23, no.

4 (2005): 14–23; Bundesministerium für Bildung und Forschung, *Kinder—Wunsch und Wirklichkeit in der Wissenschaft: Forschungsergebnisse und Konsequenzen* (Bonn, 2010); and Bundesministerium für Bildung und Forschung, *Familienfreundlichkeit.*

76. See Lunbeck, *The Status of Women.*

77. On the sources, see Table 4.3.

78. See Robert B. Townsend, "The Status of Women and Minorities in the History Profession, 2008," *Perspectives on History* (September 2008).

79. Lunbeck, *The Status of Women,* 3.

80. See Townsend, "The Status of Women and Minorities"; and Townsend, "What the Data."

81. Townsend, "The Status of Women and Minorities."

82. Curt Rice, *Six Steps to Gender Equality* (Tromsø, 2014), 18–9.

83. Sarah-Jane Leslie et al., "Women in Science: Expectations of Brilliance underlie Gender Distributions across Academic Disciplines," *Science* 347, no. 6219 (16 January 2015): 262–65; see also Ilse Costas, "Geschlechtliche Normierung von Studienfächern und Karrieren im Wandel," *Historische Sozialforschung* 25, no. 2 (2000): 23–53.

84. Rice, *Six Steps to Gender Equality,* 15; see also Stephen Benard and Shelley J. Correll, "Normative Discrimination and the Motherhood Penalty," *Gender and Society* 24, no. 5 (2010): 616–46; and Shelley J Correll and Stephen Benard, "Getting a Job: Is There a Motherhood Penalty?," *American Journal of Sociology* 112, no. 5 (2007): 1297–339.

85. Rice, *Six Steps to Gender Equality,* 16–7.

86. Townsend, "What the Data Reveal"; see also Linda Kerber, "We Must Make the Academic Workplace More Human and Equitable," *Chronicle of Higher Education,* 18 March 2005.

87. For the United States, see "History Practice Section: Conditions of Work for Women Historians in the Twenty-First Century," *Journal of Women's History* 18, no. 1 (2006): 121–80; and for Germany, Inken Lind, "Balancing Career and Family in Higher Education—New Trends and Results," in *Gender Equality Programmes in Higher Education: International Perspectives,* ed. Sabine Grenz et al. (Wiesbaden, 2008), 193–208; and Alexandra Rusconi and Heike Solga, "Karriere und Familie in der Wissenschaft," in *Zeit, Geld, Infrastruktur—Zur Zukunft der Familienpolitik,* ed. Hans Bertram and Martin Bujard (Baden Baden, 2012), 253–69.

88. On the various current Bundesministerium für Bildung und Forschung initiatives, see the website "Women in Academia," http://www.bmbf.de/de/494.php; and for the German Research Foundation, see the website "Equal Opportunities," http://www.dfg .de/en/research_funding/principles_dfg_funding/equal_opportunities/index.html; and Deutsche Forschungsgemeinschaft, "Chancengleichheits-Monitoring. Repräsentanz von Frauen in den Förderverfahren und Gremien der DFG: Berichtszeitraum 2012" (Bonn, 2013).

Bibliography

Allen, Ann Taylor. "The March through the Institutions: Women's Studies in the United States and West and East Germany, 1980–1995." *Signs* 22, no. 1 (1996): 152–80.

American Association of University Professors. "Distribution of Faculty, by Rank, Gender, Category, and Affiliation, 2011–12 (Percent)." Washington, DC: American As-

sociation of University Professors, 2012. Retrieved 1 March 2015 from http://www
.aaup.org/NR/rdonlyres/889956C2-6DBE-48A1-B64ABB69DAF4C6C6/0/Tab12
.pdf.

American Historical Association. "1970 Report of the American Historical Association Committee on the Status of Women." Washington, DC: American Historical Association, 9 November 1970. Retrieved 7 May 20157 from https://www
.historians.org/about-aha-and-membership/aha-history-and-archives/archives/
report-of-the-aha-committee-on-the-status-of-women.

Auferkorte-Michaelis, Nicole. "Junge Elternschaft und Wissenschaftskarriere: Wie
kinderfreundlich sind Wissenschaft und Universitäten?" *Zeitschrift für Frauenforschung und Geschlechterstudien* 23, no. 4 (2005): 14–23.

"Average Undergraduate Tuition and Fees and Room and Board Rates Charged for
Full-Time Students in Degree-Granting Institutions, by Level and Control of Institution: 1969–70 through 2011–12." Retrieved 4 March 2015 from http://nces
.ed.gov/programs/digest/d12/tables/dt12_381.asp.

Bauer, Quirin J., and Susanne Gruber. "Balancing and Optimising Gender Mainstream-
ing at German Universities." In *Gender Equality Programmes in Higher Education:
International Perspectives,* edited by Sabine Grenz, Beate Kortendiek, Marianne
Kriszio, Andrea Löther, 119–35. Wiesbaden: Verlag für Sozialwissenschaften, 2008.

Benard, Stephen, and Shelley J. Correll. "Normative Discrimination and the Motherhood Penalty." *Gender and Society* 24, no. 5 (2010): 616–46.

Berger, Heike Anke. *Deutsche Historikerinnen: 1920–1970: Geschichte zwischen Wissenschaft und Politik.* Frankfurt/Main: Campus Verlag, 2007.

Berkshire Conference of Women Historians, "History." Retrieved 8 March 2015 from
http://berksconference.org/about/history/.

Benard, Stephen, and Shelley J. Correll. "Normative Discrimination and the Motherhood Penalty." *Gender and Society* 24, no. 5 (2010): 616–46.

Bloom, Ida. "Forward." In *Writing Women's History: International Perspectives,* edited by
Karen Offen, Ruth Roach Pierson, and Jane Rendall, xiii-xix. Basingstoke: Macmillan, 1991.

Boris, Eileen, and Nupur Chaudhuri, eds. *Voices of Women Historians: The Personal, the
Professional, the Political.* Bloomington, IN: Indiana University Press, 1999.

Boxer, Marilyn J. *When Women Ask the Questions: Creating Women's Studies in America.*
Baltimore, MD: Johns Hopkins University Press, 1998.

Bundesministerium für Bildung und Forschung (BMBF). *Familienfreundlichkeit an
deutschen Hochschulen: Schritt für Schritt.* Bonn: BMBF, 2013.

———. *Kinder—Wunsch und Wirklichkeit in der Wissenschaft: Forschungsergebnisse und
Konsequenzen.* Bonn: BMBF, 2010.

Burkhardt, Anke, and Ruth Heidi Stein. "Frauen an ostdeutschen Hochschulen vor und
nach der Wende." In *Geschichte der Mädchen,* vol. 2, edited by Elke Kleinau and
Claudia Opitz, 497–516. Frankfurt/Main: Campus Verlag, 1996.

Coalition on the Academic Workforce. "A Portrait of Part-Time Faculty Members. A
Summary of Findings on Part-Time Faculty Respondents to the Coalition on the
Academic Workforce Survey of Contingent Faculty Members and Instructors."
June 2012. Retrieved 8 March 2015 from http://www.academicworkforce.org/sur
vey.html.

Coordinating Council for Women in History. "45th Anniversary The CCWH celebrated 45 years in 2015!" Retrieved 8 March 2015 from http://theccwh.org/about-the-ccwh/history/45th-anniversary/.

Correll, Shelley J., and Stephen Benard. "Getting a Job: Is There a Motherhood Penalty?" *American Journal of Sociology* 112, no. 5 (2007): 1297–1339.

Costas, Ilse. "Diskurse und gesellschaftliche Strukturen im Spanungsfeld von Geschlecht, Macht und Wissenschaft: Ein Erklärungsmodell für den Zugang von Frauen zu akademischen Karrieren im internationalen Vergleich." In *Frau Macht Wissenschaft: Wissenschaftlerinnen gestern und heute,* edited by Immacolata Amodeo, 157–83. Königstein/Taunus: Ulrike Helmer Verlag, 2003.

———. "Geschlechtliche Normierung von Studienfächern und Karrieren im Wandel." *Historische Sozialforschung* 25, no. 2 (2000): 23–53.

Datenbank der Zentraleinrichtung zur Förderung von Frauen- und Geschlechterforschung an der Freien Universität Berlin (ZEFG) und des Kompetenzzentrums Frauen in Wissenschaft und Forschung (CEWS)—ein Arbeitsbereich des Leibniz-Instituts für Sozialwissenschaften (GESIS), "Professuren mit einer Teil- oder Voll-Denomination für Frauen- und Geschlechterforschung / Gender Studies an deutschsprachigen Hochschulen," Retrieved 7 May 20157 from http://www.zefg.fu-berlin.de/Datenbanken/Genderprofessuren/index.html.

Des Jardins, Julie. *Women and the Historical Enterprise in America: Gender, Race, and the Politics of Memory, 1880–1945.* Chapel Hill, University of North Carolina Press, 2003.

Deutsche Forschungsgemeinschaft. *Chancengleichheits-Monitoring: Repräsentanz von Frauen in den Förderverfahren und Gremien der DFG: Berichtszeitraum 2012.* Bonn: DFG, 2013.

Eckert, Hans Andreas, Nora Hilgert, and Ulrike Lindner. *Die Situation des wissenschaftlichen Nachwuchs in der Geschichtswissenschaft,* edited by Verband der Historiker und Historikerinnen Deutschlands (VHD). Frankfurt/Main: VHD, 2012.

Epple, Angelika, and Angelika Schaser, eds. *Gendering Historiography: Beyond National Canons.* Frankfurt/Main: Campus Verlag, 2009.

European Commission. *She Figures 2012: Gender in Research and Innovation—Statistics and Indicators.* Luxembourg: European Union, 2013.

Färber, Christine, and Ulrike Spangenberg. *Wie werden Professuren besetzt?: Chancengleichheit in Berufungsverfahren.* Frankfurt/Main: Campus Verlag, 2008.

Feist, Dagmar, "Zeitschriften zur Historischen Frauenforschung." *Geschichte und Gesellschaft* 22, no. 1 (1996): 97–117.

Frevert, Ute, Heide Wunder, and Christina Vanja. "Historical Research on Women in the Federal Republic." In *Writing Women's History,* edited by Karen Offen, Ruth Roach Pierson, and Jane Rendall, 291–332. Bloomington: Indiana University Press, 1991.

Gemeinsame Wissenschaftskonferenz (GWK). *Chancengleichheit in Wissenschaft und Forschung. 16. Fortschreibung des Datenmaterials (2010/2011) zu Frauen in Hochschulen und außerschulischen Forschungseinrichtungen.* Bonn: GWK, 2012.

Glaser, Edith. "'Sind Frauen studierfähig' Vorurteile gegen das Frauenstudium." In *Geschichte der Mädchen,* vol. 2, edited by Elke Kleinau and Claudia Opitz, 299–324. Frankfurt/Main: Campus Verlag, 1996.

Goggin, Jacqueline. "Challenging Sexual Discrimination in the Historical Profession: Women Historians and the American Historical Association, 1890–1940." *American Historical Review* 97, no. 3 (1992): 769–802.

Grenz, Sabine, Beate Kortendiek, Marianne Kriszio, Andrea Löther, eds. *Gender Equality Programmes in Higher Education: International Perspectives.* Wiesbaden: Verlag für Sozialwissenschaften, 2008.

Guzy, Lidia, Anja Mihr, Rajah Scheepers, eds. *Wohin mit uns?: Wissenschaftlerinnen und Wissenschaftler der Zukunft.* Frankfurt/Main: Peter Lang, 2009.

Hagemann, Karen. "Der Arbeitskreis historische Frauenforschung." *Metis* 2, no. 1 (1993): 87–92.

———. "Gleichberechtigt? Frauen in der bundesdeutschen Geschichtswissenschaft,." *Zeithistorische Forschungen*, no. 1 (2016): 108–35.

Hagemann, Karen, and Jean H. Quataert. "Comparing Historiographies and Academic Cultures in Germany and the United States though the Lens of Gender." In *Gendering Modern German History: Rewriting Historiography*, edited by Karen Hagemann and Jean H. Quataert, 1–38. New York: Berghahn Books, 2007.

Hagemann, Karen, and Sonya Michel, eds. *Gender and the Long Postwar: Reconsiderations of the United States and the Two Germanys, 1945–1989.* Baltimore, MD: Johns Hopkins University Press, 2014.

Häntzschel, Hiltrud. "Zur Geschichte der Habilitation von Frauen in Deutschland." In *"Bedrohlich gescheit": Ein Jahrhundert Frauen und Wissenschaft in Bayern*, edited by Hiltrud Häntzschel and Hadumod Bußmann, 84–104. Munich: Beck Verlag, 1997.

Harders, Levke. "Disziplin(ierung) und Geschlecht in den Geisteswissenschaften in den USA und Deutschland." In *Das Geschlecht der Wissenschaften: Zur Geschichte von Akademikerinnen im 19. und 20. Jahrhundert*, edited by Ulrike Auga, 259–80. Frankfurt/Main: Campus Verlag, 2010.

Harwarth, Irene, Elizabeth DeBra, and Mindi Maline. *Women's Colleges in the United States: History, Issues, & Challenges.* Washington, DC: National Institute on Postsecondary Education, Libraries, and Lifelong Learning, U.S. Dept. of Education, 1997.

Hausen, Karin. "Juniorprofessuren als Allheilmittel? Ein zorniger Blick zurück auf das vermeintliche Vorwärts." *feministische studien* 20, no. 1 (2002): 87–92.

———. "Women's History in den Vereinigten Staaten." GG 7 no. 3/4 (1981): 347–63.

Hesse, Carla. "Report on the Status and Hiring of Women and Minority Historian in Academia." Prepared by the AHA's Committee on Women Historians (Washington, DC, 2014). Retrieved 7 May 20157 from https://www.historians.org/about-aha-and-membership/aha-history-and-archives/archives/report-on-the-status-and-hiring-of-women-and-minority-historians-in-academia.

Hesseltine, William B., and Louis Kaplan. "Doctors of Philosophy of History: A Statistical Study." *American Historical Review* 47, no. 4 (1942): 765–800.

Horowitz, Helen Lefkowitz. *Alma Mater: Design and Experience in the Women's Colleges from Their Nineteenth-Century Beginnings to the 1930s.* Amherst, University of Massachusetts Press: 1993.

Huerkamp, Claudia. *Bildungsbürgerinnen: Frauen im Studium und in akademischen Berufen 1900–1945.* Göttingen: Vandenhoeck & Ruprecht, 1996.

———. "Geschlechtsspezifischer Numerus Clausus—Verordnung und Realität." In *Geschichte der Frauen- und Mädchenbildung*, vol. 2: *Vom Vormärz bis zur Gegenwart*, edited by Elke Kleinau and Claudia Opitz, 325–41. Frankfurt/Main: Campus Verlag: 1996.

Hunt, Lynn. "Has the Battle Been Won? The Feminization of History." *Perspectives on History* (May 1998). Retrieved 7 May 20157 from https://www.historians.org/publications-and-directories/perspectives-on-history/may-1998/has-the-battle-been-won-the-feminization-of-history.

Kerber, Linda. "The Equitable Workplace: Not for Women Only." *Perspectives on History* (February 2006). Retrieved 7 May 2017 from https://www.historians.org/publications-and-directories/perspectives-on-history/february-2006/the-equitable-workplace-not-for-women-only.

Kerber, Linda K. et al., "History Practice Section: Conditions of Work for Women Historians in the Twenty-First Century." *Journal of Women's History* 18, no. 1 (2006): 121–80.

———. "We Must Make the Academic Workplace More Human and Equitable." *Chronicle of Higher Education,* 51, no. 28 (18 March 2005).

Kleinen, Karin. "Frauenstudium" in der Nachkriegszeit (1945–1950): Die Diskussion in der britischen Besatzungszone." *Jahrbuch für Historische Bildungsforschung* 2 (1993): 281–300.

Leslie, Sarah-Jane, Andrei Cimplian, Meredith Meyer, and Edward Freeland "Women in Science: Expectations of Brilliance underlie Gender Distributions across Academic Disciplines." *Science* 347, no. 6219 (2015): 262–65.

Lincke, Hans-Joachim, and Sylvia Paletschek. "Situation des wissenschaftlichen Nachwuchses im Fach Geschichte: Berufsaussichten und Karrierestadien von Historikern und Historikerinnen an deutschen Universitäten. Ergebnisse einer Erhebung im Jahr 2002." In *Jahrbuch der Historischen Forschung in der Bundesrepublik Deutschland 2002,* edited by Hans-Martin Hinz, 45–56. Munich: Oldenbourg Wissenschaftsverlag, 2003.

Lind, Inken. "Balancing Career and Family in Higher Education—New Trends and Results." In *Gender Equality Programmes in Higher Education: International Perspectives,* edited by Sabine Grenz Beate Kortendiek, Marianne Kriszio, Andrea Löther, 193–208. Wiesbaden: Verlag für Sozialwissenschaften, 2008.

Link, Arthur S. "The American Historical Association, 1884–1984: Retrospect and Prospect." *American Historical Review* 90, no. 1 (1985): 1–17.

Löther, Andrea, and Brigitte Mühlenbruch. "Gleichstellungspolitik in den Hochschulsonderprogrammen und im Hochschul- und Wissenschaftsprogram." In *Erfolg und Wirksamkeit von Gleichstellungsmaßnahmen an Hochschulen,* edited by Andrea Löther, 22–37. Bielefeld: USP International, 2004.

Lunbeck, Elizabeth, *The Status of Women in the Historical Profession.* Washington DC: American Historical Association, 2005.

Lundgreen, Peter. "Promotionen und Professionen." In *Examen, Titel, Promotionen. Akademisches und staatliches Qualifikationswesen vom 12. bis zum 21. Jahrhundert,* edited by Rainer C. Schwinges, 353–69. Basel: Schwabe Verlag, 2007.

Mazon, Patricia M. *Gender and the Modern Research University: The Admission to German Higher Education, 1865–1914.* Stanford, CA: Standford University Press. 2003.

Metz-Göckel, Sigrid. "Die 'deutsche Bildungskatastrophe' und die Frau als Bildungsreserve." In *Geschichte der Frauen- und Mädchenbildung,* vol. 2: *Vom Vormärz bis zur*

Gegenwart, edited by Elke Kleinau and Claudia Opitz, 373–85. Frankfurt/Main: Campus Verlag, 1996.

Müller-Benedict, Volker, ed. *Akademische Karrieren in Preußen und Deutschland 1850– 1940,* vol. 6: *Datenhandbuch zur deutschen Bildungsgeschichte.* Göttingen: Vandenhoeck & Ruprecht,2008.

National Center for Education Statistics, "Digest of Education Statistics, 1994–2012," Retrieved 7 May 20157 from http://nces.ed.gov/programs/digest/.

National Science Foundation, "Doctorate Recipients from US Institutions, 1994–2012," Retrieved 7 May 20157 from http://www.nsf.gov/statistics/sed/2012/archives.cfm, http://www.nsf.gov/statistics/sed/2012/data_table.cfm.

Opitz-Belakhal, Claudia. *Geschlechter-Geschichte.* Frankfurt/Main: Campus Verlag, 2010.

Paletschek, Sylvia. "Berufung und Geschlecht: Berufungswandel an bundesrepublikanischen Universitäten im 20. Jahrhundert." In *Professorinnen und Professoren gewinnen: Zur Geschichte des Berufungswesens an den Universitäten Mitteleuropas,* edited by Christian Hesse and Rainer Christoph Schwinges, 307–52. Basel: Schwabe Verlag, 2012.

———. "Ermtrude und ihre Schwestern: Die ersten habilitierten Historikerinnen in Deutschland." In *Politische Gesellschaftsgeschichte im 19. und 20. Jahrhundert,* edited by Henning Albrecht, Gabriele Boukrif, and Claudia Bruns, 175–87. Hamburg: Krämer Verlag, 2006.

———. "Verschärfte Risikopassage: Ein historischer Blick auf Nutzen und Nachteil der deutschen Privatdozentur." *Forschung und Lehre,* no. 11 (2004): 598–600.

Pierson, Paul. "Increasing Returns, Path Dependency, and the Study of Politics." *American Political Science Review* 94, no. 2 (2000): 251–67.

Puhle, Hans-Jürgen. "Warum gibt es so wenige Historikerinnen? Zur Situation der Frauen in der Geschichtswissenschaft." *Geschichte und Gesellschaft* 7, no. 3/4 (1981): 364–93.

Rice, Curt. *Six Steps to Gender Equality.* Tromsø: Science in Balance Group, 2014.

Riegraf, Birgit, Brigitte Aulenbacher, Edit Kirsch-Auwärter, and Ursula Müller, eds. *Gender Change in Academia: Re-Mapping the Fields of Work, Knowledge, and Politics from a Gender Perspective.* Wiesbaden: Verlag für Sozialwissenschaften, 2010.

Rusconi, Alexandra, and Heike Solga. "Karriere und Familie in der Wissenschaft." In *Zeit, Geld, Infrastruktur — Zur Zukunft der Familienpolitik,* edited by Hans Bertram and Martin Bujard, 253–69. Baden Baden: Nomos Verlag, 2012.

Schwinges, Rainer C., ed. *Examen, Titel, Promotionen: Akademisches und staatliches Qualifikationswesen vom 12. bis zum 21. Jahrhundert.* Basel: Schwabe Verlag, 2007.

Smith, Bonnie G. *The Gender of History: Men, Women, and Historical Practice.* Cambridge, MA: Harvard University Press, 1998.

Statistisches Bundesamt. *Bildung und Kultur: Personal an Hochschulen, Fachserie 11, Reihe 4.4.* Wiesbaden: Verlag Statistisches Bundesamt, 2003–11.

———. *Bildung und Kultur: Personal an Hochschulen 2012, Fachserie 11, Reihe 4.4.* Wiesbaden: Verlag Statistisches Bundesamt, 2013.

Stock-Morton, Phyllis. "Finding Our Own Ways: Different Paths to Women's History in the United States." In *Writing Women's History: International Perspectives,* edited by Karen Offen, Ruth Roach Pierson, and Jane Rendall, 50–78. Basingstoke: Macmillan, 1991.

Thelen, Kathleen. "How Institutions Evolve: Insights from Comparative Historical Analysis." In *Comparative Historical Analysis in the Social Sciences,* edited by James Mahoney and Dietrich Rueschemeer, 208–40. New York: Cambridge Uiversity Press, 2002.

Townsend, Robert B. *History's Babel: Scholarship, Professionalization, and the Historical Enterprise in the United States, 1880–1940.* Chicago: Chicago University Press, 2013.

———. "The Status of Women and Minorities in the History Profession, 2008." *Perspectives on History* (September 2008). Retrieved 7 May 2017 from https://www.his torians.org/publications-and-directories/perspectives-on-history/september-2008/ the-status-of-women-and-minorities-in-the-history-profession-2008.

———. "What's in a Label? Changing Patterns of Faculty Specialization since 1975." *Perspectives on History* (January 2010). Retrieved 7 May 2017 from https://www .historians.org/publications-and-directories/perspectives-on-history/january-2007/whats-in-a-label-changing-patterns-of-faculty-specialization-since-1975.

———."What the Data Reveal about Women Historians," *Perspectives on History* (May 2010). Retrieved 7 May 2017 from https://www.historians.org/publications-and-directories/perspectives-on-history/may-2010/what-the-data-reveals-about-women-historians

Vogt, Annette. "Wissenschaftlerinnen an deutschen Universtäten (1900–1945): Von der Ausnahme zur Normalität." In *Examen, Titel, Promotion: Akademisches und staatliches Qualifikationswesen vom 13. bis 21. Jahrhundert,* edited by Rainer C. Schwinges, 707–30. Basel: Schwabe Verlag, 2007.

Zimmer, Annette, Holger Krimmer, and Freia Stallmann. *Frauen an Hochschulen: Winners among Losers: Zur Feminisierung der deutschen Universität.* Opladen: Budrich, 2007.

Zimmermann, Karin. "Gender Knowledge Under Construction: The Case of the European Union's Science and Research Policy." In *Gender Change in Academia: Re-Mapping the Fields of Work, Knowledge, and Politics from a Gender Perspective,* edited by Birgit Riegraf, Brigitte Aulenbacher, Edit Kirsch-Auwärter, and Ursula Müller, 173–88. Wiesbaden: Verlag für Sozialwissenschaften, 2010.

Zuber, Stephanie. "Women in Cutting-Edge Research—Gender Equality and the German Excellence Initiative." In *Gender Change in Academia: Re-Mapping the Fields of Work, Knowledge, and Politics from a Gender Perspective,* edited by Birgit Riegraf, Brigitte Aulenbacher, Edit Kirsch-Auwärter, and Ursula Müller, 189–202. Wiesbaden: Verlag für Sozialwissenschaften 2010.

Chapter 5

Forms, Strategies, and Narratives of Professionalization in Western and Eastern Europe

Autonomous Profession versus
Heteronomous Professional Service Class?

Hannes Siegrist

The title of my article refers to a widely diffused master narrative about European professions which runs, that in Western Europe the members and organizations of highly qualified professions realized their claims for individual and collective *autonomy* to a high degree, while similar groups in Eastern Europe belonged to a *heteronomous* (i.e. determined by others) service class. In the following, I ask, first, whether Europe was divided so neatly with regards to the institutionalization and organization of higher learning, meritocracy, professional work, social position and status, and social inequality and cultural difference. This leads me then to the second question, namely whether and how the history of the professions should be revised after the collapse of European communism and in the actual age of Europeanization and globalization of social, cultural, scientific, and economic relations.

In my essay, I sketch a few answers for these questions on the basis of a critical reevaluation of the comparative historical and sociological research on professions, which was started in the 1970s and 1980s by a number of European and American scholars who aimed at analyzing strategies and forms of professionalization in different countries, social constellations, cultural contexts, civilizations, and political regimes.[1] Among them

Notes for this chapter begin on page 148.

was Konrad Jarausch, with his innovative studies about the rise and fall of liberal and democratic ideas, attitudes, and strategies in the history of German and Central European students, universities, and professions.[2]

During the periods of the Cold War and peaceful coexistence, the ideological debates about the professions between the Eastern and Western European countries focused on difference, distinction, and divergence. Approximations, assimilations, and cultural and institutional transfers were often ignored, understated, or criticized by political leaders, public opinion, and mainstream scientific literature, because they did not fit into the dominant bipolar ideological grid. Theories about the convergence of advanced industrial societies and about similarities between Western and Eastern professionals were marginalized by the respective ideological mainstream. More than twenty-five years after the end of the state-Socialist regimes and Soviet domination in Eastern Europe, and in view of the successful process of European integration, which has made obsolete many of the twentieth-century institutional and constitutional differences between Eastern and Western countries, it is about time to review the social structures, strategies, programs, and mentalities of professional groups in past and present times. This includes a critical reexamination of differences, similarities, functional equivalents, sociotechnical and cultural transfers, and adaptations on both sides of the Iron Curtain.

Professions and Professionalization: Definitions, Types, and Theories

I define and discuss the polyvalent term profession, which is the common point of reference in my essay on the long-term and comparative history of the professions in Europe. In general, a profession is conceived as a combination of special knowledge and skills, functional competences, and claims for a particular socioeconomic status and position of an individual and group. Concretely, we may think here of lawyers, medical doctors, engineers, teachers, painters, composers, and journalists and their traits, rules, and ambitions in a particular time, cultural context, or social constellation. On a more abstract level, "profession" refers to a social principle or an institution, which regulates social roles, relations, and hierarchies as well as processes of cooperation, inclusion, and exclusion. Professions are intermediary social institutions, which integrate individuals into work, economy, society, culture, and political systems. In modern, that is to say, competitive and meritocratic economies, societies, and cultures, they become a central institution that standardizes more and more social roles and relations and determines the society's dealings with cognitive knowledge, cultural patterns, and forms of expression.

The comparative empirical research has shown, that the difference between higher or learned professions in the narrow sense (including only science- and fine arts–based professions) and professions in a wider sense (including all kinds of more or less formally regulated "professions" or "occupations") is gradual. It depends on social and symbolic strategies of professions and interest groups, on traditions, on opportunities, and on the institutional and organizational preferences of political and economic systems, societies, and cultures.

In the following, the focus is on the highly qualified professions, whose programs and strategies of professionalization promise a specific kind of rationalization, standardization, canonization, use, and control of expert knowledge. Programs and strategies of professionalization motivate and stabilize the behavior and expectations of the individual professionals and the policies of their organizations. Social and symbolic strategies and processes of *professionalization* refer to a specific mode of making, de-making, and re-making a role-bundle, which is composed of special knowledge and skills, functions, and mentalities, and claims for a specific income, status, position, attitude.

The historical and comparative research about professions has shown that processes of professionalization are neither unilinear nor independent of their institutional, social, and political environment. They are entangled with complementary and alternative processes of institutionalizing, organizing, and moralizing social relations—such as nationalization, internationalization, liberalization, scientification, bureaucratization, building and debuilding of estates, classes and social milieus, and so on. Projects and strategies of professionalization are adapted by the actors to different institutional and political settings, are intertwined with different forms of modernization and traditionalization, and are embedded in processes of nationalization and globalization. There are not only multiple modernities in general but also multiple forms of profession and professionalization. But, modern and dynamic societies and cultures have in common, that they invest more and more in the development of sciences, engineering, humanities, and fine arts. This is the starting and reference point of the history of the highly qualified academic and artistic professions in Western and Eastern Europe from the late eighteenth to the early twenty-first century. Academically trained professionals, who dispose of a particular, higher, not easily accessible, systematic knowledge, are expected to define, handle, and solve an increasing number of social, cultural, and technical challenges, dilemmas, conflicts, and problems. Modern societies are "professional societies" in the sense that social roles and relations in and outside the sphere of work are increasingly institutionalized (regulated) as profession-based roles and profession-related relationships.

During the last two centuries, Europe has been a social, political, and cultural laboratory, where professionals, scholars, states, politicians, clients, consumers, elites, and social classes have continually argued about desirable and undesirable forms and aims of professionalization, deprofessionalization, and reprofessionalization. The contrast *liberal profession versus professional service class*, which I mention in the title, is periodically revived in modern societies and the international relations. But there are many more types, gradations, and variations of professional roles, socioeconomic positions, and sociocultural styles.[3]

With regards to socioeconomic positions, there are not only the groups of the state officials/civil servants and liberal professionals but also the groups of the professionals in an entrepreneurial or a managerial position,[4] the self-employed and dependent artists, cultural homeworkers or freelance professionals, authors, journalists, and performing artists.[5] In the long run, the numbers and variations of the latter increased in numbers and importance. Thus, the processes of institutionalizing and organizing knowledge, culture, symbolic expressions, prestige, and power resulted in an increasing extension, differentiation, and fragmentation of the original professional fields. Skills, attitudes, roles, and positions that have often been associated with academic professions—such as higher systematic or science-based knowledge, professional autonomy, self-responsibility, and disinterested professional service for the sake of science and general welfare—vary quite a lot depending on time and place, context and situation, and constellation of interest and power. In the course of history, the basic patterns and types of professions were transferred, varied, or rejected in processes of building and debuilding scientific communities, disciplines, professions and occupations, social estates and classes, nations, empires, and civilizations. The original or classic concepts, institutions, and organizations were adapted to liberal, Capitalist, democratic, nationalist, fascist, Communist, and post-Communist systems.

The histories of the liberal professions and the professional service classes are entangled and interdependent in many ways. Yet, until the 1970s, large parts of the American and British literature on professions focused on the sector of the self-employed liberal professions and their professionalization from within, while the bulk of the continental European research about highly qualified occupations was primarily interested in state officials (*Beamte*). In recent decades, the research on professions increasingly includes professionally or academically qualified entrepreneurs, managers, and white-collar employees (*Angestellte*) in both public and private manufacturing, chemical, electrical, transportation, and service industries. At the same time, the traditional differences between the research on professions and artists are blurring. Thus the research about professionalization is extended to the alumni of professional schools and academies for artists and professions with higher artistic, performing, and expressive skills, to holders of functions and occupations in the media, cultural industries, and fine arts, the development and characteristics of which are in many respects similar to the professions in the natural, engineering, social, and cultural sciences. The recent historiography and sociology of knowledge, sciences, disciplines, culture, universities, and research institutes extends and deepens the research on professionals and professionalization in particular respects.[6] The research about professions, occupations, and adjacent fields has become more colored, encompassing, and ambitious. Against this background, it becomes even more evident, that "liberal profession" and "professional service class" are just particular forms of a fundamental social institution called "profession," whose forms, meanings, and functions have multiplied in the last two centuries.

The Formative Period: Types of Professions and Professionalization in the Age of Liberalization, Nation-Building, Industrialization, and Scientification (Late Eighteenth to Early Twentieth Centuries)

The master narrative about the peculiarities of Western European liberal professions is mainly derived from memories and long-term histories of a few self-employed liberal professions in England, Italy, and France, such as medical doctors and legal practitioners (barristers, attorneys, *avocats*, *avvocati*).[7] In the research literature, the institutional, organizational, and ideological development of the English, French, and Italian liberal professions is often grasped as a professionalization that comes "from within the professions" or "from below." Their claims for professional autonomy and self-government were praised and emulated by many other highly qualified groups in the late nineteenth and in the twentieth centuries, which wanted to emancipate themselves from their—political, social, and cultural—patrons and refused to accept a "professionalization from above," which produced and reproduced heteronomous professions and professional service classes.

Liberal Professions

Liberal professions define their organization as an intermediate social agency that claims to legislate and to sanction the rules concerning access, functions, behavior, position, income, status, and other relations of its members. The professional organization integrates the professional community and demarcates its domain and jurisdiction. The individual professional's claim for autonomy is legitimated by the statute of the guild-like professional organization on the one hand, particular skills and credentials that stem from different origins—typically from the state or from a public or private agency—on the other. Liberal professionalism was from its very beginnings combined with strategies for social, economic, and cultural hegemony and exclusion, which manifest themselves in the claim for dominance over lay people, for an élite or middle-class position, for a self-governing professional organization with compulsory membership, and for an extensive control of prices, markets, and terms of trade. Professional strategies for a particular individual and collective professional autonomy are often embedded into more general claims for the independence of science, humanities, and fine arts and their subdisciplines in the modern constitutional society.

This modern concept of the liberal profession was originally developed in the processes of institutional revolutions and fundamental cultural reforms between the late eighteenth and the early twentieth century, when in Europe the aristocratic society of estates and the monopolistic regimes of premodern craft corporations and the guilds of learned professions were either abolished or by force adapted to liberal institutional and constitutional systems. In the process of liberalizing social relations in economy, society, and culture, the majority of the occupations were deregulated. Originally, liberalization led for most of the professions, trades, or occupational groups in the crafts' and commercial sectors to the loss of the privileges for professional self-administration. Their traditional forms of corporate autonomy and monopolies were substituted by the principle of formal individual autonomy and the freedom of contract. Thus, individual actors, who were involved in markets and the public sphere, risked to be determined by decisions of third parties or by anonymous processes to quite a high degree. Only a few professions succeeded to limit the heteronomy by states, legislators, employers, clients, consumers, anonymous markets forces, and the public sphere. These were the so-called liberal professions.[8]

The chance to remain or become an autonomous liberal profession depended very much on the type and level of theoretical knowledge and professional skills (rare, crucial, higher, and not easily accessible knowledge) on the one hand, and the social proximity to power, elites, and middle classes on the other. The particular functions, status, and socioeconomic position of the liberal professions—such as self-employed doctors, lawyers, engineers, architects, and artists—had to be negotiated with the state, legislators, and interest groups. Sooner or later, they were guaranteed by legislation, administrative law, jurisdiction, and constitution. In these negotiations, the liberal professionals and artists presented themselves as "disinterested" servants of science, culture, and public welfare; i.e. as an *autonomous service class* with a particular morale that contrasts with the values of "interest-driven" and "profit-oriented" merchants, industrial entrepreneurs, master-craftsmen, and shopkeepers. And they distinguished themselves from the academically trained higher civil servants and white-collar employees, whom they regarded as two segments of a dependent, patronized, or heteronomous professional service class.

Heteronomous Professional Service Class

The term heteronomous professional service class in the title of my article refers to a group of highly qualified professions, whose qualification, functions, status, position, and moral requirements (deontology) are determined to a large degree by others/third parties and whose development depends more on external forces and inference. A heteronomous professional service class is the expression or outcome of a *professionalization from above* or a *professionalization from outside,* i.e. of strategies that are driven by states, enterprises, the economy, and all kinds of national and international "nonprofessional" organizations. The professionalization from above or from outside was driven by modernizing states, market forces, and expanding enterprises, empires, and international organizations. The numbers of the members of the professional service class were rapidly expanding in the processes of modern state-building, nation-building, bureaucratization, and industrialization from the eighteenth to the twentieth century.

From the eighteenth century to the early twentieth century, it was above all the modernizing state that developed, regulated, transmitted, and used scientific and cultural knowledge and corresponding professional skills in order to strengthen the authority and power in its interior and international relations. The modern state used the professions and their knowledge and skills for social integration and economic and cultural progress. National and imperial states pursued their political aims by combining strategies of bureaucratization, professionalization, and nationalization. On the European continent, the state or legislator provided that lawyers, doctors, engineers, teachers, architects, and artistic professions were, first, trained and examined by state-run universities, schools, and examination boards; second, recruited and supervised as civil servants or public officials in the bureaucracies of the state, local authorities, and public corporations. The result was a heteronomous professional and artistic service class, which was composed of state officials, holders of a public office, and contractors, who were regarded both as a professional and as national elite.

This pattern was widely diffused in Europe—from France, to Prussia, the Habsburg Empire, and Czarist Russia on the West–East line, and from Italy to Sweden on North–South line.[9] In the nineteenth century, the pattern of the professional civil servant influenced to a certain degree even the roles, attitudes, and actions of professionals who worked in the socioeconomic positions of an entrepreneur, manager, or white-collar employee in the private sector of the rising industrial society and cultural and media industries.

Originally, market-driven and other more informal strategies of professionalization had been more diffused in the fields of industry and fine arts, e.g. in the case of engineers, media, and artistic professions; and, in rural regions and at the peripheries of states and empires, where more or less qualified legal, medical, and engineering practitioners continued their activities in more informal ways as long as they were outside the reach of the control by the state or of a self-administered professional organization, which concentrated their efforts in big and middle-sized cities and towns. Corporatist liberal professionalism was an urban phenomenon, that worked in administrative and industrial centers where there was a critical mass and density of professionals. The divide between urban centers and rural peripheries was widely diffused in nineteenth-century Europe, even in those countries, where professionalization and professions originally had been equated with market-closure and protected domains installed either by a strong state or by autonomous professional organizations.[10]

At the turn of the nineteenth and twentieth centuries, there was a shift from a state-driven to a market-driven and enterprise-driven professionalization from above. The professional qualifications, competences, and attitudes were increasingly adapted to new sociotechnical systems; cultural, commercial, and legal procedures and standards; organizational patterns; and forms of division of work. In the private manufacturing, chemical, electrical, mobility, media, and cultural industries, more or less formalized professions—such as that of the chemical scientist, mechanical or electrical engineer, corporate legal counsel, writer, journalist, composer, performing artist, painter, and designer—were periodically de- and reregulated according to the requirements of expanding enterprises and the respective branch. Thus, the processes of professionalization, deprofessionalization, and reprofessionalization were increasingly driven by market forces. The circle of those, who intervened into the negotiations and conflicts about the institutionalization and organization of so-called higher cognitive and expressive forms of knowledge, was extended. The original narrow circle of representatives of the state administration, legislative bodies, universities, and professions was complemented by representatives of employers, clients, and other users on markets and in the public sphere.

For a long time, market-driven and civil society–driven forms of professionalization had been the dominant form of institutionalization of social relations only in Great Britain and in a few continental European and Western societies and subnational regional states. Prominent examples are Switzerland and the United States, where, in the first two thirds of the nineteenth century, radical liberal and radical democratic movements had eliminated premodern corporatist institutions and at the same time hindered the expansion of professional bureaucracies.[11] The institutions and organizations of autonomous liberal profession had been swept away by radical liberal, egalitarian, and democratic movements and protests of cultural reformers, laypeople, and citizens. Only a few decades later, this wave of deprofessionalization was stopped and reversed by strategies of reprofessionalization, which were determined by the dynamics of markets for high quality goods and services, encouraged by the growth and modernization of the systems of higher education and science, and promoted by professional elites and reformist middle-class groups.

Around 1900, the reformers declared that the transfer and adaptation of elements of the German, French, or Austrian type of liberal professions and higher civil servants, combined with European models of higher education, scientific training, formal examination, self-administrative bodies, and so on, would increase at the same time the quality of professional services, the status and position of the profession, and the general wealth and welfare. In the early and middle twentieth century, the claims of the professions of lawyers, medical doctors, and a few others were sooner or later confirmed by the legislation. These were the foundations of the renaissance of corporatist liberal professions—such as lawyers and medical doctors—in the United States in the twentieth century; and, later, the foundations of American policies for the reconstruction of liberal professions and professionalism after World War II in Western Europe, and after 1990 in East Central and Eastern Europe.

Before I go on with the history of the twentieth century, I may remind here, that in the nineteenth century, there was no sharp West–East divide in the history of professions and professionals. The different professional patterns and paths of professionalization were diffused and scattered more or less all over Europe. They represented social and symbolic strategies of states, legislators, graduates of universities, highly qualified occupational and status groups, and users and clients of information, knowledge, and services. All these groups had a special interest in the question, how the fields of systematic knowledge and high culture were institutionalized and organized. Their programs and discourses about professionalization and professions dealt with the meaning and function of highly qualified professions in modern agricultural, industrial, administrative, and scientific regimes and cultures. On a more abstract or systematic level, we find that also in the particular concepts, theories, and narratives of contemporary ideological currents and sociological, cultural, and historical schools.

Besides the similarities and convergences, there were a few gradual differences, distinctions, and divergences between Eastern and Western European professions. Contemporary observers and the mainstream historiography of the twentieth century explain them first by a particular institutional path or tradition, second by differences of the economic, social, political, and cultural structures in the respective regions, and third, by the effects of a belated and distorted modernization in Central and Eastern European countries. The problem of such comparative explanations is that they are based on the often implicit assumption, that the general conditions and developments in Western and Southern European countries were not only different from those in the East, but at the same time homogeneous. Such more structuralist and evolutionist types of explanation are challenged by approaches that show that in the nineteenth century differences and tensions between urban and rural areas and between centers and peripheries were strong and widely diffused not only in Eastern but also in Western, Southern, and Northern European countries.[12] Furthermore, the effects of cross-border communication, institutional transfers, international migration of students and professionals, and economic cooperation and exchange reduced the differences between the Western and Eastern European countries. The social and cultural history of the professions, universities, higher education, and science, industrial, and financial enterprises demonstrate that exchanges and interactions produced extended zones of transition that were characterized by a specific mix of institutions, transnational mentalities, international agreements, and elements of a transnational professional regime.[13]

Professions and Service Classes in the Twentieth Century: Convergences and Divergences, Continuities, and Discontinuities

The increasing differentiation and clear distinction of Western liberal professions and the Eastern European professional service class was a result of the conflicts, crises, catastrophes, and ruptures of the twentieth century. In the early twentieth century, there were more convergences than divergences between Eastern and Western European professions. From the 1930s onward, the differences and divergences became stronger.

First, after 1918, the new and old national states in East-Central and Eastern Europe intensified their efforts for overcoming their—presumed and real—backwardness in the fields of economy, science, and culture by expanding universities, professional schools, and professional bureaucracies, whose members were strongly attached to the modernizing state. New nation-states as well as nationalist regimes intensified the links between strategies of professionalization, bureaucratization, and nationalization.[14] This was often a strategy for compensating for real or imagined deficiencies in the market, civil society, and the professional middle classes.

Second, in the decades after World War II, the peoples' republics and Communist governments in East Central, South-Eastern, and Eastern Europe countries adapted the Soviet pattern of the Communist intelligentsia. Their declared aim was to convert the so-called highly qualified bourgeois or middle-class professions—independently of their socioeconomic status as states official, liberal professional, liberal artist, cultural homeworker, or entrepreneur—into a service class that was defined as "Socialist intelligentsia" and had to fulfill particular services in the Communist project for the modernization of economy, science, culture, and society. The rise and diffusion of the regime of Communist intelligentsia in Eastern European countries was facilitated by the fact, that large parts of the indigenous professional elites and middle classes had been repressed, eliminated, or expelled for racist, political, and cultural reasons during war and German occupation.

Third, after the experience of degradation, repression, and deprofessionalization in fascist Europe, the professions' organizations claimed a special authority and role as an institution above social classes and as a mediator between interest groups, cultures, and the Western and the Eastern industrial societies. After 1945, they revived and varied the classic discourses about the governance of experts and the third way beyond of capitalism and communism that had already been disputed during the economic crises and sociopolitical conflicts in the interwar period.

Fourth, starting in the 1950s and 1960s, the distinction between "Western" professional autonomy and "Eastern" heteronomy of professions was stressed both in the Western and the Eastern historiography and sociology of professions. The dominant schools in the West conceived the professions in general, and the liberal professions in particular, as a crucial and mediating group, whose expert knowledge and affective neutrality were decisive for economic, cultural, and technical progress, social peace, and the future developments of modern societies and the mankind.[15] At the same time, the mainstream historiography and sociology of profession and intelligentsia in the Communist countries reproduced and adapted the ideological premises of a Marxist-Leninist theory of two classes, for which the profession and intelligentsia belonged as subclasses or strata to the working class.

Between the late nineteenth century and the 1930s, the differences between Eastern and Western European professions and professional regimes in general had been blurring. The pattern of the professionally trained state official remained dominant in large areas of Central and Eastern Europe. At the same time, the number and percentage of self-employed and privately employed professionals was steadily increasing, because many states expanded and liberalized the system of higher education.

Between 1870 und 1914, liberal professionalism and the role of the self-employed liberal professional became more attractive among the elites and middle classes, even in those European states, where traditionally professional civil servants had dominated—from France to Prussia and the German Empire, the Austrian-Hungarian, and the Russian Empire. This convergence continued after World War I, when the redimensioned and new nation-states in Central and East Central Europe such as in Hungary, Romania, Bulgaria, Poland, Czechoslovakia, and Yugoslavia intensified their efforts for building a modern state and professional society.

Between the late nineteenth century and the late 1920s, the European professions and their organizations learned to integrate themselves into modern liberal, democratic, and Capitalist systems by negotiating their rules and domains with all kinds of interest groups, states, and legislators. The nationalization of the professional communities was guided by cognitive and institutional standards that were discussed and diffused by journals, international congresses, and international migration of professors, students, and professional practitioners. Professional strategies and inter-professional conflicts were entangled with economic interest groups, political movements, and parties, and with aims and strategies of elites and middle classes. And the professions' strategies were embedded into policies of nationalization that aimed at creating a sovereign national system of knowledge, culture, fine arts, and the professions.[16]

During World War I, the majority of the organizations and members of scientific, cultural, and artistic professions subordinated their interests and moral and cognitive standards to nationalist ideologies and military aims. By doing so, many of them betrayed humanist values, scientific ideals, and the traditions of enlightenment, freedom, and professional solidarity. Nevertheless, after 1918, their organizations and representatives claimed the leadership of the professions in the processes of economic reconstruction, society and state-building, cultural and technical progress, understanding among nations, and peacekeeping. In the 1920s and 1930s,

conflicts about social and economic inequality and tensions between political, cultural, national, and racial majorities and minorities increased
again. They disturbed the certainty that a profession is a time- and context-
indifferent institution and reliable basis of individual identity, social community, and cultural progress.

While some professions and subcategories conquered new functions,
political positions, market segments, and cultural influence, others were
not able to compensate for their loss of status, power, and influence e.g.
after the collapse of the former imperial state. In the conflicts of classes
and in the processes of democratization, economic crises, rationalization
of work, and commodification of cultural services and goods, the professions claimed for more autonomy and better rights. Self-employed professionals strove for the institutionalization and organization of the single
professions as compulsory neo-corporatist orders. State-employed as well
as privately employed professionals tried to strengthen their voluntary
and compulsory interest organizations and bargaining power in conflicts
about working conditions and individual and collective contracts.

In the interwar period, many professions lost some of their influence
on the systems of higher education and as gatekeepers for the access to
markets for professional positions and services. Universities and professional schools expanded despite the professions' warnings for overcrowding. While the numbers of students from traditional and new middle-class
groups increased, the states periodically stopped hiring new professional
staff members. As the number of self-employed and privately employed
professionals increased, the complaints about overcrowding, deteriora-
tion of incomes, and the loss of professional autonomy and status became
louder. The tensions and conflicts between more traditional professionals, who defended corporatist values, social closure, and monopolies, and
more innovative groups, who adapted the rules, the forms of services and
products, and conquered new markets, grew.

In periods of economic depression and of profound political, social, and
cultural unrest, the professionals' attitudes and strategies were now often
overlaid by more general sociocultural tensions and conflicts about ideologies, nationality, race, class, and religious and cultural origin, among
others. Thus, anti-Semitic prejudices and policies in the context of professional matters were revived and widely diffused first in large parts of
Central and East Central Europe, later then also in more or less radical
forms, in most other countries of Europe.[17]

The profession's ability to regulate its own affairs and to settle the conflicts within and between the professions and status-groups shrank. Established concepts of homogeneous professional community, professional
identity, and solidarity eroded. The will to defend the unity and auton-

omy of the profession was diminishing. The persistence of the rhetoric and rituals of autonomy, disinterestedness and service for the common good veiled, that large groups had lost or were losing confidence in professional solidarity and autonomy. Among younger and marginal members, the inclination, to become a member of a privileged but obedient service class of a strong nationalist or racist regime increased.

In large parts of Europe, from Spain to Hungary and Poland, and from Italy to Germany, the tradition of enlightened and heroic liberal professionalism with its cult of the strong, independent, or even charismatic individual on the one hand, professional honor and solidarity on the other, was replaced by forms of a subservient nationalist, racist, and materialist professionalism. Konrad Jarausch who has studied the German case in a comparative perspective comments, "Even in the West, where more practitioners resisted the temptation of right wing politics, the underlying problem was similar. Though altruistic rhetoric proclaimed high-sounding goals of social service, professional practice was all too often centered on the crass advancement of material self-interest. Because its corruption was so blatant, the German example points more clearly to the perils of an egotistical professionalism, oblivious to ethical concerns. Capable of making enormous contributions to human welfare, the professions only deserve their privileges when they use their power with social responsibility and political liberality."[18]

From the late 1920s to the mid 1940s, radical nationalist, fascist, and national-Socialist movements and dictatorial regimes took advantage of this situation. Until 1940, most European countries had shifted from democracy to dictatorship and fascism. Therefore, they adapted the model of the liberal profession and of the professional civil servant to the functional needs and ideological purposes of dictatorial or totalitarian regimes. They undermined the autonomy of the self-employed liberal and artistic professions and limited the scope of action of professionally trained state officials, privately-employed white-collar workers, and entrepreneurs. The professional unions and compulsory chambers of the professional status groups were forced either to dissolve themselves or to merge with a compulsory nationalist or fascist corporatist organization, which was composed of different socioeconomic status groups and implemented the directives of the political authority in a particular economic branch or professional field.

Because many formal requirements concerning qualification, examination, functions, and position were unaltered, the fundamental process of deprofessionalization was veiled and not visible at first glance for everybody. The decisive elements of the dictatorial and fascist reprofessionalization were the political, moral, and racial criteria for the access to and

the exercise of the profession. Relicts of self-administration were implemented by partisans of the totalitarian regime and shared by opportun-
ists, fellow travelers, and "inner emigrants" from within the professions.

In the year 1940, there were only a few democracies left, where the traditional pluralistic professional regimes were at work; such as England,
France, Switzerland, and Sweden. In all the other countries, dictatorial
nationalist and totalitarian fascist systems merged elements of formal and
technical professional autonomy with their moral and political heteronomy. They redefined the professions as intellectual workers or *combatant
foreheads* (Kämpfer der Stirn) who served the general interest represented
by the will of the dictator, the national-Socialist, or fascist party and the
people. Such processes aimed at a deprofessionalization in the sense, that
the institution of "profession" was subordinated to fascist aims, hierarchies, and values. The fascist mode of de-grading professions, artists, and
middle classes was diffused in the late 1930s and early 1940s by armies
and administrations of national-Socialist and fascist regimes, which in-
vaded the continent and adapted the regime of knowledge and professional order in Eastern and Western Europe to their political ideology
and aims, racist agenda, institutional preferences, and arbitrary decisions.
In the occupied countries, men and women of Jewish and Slavic origin
as well as liberal, democratic, and Socialist citizens were excluded from
higher education, exams, and professional or artistic careers. Strategies of
cultural and political discrimination stressed the process of professional
closure in a particular way.

Members of the discriminated groups hoped to save their life, vision,
and professional values and careers by emigrating into one of the few remaining democracies on the European continent, or into the United States,
Turkey, or a South or Central American country.[19] Beyond the territories of
fascist dictatorships, professional, scientific, and artistic knowledge and
skills remained in principle universal values. In countries where the skills
of the exiled professionals and artists were rare and needed, emigrants
could, often with the initial support of professional, political, or confessional organizations, continue their professional career. But, not every
professionally trained emigrant was welcomed, because some of his or
her so-called indigenous colleagues feared that their exclusive claims and
incomes would be harmed by an additional competitor.

After 1945, the prefascist or prewar types of professions were reinstalled
in the democratic liberal and Socialist Western and Central European countries, which now regarded the professional freedom as a precondition, expression, and outcome of a liberal, democratic, and meritocratic society,
of scientific, cultural, and artistic freedom and progress, economic wealth,
and social welfare. Some of the organizational structures (e.g. chambers
with compulsory membership), which had been installed for the control

of the professions during the neocorporatist reforms of nationalist and fascist dictatorships in the interwar period or during the occupation by Nazi Germany, persisted and were adapted to the new contexts. Constitutions, court decisions, and international conventions guaranteed a certain degree of autonomy for academically qualified professions, experts, and artists. They were regarded as crucial for the social, cultural, technical, and political development in the democratic and Capitalist middle-class societies in post–World War II Europe.[20]

After 1945, the renaissance of liberal professionalism on the European continent was promoted by the Western Allies: France, Great Britain, and the United States. The United States, which had adopted the European patterns of a higher professional qualification, exclusive access, and self-administration in the early decades of the twentieth century, diffused in Europe an American version of liberal professions, which combined the ideas of classical liberal professionalism with strategies of market closure and a moderate entrepreneurial attitude of the single professional. Both in the defeated and liberated countries of Europe, the "universal values" of scientific, artistic, and professional freedom were guaranteed by constitutions and international conventions that forbade professional discrimination for reasons of race, gender, and religion, and promoted by international organizations and foundations. A polyvalent and multifunctional concept of professional autonomy supported the cooperation and integration of heterogeneous and fragmented professions.[21] During the Cold War, it motivated "Western" critics of the "Eastern" Communist intelligentsia and had a strong impact on the Western historiographies and sociologies of the professions.[22]

A critical review of the contemporaneous literature about programs, strategies, and narratives of professionalization shows that most Western and the Eastern historians and sociologists stressed differences and divergences. They were involved in a fundamental conflict about the role and functions of the professions in modern industrial societies, which had been started in the Russian Revolution, and determined later the development in Eastern Europe and large parts of the world.

The Rise and Diffusion of Socialist Intelligentsia and the Persistence of Claims on Professional Autonomy in Eastern and East Central Europe

The first great wave of elimination of traditional liberal, privately employed, and entrepreneurial types of professional status-roles began in the Russian Revolution, when the so-called bourgeois professions were degraded and converted into the category of useful specialists, who were tolerated and supervised by the Communist Party but should have been substituted as soon as possible by the new Communist intelligentsia and nomenklatura. The members of the Socialist intelligentsia were qualified according to classic academic, professional, and technical standards on the one hand, the revolutionary rules and aims of the Communist regime on the other.[23] The second wave of deprofessionalization and reprofessionalization according to the Soviet regime of intelligentsia-professions lasted from the mid or late 1940s to the late 1980s.[24] It revolutionized the role and status of the holders of higher scientific, technical, political, organizational, and cultural knowledge and skills in Central and Eastern European countries, which adapted the basic pattern in particular ways.[25] The Communist model of professional intelligentsia was periodically discussed also in the Western world, starting with the sputnik-shock and going on in the debates among leftist intellectuals, professionals, politicians, and students in the late 1960s and 1970s, before it was more widely discussed as an alternative and innovative model of institutionalizing and organizing science, culture, and work in modern societies.[26] From the 1960s to the 1980s, elements of Eastern practices and institutions and Western reformists' discussions were transferred into postcolonial and developing countries in Africa, Asia, and Latin America, which sent their students to Eastern European universities and professional schools and received personal, institutional, and organization support for their projects of nation building, economic and military development, and cultural emancipation.

The blueprint of the state Socialist intelligentsia program had been developed during the Russian Revolution, when the Bolsheviks implemented their program for the de- and reprofessionalization of highly qualified professionals in the natural, engineering, cultural, social, and economic sciences in the context of the reorganization of industry, administration, and agriculture. It was originally motivated by ideological, political, and practical reasons and embedded in the process of a fundamental social, economic, and cultural revolution. The de- and reprofessionalization in Russia and the Soviet Union was the work of Bolshevik leaders, who had a more general intellectual and practical training as professional organizers, agitators, or political intellectuals. In Czarist Russia, many of them had been hindered for political and ideological reasons from starting or finishing a normal higher education and professional training and career. During their exile in Central and Western European countries, they had been confronted with different systems of higher education and professions. After their return to Russia, on the one hand, they rivaled with the normal professionals, bourgeois specialists, or brainworkers, who claimed the leadership in the reformist liberal, democratic, and technocratic movements for the modernization of society and culture in the first two decades of the twentieth century; on the other hand with representatives of radical antiprofessional movements and followers of the cult of the proletarian, who wanted to eliminate the whole professional system. The Bolsheviks won the battle. They needed the so-called bourgeois specialists for their highly ambitious projects of industrialization, social revolution, and civilization-building, but negated claims for professional, managerial, or entrepreneurial autonomy, technocratic leadership, and social closure. They controlled the so-called bourgeois specialists by political commissars and treated them with methods of the carrot-and-stick style. As soon as possible, the bourgeois specialist should be replaced by the members of the new Socialist intelligentsia, whose members were preferably recruited among the children of industrial and agricultural workers and educated and trained by universities and professionals schools that imparted both professional and political competences.

The Russian revolutionaries adapted the classic pattern of the professionally qualified national service class of state and public officials to the needs of a centrally planned and nationalized economy and culture. The members of the intelligentsia professions were employed by the state administrations, state-owned enterprises, and state-controlled cooperatives. Their behavior in work, private life, social relations, and politics had to correspond to the aims and directives of the centralized planning economy and its subordinated plants and administrations, the Communist Party, and the dictatorial state.

The Soviet methods of organizing and institutionalizing particular higher knowledge and skills were inspired by the classical forms of bureaucratization and professionalization from above. The institution of the profession was used as a means for qualifying, motivating, and disciplining (in the forms of self-control and external control) highly qualified brainworkers, who were in the top and middle ranks of the economic, political, social, and cultural system. It was used also for the regulation of lower qualifications, functions, and positions, so that in the later period of advanced state socialism almost every adult hat had a—more or less demanding—formalized profession or occupation. The state-Socialist society became a society of professions or profession-based society.

Traditional differences, hierarchies, inequalities, and distinctions were leveled—such as those between agricultural, industrial, and administrative professions, between aristocratic, bourgeois, and working-class professions, as well as between science-based, technical, commercial, and fine arts–based professions. Although the differences between agricultural and industrial working-class occupations and intelligentsia professions were massively reduced, they were not completely eliminated. Communist societies, which pretended that science and culture (including fine arts) had a decisive role in the development of economy, society, and quality of life, conserved a few particularities for professions, which were based on complex knowledge, that was not easily and generally understood by third parties, and the effects of it were often ambiguous. The external controls were complemented by the self-control of the professional, who had learned and internalized the formal and informal rules during his or her professional training and career.

In the countries of Central and East-Central Europe, which introduced the Soviet concept of professions, intelligentsia, and service class and adapted in manifold ways to their traditions, conditions, and interests, some of the professions and professionals were able to conserve some professional autonomy or even to establish professional organizations, who defended particular aims and negotiated quite successfully about rights, domains, interests, and special rewards. Limited forms of a professional autonomy were practiced, as long as they did not refuse in open forms the Communist orthodoxy, the hegemony of the Communist Party, and the Soviet Union. Forms of limited self-administration and self-governance of unions of the intelligentsia professions as well as their individual members' claims on professional respect and a middle class–like position and status persisted and were periodically discussed and reestablished in new forms.[27] In many countries they controlled in fact the access of clients to professional services by informal practices ranging from preferential treatment for friends and member of particular networks, and by exchange of material and immaterial goods for professional services.[28]

The homogeneity of the single professions as well of the entire professional service class was furthered by the policies of professional education and labor, by standardized work contracts and incomes for professionals, artists, and authors and by the effects of professional mobility and migration. In the late 1940s and 1950s, the former border-crossing mobility of students and fully fledged professionals between Eastern and Western Europe was almost completely reduced to a one-way movement of refugees who left the Communist world on the one hand, and to the mobility within the Eastern, respectively Western, hemisphere on the other. The pattern of the Eastern European professional service class became a social and symbolic element of the East–West conflict because it was diffused worldwide.

Conclusion and Outlook: Similarities and Convergences in the Late Twentieth and Early Twenty-First Century

In recent decades, interest in common European institutions, traditions, and experiences has increased. International cooperation and cross-border communication as well as institutional, technical, and cultural transfers between nations and supranational organizations have been intensified both on the European and global level. Historians, political scientists, and sociologists have discovered long-term structural, institutional, and mental convergences on the one hand, and an increasing exchange and cross-border cooperation between the West and the East from the 1970s onward, on the other. Similarities and affinities that had persisted in the times of Cold War and were strengthened in the times of peaceful coexistence, facilitated then the transformation of the institutional and professional regime in Eastern Europe after 1990. This was an important precondition for the successful restructuration of professions, universities, research institutes, disciplines, and scientific communities; and for the reorganization of industrial plants, hospitals, service and cultural industries, and public administrations. Continuities in the histories of professions helped to absorb the shock that resulted from the degradation and discrimination of the Socialist intelligentsia, whose components were converted into manifold post-Socialist varieties of professions and socioeconomic status and interest groups.[29]

After 1990, many holders of academic, professional, and artistic qualifications lost their former position and were confronted with professional, social, and economic risks.[30] They experienced the transformation to a post-Socialist economic, social, political, cultural, and legal regime as a degradation or dilution of their skills and competences. Yet, diploma and titles as well as some core elements of a professional knowledge, position, prestige, and attitude were conserved as a social and cultural capital. So, the members of the former Socialist intelligentsia continued to refer to values like higher qualification, the principles of scientific procedures, academic rituals, and professional collegiality and honor. This helped them to orient themselves in the unpredictable process of transformation and during their negotiations with the post-Communist political regimes and international organizations about their functions, role, position, and status in the new organization of knowledge and culture.

Between the late 1980s and early 1990s, the efforts to destroy the intelligentsia and it subcategories were primarily directed against the omnipotent state and Communist Party, rigid targets of the centrally planned economy, research-organization and educational system, and arbitrary surveillance. The reformers relied on arguments of depoliticization, professional dignity, revival of own liberal traditions, and "return to Europe." The concepts of Communist intelligentsia and service class, certain contents, and forms of ideological, organizational, and institutional knowledge and corresponding sociocultural practices and rituals were quickly replaced by liberal institutional and organizational patterns and corresponding so-called Western sociocultural styles, which stemmed from large Western European states and the United States, the European Union, and international organizations and conventions. The reorganization of the professions and the reinstitutionalization of the professional field was at the same time a professionalization from within and from outside, from above and from below. It was a mixture of state-, market-, politics-, and knowledge-driven professionalization. The institutional reforms led to a hybrid regime of scientific and expressive knowledge and skills, and to a pluralistic professional regime.

The professional system persisted, because a good number of its rules, norms, mentalities, and practices are deeply rooted in the European system of higher education, professional organization, and institutionalization of knowledge, skills, work, and social status. During the era of transition, the professions stabilized social identities and social relations and were, therefore, able to alleviate the effects of occasional state collapse, market failure, economic crises, and institutional, legal, and cultural anomy. The social acceptance of a professions-based economic, social, and cultural system in general and of academically qualified professionals in particular was high both among traditional Communists and liberal reformers.

Thus, the thesis about long-term cross-border and cross-bloc entanglements and convergences relativizes the widely diffused opinion that the post-Communist transformation was mainly a politically motivated imposition or market-driven transfer of so-called Western institutions in Central and Eastern European countries. Eastern European professionals conceived and experienced that change rather as a renaissance of an indigenous pre-Communist liberal order or as an adaptation of "good" institutional traditions and cultural roots, that had survived or been adapted during communism. In the countries of East Central Europe, many of them interpreted the approximation, convergence, or "return to the West" more as an active process of self-Westernization than as a passive Westernization from abroad or from above.

For a while, many professionals and observers thought that the process of post-Socialist and post-dictatorial transformation seized and changed only the former "Eastern Europe" in the area from Magdeburg to Moscow. Only haltingly did they realize that the so-called liberalization in Eastern Europe was entangled with much larger and more fundamental processes of de- and reregulation on the European and worldwide level. In the 1990s and 2000s, not only the "Eastern" Socialist intelligentsia and its single professions were de- and reregulated but also the professions in the former Western sphere, where processes of change, which had been started between the 1960s and 1980s, were now intensified.

The revival of the classical concept of liberal profession in Eastern Europe in the 1990s distracted for a while from the fact, that exactly this pattern had already been challenged for some time in Western Europe, where liberal, social, and democratic reformers as well as entrepreneurs, consumers, clients, trade unions, and citizens blamed the liberal professions for arcane methods and nontransparent procedures, protective and monopolistic strategies, and for their unwillingness to cooperate with them on a more equal basis.[31] Within the framework of liberalizing markets and scientific and cultural relations, the opponents of professional autonomy strove for a certain deregulation of professional services and more heteronomy in the professional fields.[32] Some of them postulated that the professions should be more strictly regulated by law and supervised by independent mixed boards, which were composed of representatives of the professions, laypeople, selected social and cultural milieus, and relevant interest groups.

Thus, after 1990, the reform of the professions in Eastern Europe was connected with ongoing processes of de- and reconstructing professions that had been started in the 1960s and 1970s on a European and global scale. In the 1990s and 2000s, almost every profession and socioeconomic status group of them—liberal professions as well as professionals employed in private, public, and state-owned enterprises and administrations—were confronted with new technical, cultural, and social demands, forms of work, communication, and organization, which challenged social hierarchies and the role of professionals. New organizational theories and management strategies—such as management by objectives, lean management, corporate responsibility, new public management, and private-public partnerships reduced the differences between liberal professions and public and private professional service classes.[33]

The majority of the professions and their subcategories were expected to deliver their services according the rules of—more or less regulated—national and international markets. In the information, knowledge, science, cultural, and media industries, there are large international enterprises, which employ thousands of highly qualified professionals, who are urged to submit themselves to the rules of the firm's corporate identity or to comply with the corporate social responsibility programs. The profession-based or profession-related systems of knowledge, work, status, position, and power in large enterprises and administrations is challenged by systems, that focus more on entrepreneurial, sociotechnical, managerial, and property-related concerns and tend to subordinate the professionals' claims for a profession-centered status and identity to the functional, social, and cultural requirements of the enterprise, administrative, or sociotechnical working unit.

The diversified and intensified competition for power, status, income, and cultural influence reduces some of the traditional differences between liberal professions and civil servants, and between civil servants and privately employed professionals. The borderlines between public and private professional service classes are blurring. At the same time, the access to professional skills and markets as well as the rules for professional performance are denationalized to a certain degree. The assimilation and internationalization of the systems of higher learning and licensing furthers on the one side the erosion of old distinctions and conflict lines, and produces at the same time new ones. Nowadays, the professionals are divided in those who belong to the transnational or cosmopolitan private and public service classes, and those, who identify themselves with traditional local and national service classes of liberal professionals and civil servants. The functional, social, and economic roles of the professions as well as their intra-professional, inter-professional, and inter-organizational relations are increasingly under pressure. Furthermore, the remnants of the old male, national, middle-class, and urban professions are challenged by national rules and laws and international agreements on "gender mainstreaming" and management of "cultural diversity." The historiography and sociology of professions have to take note of such recent trends. They are challenged by actual changes which will—sooner or later—also motivate new research and interpretations of the past.

Hannes Siegrist is a professor emeritus of history at the University of Leipzig.

Notes

1. For an overview about problems and further literature see, Hannes Siegrist, "Professionalization, Professions in History," in *International Encyclopedia of the Social and Behavioral Sciences,* vol. 18, ed. Neil J Smelser and Paul B Baltes (Oxford, 2001), 12154–60; Hannes Siegrist: "The Professions in Nineteenth-Century Europe," in *The European Way. European Societies during the Nineteenth and Twentieth Centuries,* ed. Hartmut Kaelble (New York, 2004), 68–88; Isabella Löhr, Matthias Middell, and Hannes Siegrist, eds, *Kultur und Beruf in Europa* (Stuttgart, 2012); Dietmar Müller and Hannes Siegrist, eds, *Professionen, Eigentum und Staat. Europäische Entwicklungen im Vergleich — 19. und 20. Jahrhundert* (Göttingen, 2014); Hannes Siegrist, "Heteronome Dienstklasse oder autonome Profession? Thesen zur Geschichte der Wissensberufe und der Professionalisierung im modernen

Europa," in *Leipziger Zugänge zur rechtlichen, politischen und kulturellen Verflechtungsgeschichte Ostmitteleuropas*, ed. Dietmar Müller and Adamantios Skordos (Leipzig, 2015), 131–148.

2. Konrad H. Jarausch, *Deutsche Studenten 1800–1870* (Frankfurt, 1984); Konrad H. Jarausch, "The German Professions in History and Theory," in *German Professions, 1800–1950*, ed. Geoffrey Cocks and Konrad H. Jarausch (New York, 1990), 9–24; Konrad H. Jarausch, *The Unfree Professions. German Lawyers, Teachers and Engineers, 1900–1950* (New York, 1990); Michael Burrage, Konrad H. Jarausch, and Hannes Siegrist, "An Actor-Based Framework for the Study of the Professions," in *Professions in Theory and History. Rethinking the Study of the Professions*, ed. Michael Burrage and Rolf Torstendahl (London, 1990), 203–25; Konrad H. Jarausch, Matthias Middell, and Annette Vogel, *Sozialistisches Experiment und Erneuerung der Demokratie—Die Humboldt-Universität zu Berlin 1945–2010* (Berlin, 2012); Michael Grüttner, Rüdiger Hachtmann, Konrad H. Jarausch, Jürgen John, Matthias Middell, eds, *Gebrochene Wissenschaftskulturen. Universität und Politik im 20. Jahrhundert* (Göttingen, 2010).

3. See here and for the following Michael Burrage, "Exceptional Professions in Extraordinary Times. A Comparison of Lawyers in Four Societies," *Professionen, Eigentum und Staat. Europäische Entwicklungen im Vergleich—19. und 20. Jahrhundert*, ed. Dietmar Müller and Hannes Siegrist (Göttingen, 2014), 41–74; Siegrist, "Professionalization"; Hannes Siegrist, "Berufe im Gesellschaftsvergleich. Rechtsanwälte in Deutschland, Italien und der Schweiz," in *Geschichte und Vergleich. Ansätze und Ergebnisse international vergleichender Geschichtsschreibung*, ed. Heinz-Gerhard Haupt and Jürgen Kocka (Frankfurt, 1996), 207–38; Hannes Siegrist, "Autonomie in der modernen Gesellschaft, Wissenschaft und Kunst (18.–20. Jahrhundert)," in *Menschenbilder—Wurzeln, Krise, Orientierung*, ed. Udo Ebert, Ortrun Riha, and Lutz Zerling (Leipzig, 2012), 75–92; Hannes Siegrist, "Professionelle Autonomie in der modernen Gesellschaft, Wissenschaft und Kultur. Einführung," in *Professionen, Eigentum und Staat: Europäische Entwicklungen im Vergleich—19. und 20. Jahrhundert*, ed. Dietmar Müller and Hannes Siegrist (Göttingen, 2014), 15–38.

4. See Wolfgang König, "Staat und Industrie. Die Ingenieure in der Frühindustrialisierung 1800–1870," in *Geschichte des Ingenieurs. Ein Beruf in sechs Jahrtausenden*, ed. Walter Kaiser and Wolfgang König (Munich, 2006), 188–98; Peter Lundgreen, "Engineering Education in Europe and the U.S.A., 1750–1930. The Rise to Dominance of School Culture in the Engineering Profession," *Annals of Science* 47 (1990): 33–75; Michaela Minesso, "The Engineering Profession 1802–1923," in *Society and the Professions in Italy, 1860–1914*, ed. Maria Malatesta (Cambridge, 1995), 175–220; Manfred Späth, "Der Ingenieur als Bürger. Frankreich, Deutschland und Russland im Vergleich," in *Bürgerliche Berufe*, ed. Hannes Siegrist (Göttingen, 1988), 84–105; Galina Ul'yanova, "Engineers in the Russian Empire," in *Professionen im modernen Osteuropa. Professions in Modern Eastern Europe*, ed. Charles McClelland, Stephan Merl, and Hannes Siegrist (Berlin, 1995), 335–66; Manuel Schramm, "Vermessungsingenieure in Deutschland und den USA im 20. Jahrhundert. Wege der Professionalisierung," in *Professionen, Eigentum und Staat. Europäische Entwicklungen im Vergleich—19. und 20. Jahrhundert*, ed. Dietmar Müller and Hannes Siegrist (Göttingen, 2014), 169–86; Kees Gispen, "Der gefesselte Prometheus. Die Ingenieure in Großbritannien und in den Vereinigten Staaten 1750–1945," in *Geschichte des Ingenieurs. Ein Beruf in sechs Jahrtausenden*, ed. Walter Kaiser and Wolfgang König (Munich, 2006), 127–78; Mario König, Hannes Siegrist, and Rudolf Vetterli, *Warten und Aufrücken. Die Angestellten in der Schweiz 1870–1950* (Zürich, 1985).

5. See the essays and documents on scientific, cultural, and artistic professions in: Löhr, Middell, and Siegrist, *Kultur und Beruf in Europa*; Dorothea Trebesius, *Komponieren als Beruf. Frankreich und die DDR im Vergleich 1950–1980* (Göttingen, 2012); Charles McClelland, *Prophets, Paupers, or Professionals? A Social History of Everyday Visual Artists in Modern Germany 1850–Present* (Oxford, 2003); Walther Müller-Jentsch, *Die Kunst in der Gesellschaft* (Wiesbaden, 2011), 85–138; Juliane Scholz, *Der Geschichte des Drehbuchautors. USA und Deutschland. Ein historischer Vergleich."* Göttingen: Wallstein, 2016.
6. See Jakob Vogel, *Ein schillerndes Kristall. Eine Wissensgeschichte des Salzes zwischen Früher Neuzeit und Moderne* (Cologne, 2008); Ralph Jessen and Jakob Vogel, eds, *Wissenschaft und Nation in der europäischen Geschichte* (Frankfurt, 2002,) 97–114; Rudolf Stichweh, "Professionen und Disziplinen. Formen der Differenzierung zweier Systeme beruflichen Handelns in modernen Gesellschaften," in *Wissenschaft, Universität, Professionen. Soziologische Analysen,* ed. Rudolf Stichweh (Frankfurt, 1994), 278–336; Pierre Bourdieu, *Die Regeln der Kunst. Genese und Struktur des literarischen Feldes* (Frankfurt, 1999).
7. See with further literature Michael Burrage, "Unternehmer, Beamte und freie Berufe. Schlüsselgruppen der bürgerlichen Mittelschichten in England, Frankreich und den Vereinigten Staaten," in *Bürgerliche Berufe,* ed. Hannes Siegrist (Göttingen, 1988), 51–83; Claudia Huerkamp, "The Making of the Modern Medical Profession, 1800–1914: Prussian Doctors in the Nineteenth Century," in *German Professions 1800–1950,* ed. Geoffrey Cocks and Konrad H. Jarausch (New York, 1990), 66–84; Hannes Siegrist, "Juridicalisation, Professionalisation and the Occupational Culture of the Advocate in the Nineteenth and the Early-Twentieth Centuries. A Comparison of Germany, Italy and Switzerland," in *Lawyers and Vampires. Cultural Histories of Legal Professions,* ed. David Sugarman and Wesley Pue (Oxford, 2003), 123–50.
8. Siegrist, "The Professions in Nineteenth-Century Europe," 68–88.
9. See e.g. für lawyers and attorneys: Wolfgang Höpken, "Professionalisierung an der Peripherie: Juristen und Beamte in Bulgarien 1878–1930," in *Professionen im modernen Osteuropa/Professions in Modern Eastern Europe,* ed. Charles McClelland, Stephan Merl, and Hannes Siegrist (Berlin, 1995), 90–124; Jörg Baberowski, "Rechtsanwälte in Russland 1866–1914," in *Professionen im modernen Osteuropa/Professions in Modern Eastern Europe,* ed. Charles McClelland, Stephan Merl, and Hannes Siegrist (Berlin, 1995), 29–59; Hannes Siegrist, *Advokat, Bürger und Staat. Sozialgeschichte der Rechtsanwälte in Deutschland, Italien und der Schweiz 18.–20. Jh.* (Frankfurt, 1996).
10. Jörg Baberowski, *Autokratie und Justiz. Zum Verhältnis von Rechtsstaatlichkeit und Rückständigkeit im ausgehenden Zarenreich 1864–1914* (Frankfurt, 1996); Hannes Siegrist, "Die Advokaten auf dem Land," in *Idylle oder Aufbruch? Das Dorf im bürgerlichen 19. Jahrhundert. Ein europäischer Vergleich,* ed. Wolfgang Jacobeit, Josef Mooser, and Bo Stråht (Berlin, 1990), 169–80; Kees Gispen, "Engineers in Wilhelmian Germany. Professionalization, Deprofessionalization, and the Development of Nonacademic Technical Education," in *German Professions 1800–1950,* ed. Geoffrey Cocks and Konrad H. Jarausch (New York, 1990),104–22; Jürgen Kocka, "Kultur und Technik, Aspirationen der Ingenieure im Kaiserreich," in *Kultur und Beruf in Europa,* ed. Isabella Löhr, Matthias Middell, and Hannes Siegrist (Stuttgart, 2012), 29–36.
11. See Burrage, "Unternehmer, Beamte und freie Berufe," 51–83; Siegrist, *Advokat, Bürger und Staat*; Siegrist, "The Professions in Nineteenth-Century Europe," 68–88; Charles McClelland, "The German Model for American Medical Reform," in *Kultur und Beruf in Europa,* ed. Isabella Löhr, Matthias Middell, and Hannes Siegrist (Stuttgart, 2012),

189–96; Charles E McClelland, *Queen of the Professions. The Rise and Decline of Medical Prestige and Power in America* (Lanham, MD, 2014).

12. See e.g. Höpken, "Professionalisierung," 90–124; Dietmar Müller, "Eigentum verwalten in Rumänien. Advokaten, Geodäten und Notare (1830–1940)," in *Professionen, Eigentum und Staat. Europäische Entwicklungen im Vergleich — 19. und 20. Jahrhundert*, ed. Dietmar Müller and Hannes Siegrist (Göttingen, 2014), 75–132; Siegrist, *Advokat, Bürger und Staat*.

13. On the dynamics of territorialization of social, cultural, and political regimes in Europe, see Stefan Troebst, "Vom spatial turn zum regional turn? Geschichtsregionale Konzeptionen in den Kulturwissenschaften," in *Dimensionen der Kultur- und Gesellschaftsgeschichte*, ed. Matthias Middell (Leipzig, 2007), 143–59.

14. Vgl. Dietmar Müller and Hannes Siegrist, "Vorwort," in *Professionen, Eigentum und Staat. Europäische Entwicklungen im Vergleich — 19. und 20. Jahrhundert*, ed. Dietmar Müller and Hannes Siegrist (Göttingen, 2014), 7–14; Cornel Micu, "Professionals, Pseudo-Professionals or State Servants? The Professionalization of Romanian Agriculture 1919–1989," in *Professionen, Eigentum und Staat. Europäische Entwicklungen im Vergleich — 19. und 20. Jahrhundert*, ed. Dietmar Müller and Hannes Siegrist (Göttigen, 2014), 187–206; Höpken, "Professionalisierung an der Peripherie"; Baberowski, "Rechtsanwälte in Russland 1866–1914"; Claudia Kraft, *Europa im Blick der polnischen Juristen. Rechtsordnung und juristische Professionen in Polen im Spannungsfeld zwischen Nation und Europa* (Frankfurt, 2002); Dietmar Müller, "Die Institutionalisierung sozialwissenschaftlichen Wissens in der Zwischenkriegszeit. Das rumänische Sozialinstitut und der Verein für Socialpolitik," in *Kultur und Beruf in Europa*, ed. Isabella Löhr, Matthias Middell, and Hannes Siegrist (Stuttgart, 2012), 197–205; Frank Hadler, "Graben wie die Großen in Kleinasien: Ein frisch berufener Prager Professor umreißt mit weltpolitischen Argumenten sein archäologisches Karrierefeld," in *Kultur und Beruf in Europa*, Isabella Löhr, Matthias Middell, and Hannes Siegrist (Stuttgart, 2012), 206–16; Milan Ristovic, "In the Government's Service and in the Shadow of the State. Civil Servants in the Serbian and Yugoslav Socieal Context in the 19th and 20th Centuries," in *Kultur und Beruf in Europa*, ed. Isabella Löhr, Matthias Middell, and Hannes Siegrist (Stuttgart, 2012), 241–51.

15. See the the comprehensive discussion of contemporary scientific and popular books by Florent Champy, *La sociologie des professions* (Paris, 2009).

16. See for this and the following, Müller and Siegrist, *Professionen, Eigentum und Staat*.

17. See in a European wide comparative perspective Jarausch, "The German Professions," 20; Jarausch, *The Unfree Professions*; Victor Karady, "Professional Status, Social Background, and the Different Impact of Right Radicalism among Budapest Lawyers in the 1940s," in *Professionen im modernen Osteuropa/Professions in Modern Eastern Europe*, ed. Charles McClelland, Stephan Merl, and Hannes Siegrist (Berlin, 1995), 60–89; Maria M. Kovacs, "The Radical Right and the Hungarian Professions: The Case of Doctors and Lawyers, 1918–1945," in *Professionen im modernen Osteuropa/Professions in Modern Eastern Europe*, ed. Charles McClelland, Stephan Merl, and Hannes Siegrist (Berlin, 1995), 168–88.

18. See Jarausch, "The German Professions," 20.

19. See e.g. the following essays and documents: Isabella Löhr, "Fluchthilfe zur Rettung der Zunft. Die akademische Zwangsmigration in den 1930er Jahren," in *Kultur und Beruf in Europa*, ed. Isabella Löhr, Matthias Middell, and Hannes Siegrist (Stuttgart, 2012), 270–78; Juliane Scholz, "Deutsche Drehbuchautoren in Hollywood (1933–1945)," in *Kultur*

und Beruf in Europa, ed. Isabella Löhr, Matthias Middell, and Hannes Siegrist (Stuttgart, 2012), 61–70.

20. See for this and what follows Hannes Siegrist, "Der Wandel als Krise und Chance. Die westdeutschen Akademiker 1945–1965," in *Wege zur Geschichte des Bürgertums,* ed. Klaus Tenfelde and Hans-Ulrich Wehler (Göttingen, 1994), 289–314; Hannes Siegrist, "Der Akademiker als Bürger. Die westdeutschen gebildeten Mittelklassen 1945–1965 in historischer Perspektive," in *Biographien in Deutschland. Soziologische Rekonstruktionen gelebter Gesellschaftsgeschichte,* ed. Wolfram Fischer-Rosenthal and Peter Alheit (Opladen, 1995), 118–36; Hannes Siegrist, "From Divergence to Convergence. The Divided German Middle Class 1945–2000," in *Social Contracts under Stress. The Middle Classes of America, Europe, and Japan at the Turn of the Century,* ed. in Olivier Zunz, Leonard Schoppa, and Nobuhiro Hiwatari (New York, 2002), 21–46.

21. Claude Dubar and Pierre Tripier, *Sociologie des professions,* 2nd ed. (Paris, 2005).

22. See e.g. Champy, *La sociologie des professions.*

23. Dietrich Beyrau, *Intelligenz und Dissens. Die russischen Bildungsschichten in der Sowjetunion 1917 bis 1985* (Göttingen, 1993); Dietrich Beyrau, "Der organisierte Autor. Institutionen, Kontrolle, Fürsorge," in *Kultur im Stalinismus. Sowjetische Kultur und Kunst der 1930er bis 50er Jahre,* ed. Gabriele Gorzka (Bremen, 1994), 60–76; Dietrich Beyrau, "Bildungsschichten unter totalitären Bedingungen. Überlegungen zu einem Vergleich zwischen NS-Deutschland und der Sowjetunion unter Stalin," *Archiv für Sozialgeschichte* 34 (1994): 35–54; Dietrich Beyrau, ed., *Im Dschungel der Macht. Intellektuelle Professionen unter Stalin und Hitler* (Göttingen, 2000); Wladimir Iljitsch Lenin, "Der Aufbau des Sozialismus und die bürgerliche Intelligenz (1919)," in *Über Kultur, Ästhetik, Literatur,* ed. Karl Marx, Friedrich Engels, and Wladimir Iljitsch Lenin (Leipzig, 1975), 354–55.

24. Rafael Mrowczynski, "Rechtsberater in staatssozialistischen und post-sozialistischen Gesellschaften. Ein Vergleich zwischen Polen, der Sowjetunion und dem post-kommunistischen Russland," in *Professionen, Eigentum und Staat. Europäische Entwicklungen im Vergleich — 19. und 20. Jahrhundert,* ed. Dietmar Müller and Hannes Siegrist (Göttingen, 2014), 133–66; Dorothea Trebesius, "Künstlertum, Autorschaft und Professionalisierung. Komponisten in Frankreich und der DDR," in *Professionen, Eigentum und Staat. Europäische Entwicklungen im Vergleich — 19. und 20. Jahrhundert,* ed. Dietmar Müller and Hannes Siegrist (Göttingen, 2014), 253–71; Trebesius, *Komponieren als Beruf;* Anna Sabine Ernst, "Von der bürgerlichen zur sozialistischen Profession? Ärzte in der DDR, 1945–1961," in *Die Grenzen der Diktatur. Staat und Gesellschaft in der DDR,* ed. Richard Bessel and Ralph Jessen (Göttingen, 1996), 25–48; Ralph Jessen, *Akademische Elite und kommunistische Diktatur. Die ostdeutsche Hochschullehrerschaft in der Ulbricht-Ära* (Göttingen, 1999).

25. See e.g. for the variations in Yugoslavia, Srdan Milošević, "Between Profession and Ideology. Geodetic Professionals in Socialist Yugoslavia (1945–1953)," in *Professionen, Eigentum und Staat. Europäische Entwicklungen im Vergleich — 19. und 20. Jahrhundert,* ed. Dietmar Müller and Hannes Siegrist (Göttingen, 2014), 207–29.

26. Se e.g. Kievenheim, Christoph, André Leisewitz, eds. *Soziale Stellung und Bewusstsein der Intelligenz,* Köln: Pahl-Rugenstein,1973. Hellmuth Lange, *Wissenschaftliche Intelligenz. Neue Bourgeoisie oder neue Arbeiterklasse?,* Köln: Pahl-Rugenstein, 1972.

27. See e.g. Mrowczynski, "Rechtsberater in staatssozialistischen,"133–66; Trebesius, "Künstlertum, Autorschaft und Professionalisierung," 253–71; Maurice Aymard, "Europe from Division to Reunification. The Eastern European Middle Classes during and after

Socialism," in *Social Contracts under Stress. The Middle Classes of America, Europe, and Japan at the Turn of the Century,* ed. Olivier Zunz, Leonard Schoppa, and Nobuhiro Hiwatari (New York, 2002), 362–78.

28. See Rafael Mrowczynski. *Im Netz der Hierarchien. Russlands sozialistische und postsozialistische Mittelschichten.* Wiesbaden: VS-Verlag für Sozialwissenschaften, 2010.

29. See Mrowczynski: "Rechtsberater in staatsozialistischen," 133–66; Aymard, "Europe from Division," 362–78.

30. See for the German case Jürgen Kocka and Renate Mayntz, eds, *Wissenschaft und Wiedervereinigung. Disziplinen im Umbruch. Forschungsberichte der Interdisziplinären Arbeitsgruppen der Berlin-Brandenburgischen Akademie der Wissenschaften,* Bd. 6 (Berlin, 1998).

31. See Jürgen Gerhards, "Der Aufstand des Publikums. Eine systemtheoretische Interpretation des Kulturwandels in Deutschland zwischen 1960 und 1989," *Zeitschrift für Soziologie* 30, no. 3 (2001): 163–84.

32. See Julia Evetts, "Professions in European and UK Markets. The European Professional Federations," *International Journal of Sociology and Social Policy* 20, no. 11/12 (2000): 1–30; Julia Evetts, "Professionalism beyond the Nation-State. International Systems of Professional Regulation in Europe," *International Journal of Sociology and Social Policy* 18, no. 11/12 (1998): 47–64; Gisela Shaw, "German Lawyers and Globalisation. Changing Professional Identity," *German Life & Letters* 58, no. 2 (2005): 211–25.

33. See Dubar and Tripier, *Sociologie des professions,* 185–273. Luc Boltanski and Ève Chiapello, *Der neue Geist des Kapitalismus* (Konstanz, 2003); Peter Weingart, "Die unternehmerische Universität," in *Nach Feierabend. Zürcher Jahrbuch für Wissenschaftsgeschichte* 6 (2010): 55–72.

Bibliography

Aymard, Maurice. "Europe from Division to Reunification. The Eastern European Middle Classes during and after Socialism." In *Social Contracts under Stress. The Middle Classes of America, Europe, and Japan at the Turn of the Century,* edited by Olivier Zunz, Leonard Schoppa, and Nobuhiro Hiwatari, 362–78. New York: Russel Sage, 2002.

Baberowski, Jörg. *Autokratie und Justiz. Zum Verhältnis von Rechtsstaatlichkeit und Rückständigkeit im ausgehenden Zarenreich 1864–1914.* Frankfurt: Klostermann, 1996.

———. "Rechtsanwälte in Russland 1866–1914." In *Professionen im modernen Osteuropa/ Professions in Modern Eastern Europe,* edited by Charles McClelland, Stephan Merl, and Hannes Siegrist, 29–59. Berlin: Duncker & Humblot, 1995.

Beyrau, Dietrich. "Bildungsschichten unter totalitären Bedingungen. Überlegungen zu einem Vergleich zwischen NS-Deutschland und der Sowjetunion unter Stalin." *Archiv für Sozialgeschichte* 34 (1994): 35–54.

———. "Der organisierte Autor. Institutionen, Kontrolle, Fürsorge." In *Kultur im Stalinismus. Sowjetische Kultur und Kunst der 1930er bis 50er Jahre,* edited by Gabriele Gorzka, 60–76. Bremen: Temmen, 1994.

———. *Intelligenz und Dissens. Die russischen Bildungsschichten in der Sowjetunion 1917 bis 1985.* Göttingen: Vandenhoeck & Ruprecht, 1993.

Beyrau, Dietrich, ed. *Im Dschungel der Macht. Intellektuelle Professionen unter Stalin und Hitler.* Göttingen: Vandenhoeck & Ruprecht. 2000.

Boltanski, Luc, and Ève Chiapello. *Der neue Geist des Kapitalismus.* Konstanz: UVK, 2003.

Bourdieu, Pierre. *Die Regeln der Kunst. Genese und Struktur des literarischen Feldes.* Frankfurt: Suhrkamp, 1999.

Burrage, Michael. "Exceptional Professions in Extraordinary Times. A Comparison of Lawyers in Four Societies." In *Professionen, Eigentum und Staat, Europäische Entwicklungen im Vergleich — 19. und 20. Jahrhundert,* edited by Dietmar Müller and Hannes Siegrist, 41–74. Göttingen: Wallstein Verlag, 2014.

———. "Unternehmer, Beamte und freie Berufe. Schlüsselgruppen der bürgerlichen Mittelschichten in England, Frankreich und den Vereinigten Staaten." In *Bürgerliche Berufe,* edited by Hannes Siegrist, 51–83. Göttingen: Vandenhoeck & Ruprecht, 1988.

Burrage, Michael, Konrad H. Jarausch, and Hannes Siegrist. "An Actor-Based Framework for the Study of the Professions." In *Professions in Theory and History. Rethinking the Study of the Professions,* edited by Michael Burrage and Rolf Torstendahl, 203–25. London: Sage, 1990.

Champy, Florent. *La sociologie des professions.* Paris: Quadrige/PUF, 2009.

Dubar, Claude, and Pierre Tripier. *Sociologie des professions.* 2nd ed. Paris: Armand Colin, 2005.

Ernst, Anna Sabine. "Von der bürgerlichen zur sozialistischen Profession? Ärzte in der DDR, 1945–1961." In *Die Grenzen der Diktatur. Staat und Gesellschaft in der DDR,* edited by Richard Bessel and Ralph Jessen, 25–48. Göttingen: Vandenhoeck & Ruprecht, 1996.

Evetts, Julia. "Professionalism beyond the Nation-State. International Systems of Professional Regulation in Europe." *International Journal of Sociology and Social Policy* 18, no. 11/12 (1998): 47–64.

———. "Professions in European and UK Markets. The European Professional Federations." *International Journal of Sociology and Social Policy* 20, no. 11/12 (2000): 1–30.

Gerhards, Jürgen. "Der Aufstand des Publikums. Eine systemtheoretische Interpretation des Kulturwandels in Deutschland zwischen 1960 und 1989." *Zeitschrift für Soziologie* 30, no. 3 (2001): 163–84.

Gispen, Kees. "Der gefesselte Prometheus. Die Ingenieure in Großbritannien und in den Vereinigten Staaten 1750–1945." In *Geschichte des Ingenieurs. Ein Beruf in sechs Jahrtausenden,* edited by Walter Kaiser and Wolfgang König, 127–78. Munich: Carl Hanser Verlag, 2006.

———. "Engineers in Wilhelmian Germany. Professionalization, Deprofessionalization, and the Development of Nonacademic Technical Education." In *German Professions 1800–1950,* edited by Geoffrey Cocks and Konrad H Jarausch, 104–22. New York: Oxford University Press, 1990.

Grüttner, Michael, Rüdiger Hachtmann, Konrad H Jarausch, Jürgen John, and Matthias Middell, eds. *Gebrochene Wissenschaftskulturen. Universität und Politik im 20. Jahrhundert.* Göttingen: Vandenhoeck & Ruprecht, 2010.

Hadler, Frank. "Graben wie die Großen in Kleinasien: Ein frisch berufener Prager Professor umreißt mit weltpolitischen Argumenten sein archäologisches Karrierefeld." In *Kultur und Beruf in Europa,* edited by Isabella Löhr, Matthias Middell, and Hannes Siegrist, 206–16. Stuttgart: Steiner, 2012.

Höpken, Wolfgang. "Professionalisierung an der Peripherie: Juristen und Beamte in Bulgarien 1878–1930." In *Professionen im modernen Osteuropa/Professions in Modern*

Eastern Europe, edited by Charles McClelland, Stephan Merl, and Hannes Siegrist, 90–124. Berlin: Duncker & Humblot, 1995.

Huerkamp, Claudia. "The Making of the Modern Medical Profession, 1800–1914: Prussian Doctors in the Nineteenth Century," in *German Professions 1800–1950,* ed. Geoffrey Cocks and Konrad H Jarausch (New York, 1990), 66–84.

Jarausch, Konrad H. *Deutsche Studenten 1800–1870.* Frankfurt: Suhrkamp, 1984.

———. "The German Professions in History and Theory." In *German Professions, 1800–1950,* edited by Geoffrey Cocks and Konrad H Jarausch, 9–24. New York: Oxford University Press, 1990.

———. *The Unfree Professions. German Lawyers, Teachers and Engineers 1900–1950.* New York: Oxford University Press, 1990.

Jarausch, Konrad H., Matthias Middell, and Annette Vogel. *Sozialistisches Experiment und Erneuerung der Demokratie – Die Humboldt-Universität zu Berlin 1945–2010.* Berlin: Akademie Verlag, 2012.

Jessen, Ralph. *Akademische Elite und kommunistische Diktatur. Die ostdeutsche Hochschullehrerschaft in der Ulbricht-Ära.* Göttingen: Vandenhoeck & Ruprecht, 1999.

Jessen, Ralph, and Jakob Vogel, eds. *Wissenschaft und Nation in der europäischen Geschichte.* Frankfurt: Campus Verlag, 2002.

Karady, Victor. "Professional Status, Social Background, and the Different Impact of Right Radicalism among Budapest Lawyers in the 1940s." In *Professionen im modernen Osteuropa/Professions in Modern Eastern Europe,* edited by Charles McClelland, Stephan Merl, and Hannes Siegrist, 60–89. Berlin: Duncker & Humblot, 1995.

Kievenheim, Christoph, André Leisewitz, eds. *Soziale Stellung und Bewusstsein der Intelligenz,* Köln: Pahl-Rugenstein, 1973.

Kocka, Jürgen. "Kultur und Technik, Aspirationen der Ingenieure im Kaiserreich." In *Kultur und Beruf in Europa,* edited by Isabella Löhr, Matthias Middell, and Hannes Siegrist, 29–36. Stuttgart: Steiner, 2012.

Kocka, Jürgen, and Renate Mayntz, eds. *Wissenschaft und Wiedervereinigung. Disziplinen im Umbruch. Forschungsberichte der Interdisziplinären Arbeitsgruppen der Berlin-Brandenburgischen Akademie der Wissenschaften,* Bd. 6. Berlin: Akademie Verlag, 1998.

König, Mario, Hannes Siegrist, and Rudolf Vetterli. *Warten und Aufrücken. Die Angestellten in der Schweiz 1870–1950.* Zürich: Chronos, 1985.

König, Wolfgang. "Staat und Industrie. Die Ingenieure in der Frühindustrialisierung 1800–1870." In *Geschichte des Ingenieurs. Ein Beruf in sechs Jahrtausenden,* edited by Walter Kaiser and Wolfgang König, 188–98. Munich: Carl Hanser Verlag, 2006.

Kovacs, Maria M. "The Radical Right and the Hungarian Professions: The Case of Doctors and Lawyers, 1918–1945." In *Professionen im modernen Osteuropa/Professions in Modern Eastern Europe,* ed. Charles McClelland, Stephan Merl, and Hannes Siegrist, 168–88. Berlin: Duncker & Humblot, 1995.

Kraft, Claudia. *Europa im Blick der polnischen Juristen. Rechtsordnung und juristische Professionen in Polen im Spannungsfeld zwischen Nation und Europa.* Frankfurt: Klostermann 2002.

Lange, Hellmuth. *Wissenschaftliche Intelligenz. Neue Bourgeoisie oder neue Arbeiterklasse?,* Köln: Pahl-Rugenstein 1972.

Lenin, Wladimir Iljitsch. "Der Aufbau des Sozialismus und die bürgerliche Intelligenz (1919)." In *Über Kultur, Ästhetik, Literatur,* edited by Karl Marx, Friedrich Engels, and Wladimir Iljitsch Lenin, 354–55. Leipzig: Reclam Verlag, 1975.

Löhr, Isabella. "Fluchthilfe zur Rettung der Zunft. Die akademische Zwangsmigration in den 1930er Jahren." In *Kultur und Beruf in Europa,* edited by Isabella Löhr, Matthias Middell, and Hannes Siegrist, 270–78. Stuttgart: Steiner, 2012.

Löhr, Isabella, Matthias Middell, Hannes Siegrist, eds. *Kultur und Beruf in Europa.* Stuttgart: Steiner, 2012.

Lundgreen, Peter. "Engineering Education in Europe and the U.S.A., 1750–1930. The Rise to Dominance of School Culture in the Engineering Profession." *Annals of Science* 47 (1990): 33–75.

Marung, Steffi. "Ungleiche Schwestern in der europäischen Familie. Russische Orientalistik und sowjetische Afrikanistik als Teil der europäischen Regionalwissenschaften seit dem Ende des 19. Jahrhunderts." In *Kultur und Beruf in Europa,* edited by Isabella Löhr, Matthias Middell, and Hannes Siegrist, 227–35. Stuttgart: Steiner, 2012.

McClelland, Charles. "The German Model for American Medical Reform." In *Kultur und Beruf in Europa,* edited by Isabella Löhr, Matthias Middell, and Hannes Siegrist, 189–96. Stuttgart: Steiner, 2012.

———. *Prophets, Paupers, or Professionals? A Social History of Everyday Visual Artists in Modern Germany 1850–Present.* Oxford: Peter Lang, 2003.

———. *Queen of the Professions. The Rise and Decline of Medical Prestige and Power in America.* Lanham, MD: Roman and Littlefield, 2014.

Micu, Cornel. "Professionals, Pseudo-Professionals or State Servants? The Professionalization of Romanian Agriculture 1919–1989." In *Professionen, Eigentum und Staat. Europäische Entwicklungen im Vergleich — 19. und 20. Jahrhundert,* edited by Dietmar Müller and Hannes Siegrist, 187–206. Göttingen: Wallstein, 2014.

Milošević, Srdan. "Between Profession and Ideology. Geodetic Professionals in Socialist Yugoslavia (1945–1953)." In *Professionen, Eigentum und Staat. Europäische Entwicklungen im Vergleich — 19. und 20. Jahrhundert,* edited by Dietmar Müller and Hannes Siegrist, 207–29. Göttingen: Wallstein, 2014.

Minesso, Michaela. "The Engineering Profession 1802–1923." In *Society and the Professions in Italy 1860–1914,* edited by Maria Malatesta, 175–220. Cambridge: Cambridge University Press, 1995.

Mrowczynski, Rafael. *Im Netz der Hierarchien. Russlands sozialistische und postsozialistische Mittelschichten.* Wiesbaden: VS-Verlag für Sozialwissenschaften, 2010.

Mrowczynski, Rafael. "Rechtsberater in staatsozialistischen und post-sozialistischen Gesellschaften. Ein Vergleich zwischen Polen, der Sowjetunion und dem postkommunistischen Russland." In *Professionen, Eigentum und Staat. Europäische Entwicklungen im Vergleich — 19. und 20. Jahrhundert,* edited by Dietmar Müller and Hannes Siegrist, 133–66. Göttingen: Wallstein, 2014.

Müller, Dietmar. "Die Institutionalisierung sozialwissenschaftlichen Wissens in der Zwischenkriegszeit. Das rumänische Sozialinstitut und der Verein für Socialpolitik." In *Kultur und Beruf in Europa,* edited by Isabella Löhr, Matthias Middell, and Hannes Siegrist, 197–205. Stuttgart: Steiner, 2012.

———. "Eigentum verwalten in Rumänien. Advokaten, Geodäten und Notare (1830–1940)." In *Professionen, Eigentum und Staat. Europäische Entwicklungen im Vergleich — 19. und 20. Jahrhundert,* edited by Dietmar Müller and Hannes Siegrist, 75–132. Göttingen: Wallstein, 2014.

Müller, Dietmar, and Hannes Siegrist. "Vorwort." In *Professionen, Eigentum und Staat. Europäische Entwicklungen im Vergleich—19. und 20. Jahrhundert,* edited by Dietmar Müller and Hannes Siegrist, 7–14. Göttingen: Wallstein, 2014.

Müller, Dietmar, and Hannes Siegrist, eds. *Professionen, Eigentum und Staat. Europäische Entwicklungen im Vergleich—19. und 20. Jahrhundert.* Göttingen: Wallstein, 2014.

Müller-Jentsch, Walther. *Die Kunst in der Gesellschaft.* Wiesbaden: VS Verlag für Sozialwissenschaften, 2011.

Ristovic, Milan. "In the Government's Service and in the Shadow of the State. Civil Servants in the Serbian and Yugoslav Socieal Context in the 19th and 20th Centuries." In *Kultur und Beruf in Europa,* edited by Isabella Löhr, Matthias Middell, and Hannes Siegrist, 241–51. Stuttgart: Steiner, 2012.

Scholz, Juliane. "Deutsche Drehbuchautoren in Hollywood (1933–1945)." In *Kultur und Beruf in Europa,* edited by Isabella Löhr, Matthias Middell, and Hannes Siegrist, 61–70. Stuttgart: Steiner, 2012.

———. *Der Drehbuchautor. USA und Deutschland. Ein historischer Vergleich.* Göttingen: Wallstein, 2016.

Schramm, Manuel. "Vermessungsingenieure in Deutschland und den USA im 20. Jahrhundert. Wege der Professionalisierung." In *Professionen, Eigentum und Staat. Europäische Entwicklungen im Vergleich—19. und 20. Jahrhundert,* edited by Dietmar Müller and Hannes Siegrist, 169–86. Göttingen: Wallstein, 2014.

Shaw, Gisela. "German Lawyers and Globalisation. Changing Professional Identity." *German Life & Letters* 58, no. 2 (2005): 211–25.

Siegrist, Hannes. *Advokat, Bürger und Staat. Sozialgeschichte der Rechtsanwälte in Deutschland, Italien und der Schweiz 18.–20. Jh.* Frankfurt: Klostermann, 1996.

———. "Autonomie in der modernen Gesellschaft, Wissenschaft und Kunst (18.–20. Jahrhundert)." In *Menschenbilder—Wurzeln, Krise, Orientierung,* edited by Udo Ebert, Ortrun Riha, and Lutz Zerling, 75–92. Leipzig/Stuttgart: Hirzel Verlag, 2012.

———. "Berufe im Gesellschaftsvergleich. Rechtsanwälte in Deutschland, Italien und der Schweiz." In *Geschichte und Vergleich. Ansätze und Ergebnisse international vergleichender Geschichtsschreibung,* edited by Heinz-Gerhard Haupt and Jürgen Kocka, 207–38. Frankfurt: Campus Verlag, 1996.

———. "Der Akademiker als Bürger. Die westdeutschen gebildeten Mittelklassen 1945–1965 in historischer Perspektive." In *Biographien in Deutschland. Soziologische Rekonstruktionen gelebter Gesellschaftsgeschichte,* edited by Wolfram Fischer Rosenthal and Peter Alheit, 118–36. Opladen: Westdeutscher Verlag, 1995.

———. "Der Wandel als Krise und Chance. Die westdeutschen Akademiker 1945–1965." In *Wege zur Geschichte des Bürgertums,* edited by Klaus Tenfelde and Hans-Ulrich Wehler, 289–314. Göttingen: Vandenhoeck & Ruprecht, 1994.

———. "Die Advokaten auf dem Land." In *Idylle oder Aufbruch? Das Dorf im bürgerlichen 19. Jahrhundert. Ein europäischer Vergleich,* edited by Wolfgang Jacobeit, Josef Mooser, and Bo Stråht, 169–80. Berlin: Akademie-Verlag, 1990.

———. "From Divergence to Convergence. The Divided German Middle Class 1945–2000." In *Social Contracts under Stress. The Middle Classes of America, Europe, and Japan at the Turn of the Century,* edited by Olivier Zunz, Leonard Schoppa, and Nobuhiro Hiwatari, 21–46. New York: Russel Sage, 2002.

————. "Heteronome Dienstklasse oder autonome Profession? Thesen zur Geschichte der Wissensberufe und der Professionalisierung im modernen Europa." In *Leipziger Zugänge zur rechtlichen, politischen und kulturellen Verflechtungsgeschichte Ostmitteleuropas*, edited by Dietmar Müller and Adamantios Skordos, 131–148. Leipzig: Leipziger Universitätsverlag, 2015.

————. "Juridicalisation, Professionalisation and the Occupational Culture of the Advocate in the Nineteenth and the Early-Twentieth Centuries. A Comparison of Germany, Italy and Switzerland." In *Lawyers and Vampires. Cultural Histories of Legal Professions*, edited by David Sugarman and Wesley Pue, 123–50. Oxford: Hart, 2003.

————. "Professionalization, Professions in History." In *International Encyclopedia of the Social and Behavioral Sciences*, vol. 18, edited by Neil J Smelser and Paul B Baltes, 12152–60. Oxford: Elsevier Science, 2001.

————. "Professionelle Autonomie in der modernen Gesellschaft, Wissenschaft und Kultur. Einführung." In *Professionen, Eigentum und Staat. Europäische Entwicklungen im Vergleich—19. und 20. Jahrhundert*, edited by Dietmar Müller and Hannes Siegrist, 15–38. Göttingen: Wallstein, 2014.

————. "The Professions in Nineteenth-Century Europe." In *The European Way. European Societies during the Nineteenth and Twentieth Centuries*, edited by Hartmut Kaelble, 68–88. New York/Oxford: Berghahn Books, 2004.

Späth, Manfred. "Der Ingenieur als Bürger. Frankreich, Deutschland und Russland im Vergleich." In *Bürgerliche Berufe*, edited by Hannes Siegrist, 84–105. Göttingen: Vandenhoeck and Ruprecht, 1988.

Stichweh, Rudolf. "Professionen und Disziplinen. Formen der Differenzierung zweier Systeme beruflichen Handelns in modernen Gesellschaften." In *Wissenschaft, Universität, Professionen. Soziologische Analysen*, edited by Rudolf Stichweh, 278–336. Frankfurt: Auflage, 1994.

Trebesius, Dorothea. *Komponieren als Beruf. Frankreich und die DDR im Vergleich 1950–1980*. Göttingen: Wallstein, 2012.

————. "Künstlertum, Autorschaft und Professionalisierung. Komponisten in Frankreich und der DDR." In *Professionen, Eigentum und Staat. Europäische Entwicklungen im Vergleich—19. und 20. Jahrhundert*, edited by Dietmar Müller and Hannes Siegrist, 253–71. Göttingen: Wallstein, 2014.

Troebst, Stefan. "Vom spatial turn zum regional turn? Geschichtsregionale Konzeptionen in den Kulturwissenschaften." In *Dimensionen der Kultur- und Gesellschaftsgeschichte*, edited by Matthias Middell, 143–59. Leipzig: Leipziger Universitäts Verlag, 2007.

Ul'yanova, Galina. "Engineers in the Russian Empire." In *Professionen im modernen Osteuropa. Professions in Modern Eastern Europe*, edited by Charles McClelland, Stephan Merl, and Hannes Siegrist, 335–66. Berlin: Duncker & Humblot, 1995.

Vogel, Jakob. *Ein schillerndes Kristall. Eine Wissensgeschichte des Salzes zwischen Früher Neuzeit und Moderne*. Cologne: Böhlau Verlag, 2008.

Weingart, Peter. "Die unternehmerische Universität." *Nach Feierabend. Zürcher Jahrbuch für Wissenschaftsgeschichte* 6 (2010): 55–72.

Chapter 6

A Myth of Unity?
German Unification as a Challenge
in Contemporary History

Martin Sabrow

Translated by Jane Rafferty

At first glance, myth and historiography are not really compatible. In everyday language, myth means "a distortion of reality, a deformed, wrong image of a historical process or person, a bloated balloon of legends to be pierced by the historians' scalpel."[1] Such a "bloated balloon" also contradicts Germany's extremely sober and down-to-earth political culture that is perfectly embodied by Chancellor Merkel and best described by the term "visionless." In his recent book on German myths, the well-known political scientist Herfried Muenkler accordingly described the country as a largely myth-free zone compared with its European neighbors and the United States. Consequently, his study touches the Bonn republic only briefly, and it completely ignores the Berlin republic. Instead, it is mostly dedicated to master narratives of bygone times such as Luther's "Here I Stand, I Can Do Nothing Else," the "Miracle of the House of Brandenburg," and the "Day of Potsdam."

And indeed, if we follow Muenkler in understanding myths as historical master narratives that "express the self-confidence of a political entity," generate "trust and courage," and lay the foundation for a shared national identity,[2] then despite all attempts by the media and other "memorial entrepreneurs" not even the peaceful revolution of 1989–90 has ever gained the power of a pride-engendering myth—even though it undoubtedly had the potential. However, neither the courageous orchestral conductor Kurt Masur, who helped to diffuse the explosive situation on 9 October 1989 by calling on the citizens of Leipzig to adhere to nonviolent forms of protest, nor the two officers of the The *Ministry* for *State Security* (Ministerium für Staatssicherheit / MfS) Edwin Görlitz and Harald Jaeger who decided on their own to open the barrier at the border crossing point Bornholmer Straße only one month later, nor the brave pastor of Leipzig's St Nicolas Church, Christian Fuehrer, who had been holding prayers for peace since 1987 that later became the pivotal point for the Monday mass demonstrations against the regime—none of these brave people have ever been considered as heroic figures.

Finally, empirical evidence also belies the myth of German unity. Twenty years after the Spiegel asked "Has German unity just become a myth?" the question can be answered unambiguously: after having been regarded as a distant utopia or a political delusion for about two decades, it simply became a fact. In the year of its twenty-fifth anniversary, the level of unity and integration may still raise many questions, but certainly not the mere political act of reuniting the two countries on 3 October 1990.

So, does this essay already founder on the problem that German unity is simply not a legend but an actual fact? Well, maybe the very fact that it is so readily accepted as a historical fact should make us suspicious. The power of historical myths has always rested on the belief that their representatives and contemporaries did not consider them as delusion but as reality, as a fact that cannot be questioned at all. This assessment should cast doubt on whether our own present is really a largely myth-free zone. So, the question continues to be: German unity—a myth, or not?

The Teleological Transition from Contingency to Continuity

In a review of Tom Holland's "Rubicon: The Last Years of the Roman Republic," Michael Sommer recently defended the British author's thesis that spontaneous, irrational, and often hazardous behavior of individuals can dramatically change history. He even called it a "truth that historians don't like to face. They painstakingly search for sense and system in something that often stubbornly defies systematisation; blocking out contingency is the historians' vocational disease."[3]

However, the unification of 1990 represents just such a transition from contingency to continuity. When the Socialist experiment suddenly ended, and the German Democratic Republic (GDR) dissolved into Western society, those who were not "blessed by being born late" were ripped out of their familiar mental landscape in a way they had not anticipated.

The unopposed erosion of the SED (Sozialistische Einheitspartei Deutsch-lands) regime in 1989–90 and the development toward German unity both happened at a breath-taking pace, and had been unforeseen by any politician. It exceeded all political expectations and strategies, went be-yond public imagination, and also gave the lie to the prognostic abilities of German social and political scientists. A quote by Hans-Otto Bräuti-gam, the permanent representative of the Federal Republic in East Berlin, perfectly demonstrates everybody's cluelessness. Still in January 1989, he stated: "I cannot see that the GDR is under any external pressure to re-form." Even after a change in leadership and generation, there would be no change in policies. The GDR was not a country for dramatic change. Democratization as understood by the West was virtually unimaginable.[4] Erich Honecker was profoundly convinced of the GDR's stability as well when he declaredat a conference to mark the 500th anniversary of Thomas Münzer's birth on 19 January 1988: "The wall will still be standing in 50 and even 100 years if the reasons for it have not yet been removed." West-ern GDR experts thought along the same lines, and Gert-Joachim Glaess-ner was representing them perfectly when he maintained in 1988: "In the 15 years of the Honecker era, the GDR has gained international standing and inner stability." Even one year later, in 1989, he was still able to hold onto his analyses without receiving any criticism. According to him, what was important to the GDR was to "consolidate its achievements and to set the points for a crisis-free development of GDR society up to the turn of the century. Not without good reason, the GDR is able to confidently take stock of the era Honecker."[5] As with scholars, so with politicians: in 1989, Zbigniew Brzezinski, in summing up the "failed communist experiment," called the GDR the only Eastern bloc state with relative stability and po-tential for economic development.[6]

After 1989, we quickly agreed to regard this failure with a shake of the head and to use regrettable moral indifference or professional blindness to explain why contemporary analysts did not see the end of the GDR com-ing. The upheaval of 1989–90 became a caesura that radically transformed the thoughts and actions of contemporaries and gave it a new bench-mark that no historiography could have ever anticipated. It gave way to a ground-breaking new perspective, and the year 1989 became the end point of a historical development that challenged people to reorganize their understanding of the world. It absorbed its own historicity to such an extent that any counterfactual view became pointless. The irresistible power of this caesura steers the retrospective reorganization of historical knowledge. It has opened up new intellectual horizons that the discipline cannot cope with. It has transformed what was once considered to be impossible into the retrospectively inevitable, and it has thereby turned formerly popular studies on the German question into waste paper. The power of the factual rapidly replaced the old paradigm with a new one, and historians reacted with helpless attempts at an explanation while desperately trying to find an answer to the question as to why they did not see it coming. In polemic exaggeration, Klaus von Beyme once described the date 9 November 1989 as the "Black Friday" of social sciences.[7] However, the self-conception of historiography as a scholarly discipline has remained intact; it has only doubled its efforts to restructure its diachronic orientation toward the epochal caesura of 1989.

Only in retrospect, the many hidden omens of the approaching fall of the Eastern bloc assemble to a recognizable and meaningful pattern. Today, it all seems so obvious to us. We can only imagine the last General Secretaries of the different Soviet satellites as anachronistic gerontocrats who somehow and at some point had lost touch with reality and were simply overtaken by events. Not without reason did the alleged quote, "He who comes late is punished by life" turn into the swan song of state socialism, and did the picture of Gorbatschow showing Honecker his watch become its iconic symbol. Regardless of its actual historical relevance, the caesura of 1989 has become a regulatory power that is still actively shaping not only historiography but also our "social world" (Alfred Schütz). Thereby, it discredits possible alternative historical developments that can barely be imagined anymore. The path to German unity has become a sacrosanct master narrative of the twentieth century that it is now one of the key components of Western identity — and this is exactly what provides it with a somehow mythical significance.

The Teleological Ordering Power of the Unity Narrative

This master narrative turned 3 October 1990 into the endpoint of a long and burdensome path that finally resulted in Germany's reunification. Despite the fact that Francis Fukuyama's overstatement that the end of the Cold War would equal the end of history remained a triumphant prophecy that was quickly abandoned again,[8] the years 1989–90 are still a historical benchmark on which all political acting had been concentrated. Let me just quote the introduction of the German Unification Treaty:

> The Federal Republic of Germany and the German Democratic Republic,
>
> Resolved to achieve in free self-determination the unity of Germany in peace and freedom as an equal partner in the community of nations,
>
> ...

In grateful respect to those who peacefully helped freedom prevail and who have unswervingly adhered to the task of establishing German unity and are achieving it,

...

Have agreed to conclude a Treaty on the Establishment of German Unity."[9]

These words perfectly demonstrate the mighty power of this teleological hindsight as a leading paradigm that has absorbed, that has swallowed not only all historical alternatives but also the former validity of the German division and the existence of two German states as a benchmark of contemporary history.

The mythical quality of this narrative thus presents a challenge to contemporary history. After 1990, the "policy of détente" was subjected to intense critique because it was not longer asked whether it had made German-German coexistence easier, but whether it had held fast to the aim of German unity. Egon Bahr, for instance, who died recently, was accused of having wheeled and dealed enthusiastically with those in power and of having shown the cold shoulder to the powerless people of the GDR opposition. Asked by a Federal Commission of Enquiry in 1994, Bahr tried in vain to claim that the German policy of the SPD had aimed at stabilizing the GDR while simultaneously working toward unification. This is what he said: "Destabilising goals could not be reached without stabilising factors. Kennedy put it this way: 'You have to recognise the status quo if you want to change it.'"[10] This earned him the crucial counterquestion from former GDR civil rights lawyer Gerd Poppe if this was not rather a final hindsight? "Or, if you already saw it that way at the time, and if the later aim was supposed to be destabilisation, why were some oppositional groups still accused in 1989 of having a destabillsing and therefore destructive influence, some even called it an influence that would threaten peace."[11] Again, at the same sitting, for the opposition in the GDR the Commission Chairman Rainer Eppelmann also subjected himself to the master narrative of "unity" when he self-critically admitted: "For the time being, we understood the talks about 'German Unity,' which happened earlier in the East and then later in the West as well, as a weapon in the struggle. As a short-term political objective German unity was not topical for us."[12]

The teleological power of the unity myth finds its strongest expression when it silences opposing options. For example, the once widespread dream among the West German left and the GDR opposition of a "Third Way," a democratically revived GDR, is barely being remembered. The revolutionary upheaval of 1989–90 has not established itself as a site of memory that represents people's hope for a democratic form of socialism that would conciliate capitalism and the benefits of the GDR's planned economy. Instead, it represents a movement for national freedom and unity that consequently culminated in the end of the forty-year-long division of Germany. Public memory is dominated by a narrative that sees the opening of the border on 9 November 1989 from the point of view of German unification on 3 October 1990.[13] From a viewpoint that interprets the peaceful revolution as a linear chain of events that led from freedom to unity,[14] contemporary ideas and scenarios of a Socialist and democratic GDR shrink are marginalized and considered to be the weird phantasies of some marginal outsiders who had lost all contact with the population and the political options in the given situation.

However, this is a retrospective distortion of what really happened. Contemporary accounts teach us just how strongly the idea of unity of 3 October 1990 captured the hope for freedom of 9 November 1989. In the autumn of 1989, many observers of the radical changes in East Germany and the mood of rebellion they unleashed were quite understandably convinced that the overall consensus among the GDR population was to turn their country into a "socialistically inspired alternative to the consumer society of the FRG"[15] that sought to leave behind both Stalinism and Thatcherism in equal measure.[16] This interpretation dovetails with numerous statements published by the recently founded opposition groups: "It is not about reforms that do away with socialism, but about reforms that will continue to make it possible in this country," declared an artists' resolution of 18 September 1989. It thereby revealed what the majority of the political opposition was thinking and hoping for during the final crisis of the SED-Regime.[17] "No one ever demanded the end of socialism, no one ever thought of the end of socialism."[18] Even if the individual opposition groups were pursuing very different ideas of a third way, there can be no doubt that the movement was generally orientated toward "an alternative socialism," but not "an alternative to socialism."[19]

How incompatible this idea of a third way was with the aims and interests of the protesting masses already became clear in the first weeks after the fall of the wall when the number of GDR citizens in favor of "a way towards a better, reformed socialism" dropped from 86 percent to 56 percent, and the number of those in favor of unification rose from 48 percent to 79 percent within only four months.[20] At the same time, the leading opposition group "Neues Forum" proclaimed as its goal "that something like a GDR identity should emerge which, after 40 years of decrees from above, might now have the opportunity to grow from below."[21] In the period that followed, the hope for an improved form of socialism in the GDR turned into the irrelevant opinion of a miniscule minority that did not play any significant role in the first free elections for the People's chamber on 18 March 1990. At the same time, the ever louder growing calls for unity in East Germany not only started to pressure politicians in Bonn and Berlin, but also those in Moscow, London, and Paris who had been rather hesitant so far.

It is true: the teleological power and the historians' challenging task to deal with contingency have provided German unification with some features of a myth of contemporary history that relativizes to some degree the initially stated thesis of Germany as a largely myth-free zone. Nevertheless, there can be no doubt that the efficacy of this myth can hardly, at least not yet, be compared with other national myths of unity such as the Italian Risorgimento or the Polish rebirth of 1918, and it gets nowhere near the status of the unification of the German empire in 1870–71. The question, though, is: why?

Challenges of Unification

A first and fairly obvious reason for the low appeal of the myth of German unity is, of course, the fact that over the past quarter-century, the political unity has not yet led to a real heartfelt unity of society. To this day, the project of unification has rather proven to be a political than a societal success story, and the controversial Day of German Unity on 3 October is characterized more as a state than as a national holiday, as recent surveys have emphasized unanimously.[22] In particular, the often traumatic experiences resulting from biographical breaks caused by the transition have barely penetrated public consciousness. It was twenty years until the self-proclaimed "Third Generation East," a group of people who had been children or teenagers in 1989, insisted on addressing these experiences. And it was only in this current year, twenty-five years later, that an exhibition shown by the German National Museum of History focused on the East German's experience of having to rapidly adjust to an entirely different system. The daily lives of East Germans changed dramatically in the wake of reunification, and three years after the GDR had adapted the German Basic Law, not even one in three workers still had their old job.

It is only with the benefit of hindsight that it becomes clear how bumpy the path to inner unity has been — and how often it led to a dead end. However, shortly afterward also West Germany was subjected to far-reaching changes due to globalization, medialization, and digitization. To a certain extent, it is thus legitimate to talk about intertwined changes in a doubly divided history, in which the neoliberal reconstruction of the socialist society after 1990 eventually led to analogous "co-transformations" in the

West.[23] However, it was only in East Germany that language, values, and certainties changed drastically—and along with them people's work life, their overall outlook, familiar hierarchies, and concepts. In a historically unparalleled way did the unification of Germany not only seize the future of most East Germans—it also took hold of their past. After 1989, a certain "memory mania," strong desire for coming to terms with the past, quickly replaced the partial consensus of keeping silent after 1945. It prevented any professional continuity of the old GDR elite in such an inexorable harshness that contrasted strongly with the resolute reintegration of the German postwar society. It is not by chance that nothing undermined the reputation of the public authority of the Federal Commissioner for the Records of the State Security Service of the former GDRas much as the fact that among the almost 2,000 employees of his agency, a handful of 47 former employees of the Ministry for State Security were still employed as drivers or doormen in 2009.

From a sociopolitical and economic point of view, the result of the German unification project is ambivalent—and so is the scholarly verdict. Today, the infrastructure in Eastern Germany is generally assessed as good. But its financial power is still less, and its unemployment rate higher; these days there are 9 percent unemployed in the East versus 5.7 percent in the West. As for the economy, companies tend to use the five new federal states predominantly as a production site and a sales territory while keeping their headquarters in the West.

The delegitimization of the SED dictatorship, the debate about whether the GDR was an unjust state, a rogue state, and the public equation of the Nazi and the SED regime were additional factors that sustained cultural differences between East and the West—and probably even intensified them. Twenty-six years after the peaceful revolution of 1989, many East Germans still feel like "second-class citizens."[24]

But still, within the last ten years, conflicts over German unity have become noticeably less intense. At earlier anniversaries, the public and media discourse was dominated by how unification has rather divided the country and did thus fail. In the 1990s, the key term was "Vereinigungskrise," "unification crisis." On the fifteenth and twentieth anniversaries, it was all about how the *Treuhand* had failed and how the once promised "flourishing landscapes" were turning into abandoned landscapes: the emphasis was on division rather than on unity, and unification was generally discussed as a burden and a nuisance. Apparently, these times are over. Unification has lost its pathos, but also its potential to enrage. Finally, in the year 2015, we are witnessing an increasingly pragmatic approach, and the public discourse more and more tends to accept a continuing "diversity in unity." Scholars would call this the "simultaneity of convergence and difference … in the political and social culture" of present-day Germany.[25] Euphoria and disappointment team up in a pragmatic arrangement, and meanwhile the term "unification crisis" is viewed as an anachronism.[26] In East Germany, the trust in institutions and the overall acceptance of the political system still clearly lag behind West German values, but the former gap in identification with the German system has become smaller and smaller: in autumn 2014, "the democracy as we find it in Germany" received the support of 90 percent of the West German and even 72 percent of the East German population—and is thus 31 percent higher than in 1991.[27] Today in both East and West, four out of five Germans think that the advantages of German unification "all in all … outweigh," and a vast majority of the East German population confirms that they have personally benefited from unification.[28]

Talking about the End While Facing a New Beginning

There is a third factor that detracts from the power of the unity myth, and this lies in the historical burden that the history of German unification bore with it. The Ukraine conflict and the annexation of the Crimea by the Russian Federation brings us back to the question of whether or not the West promised Moscow not to expand NATO eastward during the course of German unification and the Two-Plus-Four talks. The Greek crisis has revived concerns about Germany having become too strong again within Europe—the same concerns that in 1990 made Margaret Thatcher, François Mitterand, and Giulio Andreotti become firm, but ultimately powerless opponents of German unification. The radicalization of the right-wing populist party, Alternative for Germany (Alternative für Deutschland), is largely attributable to the strong East German support of a Saxonian political leader who took over the party in the early summer of 2015, and who forced the former spokesman form the West to back down. Additionally, the xenophobic movement "Pegida" (Patriotic Europeans against the Islamization of the Occident), despite being an all-German phenomenon, is largely supported by those in East Germany who were disappointed by German unification. The movement does not stand for a cohesive right-wing extremist ideology, but rather addresses the diffuse feeling among the lower middle classes—and they mostly attract people from the rural regions of Eastern Germany. Frank Richter, the Director of the Saxon Regional Centre for Political Education, has conveyed and formulated this diffuse feeling of always losing: "They are dancing at the opera ball in Dresden. The wolves howl in the Lausitz. Now we're going to the demo." This gives expression to a dissatisfaction specific to those East

Germans who still have not come to terms with the politically liberal state of things that assailed them during German unification and made them feel emotionally alienated. An estimated 215 out of a total of 359 attacks on refugees and their homes took place in the East; and although only 17 percent of recent acts of violence in Germany were xenophobic in nature, 60 percent of these took place in the East.[29] "Dark Germany" (to quote an expression coined by Joachim Gauck during the last weeks) rears its ugly head predominantly in those places where people could not express themselves freely within the public sphere prior to 1989, and where life was not dominated by the culture of a civil society as it had developed in the West. This came to the fore more assertively than anywhere else in the context of the refugee wave in summer 2015 when cries such as "We are the vermin" in the "valley of the susceptible" in southern Saxony could be heard; the hateful graffiti daubed on refugee accommodations and the arson attacks from Berlin to Dresden to Usedom cannot be understood adequately without looking at the history of division and reunification of the two Germanies.

Every day it becomes more apparent that the German reunification has not been the crowning finale but rather the sinister beginning of a story that is still unfolding, as the tragedy of the refugees stranded at the edge of fortress Europe has taught us just these weeks: "Strange as it may be, the fall of the Berlin Wall wasn't the beginning of unlimited freedom for Europe, but introduced an era of fences"—this is how the Berliner Tages-spiegel recently put it.[30]

Positive and Negative Memory

The last and more deep-rooted reason why the power of the unity myth remains limited these days is the nature of German historical culture. Our predominant culture of remembrance places less emphasis on an obligat-ing tradition than on the liberating break with it. The German dialogue with the past has become cathartic and not mimetic. It thrives nowadays primarily on dissociation and overcoming, not on obligations arising from tradition and the longing for continuity. The lines involved are drawn very clearly: they separate the Western culture of distancing oneself from the past from a culture of affirmation as seen, for example, in Russia or Turkey where commissions are being created to defend the imperialistic percep-tion of history up to Stalin, or where a fifty-six-meter-high bronze statue of Peter the Great can be erected on the banks of the Moskwa, or where the Armenian genocide or the former complicity in the Jewish prosecution is considered as an attack on national honor.

This way of dealing with the past, as critical as it is obsessive, reveals a certain mind-set: the more unpleasant the memory is, the less it does evoke pride in the past, but rather generates shame and pain, the more intensely German memory culture holds on to it. So it is not the heroes who are at the center of our present historical culture, but the victims. Our time is not characterized by proud narratives about gaining unity and freedom, but by historical traumas that were suffered by some and inflicted by others. The paradigm shift from historical heroization to historical victimization is not, of course, only a German trend, but an Occidental one, and it becomes most readily understandable in the way the Holocaust has become the key reference point in Western self-understanding—at least after the famous Holocaust conference in Stockholm, in which took part more than forty European countries and which laid the foundation for the International Holocaust Remembrance Alliance and for the groundbreaking declaration, which reads as follows:

> The Holocaust (Shoah) fundamentally challenged the foundations of civilization. The unprecedented character of the Holocaust will always hold universal meaning.

Today's predominantly victim-centered commemorative culture has replaced the evocation of glory by dealing with historical guilt. The associated shift from a mimetic culture of pride to a cathartic culture of coming to terms with the past makes it much more difficult for the symbols of a glorious past to come to the fore in the public sphere than those of a dark past. "Is it possible to exhibit freedom?," asks "The Rastatt Memorial Centre," one of the key German memory sites "for the freedom movements in German history" that was founded with reference to the 1848 revolution.[31] It is not by chance that the planned "monument to freedom and unity" that is supposed to be erected at Berlin's Schlossfreiheit already has a very troubled history: after a failure at the first attempt, it was determined by the Bundestag in 2007 that the monument would be inaugurated on the twenty-fifth anniversary of the Peaceful Revolution in 2014, yet it could not be completed on that symbolic date for reasons that were more historical-political than structural in nature. The "rocking dish of unity" (*Einheitswippe*), which was mocked in public as "the elephant of the nation," is said to be a toy "which was fancied for a long time and could be seen at close range just in time." The malice shown by the "Frankfurter Allgemeine" for this "public entertainment installation" told in a symbolic way of the difficulties in strengthening public awareness of the value of positive memory: "It doesn't rock, it doesn't work."[32] Therefore, the inauguration of the monument was first postponed until the twenty-fifth anniversary of German unity in 2015, and then obviously skipped again, as has become apparent in the course of the year.[33] "The seesaw is hanging in the balance," taunted the same newspaper just recently and suggested a radical solution: "It will be expensive, it produces wrong impressions, and it has no facilities for wheelchair-users either. Would it not be better to stop the construction of the monument to unity in Berlin?"[34]

As demonstrated by this example, the deepest reason for the weakness, even failure of a new German unity myth of national pride is not the critical objection of historiography, but the culture of commemoration of our post-national German nation, which has learned to distrust any collective symbols and which in the age of an ever-growing individualization and transnationalization does not believe any more in the power of mutualizing principles such as "Volk" and "unity." This skepticism goes hand in hand with the state's cautious approach to the anniversary of German unification in the first years after 1990, which was caused by clear concerns about a new, perhaps somewhat gloating, patriotism. With this in mind, Federal President Roman Herzog warned his fellow countrymen in 1994 "not to keep love for our country secret for a moment, but to express it in a very quiet way."[35] The skeptical comments of the leading German daily newspapers regarding the planned monument to unity point in the same direction: "Big bowls, particularly if one can read on them 'We are *one* people' or 'We are *the* people' (the people par excellence?), can evoke unpleasant reminiscences of the firebowls on the Nazi Party Rally Grounds in Nuremberg." Certainly, the monument to unity will be inaugurated one day, but then it will not tell of the power of the unity myth, but rather appear as a monument whose statement has turned into its opposite, as the "Frankfurter Allgemeine" predicts: "There may be a certain truth for particular epochs included involuntarily in the monument. At the same time, the whole monument with its church congress–like anti-individualism manifests to the individual up there that he can only stand there because the mass is carrying him from underneath. This is maybe a realistic picture of the desperate aesthetic and political state of things in the Berlin Republic."[36] This kind of carping may sound ironic, but it exposes the core of our present historical culture, which has bowed out of the idea of the nation, and is now laying the foundation for future historical myths, which will rather be shaped by the idea of having to come to terms with even the most painful past than by trying to glorify even just parts of it.

Martin Sabrow is a professor of history at Humboldt University (Berlin) and the Director of the Center for Contemporary History Potsdam.

Notes

This essay originally appeared as Martin Sabrow, "A Myth of Unity? German Unification as a Challenge in Contemporary History," *German Historical Institute London Bulletin* 38, no. 2 (2016): 46–62.

1. Matthias Waechter, "Mythos," *Docupedia-Zeitgeschichte*, 11 February 2010

2. Herfried Münkler, *Die Deutschen und ihre Mythen* (Berlin, 2009), 9.

3. Michael Sommer, "Caesar als Aufmischer der Geschichte," *Frankfurter Allgemeine Zeitung*, 25 August 2015.

4. Der scheidende Vertreter der Bundesrepublik in der DDR, Hans-Otto BRÄUTIGAM, erklärte in einem Interview am 2. Januar, die DDR habe "eine relative Stabilität" erreicht. Diesen Zustand werde sie halten können. BRÄUTIGAM erklärte weiter: "Ich kann nicht erkennen, daß die DDR unter einem Reformdruck von außen steht." Auch nach einem Führungs- und Generationswechsel werde es dort keine ganz neue Politik geben. Die DDR sei kein Land für dramatische Änderungen und Wechsel. Eine Demokratisierung im westlichen Sinne sei kaum vorstellbar. Hans Otto Bräutigam, "BRD Vertreter in der DDR. Interview über die Situation in der DDR," *ADG 33140*, 2 January 1989.

5. Joachim Glaeßner, *Die DDR in der Ära Honecker. Politik—Kultur—Gesellschaft* (Opladen, 1988), 11; Joachim Glaeßner, *Die andere deutsche Republik. Gesellschaft und Politik in der DDR* (Opladen, 1989), 73.

6. Zbigniew Brzezinski, *Das gescheiterte Experiment. Der Untergang der kommunistischen Systeme* (Vienna, 1989), 239.

7. Jens Hacker, *Deutsche Irrtümer. Schönfärber und Helfershelfer der SED-Diktatur im Westen* (Frankfurt, 1993); Klaus von Beyme, *Systemwechsel in Osteuropa* (Frankfurt, 1994), 36. Eckhard Jesse,"Das Ende der DDR," *Aus Politik und Zeitgeschichte* 33–34 (2015): 28–25.

8. Francis Fukuyama, *Das Ende der Geschichte. Wo stehen wir?* (Munich, 1992).

9. http://germanhistorydocs.ghi-dc.org/sub_document.cfm?document_id=78

10. *Enquete-Kommission Aufarbeitung von Geschichte und Folgen der SED-Diktatur in Deutschland* (Baden-Baden, 1995); *Protokoll der 52. Sitzung*, 3.11.1993, 756.

11. *Protokoll der 52. Sitzung*, 794.

12. Ibid., 737.

13. Stellvertretend für eine Interpretationslinie, die die friedliche Revolution primär von der deutschen Vereinigung her betrachtet: Gerhard A Ritter, *Wir sind das Volk! Wir sind ein Volk! Geschichte der deutschen Einigung* (Munich, 2009).

14. Als Beispiel unter vielen: „Für die Deutschen ist sie schon deshalb etwas Einzigartiges, da es die erste Revolution war, die erfolgreich die Ideen von Freiheit und Nation miteinander verband. Unmittelbar und ohne Umwege ging aus ihr die Bundesrepublik als ein geeinter Nationalstaat hervor. Schon deswegen ist sie,unsere Revolution.' Aber auch weil sie sich im Zusammenhandeln und -wirken von West und Ost vollzog und vollendete." Ehrhart Neubert, *Unsere Revolution. Die Geschichte der Jahre 1989/90* (Munich, 2008), 13.

15. So die Sicht des Herausgebers auf den gemeinsamen Schnittpunkt der von ihm im Dezember 1989 veröffentlichten Anthologie regimekritischer Texte: Hubertus Knabe, "Die deutsche Oktoberrevolution," *Aufbruch in eine andere DDR. Reformer und Oppositionelle zur Zukunft ihres Landes*, edited by Hubertus Knabe (Reinbek, 1989), 9–20, 19.

16. In East Germany, New Forum and other groups are beginning to polarise along new lines. Some seek to influence the reform wing of the ruling Communist Party in a more social democratic direction. Others want to fight for a distinctive third camp, socialism based on new forms of popular democratic planning, and on social and cooperative ownership-equally opposed to Stalinism and East European-style neo-Thatcherism. John Palmer, "Eastern Bloc in Search of a Third Way," *The Guardian*, 22 November 1989, 23.

17. Quoted from: Christof Geisel, *Auf der Suche nach einem dritten Weg* (Berlin, 2005), 68.

18. Frank Eigenfeld, "Bürgerrechtsbewegungen 1988–1990 in der DDR," *Wir sind das Volk?*, edited by Andrea Pabst, Katharina Schultheiß, and Peter Bohley (Tübingen, 2001), 68.

19. Sung-Wang Choi, *Von der Dissidenz zur Opposition* (Berlin, 1998), 116. Stellvertretend für die mit zahlreichen empirischen Belegen gegen die teleologische Entfärbung der sozialistischen Oppositionsziele anschreibende Forschungsliteratur siehe des weiteren: Dirk Rochtus, *Zwischen Realität und Utopie. Das Konzept des "dritten Weges" in der DDR 1989/90* (Leipzig, 1999), 201; Geisel, *Auf der Suche nach einem dritten Weg*, 55; Thomas Klein, *"Frieden und Gerechtigkeit!" Die Politisierung der Unabhängigen Friedensbewegung in Ost-Berlin während der 80er Jahre* (Cologne, 2007), 512.

20. Peter Förster and Günter Roski, *DDR zwischen Wende und Wahl. Meinungsforscher analysieren den Umbruch* (Berlin, 1990), 53-56.

21. *Mitteilungsblatt des Neuen Forum* Nr. 5 vom 14 November 1989 quoted from: Geisel, 148.

22. Vera Caroline Simon, "Tag der Deutschen Einheit: Festakt und Live-Übertragung im Wandel," *Aus Politik und Zeitgeschichte* 33–34 (2015): 11–17.

23. Frank Bösch, "Geteilte Geschichte. Plädoyer für eine deutsch-deutsche Perspektive auf die deutsche Zeitgeschichte," *Zeithistorische Forschungen* 12 (2015): 98–114; Philipp Ther, *Die neue Ordnung auf dem alten Kontinent. Eine Geschichte des neoliberalen Europa* (Frankfurt:, 2014), 97.

24. Richard Schröder, "Versöhnung-mit wem? Warum die Linke nicht ausgegrenzt ist," *Der Spiegel*, 9 November 2009.

25. Everhard Holtmann and Tobias Jaeck, "Was denkt und meint das Volk? Deutschland im dritten Jahrzehnt der Einheit," *Aus Politik und Zeitgeschichte* 33–34 (2015): 35–45

26. Jesse, "Das Ende der DDR," 23.

27. Holtmann and Jaeck, "Was denkt und meint das Volk?," 37.

28. The corresponding figures are 77 percent of the East Germans versus 62 percent of the West Germans; Holtmann and Jaeck, "Was denkt und meint das Volk?," 42.

29. Quoted from: Florian Flade, Michael Ginsburg, and Karsten Kammholz, "Osten wehrt sich gegen Nazi-Image," *Welt am Sonntag*, 30 August 2015.

30. Nik Afanasjew, "Mauert sich Europa ein?, *Welt am Sonntag*, 30 August 2015.

31. http://www.bundesarchiv.de/imperia/md/content/dienstorte/rastatt/lerngang_freiheit .pdf.

32. Andreas Kilb, "Der Elefant der Nation. Das Einheitsdenkmal wird endgültig zur Farce," *Frankfurter Allgemeine Zeitung*, 2 July 2014.

33. It is still unclear at what date the planned monument to freedom and unity in Berlin will be inaugurated. This was being announced by the Senate Administration on Thursday. "Verzögerungen im Bau. Berliner Einheitsdenkmal kommt später," *Der Tagesspiegel*, 29 May 2015.

34. Niklas Maak, "Berliner Einheitsdenkmal Die Wippe auf der Kippe," *Frankfurter Allgemeine Zeitung*, 24 August 2015.

35. Quoted from: Simon, "Tag der Deutschen Einheit," 12.
36. Ibid.

Bibliography

Afanasjew, Nik. "Mauert sich Europa ein?" *Welt am Sonntag,* 30 August 2015.

Beyme, Klaus von. *Systemwechsel in Osteuropa.* Frankfurt: Suhrkamp, 1994.

Bösch, Frank. "Geteilte Geschichte. Plädoyer für eine deutsch-deutsche Perspektive auf die deutsche Zeitgeschichte." *Zeithistorische Forschungen* 12 (2015): 98–114.

Bräutigam, Hans Otto. "BRD Vertreter in der DDR. Interview über die Situation in der DDR."*ADG 33140,* 2 January 1989.

Brzezinski, Zbigniew. *Das gescheiterte Experiment. Der Untergang der kommunistischen Systeme.* Vienna: Wirtschaftsverlag Ueberreuter, 1989.

Choi, Sung-Wang. *Von der Dissidenz zur Opposition.* Berlin: Verlag Wissenschaft und Politik, 1998.

Eigenfeld, Frank. "Bürgerrechtsbewegungen 1988–1990 in der DDR." *Wir sind das Volk?,* edited by Andrea Pabst, Katharina Schultheiß, and Peter Bohley, Tübingen: Attempto, 2001. 65–78.

Enquete-Kommission Aufarbeitung von Geschichte und Folgen der SED-Diktatur in Deutschland. Baden-Baden: Nomos, 1995.

Flade, Florian, Michael Ginsburg, and Karsten Kammholz. "Osten wehrt sich gegen Nazi-Image." *Welt am Sonntag,* 30 August 2015.

Förster, Peter, and Günter Roski. *DDR zwischen Wende und Wahl. Meinungsforscher analysieren den Umbruch.* Berlin: Links Verlag, 1990.

Fukuyama, Francis. *Das Ende der Geschichte. Wo stehen wir?* Munich: Kindler Verlag, 1992.

Geisel, Christof. *Auf der Suche nach einem dritten Weg.* Berlin: Links Verlag, 2005.

Glaeßner, Gert-Joachim. *Die andere deutsche Republik. Gesellschaft und Politik in der DDR.* Opladen: Westdeutscher Verlag, 1989.

Glaeßner, Gert-Joachim. *Die DDR in der Ära Honecker. Politik—Kultur—Gesellschaft.* Opladen: Westdeutscher Verlag, 1988.

Hacker, Jens. *Deutsche Irrtümer. Schönfärber und Helfershelfer der SED-Diktatur im Westen.* Frankfurt: Ullstein, 1993.

Holtmann, Everhard, and Tobias Jaeck. "Was denkt und meint das Volk? Deutschland im dritten Jahrzehnt der Einheit." *Aus Politik und Zeitgeschichte* 33–34 (2015): 35–45.

Jesse, Eckhard. "Das Ende der DDR." *Aus Politik und Zeitgeschichte* 33–34 (2015): 25–28.

Kilb, Andreas. "Der Elefant der Nation. Das Einheitsdenkmal wird endgültig zur Farce." *Frankfurter Allgemeine Zeitung,* 2 July 2014.

Klein, Thomas. *"Frieden und Gerechtigkeit!" Die Politisierung der Unabhängigen Friedensbewegung in Ost-Berlin während der 80er Jahre.* Cologne: Böhlau, 2007.

Knabe, Hubertus. "Die deutsche Oktoberrevolution." *Aufbruch in eine andere DDR. Reformer und Oppositionelle zur Zukunft ihres Landes,* edited by Hubertus Knabe, 9–20. Reinbek: Rowohlt, 1989.

Maak, Niklas. "Berliner Einheitsdenkmal Die Wippe auf der Kippe." *Frankfurter Allgemeine Zeitung,* 24 August 2015.

Mitteilungsblatt des Neuen Forum 5 (1989).

Münkler, Herfried. *Die Deutschen und ihre Mythen.* Berlin: Rowohlt, 2009.

Neubert, Ehrhart. *Unsere Revolution. Die Geschichte der Jahre 1989/90.* Munich: Piper Verlag, 2008.

Palmer, John. "Eastern Bloc in Search of a Third Way." *The Guardian,* 22 November 1989.

Protokoll der 52. Sitzung. 3 November 1993.

Ritter, Gerhard A. *Wir sind das Volk! Wir sind ein Volk! Geschichte der deutschen Einigung.* Munich: C.H. Beck, 2009.

Rochtus, Dirk. *Zwischen Realität und Utopie. Das Konzept des "dritten Weges" in der DDR 1989/90.* Leipzig: Leipziger Universitätsverlag, 1999.

Schröder, Richard. "Versöhnung—mit wem? Warum die Linke nicht ausgegrenzt ist." *Der Spiegel,* 9 November 2009.

Simon, Vera Caroline. "Tag der Deutschen Einheit: Festakt und Live-Übertragung im Wandel." *Aus Politik und Zeitgeschichte* 33–34 (2015): 11–17.

Sommer, Michael. "Caesar als Aufmischer der Geschichte." *Frankfurter Allgemeine Zeitung,* 25 August 2015.

Ther, Philipp. *Die neue Ordnung auf dem alten Kontinent. Eine Geschichte des neoliberalen Europa.* Frankfurt: Suhrkamp, 2014.

"Verzögerungen im Bau. Berliner Einheitsdenkmal kommt später." *Der Tagesspiegel,* 29 May 2015.

Waechter, Matthias. "Mythos." *Docupedia-Zeitgeschichte,* 11 February 2010. Retrieved from https://docupedia.de/zg/Mythos.

Part III

Narratives of
German History

Chapter 7

A "Shattered" Religious Past
Rethinking the Master Narratives of Twentieth-Century German Christianity

Benjamin Pearson and Michael E. O'Sullivan

In his landmark book about the relationship of the secular media to religion in the Federal Republic, Nicolai Hannig compares the compelling spiritual journeys of Rudolf Augstein and Axel Springer. While Augstein, the iconoclastic editor of *Der Spiegel,* grew increasingly hostile to the Catholic confessional milieu of his youth, Springer gravitated first toward esoteric faith and astrology before returning to conservative Lutheranism later in life. Despite their differences, both men openly increased coverage of religion in the media while simultaneously calling for a retreat of the institutional churches from politics and society. In the eyes of both of these very different media giants, religious faith was a private matter.[1] Through such examples, Hannig highlights the unstable and increasingly personal nature of religious development in West Germany. While some would view Augstein's biography as a simple metaphor for the secularization thesis and Springer's story as evidence of religion's persistence, closer scrutiny indicates a far more complicated reality.

Such recent representations of West German Christianity challenge the master narrative of secularization present throughout German historiography for decades. Although not directly connected to the legacy of Konrad Jarausch, fresh research about the Christian confessions after 1945 disrupts traditional ideas about secularization in the same way that Jarausch and Michael Geyer pulled apart national histories of modern Germany in their book *Shattered Past.* Monographs appearing in the last decade disorder the mainstream consensus about postwar secularization, presenting contested new paradigms to challenge models that dominated the literature for so long. However, the ideas present in *Shattered Past,* released while the authors of this essay studied in Chapel Hill, provide insights for the path forward in the frequently isolated subfields of Protestant and Catholic history.

While some new studies illustrate the complexity of a seemingly fast decline of church institutions that wielded such influence until the late 1950s, they struggle to leave the Protestant secularization narrative and the so-called Catholic milieu model behind entirely, and some scholars openly bemoan the loss of these concepts' hegemony in the field. In a passage of their book relevant to the endurance of the secularization thesis, Jarausch and Geyer say, "The kind of linear continuity, typical of other national histories, falters in the face of the ruptures of German twentieth-century experience." They suggest an "alternative approach" that starts "with the recognition of the very instability of the German condition" and makes "it the pivotal concern of historical reconstruction."[2] The application of this idea to religious history might resolve much of the current tension. By embracing the volatility of faith in an age of war, genocide, and modernity, then a more flexible and inclusive history of Christianity's evolution becomes possible. New research should combine the ideas of the last decade in confessional history with the conclusions of *Shattered Past* to conceptualize modern religious experience as a "mosaic" of diffuse, evolving, and conflicting experiences involving both the transformation and continuation of Christian traditions. This essay supports decentralized religious histories of the twentieth century open to the inconsistencies inherent to lived spiritualties. Encouraging freedom from rigid archetypes, we favor studies with room for malleable chronologies and deep ambiguity that more genuinely reflect German Christian outlooks.

A Modern Myth?

It is widely accepted by both scholars and the general public that contemporary German society is thoroughly secular. Formal membership in Germany's semi-established Catholic and Protestant regional churches has followed a trend of steady decline—with brief periods of stability or small-scale growth—across the course of the twentieth century. The number of Germans renouncing their formal church membership has risen greatly in the last two decades. And church attendance rates have plummeted from their (already low in the case of Protestants) nineteenth-century levels to the point where both Catholic and Protestant attendance numbers hover around 10 percent.[3]

Yet the place of religion in German society is not as clear-cut as these statistics might suggest. Approximately 60 percent of Germans continue to belong to the Catholic or Protestant established churches. Many others have joined smaller free churches and other nonestablished religious organizations. A similar percentage of former West Germans claim to believe in God (the numbers are much lower in the states of the former German Democratic Republic, GDR), and according to at least some surveys, these numbers have actually increased slightly over the last ten years. Furthermore, in a recent survey by Bertelsmann, 70 percent of Germans described themselves as "religious," including 18 percent who consider themselves "very religious."[4]

Religion also continues to play an important role in German public life. The Catholic and Protestant *Grosskirchen* still maintain a privileged legal status and elevated social prestige. Active church members hold positions of high leadership not only in the Christian Democratic Union/Christian Social Union (CDU/CSU), but also in the Social Democratic Party (SPD) and Green Party.[5] And parachurch organizations such as the Kirchentag and Katholikentag—as well as newer gatherings of Evangelical and Pentecostal Christians—attract massive crowds, garner considerable press coverage, and play an active role in social and political life. Indeed, one commentator has recently remarked that the Protestant Kirchentag has been so successful in promoting its political agenda that "the Protestants no longer swim against the stream, they are the stream."[6]

How is one to make sense of these seemingly contradictory trends? To put the question more pointedly, is secularization—as has long been asserted—the dominant religious trend of the twentieth century? Or is it merely a "modern myth," a triumphant account of the rise of the modern world that serves to obscure any countervailing tendencies? Especially in the last ten years, many scholars have addressed this question with new interest, some questioning the explanatory power of "secularization" master narratives, declaring "the return of religion," while others have insisted that secularization remains *the* foundational fact of modern German religious life.[7]

On a theoretical level, this debate goes back to the early days of the "secularization paradigm," the still-influential framework for thinking about modern religious change pioneered by sociologists in the 1960s and 1970s and drawing on the earlier work of Emile Durkheim and Max Weber among others.[8] Interpretations of the role of religion in the modern world depend to an extraordinary extent on how one defines such basic terms as "religion" and "the secular." Functionalist understandings of religion, including the accounts of Thomas Luckmann and Niklas Luhmann, understand religion as fulfilling a basic and necessary social function such as social integration, the production of "meaning," or the management of contingency. Even when traditional religious belief and practice decline, these social functions must still take place. Therefore, by definition, *something* must still be carrying out the role of religion in the modern world; religion simply cannot go away. Critics of this approach emphasize its tautological reasoning and questionable empirical basis. However, they have often erred in the opposite direction, reducing the entire phenomenon of religion to a few easily measurable variables that chart the decline of officially sanctioned state religion, while ignoring the possibility that the meaning of religion itself might be historically contingent, changing over time in ways that are hard to capture in official statistics.[9]

Perhaps the most basic methodological difficulty for this approach is establishing a baseline from which to measure secularization. Not only do scholars lack good quality data on religious beliefs in the premodern era against which to compare contemporary tendencies, they also lack an agreed-upon empirical framework for defining terms such as "Christianity" itself.[10] This failure to empirically define such basic terms—and the theoretical impasse to which it has led—serves only to underline the need for more careful social- and cultural-historical work on religious phenomena in both the premodern and modern world. And this is where the "modern myth" of secularization has become most damaging, especially at a popular level. By offering a simple, teleological explanation for the decline of religion, the concept of "secularization" discourages the actual study of modern religious phenomena and provides an easy justification for scholars to simply ignore religion as an insignificant vestige of an earlier age.[11] As Jeffrey Cox has argued, secularization often operates as an "invocatory theory" that enables scholars to avoid confronting modern religious realities.[12] This can be seen especially clearly in much of the liberal West German historiography of the 1960s and 1970s, where religion rarely made an appearance, except as a regressive force obstructing social modernization.[13]

More recently, sociologists and historians have reconsidered these assumptions, shifting their attention from the decline of religion *per se* to the "differentiation" of religion from other areas of modern social life, including politics, the economy, and the sciences. According to this perspective, religion no longer occupies a privileged status above these other spheres, as it is assumed to have done in the premodern era. Instead religion in the modern word has become just one form of discourse alongside many others. Yet even here, as José Casanova has argued, the boundaries between different areas of social life are much more permeable in practice than is often acknowledged. Even in the modern world, religious movements have continued to successfully assert the ongoing relevance of religiously derived "values" as a foundation for activity in all other spheres of life, thereby taking upon themselves a crucial critical task within modern civil society.[14] It is only in the last ten years that historians of twentieth-century Germany have really begun to explore these phenomena.

A Protestant Sonderweg?

For a variety of reasons probably related to the presence of a more active and well-defined Catholic milieu with its associated social, political, and scholarly organizations, studies of religion in twentieth-century Germany have focused more on the role of Catholics than Protestants. Indeed, developments in the Protestant churches, and in the Protestant public more generally, have often been assimilated into an essentially Catholic narrative. Protestants have been seen as junior partners in 1950s conservative circles, inhabitants of a weaker and more porous milieu, whose continued adherence to authoritarian conservatism in the late 1950s and 1960s and whose unwillingness to confront their legacy of complicity under Nazism, led to the generational conflict and increasing secularization of the late 1960s and 1970s. While there is, of course, some validity to this narrative (especially when considering the most conservative elements of West German Protestantism), it also obscures several important differences between the Catholic and Protestant experiences in twentieth-century Germany.

In the first half of the twentieth century, these differences can be seen most easily in the greater centrality of German nationalism to Protestant than Catholic identity, leading to disastrous complicity in two World Wars and the Holocaust.[15] Because of this legacy of greater complicity, the internal divisions and institutional disruptions of the Nazi era, and the shifting balance of power between the confessions, German Protestants entered the postwar era with a weaker institutional and social foundation than German Catholics. This institutional weakness, in turn, created space for critical voices to gain a more prominent place in West German Protestant culture and in the church institutions themselves. While mainstream German Protestantism remained deeply conservative in many ways, dissenting figures such as Martin Niemöller enjoyed unprecedented prestige and publicity. Moreover, although this has often been overlooked by historians, even many more conservative Protestants soon found themselves disillusioned by the authoritarian politics of the Adenauer CDU, leading to the gradual "social democratization" of both left-leaning and moderate Protestant intellectuals.[16] Long before Vatican II created new space for dissenting Catholic voices, a highly self-critical brand of Protestantism had begun to gain an institutional foothold in the Protestant churches. This probably explains the otherwise odd fact that the Protestant churches received less outside criticism in the late 1950s and 1960s than the Catholic Church, despite Protestants' greater complicity in the crimes of the Nazis and their own imperfect process of "mastering the past." This can be seen, for example, in the Protestant playwright Rolf Hochhuth, who directed his ire at the supposed complicity of the Roman Catholic Church in the Holocaust, when his own confession was clearly much more directly implicated.[17]

A different Protestant trajectory can also be seen on the question of secularization. While secularization was seen by conservative Catholics and conservative Protestants alike as the foundational disaster of the modern world, the Protestant churches also contained an influential tradition that viewed "secularization" in a much more positive light, and even integrated the idea into the very concept of Protestant Christianity itself. German cultural Protestants such as Max Weber and Ernst Troeltsch were among the initial pioneers of what has become known as the "secularization thesis," while Protestant intellectuals and theologians such as Carl Friedrich von Weizsäcker, Friedrich Gogarten, and Dietrich Bonhoeffer all wrote positively of secularization as a logical outgrowth of the Gospel message, leading to what Bonhoeffer famously referred to as "religionless Christianity" in a "world that has come of age."[18] Following this lead, radical Protestants in the 1960s made "secularization theology" central to their program, minimizing the transcendent elements of Christianity, while focusing on God's immanence in the world.[19] Combined with the influence of post-Holocaust theology and liberation theology, this provided a solid foundation for thinking of the Christian faith in more "worldly" and often political terms.[20] This Protestant openness to the world has sometimes been understood as a form of "self-secularization." But it could just as easily be seen as a new way of asserting the relevance of religious values in public life.[21] In recent years, declining membership and uncertain finances have caused Protestant leaders to revisit and revise this model, once again emphasizing personal faith as the foundation for political and social action.[22] But Protestant culture more broadly remains closely associated with "modern" political and social causes, and "Protestant" values seem dominant to an unprecedented extent in contemporary German political culture.[23]

The Institutionalization of Ongoing Self-Reflection?

In his 1957 essay, "Is Ongoing Self-Reflection Institutionalizable?," the prominent West German sociologist Helmut Schelsky argued strongly against the proposition that Christianity was incompatible with the social realities of the modern world. While recognizing that Christianity would need to adapt to the new circumstances of the postwar era, including the independence of the state and of society from formal church control, he also suggested that the churches could take on a new, critical social role within this changed environment. This task would require not just superficial modernization (modern worship, modern communications media), but rather a fundamental shift in the *way* in which Christians held their basic beliefs. In the modern world, characterized by multiple competing belief systems, it was no longer possible for Christians to hold unconsciously and unreflectively to traditional Christian teachings. Rather, Christians had to *consciously* choose between affirming an uncritical and dogmatic Christian "ideology," on the one hand, or embracing the ideals of "continual self-questioning" and openness to the world, on the other. If the institutions of the church could not adapt to this new reality, Schelsky argued, they would continue to exist as formal institutions, but they would lose their vital place in society. If, on the other hand, they could find a way to build their institutions around the concept of ongoing self-reflection, they could survive and thrive in the changing social circumstances.[24]

From the standpoint of the early twenty-first century, it appears that the institutional structures of the Roman Catholic Church and the established Protestant regional churches continue to struggle with the task of maintaining some form of social relevance. But new institutions, founded after the end of World War II, such as the Protestant Academies and the German Protestant Kirchentag (along with their Catholic equivalents) have maintained a prominent place in postwar society, which continues up to the present day. They have done this by embracing Schelsky's formula and creating an institutional space for experience, encounter, exploration, and reflection, cultivating a loyal membership of what former-*Bundespräsident* Richard von Weizsäcker has described as "professionals active in secular society who take their bearings for life in this world from the Christian faith as best they can."[25] They have also, at times in their histories, been centers of controversy and political action, the work of exposing and grappling with the legacies of the Nazi past, and the work of reconciliation between Jews and Christians. They have served as crucial forums for the early development of Willy Brandt's Ostpolitik, for peace and development work around the world, and since the early 1980s centers of antinuclear and ecological activism.[26] Most importantly for our purposes here, they have consistently occupied a central space in public life. If "religion" is defined in a way that excludes these forms of modern Christianity, then the secularization narrative becomes much more plausible. But if these forms of modern religious experience are included in our definition, then they seem to offer a significant challenge to the master narratives of secularization.

New Narratives of Catholic Secularization: From Catholic Milieu to Catholic Pluralism

The field of German Catholic history enjoyed incredible attention during the last three decades, but much of this innovative research still embraced some version of a secularization narrative. The religious turn in Catholic historiography of Germany began in earnest during the 1980s, but focused at first on the nineteenth century. Previous to this decade, work on religion largely included theologians who approached the church within the framework of Catholic doctrine, rarely engaging with so-called "profane" historians that perpetuated ideas about a teleological secularization of modern Germany. This latter and more mainstream narrative represented Catholic social and political influence as part of an unhealthy political structure that contradicted Germany's rapid industrialization. Organizing their writing around modernization theory and class analysis, the so-called Bielefeld school of Hans-Ulrich Wehler suggested an inevitability inherent to secularization through its disparaging depictions of the Catholic Center Party.[27]

A new direction emerged thanks to the work of scholars who complicated Catholic history during the nineteenth century, but the new focus on Catholic social history reached the twentieth century through an intense focus on the milieu concept in the late 1980s and 1990s.[28] The mixture of work about the nineteenth century with a historiography focused on the rise and fall of the Catholic milieu during the twentieth century combated notions of a gradual secularization process starting with the Enlightenment and quickening with industrialization and modern politics. Rather Catholics utilized modern tools to defend their faith. Yet these histories only delayed the teleology of secularization to a later date. The religious turn uncovered the persistent influence of German Catholicism, but still adopted modernist assumptions that religious faith itself represented a premodern mind-set that could only be prolonged for so long. Most milieu historians highlighted the importance of Catholicism in the twentieth century but disagreed only on when the decline of the milieu structure that propagated its mentalities began.[29]

The origins of the milieu model lay outside the field of Catholic history, and the concept only gradually made its ways into studies of German religion. Upon its arrival, it abetted mainstream narratives about secularization as much as it contradicted them. M. Rainer Lespius first characterized German politics and society as composed of Socialist, Catholic, liberal-Protestant, and aristocratic milieus in 1966 to account for a segmented political system that resulted in the rise of Nazism.[30] Many scholars then applied the term in studies of Catholicism to explain an insular confessional subculture of associations, devotional societies, labor unions, and youth groups that underpinned the electoral success of the Catholic Center Party from the 1870s until the 1920s. The earliest practitioners of milieu history put little distance between themselves and the assumptions about secularization long present in the perspective of the Bielefeld School. Adopting a paradigm of modernization that viewed the Center Party as representing antiquated ideals, Wilfried Loth argued that the party's influence already waned prior to World War I. Several other historians used the milieu idea to promote a narrative of early Catholic decline as Oded Heilbronner, Gotthard Klein, Gerhard Paul, and Klaus-Michael Mallman all suggest that splintering and internal weakness of the anachronistic Catholic milieu made it impossible for Catholics to prevent the rise of Nazism.[31] While these historians focused attention on the history of religion, they embedded their findings firmly in the secularization thesis.

Another set of historians with connections to the Commission for Contemporary History in Bonn and its "blue series" of monographs about Catholic history used the milieu thesis to alter the secularization story if not eliminate it. The most influential researchers in this regard started a collaborative effort known as the *Arbeitskreis für kirchliche Zeitgeschichte* (AKKZG). Together, they built upon the ideas of Swiss historian Urs Altermatt and sociologist Karl Gabriel to develop a sophisticated and coherent understanding of how the Catholic milieu shaped social structures, cultural beliefs, religious mentalities, and political action by those Germans who fell under its influence in regions with Catholic majorities. Led by largely by Wilhelm Damberg, this group analyzed the Catholic milieu as an intermediary phase in the modernization process where "elements of traditional society mixed with modern forms of production in bourgeois industrial societies." The AKKZG also contended that the Catholic milieu was a "phenomenon of the modern world" and a "carrier of collective understanding" for a marginalized subculture.[32] The strength of this model rested in the depth of its sophistication, as it theorized about a cultural system with multiple layers shaped both by social structures and cultural beliefs and highlighted the persistence of Catholicism beyond the fall of the Center Party in 1933.

Through an immense collection of dissertations and monographs, the participants in the AKKZG and some of their students built an intimidating empirical edifice to support their convincing analytical framework, making the Catholic milieu hegemonic in almost all narratives about German Catholicism in the last twenty years. The milieu model reached its most influential period with the publication of books by Wilhelm Damberg and Mark Edward Ruff. By continuing research into post-1945 West Germany, these scholars completed the narrative of the Catholic milieu's rise and fall. Looking at the Diocese of Münster in comparative perspective, Damberg argues that an elite core of Catholics carried religious values successfully into the world of Christian Democratic politics after the war, but the milieu faded rapidly in the 1950s as it lost social influence in an increasingly individualistic and consumerist culture. Ruff largely confirms these findings by extending research to the youth of the Rhineland and Bavaria and to Catholic girls as well as boys.[33] With the assistance of scholars like Ruff, the AKKZG constructed a deeply influential narrative that largely replaced the secularization thesis inherent to German history prior to the religious turn. By taking the worldviews of Catholics seriously, these scholars illustrated how a religious minority became so influential to a rapidly urbanizing and industrializing nation. While challenged by external threats and internal divisions at several points, these scholars feel the milieu continued its influence into postwar West Germany where it ultimately submitted to the irresistible forces of modernity as the Federal Republic adopted fully democratic values and an advanced consumer economy. While this new paradigm challenged the Weberian secularism of the Bielefeld School, it ultimately replaced one secularization narrative with another. It tied itself to a concept intimately linked to modernization theory.

Despite its prominence, the milieu thesis faced criticism. While some historians questioned the linkage between social networks of Catholics and their somewhat unpredictable voting behavior, others criticized the AKKZG historians for relying too heavily on analysis of institutional structures, creating a top-down analysis. Still more scholars questioned why academics inspired by the concept of the Catholic milieu seemed hesitant to examine women's history, gendered analysis, and cultural histories of mentalities.[34] In another example of criticism, Derek Hastings and Thomas Forstner found the Catholic population that dominated Munich and Upper Bavaria during the 1920s and 1930s far too diverse to converge with the findings of the AKKZG, Damberg, and Ruff about northwestern Germany. Forstner suggests that Munich Catholics experienced "clusters of varied *Lebenswelten*" rather than one exclusive religious subculture. While he usefully probes the weaknesses of a concept that frequently invokes the monolithic control of clergy and lay elites over Catholic congregants, Forster still suggests a secularization process at work. He agrees with the findings of Karl Heinrich Pohl that Munich reached a point with the erosion of Catholic religious practice before World War I that did not affect

Catholics in other regions until the era of Konrad Adenauer.[35] While a growing chorus of criticism about the milieu concept arose over several years, few scholars have displaced it entirely, and fewer still question its new chronology of German Catholic secularization.

Representative of such a trend, Benjamin Ziemann's recent work both attacks the milieu thesis while offering an aggressive defense of the secularization thesis for Catholic West Germany after 1945. It forcefully brushes aside the years of milieu-inspired research, suggesting the concept works more effectively for the late nineteenth century than the twentieth century. Ziemann feels milieu historians isolate Catholicism from mainstream narratives about German history by constructing a story that ends with erosion and a "religious vacuum" by the 1950s. Instead, Ziemann reintroduces Weberian-inspired sociology to the study of religion, viewing a "functional differentiation" where religion becomes but one "subsystem" among many as a natural consequence of modernization. He suggests that the Catholic Church in West Germany succumbed to secularization as it adopted social scientific techniques in search of stabilizing its declining popularity among worshipers. According to Ziemann, the further the church embedded itself in "scientization," such as statistically quantifying religious practice and systematically polling Catholic opinion, the more it replaced "traditional pastoral metaphors with others coined by the social sciences." In other words, the Roman Catholic Church ironically secularized itself from within as it tried to prevent its own downfall.[36]

Ziemann's critique of the milieu thesis poses a potential point of departure for the field of German Catholic history, but few scholars seem willing to build upon his approach. Ziemann's theoretical sophistication and complex empiricism coalesce with his position as a church outsider to create an intriguing alternative, but the separation he seeks from milieu historians ultimately seems superficial. His chronology of secularization lines up almost identically to that of Wilhelm Damberg and Mark Ruff, as he views the 1950s as the start of a secularizing trend that increased in the 1960s and 1970s. Much as the milieu concept's focus of church associational life drives its narrative, Ziemann also views the methods of the institutional church from above as decisive in the behavior of its increasingly disinterested believers. While Ziemann opens a new perspective on the church's use of modern techniques to stave off irrelevance, his viewpoint fails to consider more individualized notions of religiosity and diverse expressions of transcendence that shape the current Federal Republic just as much as an indifference to institutional religious ritual.

Such criticism of the milieu model causes concern among some scholars of religion. Mark Ruff recently expressed concern that the "metanarrative" of the rise and fall of the Catholic milieu has been deconstructed without a viable alternative in place, leaving the field somewhat rudder-less.[37] However, the combined work of Christian Schmidtmann, Nicolai Hannig, and Thomas Großbölting presents a variation of the milieu thesis that has more coherence and flexibility than the social scientific theory of Ziemann and therefore offers a potential building block for the future. Although Hannig and Großbölting examine Protestantism as well as Ca-tholicism, they both place slightly more emphasis on Catholic themes and therefore engage debates about the milieu forthrightly. Through ex-aminations of post-1945 Catholicism and religion, these scholars endorse elements of the secularization narrative. They all suggest a decline in re-ligious worship with clear beginnings in the early 1950s that evolved into an outright crisis for the Roman Catholic Church by the 1970s. However, all three scholars mix social scientific theory with cultural analysis to un-cover much nuance in this religious transformation. They also suggest a process where religion became more individual and more plural rather than completely secular.

Schmidtmann partially persists with the milieu model's emphasis on institutional history, examining how the *Katholische Deutschen Studenteini-gung* (KDSE), a national umbrella organization for German Catholic stu-dents, and some of its individual clubs evolved during the Federal Repub-lic. As in other histories, Schmidtmann depicts a breakdown in the late 1950s that led to the ultimate dissolution of the KDSE in the 1970s. What separates this dissertation from countless others that link institutions to a declining milieu is his theoretical outlook and use of twenty-four oral histories and eight autobiographies of Catholic elites. He creates a post-modern depiction of religious pluralization, uncovers competing notions of Catholic identity in postwar West Germany, and concludes that Cath-olics eventually articulated a discourse that could not be distinguished from that of non-Catholics.[38] While his study replicates aspects of a milieu decline, he calls for theories that leave room for multiple viewpoints of religion and thick descriptions of unstable and competing understandings of Catholicism.

Hannig's already cited examination of Christianity in the media of the Federal Republic is less postmodern than Schmidtmann's interpretation of students. The premise of this book turns on the paradox that the Christian churches have declined by all statistical measures throughout the Fed-eral Republic while their continued importance in the media and the pub-lic sphere have led some to even theorize about the "return of religion" during the 1970s. This viewpoint creates an adaptable account that ex-plores how church dominance of the media hid signs of religious decline in the 1950s while attempts by younger journalists to restrict the influence of churches from politics and society actually increased media coverage of religion at times during the 1960s. Much like Schmidtmann, Hannig views the 1970s and 1980s as a period of individualization and pluralization of religion as the media devoted countless stories to noninstitutional sacred experiences and religious sects. Hannig seeks to reconcile recent media attention to religious events, such as the election of Benedict XVI, with the more diffuse religious mentalities of the German people.[39] While contributing to a narrative about the modern individualization of religion, he also captures the complexity of Christian influence in the Federal Republic in a coherent manner.

By constructing a sweeping synthesis of recent work on religion of both Christian denominations in East and West Germany, Thomas Großbölting solidifies the shift from milieu to pluralization as the new model for understandings of religion after 1945. Along with Klaus Große Kracht, Großbölting rejects notions that religion disappeared with the modernity of Germany, citing the recent upswing of Islam in the public sphere, the transformation of Jewish communities in Germany from the migration of Eastern European Jews, and the major presence of priests and nuns in German television.[40] Much like Hannig's monograph, Großbölting's book embraces the contradictions of religious development. For example, he notes the simultaneous existence of Catholic milieu erosion and religious revival in the 1950s as well as the growth of individualized faith alongside the decline of institutional strength that accompanied the changes of the Second Vatican Council. Taking his study to the post-unification era, Großbölting explores how the church structures have fallen more deeply into crisis even as many Germans articulate ill-defined notions of religiosity and the Roman Catholic Church remains one of the largest employers in the entire country through its charities, schools, and hospitals. Generally, the book depicts Christianity as pushed increasingly to the margins but not entirely eliminated from the realms that matter most in Germany, especially in the territories of the former Bonn Republic.[41]

While Schmidtmann, Hannig, and Großbölting possess some differences over how segmented and undifferentiated religious belief became over time, they create a new chronology for the post-1945 period. They all find common ground with milieu theorists in locating the institutional decline of the church in the 1950s. However, they formulate a new narrative for what came after the milieu, suggesting a layered and complicated evolution from doctrinaire Catholicism transmitted from clergy to congregants into competing understandings of Catholicism that became increasingly individualized and numerous. A large community of practicing Catholics divided internally between reformers and traditionalists transformed to an even more segmented group with a looser affiliation to one another, a varied spectrum of faith, and an increasing tendency not to see Roman Catholicism as the one true faith. While this perspective converges somewhat with the secularization thesis, it leaves space for the persistent influence of Christianity in the media, the political sphere, and the cluttered modern worldviews of Federal Republic citizens.

Despite the dynamism of this new work on Catholicism, more needs to be done in order to resolve the tension between secular impulses and the stubborn presence of Catholicism in Germany. For example, scholars should join Derek Hastings and Thomas Forstner in destabilizing the milieu narrative prior to 1945. The multiplicity of Catholic mentalities and competing religious identities did not begin with the Federal Republic of Germany or the decrease in Catholic associational life. By further deconstructing the master narrative of the Catholic milieu, historians will better grasp the full scope of religious belief when Catholicism was more dynamic and also make the seemingly rapid individualization of belief at the end of the 1950s more comprehensible. In particular, future research should uncover the mentalities of those further from the centers of power in milieu structures, including women, rural populations, and members of the working class who left the church for political reasons yet retained aspects of faith. Furthermore, future books should follow the example of Schmidtmann's oral histories to carefully recreate the viewpoints of Catholics as they evolved in the postwar era. Postmodern notions of countless competing attitudes about religion could devolve into incomprehension. Instead, historians should fashion detailed "mosaics," such as those suggested by Jarausch and Geyer in *Shattered Past* for German national histories, of these diverse religious mentalities supported by careful oral histories and assessments of personal papers. In sum, the field of Catholic history seems on track to "shatter" past assumptions about secularization to uncover experiences and beliefs previously hidden by hegemonic master narratives without decentering this history to the point of incoherence.

Conclusion: Beyond Metanarratives?

In 1979, Jean-François Lyotard famously defined postmodernism as "an incredulity toward metanarratives."[42] In this chapter, we have argued that such incredulity is warranted when it comes to the metanarratives (or master narratives) that have come to dominate historical research on religion in twentieth-century Germany. As postmodern philosophers such as Lyotard have argued, metanarratives do not simply provide a framework for organizing and evaluating information. Rather, by their very nature, they privilege certain truths while crowding out other truths. In effect, whether maliciously or unintentionally, they set the parameters of what can be said about a topic and even of what can be thought. This has certainly been the case with secularization theory and the study of modern religious phenomena. Because such phenomena have often been assumed, by definition, to be peripheral to the truly "important" aspects of modern life, historians have then considered it legitimate to ignore them.

Even more problematic, historians and other scholars who *are* interested in the study of modern religious phenomena, have often found it difficult to escape the conceptual confines of secularization theory. Studies of twentieth-century German Protestantism have tended to limit their scope to "official" institutional forms of religion, ignoring many manifestations of real exiting religion in the world, including the work of individuals and groups outside of the churches' institutional hierarchies. Because many scholars have lacked a conceptual framework for thinking about religious faith as something that can be both genuinely religious and authentically modern, they have also often forced religious phenomena into one of two categories: the traditional/reactionary and the self-secularizing. Scholars of modern Catholicism have partially overcome this difficulty by developing the concept of the Catholic milieu, which has allowed them to explore the continued relevance of Catholic faith to modern society and politics. But in the process, they too have tacitly accepted a narrative that marginalizes the Catholic experience from mainstream historiography; that accepts an essentialized, institutionally centralized, and hierarchicalized definition of what is "Catholic"; and that thereby threatens to exclude from consideration forms of real existing religious life that do not fit easily into this framework.

One solution to this problem would be to adopt an aggressively postmodern stance, rejecting all metanarratives as distortions of historical knowledge. But this seems both impractical and potentially harmful. The formation of narratives is central to the way that humans understand themselves in time.[43] It is unlikely that historians will ever fully dispense with narrative approaches to knowledge, and attempts to do so are likely to be illusory.[44] Moreover, the narratives of secularization and of the Catholic milieu serve useful functions, illuminating important facets of the twentieth-century religious experience. Even if they fail to tell the whole story, the trends of declining membership and practice certainly lie near the center of any understanding of twentieth-century German Christianity. The differentiation of religion from other areas of social life in the modern world—and especially the different paths that this process has taken in different contexts—remains a fruitful area for continuing historical research. Twentieth-century German Christianity certainly exhibits many signs of the privatization and individualization of belief (though also some signs of deprivatization and ongoing public influence). And even nonreligious

Germans continue to adhere to values derived from but now (partially) separated from their religious roots. All of these concepts have been proposed by scholars working within the broad secularization paradigm.[45]

Rather than rejecting these narrative frameworks outright, we might instead borrow from the approach taken by Konrad Jarausch and Michael Geyer in their attempts to make sense of the shattered master narratives of twentieth-century German historiography. Instead of seeking to reconstitute the problematic narratives of secularization and of the Catholic milieu or seeking to simply supplant them with newer alternatives, perhaps we could instead acknowledge the ways in which these narratives inevitably break down, without necessarily discarding them. This acknowledgement of their partial and limited usefulness, might, in turn, open up new space for pursuing alternative—complementary or even incompatible—perspectives that may uncover different and equally valid aspects of twentieth-century religion. In this chapter, we have attempted to set out a loose framework for how several such projects might be approached.

Benjamin Pearson is the Program Director for the Master of Arts in Liberal Studies Program at Excelsior College.

Michael E. O'Sullivan is an associate professor of history at Marist College.

Notes

1. Nicolai Hannig, *Die Religion der Öffentlichkeit. Kirche, Religion und Medien in der Bundesrepublik 1945–1980* (Göttingen, 2010), 343–54.
2. Konrad H Jarausch and Michael Geyer, *Shattered Past: Reconstructing German Histories* (Princeton, NJ, 2002), 17.
3. Antonius Liedhegener, "Säkularisierung als Entkirchlichung. Trends und Konjukturen in Deutschland von der Mitte des 19. Jahrhunderts bis zur Gegenwart," in *Umstrittener Säkularisierung. Soziologische und historische Analysen zur Differenzierung von Religion und Politik*, ed. Karl Gabriel, Christel Gärtner, and Detlef Pollack (Berlin, 2012), 481–531. For slightly different numbers, see Detlef Pollack, "Wiederkehr der Religion oder Säkularisierung: Zum religiösen Wandel in Deutschland," *Ost-West Europäischen Perspektiven* 1 (2007): 11–19.
4. Pollack, "Wiederkehr der Religion"; Detlef Pollack and Olaf Müller, *Religionsmonitor. Verstehen was Verbindet. Religiosität und Zusammenhalt in Deutschland* (Gütersloh, 2013), 12; and *Religion Monitor 2008. Europe. Overview of Religious Attitudes and Practices* (Gütersloh, 2008), 8, 18.

5. Ingrid Mathhäus-Maier, "Wie der Staat der Kirche dient. Gerhard Czermaks Religions-Lexikon enthüllt die Langlebigkeit alter Privilegen," *Frankfurter Rundschau*, 2 January 2010; Agathe Lukassek, "Kabinett ohne Konfessionslose," *Katholisch.de*, 16 December 2013, http://www.katholisch.de/de/katholisch/themen/politik/131216_christliches_kab inett_groko.php.

6. Malte Lehming, "34. Evangelischer Kirchentag. Glaube ohne Kampf," *Der Tagesspiegel*, 28 April 2013; Peter Wensierski, "Aufschwung Jesu," *Der Spiegel* 18 (2008): 38–41.

7. For the two sides of this debate, see Karl Gabriel, "Jenseits von Säkularisierung und Wiederkehr der Götter," *Aus Politik und Zeitgeschichte*, 12 December 2008; and Detlef Pollack, *"Säkularisierung—ein moderner Mythos?" Studien zum religiösen Wandel in Deutschland* (Tübingen, 2003).

8. See Olivier Tschannen, "The Secularization Paradigm: A Systematization," *Journal for the Scientific Study of Religion* 30, no. 4 (1991): 395–415 and especially Tschannen, *Les Théories de la sécularisation* (Geneva, 1992); for an English language manuscript of the latter, see Olivier Tschannen, "A History of the Secularization Issue" (PhD diss., University of Lausanne, 1991).

9. Tschannen, "A History of the Secularization Issue"; and Pollack, "Wiederkehr der Religion."

10. See Lucien Hölscher, *Geschichte der protestantischen Frömmigkeit in Deutschland* (Munich, 2005); Lucien Hölscher, "Europe in the Age of Secularisation," in *Secularisation in the Christian World*, ed. Callum Brown and Michael Snape (Burlington, VT, 2010), 197–204; Werner Ustorf, "A Missiological Postscript," in *The Decline of Christendom in Western Europe, 1750–2000*, ed. Hugh Mcleod and Werner Ustorf (Cambridge, 2003), 218–25; and José Casanova, "Public Religions Revisited," in *Public Religions Revisited*, ed. Hent de Vries (New York, 2008), 107.

11. To be clear, many secularization theorists deny that secularization is a teleological, theoretically irreversible process, but the term is frequently understood this way in popular and academic culture.

12. Jeffrey Cox, "Master Narratives of Long-Term Religious Change," in *The Decline of Christendom in Western Europe, 1750–2000*, ed. Hugh McLeod and Werner Ustorf (Cambridge, 2003), 205, 207.

13. See, for example, Hans-Ulrich Wehler, *The German Empire, 1871–1918* (Dover, NH, 1985); and Ralf Dahrendorf, *Society and Democracy in Germany* (Garden City, NY, 1969).

14. José Casanova, *Public Religions in the Modern World* (Chicago, 1994), 41, 62; see also Casanova, "Public Religions Revisited."

15. The literature here is vast. See Wolfgang Altgeld, *Katholizismus, Protestantismus, Judentum: Über religios begründete Gegensätze und nationalreligiöse Ideen in der Geschichte des deutschen Nationalismus* (Mainz, 1992); Manfred Gaius and Hartmut Lehmann, eds, *Nationalprotestantische Mentalitäten. Konturen, Entwicklungslinien und Umbrüche eines Weltbildes* (Göttingen, 2005).

16. See Benjamin Pearson, "The Pluralization of Protestant Politics: Public Responsibility, Rearmament, and Division at the 1950s Kirchentage," *Central European History* 43 (2010): 270–300.

17. Hannig, *Die Religion der Öffentlichkeit*, 163–304, especially 240–241.

18. Hölscher, "Europe in the Age of Secularisation"; Heinz Zahrnt, *The Question of God: Protestant Theology in the Twentieth Century*, trans. RA Wilson (New York, 1969), 123–69; Dietrich Bonhoeffer, *Letters and Papers from Prison: The Enlarged Edition*, ed. Eberhard

Bethge (New York, 1953), 280, 327. For more on Bonhoeffer and secularization, see Peter Selby, "Christianity in a World Come of Age," in *The Cambridge Companion to Dietrich Bonhoeffer*, ed. John W de Gruchy (Cambridge, 1999): 226–45.

19. See, for example, Dorothee Sölle, *Against the Wind: Memoirs of a Radical Christian* (Minneapolis, MN, 1999); Angela Hager, "Rudi Dutschke: Radikal Fromm," in *Frömmigkeit — Theologie — Frömmigkeitstheologie. Contributions to European Church History*, ed. Gudrun Litz, Heidrun Munzert, and Roland Liebenberg (Leiden, 2005); and Klaus Fischen et al., *Die Politisierung des Protestantismus. Entwicklungen in der Bundesrepublik Deutschland während der 1960er und 70er Jahre* (Göttingen, 2011).

20. Dagmar Herzog, "The Death of God in West Germany: Between Secularization, Postfascism, and the Rise of Liberation Theology," in *Die Gegenwart Gottes in der Modernen Gesellschaft*, ed. Martin Geyer and Lucien Hölscher (Göttingen, 2006); Katharina Kunter and Annegreth Schilling, eds, *Globalisierung der Kirchen. Der Ökumenischen Rat der Kirchen und die Entdeckung der Dritten Welt in den 1960er und 1970er Jahren* (Göttingen, 2014).

21. In actual practice, "secularization theology" often coexisted with more traditional missionary theology, and the two were often used together. See, for example, World Council of Churches, *The Church for Others and the Church for the World: A Quest for Structures for Missionary Congregations* (Geneva, 1968).

22. Evangelische Kirche in Deutschland, "Beschlüsse. Kundgebung zum Schwerpunktthema 'Reden von Gott in der Welt — Der missionarische Auftrag der Kirche an der Schwelle zum 3. Jahrtausend,'" 11 November 1999, http://www.ekd.de/synode99/beschluesse_kundgebung.html.

23. See Gerd Langguth, "Den Katholiken geht das politische Personal aus," *Spiegel Online*, 11 March 2012, http://www.spiegel.de/politik/deutschland/cdu-und-kirche-den-katholiken-geht-das-politische-personal-aus-a-819695.html.

24. Helmut Schelsky, "Ist die Dauerreflexion institutionalisierbar?," in *Auf der Suche nach Wirklichkeit. Gesammalte Aufsätze*, ed. Helmut Schelsky (Düsseldorf, 1965), 250–75.

25. Richard von Weizsäcker, *From Weimar to the Wall. My Life in German Politics*, trans. Ruth Hein (New York, 1999), 133.

26. See Martin Greschat, "Protestantismus und Evangelische Kirche in den 60er Jahren," in *Dynamische Zeiten. Die 60er Jahre in den beiden deutschen Gesellschaften*, ed. Axel Schildt, Detlef Siegfried, and Karl Christian Lammers (Hamburg, 2000); Thomas Mittmann, *Kirchliche Akademien in der Bundesrepublik. Gesellschaftliche, politische und religiöse Selbstverortungen* (Göttingen, 2011); Rüdiger Runge and Margot Käßmann, eds, *Kirche in Bewegung. 50 Jahre Deutscher Evangelischer Kirchentag* (Gütersloh, 1999); and Benjamin Pearson, "Faith and Democracy: Political Transformations at the German Protestant Kirchentag" (PhD diss., University of North Carolina at Chapel Hill, 2007); a book manuscript based upon the latter is in process.

27. Jonathan Sperber, "*Kirchengeschichte* or the Social and Cultural History of Religion?" *Neue Politische Literatur* 43 (1998): 13–35.

28. Margaret Lavinia Anderson, "Piety and Politics: Recent Work on German Catholicism," *The Journal of Modern History* 63 (1991): 681–716; Werner Blessing, *Staat und Kirche in der Gesellschaft. Institutionelle Authorität und mentaler Wandel in Bayern während des 19. Jahrhunderts* (Göttingen, 1982); Wolfgang Schieder, "Kirche und Revolution. Sozialgeschichtliche Aspekte der Trierer Wallfahrt von 1844," *Archiv für Sozialgeschichte* 14 (1974): 419–54; Jonathan Sperber, *Popular Catholicism in Nineteenth-Century Germany* (Princeton, NJ, 1984).

29. Michael O'Sullivan, "From Catholic Milieu to Lived Religion: The Social and Cultural History of Modern German Catholicism," *History Compass* 7, no. 3 (2009): 837–61.

30. M. Rainer Lepsius, "Partiensystem und Sozialstruktur. Zum Problem der Demokratisierung der deutschen Gesellschaft," in *Wirtschaft, Geschichte und Wirtschaftsgeschichte*, ed. W Abel (Stuttgart, 1966), 371–93.

31. Wilfried Loth, *Katholiken im Kaiserreich. Der politische Katholizismus in der Krise des wilhelminischen Deutschlands* (Düsseldorf, 1984); Gerhard Paul and Klaus-Michael Mallmann, *Milieus und Widerstand. Eine Verhaltensgeschichte der Gesellschaft im Nationalsozialismus, Widerstand und Verweigerung im Saarland, 1935–1945* (Bonn, 1995); Oded Heilbronner, *Catholicism, Political Culture, and the Countryside: A Social History of the Nazi Party in the Countryside* (Ann Arbor, MI, 1998), 202; Gotthard Klein, *Der Volksverein für das katholische Deutschland, 1890–1933. Geschichte, Bedeutung, Untergang* (Paderborn, 1996).

32. Arbeitskreis für kirchliche Zeitgeschichte (AKKZG), Münster, "Katholiken zwischen Tradition und Moderne. Das katholische Milieu als Forschungsaufgabe," *Westfälische Forschungen* 43 (1993): 592–93.

33. Antonius Liedhegener, *Christentum und Urbanisierung. Katholiken und Protestanten in Münster und Bochum 1830–1930* (Paderborn, 1997); Wilhelm Damberg, *Abschied von Milieu? Katholizismus im Bistum Münster und in den Niederlanden 1945–1980* (Paderborn, 1997); Mark Edward Ruff, *The Wayward Flock: Catholic Youth in Postwar West Germany, 1945–1965* (Chapel Hill, NC, 2005).

34. Jonathan Sperber, *The Kaiser's Voters: Electors and Elections in Imperial Germany* (Cambridge, 1997); Helmut Walser Smith and C Clark, "The Fate of Nathan," in *Protestants, Catholics, and Jews in Germany, 1800–1914*, ed. HW Smith (Oxford, 2001), 8–12.

35. Thomas Forster, *Priester in Zeiten des Umbruchs. Identität und Lebenswelt des katholischen Pfarrklerus in Oberbayern 1918 bis 1945* (Göttingen, 2014), 19–22, 39–44; Derek Hastings, *Catholicism and the Roots of Nazism: Religious Identity and National Socialism* (Oxford, 2010).

36. Benjamin Ziemann, *Encounters with Modernity: The Catholic Church in West Germany, 1945–1975*, trans. Andrew Evans (New York, 2014), 1–20.

37. Mark Edward Ruff, "Integrating Religion into the Historical Mainstream: Recent Literature on Religion in the Federal Republic of Germany," *Central European History* 42 (2009): 330–31.

38. Christian Schmidtmann, *Katholische Studierende 1945–1973. Ein Beitrag zur Kultur- und Sozialgeschichte der Bundesrepublik Deutschland* (Paderborn, 2005).

39. Hannig, *Die Religion der Öffentlichkeit*, 7–41.

40. Thomas Großbölting and Klaus Große Kracht, "Religion inder Bundesrepublik Deutschland. Eine Einleitung," *Zeithistorische Forschungen/Studies in Contemporary History* 7, no. 3 (2010), www.zeithistosche-forschunen.de.

41. Thomas Großbölting, *Der verlorene Himmel. Glaube in Deutschland seit 1945* (Göttingen, 2013).

42. Jean-François Lyotard, *The Postmodern Condition: A Report on Knowledge* (Manchester, 1984), xxiv.

43. See David Carr, *Time, Narrative, and History* (Bloomington, IN, 1986).

44. See Paul Ricouer, *Time and Narrative*, Vol. 1, trans. Kathleen McLaughlin and David Pellauer (Chicago, 1990).

45. Tschannen, "A History of the Secularization Issue."

Bibliography

Altgeld, Wolfgang. *Katholizismus, Protestantismus, Judentum: Über religios begründete Gegensätze und nationalreligiöse Ideen in der Geschichte des deutschen Nationalismus.* Mainz: Grünewald, 1992.

Anderson, Margaret Lavinia. "Piety and Politics: Recent Work on German Catholicism." *The Journal of Modern History* 63 (1991): 681–716.

Arbeitskreis für kirchliche Zeitgeschichte (AKKZG), Münster. "Katholiken zwischen Tradition und Moderne. Das katholische Milieu als Forschungsaufgabe." *Westfälische Forschungen* 43 (1993): 592–93.

Blessing, Werner. *Staat und Kirche in der Gesellschaft. Institutionelle Authorität und mentaler Wandel in Bayern während des 19. Jahrhunderts.* Göttingen: Vandenhoeck & Ruprecht, 1982.

Bonhoeffer, Dietrich. *Letters and Papers from Prison: The Enlarged Edition,* edited by Eberhard Bethge. New York: Macmillan, 1953.

Carr, David. *Time, Narrative, and History.* Bloomington: Indiana University Press, 1986.

Casanova, José. *Public Religions in the Modern World.* Chicago: University of Chicago Press, 1994.

———. "Public Religions Revisited." In *Public Religions Revisited,* edited by Hent de Vries, 101–19. New York: Fordham, 2008.

Cox, Jeffrey. "Master Narratives of Long-Term Religious Change." In *The Decline of Christendom in Western Europe, 1750–2000,* edited by Hugh Mcleod and Werner Ustorf, 205–7. Cambridge: Cambridge University Press, 2003.

Dahrendorf, Ralf. *Society and Democracy in Germany.* Garden City, NY: Anchor Books, 1969.

Damberg, Wilhelm. *Abschied von Milieu? Katholizismus im Bistum Münster und in den Niederlanden 1945–1980.* Paderborn: F Schöningh, 1997.

Evangelische Kirche in Deutschland. "Beschlüsse. Kundgebung zum Schwerpunktthema 'Reden von Gott in der Welt—Der missionarische Auftrag der Kirche an der Schwelle zum 3. Jahrtausend.'" 11 November 1999. Retrieved from http://www.ekd.de/synode99/beschluesse_kundgebung.html.

Fischen, Klaus, et al. *Die Politisierung des Protestantismus. Entwicklungen in der Bundesrepublik Deutschland während der 1960er und 70er Jahre.* Göttingen: Vandenhoeck & Ruprecht, 2011.

Forster, Thomas. *Priester in Zeiten des Umbruchs. Identität und Lebenswelt des katholischen Pfarrklerus in Oberbayern 1918 bis 1945.* Göttingen: Vandenhoek & Ruprecht, 2014.

Gabriel, Karl. "Jenseits von Säkularisierung und Wiederkehr der Götter." *Aus Politik und Zeitgeschichte,* 12 December 2008.

Gaius, Manfred, and Hartmut Lehmann, eds. *Nationalprotestantische Mentalitäten. Konturen, Entwicklungslinien und Umbrüche eines Weltbildes.* Göttingen: Vandenhoeck & Ruprecht, 2005.

Greschat, Martin. "Protestantismus und Evangelische Kirche in den 60er Jahren." In *Dynamische Zeiten. Die 60er Jahre in den beiden deutschen Gesellschaften,* edited by Axel Schildt, Detlef Siegfried, and Karl Christian Lammers, 544–81. Hamburg: Christians, 2000.

Großbölting, Thomas. *Der verlorene Himmel. Glaube in Deutschland seit 1945.* Göttingen: Vandenhoek & Ruprecht, 2013.

Großbölting, Thomas, and Klaus Große Kracht. "Religion inder Bundesrepublik Deutschland. Eine Einleitung." *Zeithistorische Forschungen/Studies in Contemporary History* 7, no. 3 (2010). Retrieved from www.zeithistosche-forschunen.de.

Hager, Angela. "Rudi Dutschke: Radikal Fromm." In *Frömmigkeit—Theologie— Frömmigkeitstheologie. Contributions to European Church History,* edited by Gudrun Litz, Heidrun Munzert, and Roland Liebenberg, 779–96. Leiden: Brill, 2005.

Hannig, Nicolai. *Die Religion der Öffentlichkeit. Kirche, Religion und Medien in der Bundesrepublik 1945–1980.* Göttingen: Wallstein Verlag, 2010.

Hastings, Derek. *Catholicism and the Roots of Nazism: Religious Identity and National Socialism.* Oxford: Oxford University Press, 2010.

Heilbronner, Oded. *Catholicism, Political Culture, and the Countryside: A Social History of the Nazi Party in the Countryside.* Ann Arbor: University of Michigan Press, 1998.

Herzog, Dagmar. "The Death of God in West Germany: Between Secularization, Postfascism, and the Rise of Liberation Theology." In *Die Gegenwart Gottes in der Modernen Gesellschaft,* edited by Martin Geyer and Lucien Hölscher. Göttingen: Wallstein, 2006.

Hölscher, Lucien. "Europe in the Age of Secularisation." In *Secularisation in the Christian World,* edited by Callum Brown and Michael Snape, 197–204. Burlington, VT: Ashgate, 2010.

———. *Geschichte der protestantischen Frömmigkeit in Deutschland.* Munich: Beck, 2005.

Jarausch, Konrad H., and Michael Geyer. *Shattered Past: Reconstructing German Histories.* Princeton, NJ: Princeton University Press, 2002.

Klein, Gotthard. *Der Volksverein für das katholische Deutschland, 1890–1933. Geschichte, Bedeutung, Untergang.* Paderborn: F Schöningh, 1996.

Kunter, Katharina, and Annegreth Schilling, eds. *Globalisierung der Kirchen. Der Ökumenischen Rat der Kirchen und die Entdeckung der Dritten Welt in den 1960er und 1970er Jahren.* Göttingen: Vandenhoech & Ruprecht, 2014.

Langguth, Gerd. "Den Katholiken geht das politische Personal aus." *Spiegel Online,* 11 March 2012. Retrieved from http://www.spiegel.de/politik/deutschland/cdu-und-kirche-denkatholiken-geht-das-politische-personal-aus-a-819695.html.

Lehming, Malte. "34. Evangelischer Kirchentag. Glaube ohne Kampf." *Der Tagesspiegel,* 28 April 2013.

Lepsius, M. Rainer. "Partiensystem und Sozialstruktur. Zum Problem der Demokratisierung der deutschen Gesellschaft." In *Wirtschaft, Geschichte und Wirtschaftsgeschichte,* edited by W Abel, 371–93. Stuttgart: G Fischer, 1966.

Liedhegener, Antonius. *Christentum und Urbanisierung. Katholiken und Protestanten in Münster und Bochum 1830–1930.* Paderborn: F Schöningh, 1997.

———. "Säkularisierung als Entkirchlichung. Trends und Konjukturen in Deutschland von der Mitte des 19. Jahrhunderts bis zur Gegenwart." In *Umstrittener Säkularisierung. Soziologische und historische Analysen zur Differenzierung von Religion und Politik,* edited by Karl Gabriel, Christel Gärtner, and Detlef Pollack, 481–531. Berlin: Berlin University Press, 2012.

Loth, Wilfried. *Katholiken im Kaiserreich. Der politische Katholizismus in der Krise des wilhelminischen Deutschlands.* Düsseldorf: Droste, 1984.

Lukassek, Agathe. "Kabinett ohne Konfessionslose." *Katholisch.de,* 16 December 2013. Retrieved from http://www.katholisch.de/de/katholisch/themen/politik/131216_christliches_kabinett_grko.php.

Lyotard, Jean-François. *The Postmodern Condition: A Report on Knowledge.* Manchester: Manchester University Press, 1984.

Mathhäus-Maier, Ingrid. "Wie der Staat der Kirche dient. Gerhard Czermaks Religions-Lexikon enthüllt die Langlebigkeit alter Privilegen." *Frankfurter Rundschau,* 2 January 2010.

Mittmann, Thomas. *Kirchliche Akademien in der Bundesrepublik. Gesellschaftliche, politische und religiöse Selbstverortungen.* Göttingen: Wallstein, 2011.

O'Sullivan, Michael. "From Catholic Milieu to Lived Religion: The Social and Cultural History of Modern German Catholicism." *History Compass* 7, no. 3 (2009): 837–61.

Paul, Gerhard, and Klaus-Michael Mallmann. *Milieus und Widerstand. Eine Verhaltensgeschichte der Gesellschaft im Nationalsozialismus, Widerstand und Verweigerung im Saarland, 1935–1945.* Bonn: Dietz, 1995.

Pearson, Benjamin. "Faith and Democracy: Political Transformations at the German Protestant Kirchentag." PhD diss. University of North Carolina at Chapel Hill, 2007.

———. "The Pluralization of Protestant Politics: Public Responsibility, Rearmament, and Division at the 1950s Kirchentage." *Central European History* 43 (2010): 270–300.

Pollack, Detlef. *"Säkularisierung—ein moderner Mythos?" Studien zum religiösen Wandel in Deutschland.* Tübingen: Mohr Siebeck Verlag, 2003.

———. "Wiederkehr der Religion oder Säkularisierung: Zum religiösen Wandel in Deutschland." *Ost-West Europäischen Perspektiven* 1 (2007): 11–19.

Pollack, Detlef, and Olaf Müller. *Religionsmonitor. Verstehen was Verbindet. Religionsität und Zusammenhalt in Deutschland.* Gütersloh: Bertelsmann Stiftung, 2013.

Religion Monitor 2008. Europe. Overview of Religious Attitudes and Practices. Gütersloh: Bertelsmann Stiftung, 2008.

Ricouer, Paul. *Time and Narrative,* Vol. 1. Translated by Kathleen McLaughlin and David Pellauer. Chicago: University of Chicago Press, 1990.

Ruff, Mark Edward. "Integrating Religion into the Historical Mainstream: Recent Literature on Religion in the Federal Republic of Germany." *Central European History* 42 (2009): 330–31.

———. *The Wayward Flock: Catholic Youth in Postwar West Germany, 1945–1965.* Chapel Hill: University of North Carolina Press, 2005.

Runge, Rüdiger, and Margot Käßmann, eds. *Kirche in Bewegung. 50 Jahre Deutscher Evangelischer Kirchentag.* Gütersloh: Gutersloher Verlagshaus, 1999.

Schelsky, Helmut. "Ist die Dauerreflexion institutionalisierbar?" In *Auf der Suche nach Wirklichkeit. Gesammalte Aufsätze,* edited by Helmut Schelsky, 250–75. Düsseldorf: Eugen Diederichs, 1965.

Schieder, Wolfgang. "Kirche und Revolution. Sozialgeschichtliche Aspekte der Trierer Wallfahrt von 1844." *Archiv für Sozialgeschichte* 14 (1974): 419–54.

Schmidtmann, Christian. *Katholische Studierende 1945–1973. Ein Beitrag zur Kultur- und Sozialgeschichte der Bundesrepublik Deutschland.* Paderborn: F Schöningh, 2005.

Selby, Peter. "Christianity in a World Come of Age." In *The Cambridge Companion to Dietrich Bonhoeffer,* edited by John W de Gruchy, 226–45. Cambridge: Cambridge University Press, 1999.

Smith, Helmut Walser, and C Clark. "The Fate of Nathan." In *Protestants, Catholics, and Jews in Germany, 1800–1914,* edited by HW Smith, 8–12. Oxford: Berg, 2001.

Sölle, Dorothee. *Against the Wind: Memoirs of a Radical Christian*. Minneapolis, MN: Fortress, 1999.

Sperber, Jonathan. *The Kaiser's Voters: Electors and Elections in Imperial Germany*. Cambridge: Cambridge University Press, 1997.

———. "*Kirchengeschichte* or the Social and Cultural History of Religion?" *Neu Politische Literatur* 43 (1998): 13–35.

———. *Popular Catholicism in Nineteenth-Century Germany*. Princeton, NJ: Princeton University Press, 1984.

Tschannen, Olivier. "A History of the Secularization Issue." PhD diss., University of Lausanne, 1991.

———. *Les Théories de la sécularisation*. Geneva: Droz, 1992.

———. "The Secularization Paradigm: A Systematization." *Journal for the Scientific Study of Religion* 30, no. 4 (1991): 395–415.

Ustorf, Werner. "A Missiological Postscript." In *The Decline of Christendom in Western Europe, 1750–2000*, edited by Hugh Mcleod and Werner Ustorf, 218–25. Cambridge: Cambridge University Press, 2003.

Wehler, Hans-Ulrich. *The German Empire, 1871–1918*. Dover, NH: Berg Publishers, 1985.

Weizsäcker, Richard von. *From Weimar to the Wall. My Life in German Politics*. Translated by Ruth Hein. New York: Broadway Books, 1999.

Wensierski, Peter. "Aufschwung Jesu." *Der Spiegel* 18 (2008): 38–41.

World Council of Churches. *The Church for Others and the Church for the World: A Quest for Structures for Missionary Congregations*. Geneva: World Council of Churches, 1968.

Zahrnt, Heinz. *The Question of God: Protestant Theology in the Twentieth Century*. Translated by R. A. Wilson. New York: Harcourt, Brace, and World, 1969.

Ziemann, Benjamin. *Encounters with Modernity: The Catholic Church in West Germany, 1945–1975*. Translated by Andrew Evans. New York: Berghahn Books, 2014.

Chapter 8

Central, Not Subsidiary
Migration as a Master Narrative in Modern German History

Sarah Thomsen Vierra

The histories of migrants often exist around the edges of German national narratives. Like the people whose stories they tell, they are seen as secondary to the political actors and social movements considered more significant to the shaping of the state and the national body. However, in *Shattered Past: Reconstructing German Histories*, Konrad Jarausch called for the incorporation of migrant histories more directly into the landscape of modern German historical narratives, recognizing the importance of migration as a factor in postwar politics, economics, and culture.[1] Migration as a "subsidiary theme" in German master narratives, Jarausch argues, discounts the roles that migrants—and perceptions of migrants—have played in influencing the course and character of Germany throughout the twentieth century.

Since the publication of *Shattered Past,* studies have continued to proliferate that have examined the causes and consequences of migration and minority communities, with historians adding their voices in ever-growing numbers. Scholarship on the Federal Republic's *Gastarbeiter* (guest worker) program and the subsequent immigrant populations has been particularly rich. Yet, while dynamic debate exists within scholarship pertaining to migration and migration issues, Jarausch's call for the general inclusion of migrants into broader German history remains salient. That the histories of migrants have become an important part of current German historiography is certain. The extent to which migration is a central part of our understanding of modern German history is still up for debate.

This essay examines the broader dynamics and consequences of German immigration over the course of the last century in order to demonstrate how migration and immigrant communities have both shaped and reflected Germany's internal dynamics and its relations with the outside world. Beginning with the Kaiserreich (German Empire), I trace the topic of migration and German history through the dramatic political and social upheavals of the twentieth century, and explore how, in particular, the use of foreign laborers represented a constant and common thread despite the tumult. Even in the horrifying excesses and violence of the Third Reich, one can see connections both to Imperial Germany's and the Federal Republic's recruitment and employment of migrant workers. And, just as the *Gastarbeiter* program in West Germany broadly reflected Cold War alliances and domestic political forces, so, too, did the contract worker program in the East demonstrate political priorities and abiding ethnic hierarchies.

Yet, the inclusion of migrant histories into the narratives of twentieth-century Germany does more than illuminate continuities. It reveals how migrants and immigrant communities played a critical role in shaping the social, political, and physical landscapes of modern Germany. While immigrants most often reside on the margins of power in any society, from those margins they have exerted significant influence on German life at the local and national levels.

This essay represents an effort to address Jarausch's call for the inclusion of migrant histories, but also to reflect the ways he has been involved in the development of scholarly approaches to and studies of migration in German history. While his chapter in *Shattered Past* constitutes his most direct engagement in this area, Jarausch has contributed to the field through his promotion of transatlantic cooperation and approaches to German history in general and minority issues in particular, his support of studies concerning migration issues in institutional contexts including the Zentrum für Zeithistorische Forschung Potsdam and the Berlin Program for Advanced German and European Studies at Freie Üniversität, and in his role as an advisor of graduate students at The University of North Carolina at Chapel Hill. Through these venues, Jarausch's influence on and support of scholarly investigations into minority communities in German history have been subtle but significant. And so, while not every study mentioned here can be traced directly back to Jarausch, I hope in this essay to illuminate the important consequences his support has had on the field.

To bring migrant histories in from the margins, it is critical to demonstrate how those histories impact key sites of struggle at the center of

German history, or—considering the multiple iterations of the German state in the last century—German histories. As such, I attempt to focus on three main threads woven throughout the history and historiography of twentieth-century Germany: state authority, German identity, and the role of business interests and the economy. Ultimately, through situating migrant histories within the narrative landscapes of the twentieth century, we gain a better understanding of how this "marginal" population has played a consistently central role in the development of modern Germany.

Migration from Empire to Republic

One of the reasons that immigration has been so slow to become a part of master narratives of Germany's past has been the focus on Germans' emigration to other parts of the world. Until recently, leaving Germany— with all the promise and trauma attached to that move—has occupied a larger share of the collective memory, as well as a significant segment of the scholarship. Throughout the nineteenth century, for example, waves of Germans braved the Atlantic to make homes and communities in the cities and growing towns across the United States. While some, such as the forty-eighters, left Germany for political reasons, the majority of emigrants were prompted by more pragmatic concerns and hoped a change of place would improve their social and economic conditions. They entered the factories on the East Coast, pushed west to establish new cities and cultivate farmland, participated in the cataclysmic and nation-defining Civil War, and wrote innumerable letters "home" to share their experiences and insights with the families and friends they left behind.[2] This has been Germany's migration story.

Yet mobility was an increasingly common element of life within the borders of the newly united German Empire. Prior to industrialization, migration within German lands was generally seasonal and more limited in terms of distance. Industrialization, however, attracted more and more people—men as well as women—from the countryside to cities to fill the ranks as factory workers, a trip that many made multiple times, preferring to maintain connections to their rural roots. Indeed, as James H. Jackson found in his study of industrial Duisburg, between 1821 and 1914 upward of one fifth of the city's population turned over every year.[3] While these internal migrants were motivated by financial reasons, Jackson argues that they constituted "a powerful force that changed social relationships in industrial Duisburg, making the city a more heterogeneous place to live," particularly in regard to confession.[4] German migrants were shaping the development of German cities just as they were doing thousands of miles away in American ones.

Internal migration, though, could not cover the growing needs of agriculture and industry. Nor was it foremost on the minds and agendas of German politicians, or perhaps not even what most concerned the public. In this country of emigration, it was the presence of *ausländische Wanderarbeiter* (foreign migrant workers) that proved both an economic advantage and a political challenge. Polish labor immigration was especially charged, and prompted not only conflict between business interests and the state over the employment of Polish workers but also public fears of Überfremdung (over-foreignization). Rural employers wanted Polish workers for agriculture; industrial employers needed more manpower to fuel production in their urban factories. In this situation, we see the beginnings of the clash of business and political interests that would come to define the employment of foreign labor in the coming decades.[5]

A compulsory rotation system restricting immigrants to seasonal employment appeared to resolve the issue, though industrial employers were less enthusiastic about the compromise than agricultural interests.[6] This effort by the state to regulate immigration and avoid settlement, however, did not affect a particular community known as the Ruhr Poles. Working in the mines of the Ruhr region, these migrants held Prussian citizenship, and so were exempt from the compulsory rotation program. Yet, they were also Polish in national culture and language, which made them targets of the government's Germanization campaign. Interestingly, the Reich's efforts to assimilate them culturally prompted a defensive reaction that resulted in the formation of cohesive and separate ethnic communities based on their Polish identities,[7] causing further anxieties about a *Polonisierung des Westens* (polonization of the West).[8]

Back in Berlin, that city's immigrants responded to the Germanization campaign in ways that adopted elements of German culture even as it reinforced their community identities. Immigrants came into contact with Germans and other ethnic minorities in nearly every aspect of their daily lives, and yet "what on the surface appeared to be Germanization, the effort to completely conform to the surrounding German culture," Charles Robert Garris writes, "was in fact the recreation of the community around new (sub)cultural symbols that only partially masked surviving (sub)cultural bonds, relationships, and practices."[9] Furthermore, Garris argues that the Germanization campaign and the promotion of assimilation reflected a belief in the malleability of identity—in other words, the acceptance, among some at least, that national identity was not biologically determined.

At the same time, concerns about a loss of German identity, both at home and abroad, motivated a revision of the Reich's citizenship law in 1913 to one largely based on the concept of *jus sanguinis*. The purpose of the new citizenship law was twofold: first, the state wanted to bar all but a very few foreigners from citizenship; and second, it wanted to promote and prolong the citizenship of Germans abroad and their descendants. While ethnic-based citizenship was not a new idea in the Reich, the state, through the 1913 law, set aside other statutes that had acknowledged both "blood" and territory in their legal definitions of belonging.

The state continued to flex its authority over the regulation of foreign residents and their labor as the Reich entered and found itself increasingly mired in World War I. When the need for labor skyrocketed in the course of the war and German workers could not fill the widening gap, the Prussian Ministry of War put out an order that all foreign agricultural workers were to be kept from leaving their jobs in the Reich. Workers of Russian-Polish background who attempted to refuse the order were either coerced by police into changing their minds or faced arrest.[10] Migrant workers became forced laborers—a new development but one that built on preexisting networks and patterns of employment, as well as on preexisting prejudice against migrants from the East.

While state authority in questions of migration continued after the end of the war, government control over mobility and the employment of foreign workers tightened and became more institutionalized under the Weimar Republic. In May 1918, the Reich Migration Agency (later called the Reich Migration Office and then demoted to a less powerful Reich Emigration Agency) was created to deal directly with issues of migration. The Reich Migration Agency's first interest was German emigration—the advising, protection, and control of ethnic German emigrants—but its creation reflected the growing centralization of state power over both the labor market and the employment of foreign workers.[11] Despite high domestic unemployment, Eastern landowners still demanded the use of seasonal labor. The government responded with legislation for the regulation and control of foreign workers, developed in concert with the labor movement's demands that both prioritized the employment of domestic workers and guaranteed, in theory at least, better conditions for labor migrants. Now, all aspects of foreign labor—from workers' employment and housing to their deportation—were centralized under the authority of the government. What the Kaiserreich had started with its massive state interventions into the economy and society during World War I, the Weimar Republic continued through its "governmentalization of the labor market" and its consequent control of the foreign workforce critical to the nation's economy.[12]

Foreign Labor to Forced Labor in Nazi Germany

Narratives of German immigration seem to consider the labor of migrants in Germany during the Third Reich as something distinctly different from what existed under the preceding Kaiserreich and the divided Germany that would follow. Certainly, the extreme levels of racism and compulsion do set those twelve years of German history apart. Yet, that these workers were victims of Nazi coercion, compulsion, and brutality does not divorce them from the broader story of immigrants in modern Germany. As Klaus Bade noted in the revised version of his opening address to the Joint German-American Project on Migration and Refugee Policies, "The era of National Socialism in the history of transnational migration was characterized neither by continuity nor by discontinuity." "In fact," Bade continued, "existing continuities were augmented gradually and, culminating during World War II, were aggravated and distorted almost beyond recognition."[13] Those continuities and distortions reveal themselves in the defining of German identity, the vast extension of state power, and collusion of business with the state.

A strong and exclusionary conception of German identity constituted a central pillar of Nazi ideology and one that had direct consequences on immigrants and the employment of foreign labor. The definition, articulated and institutionalized in the 1935 Nuremberg Laws, built upon the 1913 citizenship law's ethnocultural basis of Germanness, but went beyond it in its focus on a pseudoscientific, biological understanding of national identity.[14] German identity was literally tied to one's blood, the consequence of which was that it became impossible for non-Germans to attain that identity. While the main focus of the Nuremberg Laws was the differentiation of Germans and Jews, this understanding of German identity and supremacy had direct consequences for immigrants and foreign workers. It established a racial hierarchy that placed foreign workers—and particularly those from the East—near the bottom, and justified the Nazis' use of coercion and violence in extracting their labor.

Initially after the Nazis came to power, little changed in the recruitment and migration of Polish workers. The new government continued to use the mechanisms set in place by the previous one for the employment of foreign labor. Rearmament, however, led to an increasing need for manpower, which the annexations of Austria and Czechoslovakia only partially eased. In the late 1930s, then, Nazi Germany began to shift its focus from intensifying the labor of its own citizens to looking outside its borders for the manpower necessary to step up production for the war effort while maintaining availability of certain consumer goods and restricting the full-time employment of women. By the late summer of 1944, there were over 7.5 million foreign laborers from all over Europe toiling for the Third Reich, three quarters of whom were civilians, both men and women, and the remainder prisoners of war.[15] The experiences of these forced migrant workers—the level of compulsion in their "recruitment," their living and working conditions, their interactions with Germans—were directly affected by the vast expansion of state control over migration and production as well as their place within Nazi racial hierarchy.

The labor of foreign workers—who accounted for one quarter of the entire workforce within Germany by 1944—was critical to the war effort, and while the state undertook their "recruitment," many were put to work in the factories of privately owned businesses.[16] The role of industry and its relationship to the state during this time reflect the importance of migrants in both shaping Germany's past and helping us to understand it. Historians of the period have found industry's use of foreign and forced labor during this time to demonstrate the extension of state power into private enterprise and to show how businessmen's response was a mixture of self-preservation and promotion. For example, when faced with the decision of letting go of significant commercial business (necessary for postwar viability) or replacing its workers who were being called up with foreign labor, IG Farben "never even debated it," and eventually became one of the largest employers of forced and slave labor in the country.[17] In the case of Daimler-Benz, an initial unwillingness to use foreign workers was, by the early 1940s, replaced with its acceptance as a critical facet of the firm's labor policy. By the end of 1942, almost half of all workers at the core plants were forced; two years later that percentage increased to 67.5 percent.[18] Business executives viewed these foreign workers as a temporary, expendable labor force, which would enable them to achieve short-term production goals while maintaining long-term viability. The loss of the war and exposure of the brutality of Nazis and their collaborators would prompt businesses, along with many other German institutions and individuals, to shape a postwar narrative distancing themselves from the inhumanity of the Third Reich.[19]

Guest Workers and a Workers' Paradise

Europe, and Germany especially, roiled with the movement of peoples and borders in the wake of World War II. Hundreds of thousands were on the move, displaced from their homes either as a result of the war or as a consequence of its end. It took years for the humanitarian and political situations to begin to settle. As borders once again became fixed, if not uncontested, two regimes with markedly different political and economic orientations began to govern the increasingly separate German states that emerged as a result of the burgeoning Cold War. Both the Federal Republic of Germany and the German Democratic Republic would continue the practice of employing foreign laborers, and the histories of those workers demonstrate not only how the two Germanies developed along different lines, but also how they remained related to each other and to their shared past.

The Federal Republic was the first to revert to the broadscale employment of migrant workers as a remedy for domestic economic challenges. By the early to mid 1950s, the "Economic Miracle" had created a labor shortage in West Germany, and officials in Bonn decided that a temporary foreign labor program—a "guest worker" program—would provide a useful army of manpower that could fill the positions passed over by German workers and could be sent home once their labor was no longer needed. The state initiated the first bilateral labor contract of the *Gastarbeiter* program with Italy in 1955, and extended the program to include seven other countries over the course of the late 1950s and 1960s.

Particularly in the early stages, the government exerted significant control over the guest worker program, including the terms of the contracts, the regulation of recruitment practices, and the participation of German businesses. The state's concern with the role of these guest workers in the German economy and society extended beyond the boundaries of the workplace, however. Maren Möhring explores the reach of the state into the lives and activities of guest workers in her study on the government's responses to *Gastarbeiter* restaurateurs' business endeavors. Möhring highlights the state's efforts to confine these entrepreneurs to their specific ethnic niche and prevent them from owning and operating "German" restaurants. Her study demonstrates not only that "the basic ethnic or racial order of German society remained largely unchanged" through state control of foreign workers, but also that those workers were challenging that control and redefining their place in German society.[20] Moreover, as Monika Mattes has shown, the West German government and the business community used the guest worker program to reinforce traditional gender roles by avoiding the broadscale employment of German women through the employment of female migrant laborers.[21] The West German government, then, crafted and carried out the guest worker program as a way to shape both the economy and society of the Federal Republic.

Yet, the various participants challenged and weakened the state's control of the program in significant ways. First, West German businesses involved often resisted implementing the rotation principle, preferring to keep their now skilled workers rather than sending them home in return for a new wave of *Gastarbeiter* who would need to be trained. Instead, some companies took an active role in educating their foreign workforce in how to extend their work and residence permits, which in turn facilitated the longer-term settlement the government wished to avoid.[22] The West German state also had to contend with not only its own provincial governments and the governments of the sending countries, but also increasingly the European Economic Community and the subsequent European Union. The education of migrant children, Brittany Lehmann points out, reflected the conflicting expectations and goals of the various parties involved and served to challenge the state's authority over its growing immigrant community.[23] Debates over the educational goals for guest workers' children exposed one of the consequences of the Gastarbeiter program and the shortcoming of state power: the settlement of the so-called guest workers into permanent minority communities. The government's refusal to acknowledge, engage with, and shape that development resulted in significant challenges to the successful integration of the former guest worker population, particularly for the Turkish community.[24]

This increasingly multicultural environment, particularly in light of the crimes of the recent past, prompted Germans to confront and seek to redefine their national political, social, and cultural values—in other words, to address the perennial and problematic question "What is German?" German national identity could not and should not be connected with the Nazi conception, that much was clear. However, to what degree were "German" values reflected in the seemingly alien cultures of the immigrant communities, especially the Turks? Could the guest workers and their children become German, and if so, what did that mean? Far from being a temporary and marginal community, guest workers—by their presence and their active interventions—Rita Chin argues, "forced a major rethinking of the definitions of German identity and culture."[25] Writers such as Aras Ören, Saliha Scheinhardt, and Zafer Şenocak challenged popular German perceptions of ethnic minorities and suggested alternatives for a German identity "distinct from one's lineage or range of affiliations."[26]

Even as these debates took place among political and cultural elites, guest workers and their children were challenging and reshaping their assigned roles in German society through the course of their daily lives. To become "German," for example, one had to first cease being a "guest." This, Jennifer Miller demonstrates, is what foreign workers were doing through a series of strikes at the Pierburg Auto Parts Factory from 1971–73.[27] Guest workers' demands for better wages and working conditions, as well as solidarity with native German workers, signaled their claim as part of the "occupational community." Further, the strikes themselves threw into question "who was a *de facto* German citizen and 'German'

worker long before the immigration population dominated public political debates."[28] Similarly, Turkish-German youth challenged the "guest"
label by forging spaces of belonging that stretched and challenged the expectations of both German society and the Turkish-German community.
Their daily negotiations in their schools and neighborhoods embedded
their belonging in and began to reshape notions of identity at the local
level.[29] Migrant workers and their children, then, were provoking a reassessment of German identity at all levels of society.

As with West Germany, the German Democratic Republic (GDR) faced
severe labor shortages in the early postwar period, in no small part due
to the significant migration of German citizens from East to West. The
sealing of the border and the construction of the Berlin Wall staunched the
outflow of workers, but did not solve the immediate labor shortage. To
address the dearth of manpower, the East German government followed
the example of its Western counterpart and fell back on the tradition of
employing foreign workers, now called *Vertragsarbeiter* (contract workers),
on a temporary basis. It began its contract worker program in 1963 with
a long-time supplier of migrant laborers, Poland,[30] and extended farther
east to Hungary in 1967. Throughout the 1970s and into the early 1980s,
the East German government turned to socialist allies overseas for more
workers, including Algeria, Cuba, Mozambique, and Vietnam.[31] These
"Socialist friends" not only supplemented the East German workforce,
but also served as a stopgap measure against the country's ageing and
labor-intensive industrial infrastructure.[32]

While there are many points of comparison between the West and East
German foreign labor programs, those migrants working for the GDR
felt the influence of state authority more directly in the course of their
daily lives. Despite the internationalist rhetoric accompanying official
representations of the program, the state adopted a paternalist and controlling stance reflected in the migrants' working and living conditions.
In an edited volume resulting from a 2000 conference at the Zentrum für
Zeithistorische Forschung Potsdam, Dennis Kuck demonstrates the extent
of state control, including the restriction of workers to single-sex dormitories, the close oversight and regulation of behaviors both during the work-
day and after, and the curtailing of contact with Germans other than their
supervisors at work and in the dormitories.[33]

The strict regulation of interactions between Germans and foreign
workers reflected, at least in part, the economic interests of the East German government, who did not want the financial burden of pregnancies
and childbirth, and the sending countries, who looked forward to the return of productive, skilled workers. "These economic concerns, moreover,
provided convenient political cover to ordinary East Germans," Jonathan

Zatlin writes, "who could cloak their hostility to miscegenation by citing financial concerns."[34] Those found to have had sexual relations with
Germans faced deportation. Women who became pregnant by a fellow
contract worker faced either an abortion or deportation.[35] State power,
however, had its limits. Particularly in the mid to late 1980s, the dormitory
supervisors became overwhelmed by the sheer scope of surveillance the
Vertragsarbeiter program required, which opened up spaces for Vietnamese contract workers to conduct business on the black market as well as to
house family members with them in the dorms.[36]

Given the relatively small numbers of contract workers employed in
East Germany as well as their strict segregation from German society,
the question of their effect on German identity is a difficult one. The East
German government intended that the foreign workers would have "no
negative influence" on the broader population, and kept them as separate
as possible. This goal and the government's efforts to achieve it hindered
the possibility of the vast majority of East Germans from coming into contact with and getting to know the foreign workers.[37] And those Germans
who did work with some of the Vietnamese, Mozambican, or Algerian
participants in the *Vertragsarbeiter* program often gained only a superficial
understanding of their coworkers and saw instead the stereotypes they
had brought to work with them.[38] Indeed, in addition to tolerating dis-
plays of xenophobia, the East German state used this hostility to deflect
"their responsibility for the mismanagement of the East German economy
onto foreigners in a way that converged conveniently with the xenophobic
and racist undercurrents of German culture to overwhelm its internationalist impulses."[39] The employment of foreign workers, therefore, served to
confirm German superiority under the guise of solidarity.

Conclusion

The fall of the Berlin Wall in 1989 and the official reunification of Germany the following year propelled the reincarnated Federal Republic into
another period of dynamic mobility. Within the country, Germans from
both East and West crossed over the once nearly impenetrable border to
seek out family members and economic opportunities, as well as to satisfy desires to see and experience "the other Germany." Internationally,
ethnic Germans from Eastern Europe and Russia poured into the Federal
Republic in ever-growing numbers, while the numbers of refugees and
asylum seekers also spiked. And, while technically not immigrants, former East German citizens faced many of the same challenges as the country's newer foreign residents. Without leaving their homes, a border had

moved over them. Suddenly, East Germans found themselves living in a new state with a different form of government, different economic rules and relationships, different social norms. The level of upheaval in the new Germany was intense.

It came as no surprise, therefore, that reunification prompted yet another revisiting of the question of German identity. While the former West had been developing a discourse of multiculturalism, the political imperative now became reconciling Eastern and Western Germans with each other, and "foreign" residents viewed these discussions with trepidation. The former guest workers and their children, many of whom had lived in the Federal Republic for decades, grew especially concerned that the new German identity to emerge—the *ein Volk* (one people) promoted in the ground-shaking demonstrations in the East—would erase the gains they had made toward inclusion in German society.[40] Moreover, under the Basic Law, the *Aussiedler* (resettlers) were automatically granted German citizenship and government assistance with their settlement based on their ethnic German identity. Yet, the children of former guest workers—many of them having lived their entire lives in the Federal Republic—were still considered citizens of their parents' countries of origin, not their own. A dramatic increase of violence against "foreigners" in both Eastern and Western Germany threw the precarious position of minority communities in German society into sharp relief and drew national attention.

Grappling with facts such as these propelled German politicians and the public into intense debate about the necessity of significantly reforming the nation's citizenship law. After years of debate, a compromise was reached, and in January 2000, the new citizenship law came into effect that included the principles of *jus sanguinis* and *jus soli*. Fourteen years later, the *Bundestag* passed a law allowing for dual citizenship in limited situations. While these legislative reforms do not lay to rest debates about the nature of German identity or resolve the social and economic challenges those with immigrant background face, the (relatively) easier acquisition of citizenship represents a new development in the history of immigrant communities in Germany and provides a platform from which members of those communities can continue to challenge their marginalized position in German society.

Migration, Jarausch notes, unsettles.[41] Whether in the form of people or ideas, migration challenges established norms and brings us into contact with the new and unexpected. In the course of the twentieth century, immigrant workers and the communities they formed played a vital role in each step of Germany's development. They contributed to the country's economic strength by filling the ranks of agricultural and industrial workers, in addition to owning and operating independent businesses.

Indirectly, their employment prompted the extension of state control over the labor market and served as a connection point between the government, business interests, and unions. Perhaps most significantly, immigrants and their children have served as a constant catalyst to the debate about the nature of German identity, not only by their presence but also their active interventions in those discussions. Ultimately, the landscape of modern German history has been shaped by motion, not stability, and that should be a central theme of our historical narratives of the past.

Sarah Thomsen Vierra is an assistant professor of history at New England College.

Notes

1. Konrad H. Jarausch and Michael Geyer, *Shattered Past: Reconstructing German Histories* (Princeton, NJ, 2003), 197–220.
2. For examples, see Kathleen Neils Conzen, *Immigrant Milwaukee, 1836–1860: Accommodation and Community in a Frontier City* (Cambridge, MA, 1976); Klaus J Bade, ed., *Population, Labour and Migration in 19th and 20th Century Germany* (Leamington Spa, UK, 1987); Walter D. Kamphoefner, *The Westfalians: From Germany to Missouri* (Princeton, NJ, 1987); and Walter D. Kamphoefner, *Germans in the Civil War: The Letters They Wrote Home* (Chapel Hill, NC, 2006); Dirk Hoerder and Jörg Nagler, eds, *People in Transit: German Migrations in Comparative Perspective, 1820–1930* (Cambridge, 1995); Russell A. Kazal, *Becoming Old Stock: The Paradox of German-American Identity* (Princeton, NJ, 2004); Susannah J. Ural, *Civil War Citizens: Race, Ethnicity, and Identity in America's Bloodiest Conflict* (New York, 2010).
3. James H. Jackson, "Migration in Duisburg, 1821–1914," in *People in Transit: German Migrations in Comparative Perspective, 1820–1930*, ed. Dirk Hoerder and Jörg Nagler (Cambridge, 1995), 158.
4. Jackson, "Migration in Duisburg," 168. As a result of this migration, Duisburg shifted from being a majority Protestant to Catholic city.
5. Ulrich Herbert, *A History of Foreign Labor in Germany, 1880–1980: Seasonal Workers, Forced Laborers, Guest Workers,* trans. William Templer (Ann Arbor, MI, 1990), 11.
6. Klaus J. Bade, "From Emigration to Immigration: The German Experience in the Nineteenth and Twentieth Centuries," *Central European History* 28, no. 4 (1995): 516.
7. Christoph Klessmann, "Long-Distance Migration, Integration and Segregation of an Ethnic Minority in Industrial Germany: The Case of the 'Ruhr-Poles,'" in *Population, Labour and Migration in 19th- and 20th-Century Germany,* ed. Klaus Bade (Leamington Spa, UK, 1987), 101–14.
8. Bade, "From Emigration to Immigration," 517.

9. Charles Robert Garris, "Becoming German: Immigration, Conformity, and Identity Politics in Wilhelminian Berlin, 1880–1914" (PhD diss., University of North Carolina at Chapel Hill, 1998), 225.

10. Herbert, *A History of Foreign Labor in Germany,* 87–119.

11. Jochen Oltmer, "Migration and Public Policy in Germany, 1918–1939," in *Crossing Boundaries: The Exclusion and Inclusion of Minorities in Germany and the United States,* ed. Larry Eugene Jones (New York, 2001), 50–56.

12. Herbert, *A History of Foreign Labor in Germany,* 121–25.

13. Bade, "From Emigration to Immigration," 524.

14. Saul Friedländer, *Nazi Germany and the Jews, Volume I: The Years of Persecution, 1933–1939* (New York, 1998).

15. Ulrich Herbert, *Hitler's Foreign Workers: Enforced Foreign Labor in Germany under the Third Reich,* trans. William Templer (Cambridge, 1997), 1.

16. Herbert, *Hitler's Foreign Workers,* 153.

17. Peter Hayes, *Industry and Ideology: IG Farben in the Nazi Era* (Cambridge, 1987), 343.

18. Neil Gregor, *Daimler-Benz in the Third Reich* (New Haven, CT, 1998), 184.

19. For example, see S. Jonathan Wiesen, *West German Industry and the Challenge of the Nazi Past, 1945–1955* (Chapel Hill, NC, 2001).

20. Maren Möhring, "Food for Thought: Rethinking the History of Migration to West Germany through the Migrant Restaurant Business," *Journal of Contemporary History* 49, no. 1 (2014): 226.

21. Monika Mattes, *"Gastarbeiterinnen" in der Bundesrepublik: Anwerbepolitik, Migration und Geschlecht in den 50ers bis 70er Jahren* (Frankfurt, 2005).

22. Sarah Thomsen Vierra, "At Home in Almanya? Turkish-German Spaces of Belonging in the Federal Republic of Germany, 1961–1990," (PhD diss., University of North Carolina at Chapel Hill, 2011).

23. Brittany Lehmann, "Teaching Migrant Children: Debates, Policies, and Practices in West Germany and Europe, 1949–1992" (PhD diss., University of North Carolina at Chapel Hill, 2014).

24. Karin Hunn, *"Nächstes Jahr kehren wir zurück …": Die Geschichte der türkischen "Gastarbeiter" in der Bundesrepublik* (Göttingen, 2005), 528–40.

25. Rita Chin, *The Guest Worker Question in Postwar Germany* (Cambridge, 2007), 14.

26. Ibid., 243.

27. Jennifer Miller, "Her Fight Is Your Fight: 'Guest Worker' Labor Activism in the Early 1970s West Germany," *International Labor and Working-Class History* 84 (Fall 2013): 226–47.

28. Ibid., 243.

29. Vierra, "At Home in Almanya?"

30. Rita Röhr, "Ideologie, Plantwirtschaft und Akzeptanz: Die Beschäftigung polnischer Arbeitskräfte in Betrieben des Bezirkes Frankfurt/Oder," in *Fremde und Fremd-Sein in der DDR,* ed. Jan C. Behrends, Thomas Lindberger, and Patrice C. Poutrus (Berlin, 2003), 257–81.

31. Deniz Göktürk, David Gramling, and Anton Kaes, eds, *Germany in Transit: Nation and Migration, 1955–2005* (Berkeley, CA, 2007), 67–69.

32. Jonathan R. Zatlin, "Scarcity and Resentment: Economic Sources of Xenophobia in the GDR, 1971–1989," *Central European History* 40, no. 4 (December 2007): 708.

33. Dennis Kuck, "'Für den sozialistischen Aufbau ihrer Heimat?' Ausländische Vertragsarbeitkräfte in der DDR," in *Fremde und Fremd-Sein in der DDR,* ed. Jan C Behrends,

Thomas Lindberger, and Patrice C Poutrus (Berlin, 2003), 245–56. See also, Mike Dennis, "Die vietnamesische Vertragarbeiter und Vertragsarbeiterinnin in der DDR, 1980–1989," in *Erfolg in der Nische? Die Vietnamesen in der DDR und in Ostdeutschland,* ed. Karin Weiss and Mike Dennis (Münster, 2005), 15–50; and Damian Mac Con Uladh, "Die Alltagserfahrungen ausländischer Vertragsarbeiter in der DDR: Vietnamesen, Mozambikaner, Ungarn, und andere," in *Erfolg in der Nische? Die Vietnamesen in der DDR und in Ostdeutschland,* ed. Karin Weiss and Mike Dennis (Münster, 2005).

34. Zatlin, "Scarcity and Resentment," 715.
35. Kuck, "Für den sozialistischen Aufbau ihrer Heimat?," 249.
36. Dennis, "Die vietnamesische Vertragarbeiter und Vertragsarbeiterinnin in der DDR," 15–50.
37. Kuck, "Für den sozialistischen Aufbau ihrer Heimat?," 255.
38. Annegret Schüle, "'Die ham se sozusagen aus dem Busch geholt.' Die Wahrnehmung der Vertragsarbeitskräfte aus Schwarzafrika und Vietnam durch Deutsche im VEB Leipziger Baumwollspinnerei," in *Fremde und Fremd-Sein in der DDR,* ed. Jan C. Behrends, Thomas Lindberger, and Patrice C. Poutrus (Berlin, 2003), 283–98.
39. Zatlin, "Scarcity and Resentment," 719.
40. Nevim Çil, *Topographie des Außenseiters: Türkische Generationen und der deutsch-deutsche Wiedervereinigungsprozess* (Berlin, 2007).
41. Jarausch and Geyer, *Shattered Past,* 197.

Bibliography

Bade, Klaus J. "From Emigration to Immigration: The German Experience in the Nineteenth and Twentieth Centuries." *Central European History* 28, no. 4 (1995): 516.

Bade, Klaus J., ed. *Population, Labour and Migration in 19th and 20th Century Germany.* Leamington Spa, UK: Berg Publishers, 1987.

Chin, Rita. *The Guest Worker Question in Postwar Germany.* Cambridge: Cambridge University Press, 2007.

Çil, Nevim. *Topographie des Außenseiters: Türkische Generationen und der deutsch-deutsche Wiedervereinigungsprozess.* Berlin: Schiller Verlag, 2007.

Conzen, Kathleen Neils. *Immigrant Milwaukee, 1836–1860: Accommodation and Community in a Frontier City.* Cambridge, MA: Harvard University Press, 1976.

Dennis, Mike. "Die vietnamesische Vertragarbeiter und Vertragsarbeiterinnin in der DDR, 1980–1989." In *Erfolg in der Nische? Die Vietnamesen in der DDR und in Ostdeutschland,* edited by Karin Weiss and Mike Dennis, 15–50. Münster: LIT Verlag, 2005.

Friedländer, Saul. *Nazi Germany and the Jews, Volume I: The Years of Persecution, 1933–1939.* New York: Harper Perennial, 1998.

Garris, Charles Robert. "Becoming German: Immigration, Conformity, and Identity Politics in Wilhelminian Berlin, 1880–1914." PhD diss., University of North Carolina at Chapel Hill, 1998.

Göktürk, Deniz, David Gramling, and Anton Kaes, eds. *Germany in Transit: Nation and Migration, 1955–2005.* Berkeley: University of California Press, 2007.

Gregor, Neil. *Daimler-Benz in the Third Reich.* New Haven, CT: Yale University Press, 1998.

Hayes, Peter. *Industry and Ideology: IG Farben in the Nazi Era.* Cambridge: Cambridge University Press, 1987.

Herbert, Ulrich. *A History of Foreign Labor in Germany, 1880–1980: Seasonal Workers, Forced Laborers, Guest Workers.* Translated by William Templer. Ann Arbor: University of Michigan Press, 1990.

———. *Hitler's Foreign Workers: Enforced Foreign Labor in Germany under the Third Reich.* Translated by William Templer. Cambridge: Cambridge University Press, 1997.

Hoerder, Dirk, and Jörg Nagler, eds. *People in Transit: German Migrations in Comparative Perspective, 1820–1930.* Cambridge: Cambridge University Press, 1995.

Hunn, Karin. *"Nächstes Jahr kehren wir zurück …": Die Geschichte der türkischen "Gastarbeiter" in der Bundesrepublik.* Göttingen: Wallstein Verlag, 2005.

Jackson, James H. "Migration in Duisburg, 1821–1914." In *People in Transit: German Migrations in Comparative Perspective, 1820–1930,* edited by Dirk Hoerder and Jörg Nagler, 147–76. Cambridge: Cambridge University Press, 1995.

Jarausch, Konrad H., and Michael Geyer. *Shattered Past: Reconstructing German Histories.* Princeton, NJ: Princeton University Press, 2003.

Kamphoefner, Walter D. *Germans in the Civil War: The Letters They Wrote Home.* Chapel Hill: University of North Carolina Press, 2006.

———. *The Westfalians: From Germany to Missouri.* Princeton, NJ: Princeton University Press, 1987.

Kazal, Russell A. *Becoming Old Stock: The Paradox of German-American Identity.* Princeton, NJ: Princeton University Press, 2004

Klessmann, Christoph. "Long-Distance Migration, Integration and Segregation of an Ethnic Minority in Industrial Germany: The Case of the 'Ruhr-Poles.'" In *Population, Labour and Migration in 19th- and 20th-Century Germany,* edited by Klaus Bade, 101–14. Leamington Spa, UK: Berg Publishers, 1987.

Kuck, Dennis. "'Für den sozialistischen Aufbau ihrer Heimat?' Ausländische Vertragsarbeitkräfte in der DDR." In *Fremde und Fremd-Sein in der DDR,* edited by Jan C Behrends, Thomas Lindberger, and Patrice C Poutrus, 245–56. Berlin: Metropol Verlag, 2003.

Lehmann, Brittany. "Teaching Migrant Children: Debates, Policies, and Practices in West Germany and Europe, 1949–1992." PhD diss., University of North Carolina at Chapel Hill, 2014.

Mac Con Uladh, Damian. "Die Alltagserfahrungen ausländischer Vertragsarbeiter in der DDR: Vietnamesen, Mozambikaner, Ungarn, und andere." In *Erfolg in der Nische? Die Vietnamesen in der DDR und in Ostdeutschland,* edited by Karin Weiss and Mike Dennis, 51–68. Münster: LIT Verlag, 2005.

Mattes, Monika. *"Gastarbeiterinnen" in der Bundesrepublik: Anwerbepolitik, Migration und Geschlecht in den 50ers bis 70er Jahren.* Frankfurt: Campus Verlag, 2005.

Miller, Jennifer. "Her Fight Is Your Fight: 'Guest Worker' Labor Activism in the Early 1970s West Germany." *International Labor and Working-Class History* 84 (Fall 2013): 226–47.

Möhring, Maren. "Food for Thought: Rethinking the History of Migration to West Germany through the Migrant Restaurant Business." *Journal of Contemporary History* 49, no. 1 (2014): 226.

Oltmer, Jochen. "Migration and Public Policy in Germany, 1918–1939." In *Crossing Boundaries: The Exclusion and Inclusion of Minorities in Germany and the United States,* edited by Larry Eugene Jones, 50–56. New York: Berghahn Books, 2001.

Röhr, Rita. "Ideologie, Plantwirtschaft und Akzeptanz: Die Beschäftigung polnischer Arbeitskräfte in Betrieben des Bezirkes Frankfurt/Oder." In *Fremde und Fremd-Sein in der DDR,* edited by Jan C Behrends, Thomas Lindberger, and Patrice C Poutrus, 257–81. Berlin: Metropol Verlag, 2003.

Schüle, Annegret. "'Die ham se sozusagen aus dem Busch geholt.' Die Wahrnehmung der Vertragsarbeitskräfte aus Schwarzafrika und Vietnam durch Deutsche im VEB Leipziger Baumwollspinnerei." In *Fremde und Fremd-Sein in der DDR,* edited by Jan C Behrends, Thomas Lindberger, and Patrice C Poutrus, 238–98. Berlin: Metropol Verlag, 2003.

Ural, Susannah J. *Civil War Citizens: Race, Ethnicity, and Identity in America's Bloodiest Conflict.* New York: New York University Press, 2010.

Vierra, Sarah Thomsen. "At Home in Almanya? Turkish-German Spaces of Belonging in the Federal Republic of Germany, 1961–1990." PhD diss., University of North Carolina at Chapel Hill, 2011.

Wiesen, S Jonathan. *West German Industry and the Challenge of the Nazi Past, 1945–1955.* Chapel Hill: The University of North Carolina Press, 2001.

Zatlin, Jonathan R. "Scarcity and Resentment: Economic Sources of Xenophobia in the GDR, 1971–1989." *Central European History* 40, no. 4 (December 2007): 708.

Chapter 9

Protest and Participation
The Transformation of Democratic Praxis in the Federal Republic of Germany, 1968–83

Stephen Milder

A July 1974 public hearing on the Wyhl nuclear reactor ended abruptly when government officials suspended debate and angered citizens walked out. "If the licensing hearing that took place in Wyhl is allowed to serve as an example in our Federal Republic," the Reverend Peter Bloch warned in a letter to the *Badische Zeitung,* "wide circles of the population will lose their trust in the democratic order of our state." Bloch's connection between reactor licensing and the fate of German democracy seems surprising. But in the eyes of the reactor's opponents, whose ranks included many of his congregants, the failed hearing was the latest evidence of their inability to get government officials to consider their concerns. This failure caused many opponents of the proposed Wyhl reactor to reconsider their democracy's efficacy.

Though questioning West German democracy went hand in hand with the growth of antireactor protest, many opponents of nuclear energy emerged from the movement as committed democrats. The rise of the Green Party is the most frequently cited evidence of antinuclear activists' resurgent dedication to parliamentary democracy. In the early 1980s, the Greens worked tirelessly to win seats in local, state, federal, and European parliaments. Though they initially announced that they would serve as "basic opposition" if elected, cooperation with other parties became a heated topic of intraparty debate as soon as the first Greens took their seats in parliament. Already in 1985, those in favor of cooperation notched

Notes for this chapter begin on page 235.

a major victory when the Greens entered into a governing coalition in the state of Hesse. The Red-Green coalition in Hesse seemed to mark a major turning point: the state's new Green Minister of the Environment, Joschka Fischer, had in the 1970s "been a street-fighting anarchist who deemed the Federal Republic so flawed that it had to be subverted—its parliamentary democracy replaced with a socialist alternative."[1]

In his "alternative history" of postwar Germany, Paul Hockenos uses Fischer's biography as the seminal example of the "long march through the institutions" undertaken by West Germany's "disenchanted postwar generations." The long march, Hockenos argues, "contributed decisively to Germany's remarkable transformation from an occupied post-Nazi state into a healthy, democratic country."[2] Hockenos is far from alone in singling Fischer out in order to make a point about German democracy. "Joschka Fischer in particular," Edgar Wolfrum maintains in *Die geglückte Demokratie,* "embodies the integrative achievement of the Federal Republic's democracy."[3] Though both authors use Fischer's biography to explain the Federal Republic of Germany's (FRG) democratization, Hockenos credits the sixty-eighters with reforming German democracy while Wolfrum gives agency to democracy itself, which incorporated dissenters. The rancorous debate over the sixty-eighters' role in Germany's "democratization," therefore, could be said to turn on the extent to which the FRG was democratized before 1968, and thus whether the sixty-eighters nearly destroyed a functioning democratic system or helped "found" the stable German democracy we know today. Heinrich August Winkler takes a middle path by arguing that, "the extra-parliamentary opposition proved what it sought to disprove: the reformability of the democratic system."[4] Yet, by emphasizing the supple strength of the FRG's democratic institutions, Winkler's thesis helps us to see what is missing from whiggish narratives of the Federal Republic's history that end in the establishment of a "successful democracy," with a country that has made its long way to the West, or with the emergence of a German state that is "not only rich, but also a respected, democratic country."[5] With the exception of Joschka Fischer and a few of his comrades on the long march, the German people have no place in these narratives that equate the process of democratization with state-building and the attainment of a respectable place in the international community.

And yet, analyzing the way that people participate in self-governance is essential to assessing a democracy's health. Even though the institutions of German democracy are unquestionably more stable and more firmly ensconced today than they were in 1949, criticisms of the way Germans utilize them are on the rise. In their recent, widely discussed study of "unpolitical democracy," for example, Franz Walther and Danny Michelsen argue that Germans have withdrawn from politics and begun to consider democratic government impotent and ineffective.[6] Critics—including some erstwhile supporters—of the sixty-eighters now argue that the emergence of new social movements from the remnants of the student movement marked not only the realization that German democracy was durable and reformable, but also the beginning of this lamentable move away from proper political participation.[7] Reconciling the unquestionable entrenchment of Germany's democratic institutions with a widely diagnosed decline in democratic participation is difficult within the aforementioned whiggish histories that fuse Germany's postwar success to increased democratization and see a normalized, democratic, or Westernized country as the endpoint of that process.

The story of the antinuclear protesters who walked out of the Wyhl hearing opens the door to another history of democracy's career in postwar Germany. It foregrounds individual citizens' experiences, shedding light on the way that Germans thought about and practiced democracy, and the extent to which both changed markedly during the 1970s.[8] These activists' relationship to democracy was quite different from Fischer's. The rural people who opposed the construction of nuclear reactors on the Upper Rhine, after all, did not begin the 1970s training fellow anarchists for armed struggle in the woods outside Frankfurt. They were upstanding citizens who always went to the polls on election day and proudly supported the Christian Democratic Union (CDU), which governed Baden-Württemberg. Like many of the sixty-eighters' critics, they considered the FRG a legitimate, firmly established democracy well before the student movement began. Thus, this essay seeks to explain how and why individuals who seemed committed to democracy as it existed in the 1950s and early 1960s began questioning the democratic order during the mid 1970s, and how their reckoning with ideas about protest and participation resulted in increased commitment to a more broadly conceived parliamentary democracy. It shows that realizations about the connections between democracy and their own lives and interests were essential to changes in citizens' understanding of democracy and the way they practiced self-governance.

The Promise of One-Party Democracy

The record 80 percent turnout at Baden-Württemberg's April 1972 state elections suggested that parliamentary democracy was popular and well-entrenched. The southwest state was thriving economically, too. Its stunning 5.5 percent annual growth rate outpaced the average across the FRG during the economic miracle; "an end to the ascent is not in sight" reported *Der Spiegel* a week before voters went to the polls.[9] Unsurprisingly, Christian Democratic Premier Hans Filbinger associated his party, whose history he proposed "was closely linked to the history of the state of Baden-Württemberg," with both upward trends.[10] At a campaign stop in early April, the Premier warned against voting for the Social Democratic Party of Germany (SPD) because "those socialists want to institute Marxism, Leninism, Maoism, or some other kind of –ism in place of the successful system of a humane meritocracy."[11] Despite the gradual decrease in Cold War tensions and the SPD's disavowal of Marxism more than a decade earlier at Bad Godesberg, more than 2.5 million of nearly 4.8 million voters heeded Filbinger's warning.[12] His Christian Democrats, who had governed the state for the past two decades, received almost 800,000 more votes than they had in 1968, and won their first absolute majority in the *Landtag*. The potential for widespread distrust in the democratic order about which Reverend Bloch would warn readers of the *Badische Zeitung* (*BZ*) just two years later was nowhere to be found in analyses of the April 1972 election. Instead, the *Frankfurter Allgemeine Zeitung* (*FAZ*) reported that the "most striking" feature of recent state elections across the FRG was "the stability of political conditions" and opined that the result in Baden-Württemberg could easily "have been predicted from earlier election returns."[13]

In short, increases in voter turnout and in support for the ruling CDU suggest widespread—even growing—contentment with the status quo. This was partially a function of the remarkable postwar boom. Even the rural Upper Rhine Valley, which planners classified as "underdeveloped," was—due in no small part to government policies designed to benefit winegrowers—home to a thriving viticultural industry.[14] A lack of options at the polls also contributed to voters' support for the CDU. The Christian Democrats' only real challenger, the SPD, was discredited by Filbinger's allusions to its Marxism. The Federal Republic's political margins, meanwhile, were strictly policed by the German Constitutional Court, which had banned parties on both Left and Right for opposition to the Basic Law, making the emergence of new political options unlikely. Even the far-right National Democratic Party of Germany (NPD), which had evaded the Constitutional Court's scrutiny and received nearly 10 percent of the vote in Baden-Württemberg's 1968 *Landtag* election, decided to support the CDU's candidates in 1972 rather than run its own campaign.[15]

Voters themselves narrowed their options further. Support for the CDU remained a matter of confessional identity in heavily Catholic Southern Baden. Parish churches contributed greatly to the CDU's initial growth after its founding in 1945, serving as a "communications network" amid the rubble of the chaotic postwar years.[16] In Southern Baden, which had been one of the Catholic Center Party's foremost strongholds before 1933, this sort of "parish politics" had a longstanding tradition.[17] Even in the 1970s, Catholic villagers reliably voted overwhelmingly for the CDU while the SPD received significant support only in the area's few Protestant communities.[18] One voter in the Protestant village of Weisweil described her support for the SPD as a defensive maneuver. "Everything all around was Catholic," she recalled, "and so we had to vote against Catholicism, even though grandfather always said, 'The Socialists are bums!'"[19] While election returns alone provide clear evidence of Christian Democracy's strength in Southern Baden, the confessional underpinnings of electoral politics in the region help explain high voter turnout and the extent to which the majority Catholic population identified with its Christian Democratic government.

Saying that Southern Badensians' engagement in party politics and their regular trips to the polls were motivated by economic success and religious identity is not meant to imply that the region's inhabitants were somehow "undemocratic." Nonetheless, these regular voters acted on a far different conception of democracy than did Joschka Fischer and his *Sponti* comrades in Frankfurt. Badensians embrace the CDU because they considered it supportive of their livelihoods and connected to their communities; they essentially accepted Filbinger's rhetoric that so closely linked the party to the development and successes of the state itself. These same attributes had helped the Christian Democrats to build support for the Federal Republic, under which so many Germans had prospered. Because it was so closely associated with the state, the CDU's predominance in rural Southern Baden left precious little space for productive opposition or even open-ended debate among voters. This shortcoming would become readily apparent in the early 1970s as a struggle developed over plans to build several nuclear reactors in the region.

Nuclear Democracy and Its Discontents

Badensians' strong support for the governing CDU tempered their reaction to the news that the quasi-public *Badenwerk* utility planned to build a reactor in the town of Breisach.[20] When the reactor project was first announced in 1970, CDU supporters considered it unlikely that trusted government officials would promote an undertaking likely to harm rural people or their interests; only a handful of locals concerned themselves with the potential dangers of daily radiation leakage or the potential for an accident at the proposed plant.[21] It was precisely because of this initial lack of concern and rural Badensians' deep faith in their elected officials that the struggle over the reactor later provoked a major reconsideration of democracy in the Upper Rhine Valley.

Badensians' nonchalance about the proposed reactor melted away when they began to see it as a threat to their livelihoods and the future of their communities. The idea that steam discharged by the reactor's cooling towers might affect the local climate was the primary source of concern for agriculturalists. Since Breisach was located near the Kaiserstuhl, an outcropping of volcanic rock considered by its inhabitants to be a "unique production area for European wines of the highest quality," the link between the proposed reactor and viticulture struck at the heart of the local economy.[22] To concerned citizens' surprise, simply having the public comment period on the reactor project moved from August to September, when children would be back in school and families home from vacation, necessitated a protracted struggle with government officials. Motivated to show the breadth of public concern by the difficulty of this initial wrangling, the project's opponents collected 59,647 petition signatures within the four-week comment period. In availing themselves of legal recourse as foreseen by the FRG's Atomic Law, rural people displayed a willingness to follow the rules of the liberal democratic order so as to insure that their concerns would be heeded. Their actions, in fact, evidenced their belief that once government officials were fully aware of the threat the Breisach reactor posed to local viticulture, they would most certainly solve the problem or cancel the project.

Though Southern Badensians spoke up clearly on behalf of their interests, government officials did not change their plans to license the reactor. Nonetheless, the farmers and vintners remained committed to the democratic order and stopped far short of holding the officials' feet to the fire. At a tractor parade organized to rally rural support at the height of the antireactor signature drive, farmers decorated their tractors with signs that read "Help us [Minister of Economics] Eberle!" As one condescending report in the Communist press put it, the closest to anti-government protest the rural reactor opponents came was the "moralizing letter" they sent to Breisach's Christian Democratic Mayor, Fritz Schanno.[23] As the signature drive concluded, there were murmurings that vintners would abstain from the November *Bundestag* election, but not even so much as a rumor that these long-time CDU voters might turn to another party; a state of affairs that evidenced the extent to which Christian Democracy had become synonymous with democracy itself in the region.[24]

Government officials challenged rural people's strong support for the CDU by bullishly promoting the reactor regardless of the difficulties it might create for its neighbors. That approach was made clear in an article published in the government-sponsored *Staatsanzeiger für Baden-Württem-*

berg, which described the proposed Breisach reactor as part of a much larger development plan that would turn the "the Upper Rhine Valley between Frankfurt and Basel" into the European Economic Community's new "primary economic axis," essentially transforming the region into a "second Ruhr." To achieve this transformation, the article explained, "lowlands should be held free for commercial and industrial use while the functions 'living,' 'recreation,' etc. should be re-settled to the 'pre-mountainous zone' and the side-valleys of the Rhine."[25] Rural people and agricultural interests had no place in this commercial and industrial vision.

Being written out of their hometowns' future was too much for proud inhabitants of the Rhine Valley to bear. Ida Tittmann, who had endured World War II in the region, recalled having twice been evacuated "to the so-called pre-mountainous zone of the Black Forest."[26] The thought of being forced into the hills yet again was unsettling.[27] "They say that 'Children who have been burned fear the fire,'" she explained, "and we still fear it today."[28] That it was now her own government holding the matches and threatening all that she had "toiled for and achieved—one's own four walls and a roof over one's head" was startling to Tittmann and her neighbors, who counted on the CDU-led government to protect the livelihoods and communities they had arduously rebuilt.[29] In fact, because the CDU had become so deeply linked with Baden-Württemberg's wildly successful rise from the ruins of 1945, this government-sponsored threat to that very ascent had the potential to throw rural Badensians' faith in the democratic order into doubt. Surprisingly, however, rural Badensians' identification with democracy instead provided the basis for their criticisms of the CDU.

The targets of rural citizens' questions and criticism became apparent after the completion of the petition drive, when a hearing on the Breisach reactor project devolved into chaos. Scheduled by government officials for late October, the hearing came at the height of the grape harvest, making participation a real challenge for vintners. Those who managed to leave their vines for the day in order to attend the meeting were outraged when the Stuttgart official controlling the proceedings suddenly shut off the audience microphones, despite a long queue of patiently waiting concerned citizens. These would-be complainants quickly realized their irrelevance to government officials. Unable to express themselves verbally, incensed farmers stormed the podium and lobbed rotten tomatoes at bureaucrats. Officials responded in kind, calling upon a waiting state police unit to halt the melee.[30]

Immediately after the hearing's disastrous conclusion, Minister of Economics Rudolf Eberle, whose office held primary responsibility for the reactor project, publicly suggested that rural concerns might just have to be taken more seriously. His ministry, he announced, "would take the nec-

essary time to study the issues" related to the Breisach project.[31] It may
have taken the complete breakdown of civil discourse, but it seemed as
though Rhenish reactor opponents' well-coordinated efforts to lobby government officials had finally worked and that their concerns would in fact
be heeded.[32] Many local people were relieved to learn that further studies
would be conducted and quickly concluded that any objective scientific
study was certain to reveal eminent threats to local agriculture and thus
result in the quick cancellation of the project.

Other reactor opponents were not so easily convinced that their concerns would now be taken into account. Freiburg's *Aktionsgemeinschaft
gegen Umweltgefährdung durch Atomkraftwerke* responded to Eberle's equiv-
ocal statement in an angry open letter addressed to "Those responsible
in our democracy." The letter carefully described several particular technical concerns about the Breisach project, but it emphasized the fact that
despite a plethora of formal complaints, including nearly 60,000 petition
signatures, a warning signed by thirty scientists, and concerns voiced at
the hearing itself, government officials had provided "no certainty that
all necessary scientific data will actually be collected and published." To
remedy this situation, the *Aktionsgemeinschaft* demanded that the government give "independent citizens' groups … the right to participate in the
decision-making process in all aspects (environmental protection, zoning
and energy distribution planning, information, etc.)."[33]

Even well-heeled citizens in a region long regarded as a CDU stronghold
promoted new forms of public participation as a means of checking the
trusted representatives who had so blatantly failed to heed their concerns.
Confronted with a government-supported project that they believed ran
counter to their interests, the inhabitants of Southern Baden found reasons
to question the strength of their democracy for the first time. Their changing attitudes revealed the extent to which their earlier belief in democracy
depended not so much on the well-functioning infrastructure of elections
and parliaments as it did on the CDU itself and the Christian Democrats'
leading role in Baden-Württemberg's breathtaking rise to prosperity. In
essence, voters who had gladly embraced Christian Democracy because it
supported their interests were caused by its shortcomings to question the
liberal democratic order that the CDU had long dominated.

Rethinking Democracy from "Out of Bounds"

Questions about the ramifications of CDU politicians' support for nuclear
energy became full-fledged doubts in the efficacy of the FRG's democratic
order after plans to site another reactor in the region were made public on

a radio newscast in July 1973. At first, people in the Upper Rhine Valley were uncertain whether this new reactor, to be built less than twenty kilometers North of Breisach in the village of Wyhl, was a replacement for the Breisach project. Lacking any official explanation, some worried that Wyhl might be yet another "pearl" in the necklace of reactors proposed for the Rhine. With so little information about the project, most of the region's inhabitants struggled even to determine how they ought best to respond to the unexpected announcement. Their uncertainty about the proposed reactor caused rural Badensians to rethink their relationship to both CDU politicians and the democratic order as a whole.

In the village of Weisweil, however, uncertainty was not on the agenda the night the project was announced. An organizing meeting was underway in the village within half an hour of the newscast.[34] Shortly before midnight, the Weisweilers sent an incredulous telegram to Premier Filbinger. Their message trotted out yet again the issue of disrespect at the hands of government officials, explaining that the people of Weisweil had been "alienated by the manner in which planning for this mass project had proceeded" and planned, therefore, to "protest against [Filbinger's] undemocratic behavior."[35] The group met again the very next day and made good on its pledge to continue protesting by organizing itself as the Citizens' Initiative Weisweil.[36] The inhabitants of Weisweil, one of the region's few Protestant villages, were predisposed to distrust the CDU, which they considered the party of the Catholic majority; nevertheless, the embattled village quickly became a central node in a growing inter-confessional movement against nuclear energy that extended throughout much of Southern Baden and into Alsace as well. The movement adopted the Weisweilers' rhetoric in order to use perceived democratic failings as a weapon against the CDU.

The ways and means by which Filbinger's government, local officials, and representatives of the *Badenwerk* sought to push through the Wyhl reactor soon alienated Catholic villagers and vintners who had long supported the CDU. The project's supporters pursued their case ruthlessly, labeling the reactor's opponents ignorant rural people or "troublemakers" interested only in "promoting 'righteous popular anger' at any cost."[37] Already in the struggle over the Breisach reactor, the government had alienated rural people by treating them as ignoramuses—even when it came to matters essential to their own livelihoods. A professor of agriculture sent by government officials to meliorate rural concerns had sought to explain that prized local grapes should not be considered a "sun crop" since potatoes required more sunlight to ripen. The idea that this outsider, "simply because he was a professor … had to tell the dumb people where the wind came from, when the sun shines," one reactor opponent recalled, was an insult to proud and knowledgeable vintners.[38] Instead of quieting their concerns, the professor's dismissal of their firsthand knowledge of their crops goaded vintners to active resistance. Attempts to deal with perceived outside troublemakers backfired similarly. Public debates on the Wyhl reactor were meticulously managed so as to exclude any such outsiders. Problematically, however, many of those targeted as outsiders were in fact concerned rural people who just happened to live in the next village. They were outraged to be cast as radicals and excluded from debates over their region's future. The government's damage control strategies created a growing sense among local voters that officials considered them unintelligent and incapable of understanding their own best interests, let alone defending themselves in a political debate.

The July 1974 licensing hearing, which motivated Reverend Bloch to publish his concerns in an open letter to the *Badische Zeitung,* was the final act in what had become a drama of disenfranchisement. The curtain opened to a scene of people from all over Southern Baden streaming into the hearing past two men on horseback shrouded in dark hoods and brandishing scythes.[39] Once the hearing was underway, it devolved quickly into a showdown between agriculturalists, who felt they were being ignored yet again, and government officials, who sought to downplay popular concerns in order to push the project through. As had been the case at Breisach, the hearing's chairman acted with dictatorial authority:

> He condescendingly suggested to an excited farmer that he should simply submit his concerns in writing. Or he made it apparent that he was only listening to an environmentalist's chitchat for the sake of form. Or he switched off all the microphones in the hall.[40]

In response to the chair's obvious lack of compunction about ignoring or dismissing comments that did not suit him, Hans-Helmuth Wüstenhagen of the *Bundesverband Bürgerinitiativen Umweltschutz* (Federal Association of Citizens' Initiatives for the Protection of Nature, BBU) stood up and denounced the hearing as a "show trial." He proclaimed that, "We are leaving and we will see to it that our democratic claims are fulfilled at a higher level!"[41] Silently, in Wüstenhagen's wake, "the complainants almost unanimously left the hall."[42]

The curtain failed to drop. "The *Badenwerk's* shock troops, the police, and 'the big-wigs' on the podium" simply remained in their places.[43] As Stuttgart officials shepherded the hearing to a hasty conclusion before a sea of empty seats, a band of protesters returned to the meeting hall bearing a black coffin onto which they had painted the word "Democracy."[44] Their protest targeted not only the Stuttgart bureaucrats seated on the dais, but also Wyhl's Mayor Zimmer, who had spent only a few minutes at the hearing before returning home. The mock cortege marched next to the mayor's house where protesters eulogized democracy as Zimmer sunbathed behind his garden wall.[45] Their procession through the village of Wyhl evidenced the rootedness of activists' concerns about not only the dangers of nuclear energy, but also the troubled state of their democracy. While both issues were frequently discussed in theoretical or abstract language, reactor opponents connected the problems of nuclear development and the characteristics of a functional democracy with their livelihoods and the village government. As a result, both nuclear energy and democracy became palpable, existential matters.

In its coverage of the failed hearing, Freiburg's *Badische Zeitung* emphasized the growing animosity with which reactor opponents viewed government officials, effectively suggesting that the problem amounted to little more than a feud between provincial NIMBYs and the Stuttgart government. But the newspaper's allegation that protesters had "maneuvered out of bounds" by misbehaving at the hearing was actually an insightful description of their changed relationship with democracy. No longer willing to put up with the opaque and unfairly managed licensing process, reactor opponents moved away from liberal democratic procedure and the CDU, which controlled that procedure. But they did so in the name of democracy. Outside the boundaries of the formal, liberal democratic process, in fact, antinuclear activists added new, participatory elements to their conception of proper democratic praxis.

This transformation began shortly after the Wyhl hearing, when Badensian reactor opponents helped launch the occupation of a lead processing plant construction site just across the Rhine in September 1974. Badensian farmers considered the plant, which was to be built near the village of Marckolsheim, a threat to their crops, similar to the reactors they had now been working against for several years. Outside the political boundaries of their state—and even the FRG—they helped facilitate the six-month Marckolsheim occupation by building a "Friendship House" on the lead plant's construction site, setting up a tent city, and spending time there cooking, talking, and knitting. As mundane as they seemed, and as far away from Baden-Württemberg's voting booths and centers of government as they occurred, these activities helped change local people's ideas about participation in public affairs.

The Alsatian poet and activist Andre Weckmann, who was deeply involved in the protests now taking place on both sides of the Rhine, went so far as to call the Marckolsheim occupation the place where "we discovered democracy."[46] Weckmann's assertion that the occupation protest, which was not only illegal and extra-parliamentary but also transnational, was a site of democratic discovery emphasized the extent of the break that it represented in the lives of rural people. His description suggested that Badensians' understanding of democratic praxis changed from regular trips to the polls and silent support for the CDU to a radical sort of participation in community affairs that occurred when one lived one's life in the open air of an occupied construction site.

This process of democratic discovery continued throughout most of the following year. Local people occupied the reactor construction site at Wyhl beginning in February 1975. After being cleared from the site for several days by a ruthless police intervention, they created an even more extensive settlement there over the spring and summer of 1975. For nearly nine months, they made antinuclear protest part of their daily lives by building infrastructure, cooking meals, attending lectures at the newly founded Wyhl Forest Community College, and organizing Sunday outings to the occupied site. The Wyhl protest camp's inclusive and informal atmosphere brought together people from many walks of life and created new opportunities for dialogue and debate.[47]

After it was built, infrastructure like the encampment's central Friendship House made the occupied site a new focal point in the region's community life. Under normal circumstances, middle-aged vintners and Freiburg students rarely even spoke with one another; collaboration on a political project was out of the question. In the Wyhl forest, however, they were forced to work together just to keep the occupation going. Young people, many of whom were students or unemployed, remained on the site for weeks and even months at a time. These "permanent occupiers" pitched their tents all around the central Friendship House. Local farmers and vintners also played an essential role in the occupation. They devised a rotating schedule that called on the inhabitants of each nearby village as well as members of Freiburg antinuclear organizations to "appear regularly and in great numbers" on the site at specified times and remain there for a twenty-four-hour shift.[48] Such "orderliness and good planning," was considered key to the occupation's success.[49] It also offered opportunities for young Freiburg activists to discuss Premier Filbinger's latest missteps with rural women or to work collaboratively on craft projects to be sold at fundraisers.[50]

The rural people who organized the Marckolsheim and Wyhl occupations did not perceive these actions as attempts to rebuild democracy. Because they did consider them protests against the Filbinger government's pronuclear policy, however, the stage for a confrontation between conflicting views of democratic participation was set. Acting on his own conception of democracy, Filbinger dismissed the Wyhl occupation according to precisely the formula by which he had previously articulated the imperative that Baden-Württemberg voters support his CDU. His worldview had room only for democratic supporters of the CDU and antidemocratic radicals, who sought to replace highly functioning, economically success-ful Christian Democracy with "Marxism, Leninism, or Maoism." In ef-fect, Filbinger cast people who had long numbered among his strongest supporters as the sort of enemies of order against whom he had worked throughout his political career.[51]

Filbinger acted forcefully on his conception of democracy when he ordered police to disperse protesters from the Wyhl site just forty-eight hours after the occupation began. Because the Premier reasoned that out-side agitators were behind the protests, he expected that using police power to clear the site would return the Upper Rhine Valley to a state of bucolic peace. His plans backfired badly. A television journalist filmed the terrify-ing scene in the Wyhl forest, where police attacked middle-aged farmers with German shepherds and water cannons. One week later, after activists had already reoccupied the site, the footage was broadcast across the Fed-eral Republic as part of a prime-time special entitled "Citizens against the Reactor at Wyhl." After viewing the broadcast, even the arch-conservative *Weltbund zum Schutze des Lebens* decried the logic that had led Filbinger to send in the police. The "disappointment in the eyes of the protesters in the representatives that they themselves had elected," the group explained, "proved that the Premier of Baden-Württemberg's claim that these people were all 'extremists' was a bald-faced lie."[52]

Rural activists were taken aback by this latest evidence that government officials considered their attempts to speak up for themselves beyond the pale of democratic engagement. Many found themselves unable to sup-port the Filbinger government any longer. For some, breaking course with the CDU also meant withdrawing from liberal democracy. Josef Aschen-brenner, who had chaired the CDU's Sasbach chapter for a quarter cen-tury, had long held private concerns about the reactor project, but sought "to calm the waves [of opposition] out of solidarity with the government." When "the wife of a candidate for town council was attacked by a water cannon" on the Wyhl construction site, however, Aschenbrenner became "hot under the collar." The loyal CDU man announced that he would not seek reelection to his party post. Along with Aschenbrenner, five of the party's eight village council candidates announced that they would no longer run; three resigned from the CDU altogether.[53] The situation was similar across the Kaiserstuhl. The Bischoffingen chapter "voted by an overwhelming majority" to dissolve itself.[54] Twenty prominent local people, most of them vintners, took out an advertisement in the *Badische Zeitung* (*BZ*) announcing their resignations from the CDU on account of the "reprehensible behavior of the state government in union with the utility company through the brutal police actions."[55]

After they reoccupied the site two days later, protesters proudly displayed signs that singled the government of Baden-Württemberg out for its democratic shortcomings. This attitude emphasized the extent to which protesters' loss of faith in the Filbinger government instigated their broader criticisms of Baden-Württemberg's democratic order. Yet, slogans like, "Germany Is a Democracy, Baden-Württemberg a DICTATORSHIP [*sic*]" or comparisons between the fortified reactor site and the German Democratic Republic hinted at protesters' deep identification with democracy over dictatorship. In one sense, it might seem that by labeling the CDU-dominated state in which they lived a dictatorship, rural activists had adopted Filbinger's own Manichean conception of politics, within which the sole alternative to Christian Democracy was socialist dictatorship. Indeed, their own search for alternatives took them beyond the boundaries of Baden-Württemberg's democratic order, reinforcing Filbinger's association of political democracy with Christian Democracy but also the notion that alternatives to that order were by definition opposed to it. Over time, however, it was precisely this break with the way that they had practiced democracy for the past twenty-five years that caused Badensians to readjust their conceptions of democracy and to change the way they participated in political debates and self-governance.

Finding New Forms of Participation

The brutal police raid on the occupied site, and Filbinger's continued red-baiting, suggested a stark contrast between antinuclear protesters and the liberal democratic order. But the idea that local people "discovered" how to be democrats by being pushed out of liberal democracy and created their own "alternative" to it on rural construction sites implies that "grassroots" or "participatory" democracy exists only beyond parliaments and elections and that it comprises little more than ephemeral meetings and discussions. Placing participatory and grassroots democracy in opposition to one another, in other words, can legitimize the idea that liberal democracy, by definition, limits options for political expression and participation. Yet, the people who organized the Marckolsheim and Wyhl occupations never intended their actions to replace the liberal democratic order. Nor did they wish to create some sort of alternative utopia. Instead, they took radical action to further their interests because they believed that state government officials were mismanaging liberal democratic procedure because they were unwilling to heed citizens' concerns via normal channels. Occupied spaces, therefore, were most important in the long run as stages in the transformation of reactor opponents' understanding of the liberal democratic order and their perceptions of its legitimacy. The militant challenge posed by occupation protests revealed that even rural conservatives could strongly disagree with their Christian Democratic government; an important departure from earlier attitudes premised on the expectation that trusted leaders would do what was right for their constituents as a matter of course. At the same time, the productive, community-building aspects of occupation protests outlined new forms of participation more compatible with established liberal democratic frameworks.

Asked in 1981 to describe the way she had changed on account of her participation in the struggle against the Wyhl reactor, the vintner Anne-Marie Sacherer described how "the discussion about atomic energy" had caused her and her family "to open up their eyes." Her family "came to realize," she explained, "that the values of health, life, and peace are not to be taken for granted." All at once, they saw environmental destruction all around them. The restructuring of local vineyards, which they had formerly celebrated as a boon for local viticulture, was now grouped together with "exaggerated road construction, pollution of the Rhine, and the reckless use of pesticides" as wasteful and destructive. This newfound consciousness of environmental threats led Sacherer to begin baking whole-grain bread, to adopt organic gardening methods, and to utilize medicinal plants that she had previously considered weeds. This reassessment of her lifestyle coincided with Sacherer's changing perception of politics, since she had now seen that basic values "may not even be guaranteed by democratically elected governments." In 1975, therefore, Sacherer determined to run for the village council in her hometown of Oberrotweil in order to foster health, life, and peace.[56]

Sacherer's response to her maturing distrust of "democratically elected governments" was hardly unique. All around the region, reactor opponents sought to take the reins of local government in order to guarantee the protection of their livelihoods and their values. Already in 1975, Sasbach reactor opponents organized a campaign for the village council and took all the seats; that same year in Wyhl, a new independent ticket scored 72.9 percent of the vote. The following year, an Endingen pharmacist joined the Free Democratic Party (FDP). He was elected to two terms in the state parliament before running for the *Bundestag*. The 8,774 votes he received in the 1976 *Landtag* election were the second highest total received by an FDP candidate anywhere in Baden-Württemberg, and a 60 percent increase over the 5,469 votes the FDP had received in that same district in 1972.[57] An SPD chapter was founded in Catholic Wyhl for the first time in the party's century-long history.[58] All told, the emergence of new parties and first-time candidates amounted to an unprecedented broadening of liberal democratic participation in rural Southern Baden.

And yet, all of these new modes of participation were easily overlooked. Even as new parties and independent candidates won local elections, the CDU's vote in the 1976 *Landtag* elections decreased by only 2.3 percent in comparison with its record high of 1972; despite the resignations of spring 1975, membership in its Emmendingen Chapter actually grew marginally during the late 1970s.[59] The protests against the Wyhl reactor did not shatter the CDU. Nor did they permanently delegitimize its politics or its approach to governance. Even had such a disintegration occurred, however, it may well have been evidence of a different relationship to democracy in Southern Baden, but it would hardly have been evidence of increased democratization. Instead, the resurgence of a more responsive CDU that could, for the first time, be described as a party of "mass participation," alongside new parties and independent options amounted to an important shift in the way democracy was practiced—even in rural Southern Baden.[60] Though the rise of a new generation to party leadership positions played an important part in changes within the CDU, Rhenish antireactor protests evidence the extent to which such changes were also affected from the grassroots.

In fact, the deepest change wrought by the antinuclear protests came in terms of the way that local people thought about politics and practiced democracy. Specifically, experiences within and beyond the bounds of the liberal democratic order allowed Badensians to connect extra-parliamentary discussions, organizations, and even protests with formalized liberal democratic praxis. The network of civil society bodies and institutions that complemented parliamentary democracy in Southern Baden by the late 1970s was expansive. Meetings of the Wyhl Forest Community College continued for more than a decade after the end of the occupation. The pirate station *Radio Verte Fessenheim* began broadcasting alternative news and antinuclear information across the Franco-German frontier in 1977; it was still active thirty years later. Members of a newly formed rural women's group discussed the threat nuclear energy posed to them and their children and lobbied Stuttgart officials. All of these activities, and many others besides, provided space to think about political involvement that went beyond the stark choice of either support for the CDU or opposition to not only the governing party, but also to the democratic order as a whole.

By the end of the decade, people who had never participated in a protest before becoming involved in the antireactor struggle were traveling across the country to participate in mass antinuclear rallies. One farmer drove his all-terrain vehicle nearly 600 kilometers to participate in a tractor "trek" from Gorleben, the prospective site of the FRG's nuclear waste reprocessing and storage center, to Lower Saxony's capital of Hanover.[61]

Others boarded chartered trains to a national protest in Bonn, bearing native flowers and reinvigorating the spirit of the occupied sites by talking, sharing wine and tea, and singing together with friends, neighbors, and fellow activists en route to the capital.[62] These rallies addressed not just individual reactor projects, but also the FRG's nuclear program as a whole. On the Bonner Hofgarten in 1979, activists called for an end to nuclear energy throughout the FRG. Emcee Walter Mossmann, a veteran of Rhenish antireactor protests, called for "resistance at every level" from the stage. Though he intended the phrase as a thinly veiled criticism of the nascent Green lists that were winning their first seats in state parliaments, it actually described well the multiple modes of participation that could link the formal liberal democratic praxis embodied by the Greens with discussions, debates, and protest actions occurring outside of parliament. The Bonn rally and the Greens' myriad campaigns during the late 1970s and early 1980s provided evidence that reactor opponents' focus on immediately local problems was shifting to a larger antinuclear project that required a more broadly conceived sort of participation in liberal democracy. The very fact that protesters once again considered change possible through formal channels was important evidence of their renewed—and expanded—commitment to liberal democracy.

Conclusion

Mossmann explained this will to participate as evidence that the population was "wide awake." It was distrust of their government, not contented trips to the polls, that awoke Badensians and accompanied their reconceptualization of democracy as a means of participation in a system that not only allowed, but in fact required them to take charge of their own affairs. Differently put, it was the pursuit of self-interest that led local people toward their grappling with democracy. In order to defend themselves and their vineyards from public officials whom they had previously trusted, Rhine valley agriculturalists began to differentiate democratic processes from the remarkable postwar successes of Christian Democracy. Rhenish activists' transformation, therefore, underscores the importance of the way citizens conceived of democracy and participated in self-governance for Germany's postwar democratization.

The role of antireactor activism in this transformation is noteworthy. After all, material concerns had also shaped Badensian voters' previous democratic engagement, underpinning their support for beloved CDU officials, whom they felt had backed postwar rebuilding efforts and fostered the economic miracle. It follows that simply acting in one's own interest guarantees neither a vibrant array of democratic options nor absorption in self-governance. It was only after they failed to get their way that these citizens began to question democratic processes and to doubt the motives of government officials. Yet it was not the democratic system, as Reverend Bloch feared, that became the object of their protestations. Instead, the CDU, which had worked tirelessly to associate itself with the success of the West German state, but also firmly backed the proposed Breisach and Wyhl reactors, became the object of their scorn and distrust. Reactor opponents saw more democracy as the antidote to what they considered officials' misbehavior. Identification with the democratic system became a means of holding government officials to a higher standard. In so doing, protesters began to distinguish the CDU and its successful economic and state-building policies from democracy itself.

The fact that a "single issue" movement served as the forum for this wrestling with democracy suggests that we must rethink the way we narrate both the FRG's impressive postwar democratization and the widely reported recent decline in political participation. The emergence of the new social movements—including most notably the environmental movement and the women's movement—has been considered evidence of a retreat from real politics and a move toward implicitly less important "postmaterial" concerns. Hence, these movements' rise during the 1970s has come to be seen as the point at which democracy's forward march was stopped and the insufficient participation of the present began to emerge. Yet, by personalizing the political, these movements deeply altered the attitudes of "broad circles of the West German population" toward their democracy. Germans who had seen what would happen if they failed to stand up for their own interests began participating in self-government and democratic debate on every level—parliamentary and extra-parliamentary—that they could.

The broader spectrum of parties active in the Federal Republic today is a clear legacy of the way in which such doubts in government officials' stewardship of German democracy spurred participation. The broadening of the liberal democratic system that began in the minds of grassroots activists and extended into the nascent Green Party's first forays into parliament has brought a fuller and more vibrant democracy, but also one that is more dependent on individuals' interests and thus, arguably, more neoliberal. As a result, these developments suggest that postwar Germany's most celebrated achievement—its emergence as a stable democracy—is not simply the obvious endpoint of a whiggish state-building narrative that it is frequently made out to be. This achievement should not be described first and foremost as evidence of the success of the FRG's democratic institutions, but rather as evidence of Germans' changed attitudes toward participation in public affairs and self-advocacy. Precisely because it is so dependent on individuals' attitudes and their conceptions of democracy, this "fulfilled democracy" has the potential to foster individuals' inclusion in political debates, but also to devolve into apathy. Unlike the Basic Law and the institutions of German democracy, which remain firmly entrenched, citizens' part in fostering democracy is simultaneously a remarkable achievement and a fragile compromise that depends on their commitment to the system, but also their willingness to question it and to take part in debates and discussions both within party politics and beyond the bounds of parliamentary democracy. In this sense, democratization is not a trajectory that has reached its endpoint, but rather an ongoing process in which citizens must continuously engage themselves.

Stephen Milder is assistant professor of politics and society at the University of Groningen.

Notes

I would like to thank Peter Caldwell, Karrin Hanshew, Konrad Jarausch, and the audience at the 2013 GSA Panel, "Daring More Democracy, Building Militant Democracy" for a very productive discussion of an early draft of this chapter. Thanks are also due to James Chappel, who read a later draft and offered many helpful suggestions.

1. Paul Hockenos, *Joschka Fischer and the Making of the Berlin Republic* (Oxford, 2008), 4.
2. Ibid., 5.
3. Edgar Wolfrum, *Die geglückte Demokratie: Geschichte der Bundesrepublik Deutschland von ihren Anfängen bis zur Gegenwart* (Stuttgart, 2006), 479.
4. Heinrich August Winkler, *Der Lange Weg nach Westen*, vol. II (Munich, 2000), 252.
5. Wolfrum, *Die geglückte Demokratie*; Winkler, *Der Lange Weg*; Ulrich Herbert, *Geschichte Deutschlands im 20. Jahrhundert* (Munich, 2014), 1251.
6. Danny Michelsen and Franz Walter, *Unpolitische Demokratie. Zur Krise der Repräsentation* (Berlin, 2013), 10.
7. See for example Götz Aly, *Unser Kampf: 1968—ein irritierter Blick Zurück* (Frankfurt, 2008). The new social movements have been blamed for the "disaggregation" of society well beyond the FRG. See Tony Judt and Timothy Snyder, *Thinking the Twentieth Century* (New York, 2012); and Daniel Rodgers, *Age of Fracture* (Cambridge, MA, 2011).
8. In so doing, it follows Konrad Jarausch's suggestion that historians analyze "the gradual recovery of democracy's legitimacy during the postwar period." Jarausch, *After Hitler: Recivilizing Germans 1945–1995* (Oxford, 2006), 132.
9. Baden-Württemberg's yearly economic growth was second only to Bavaria in the FRG. Udo Vullhorst, "Strukturwandel und Wirtschaftsentwicklung," *Statistisches Monatsheft*

Baden-Württemberg 65, no. 4 (2012), 54. See also: "Im Südwesten ein achtes Weltwunder," *Der Spiegel,* 17 April 1972.

10. Hans Filbinger, "Geleitwort des Landesvorsitzenden der CDU," in *Die CDU in Baden-Württemberg und ihre Geschichte,* ed. Paul-Ludwig Weinacht (Stuttgart, 1978), 5.

11. Filbinger, quoted in "Alle blicken wie gebannt auf dem 23," *Der Spiegel,* 17 April 1972.

12. The CDU's bitter criticisms of the Brandt government's *Ostpolitik* may well have helped Filbinger to reinvigorate the specter of socialism. Bösch argues that a rise in inflation since Brandt entered office in 1969 also contributed to CDU supporters' sense of an SPD-caused crisis before the 1973 oil shock. Frank Bösch, "Die Krise als Chance," in *Das Ende der Zuversicht. Die siebziger Jahre als Geschichte,* ed. Konrad H. Jarausch (Göttingen, 2008), 299.

13. Peter Diehl-Thiele, "Die Hoffnung auf einen Erdrutsch bleibt unerfüllt," *Frankfurter Allgemeine Zeitung,* 25 April 1972. Hermann Rudolph, "Kein Vergleich mit 1968," *Frankfurter Allgemeine Zeitung,* 26 April 1972.

14. Vintners were supported by laws to renovate local vineyards (*Rebflurneuordnungen*), which were passed at the local level, but also by the Federal *Marktstrukturgesetz* and through European subsidies received through the Common Agricultural Policy. Interestingly enough, none of these programs were implemented or directed by the state government. Jennifer Hladio (*Ministerium für Ländlichen Raum und Verbraucherschutz,* Baden-Württemberg), e-mail message to author, 17 October 2014.

15. Rumors that the NPD withdrew from the election on account of pressure from the Christian Democrats or even a bribe were given credence in *Der Spiegel.* See: "Ganze Wahrheit," *Der Spiegel,* 17 April 1972; and "Der Sündenfall," *Der Spiegel,* 10 April 1972.

16. Frank Bösch, *Macht und Machterverlust. Die Geschichte der CDU* (Stuttgart, 2002), 193.

17. Paul-Ludwig Weinacht, "BCSV und CDU in Baden," in *Die CDU in Baden-Württemberg und ihre Geschichte,* ed. Paul-Ludwig Weinacht (Stuttgart, 1978), 86. See also: Weinacht, "Einführung Südwestdeutsche CDU," in *Die CDU in Baden-Württemberg und ihre Geschichte,* ed. Paul-Ludwig Weinacht (Stuttgart, 1978), 21.

18. In the Catholic village of Wyhl, for example, the SPD did not even have a local chapter until 1975. Ortsverein Wyhl, *10 Jahre SPD-Ortsverein Wyhl* (Wyhl, 1985). Almost all of the CDU's officeholders in Southern Baden in the 1950s and 1960s were Catholic, and yet the few "Protestant officeholders at the state and federal levels were far more numerous than their numbers in party membership and voters." See Paul-Ludwig Weinacht, "Die Badische CDU in Südbaden," in *Die CDU in Baden-Württemberg und ihre Geschichte,* ed. Paul-Ludwig Weinacht (Stuttgart, 1978), 205 and 210n51.

19. Lore Haag, quoted in Gerhard Auer and Jochen Reich, "Gebrannte Kinder. Vorgeschichten vom Kampf gegen das Atomkraftwerk Wyhl," *S'Eige zeige* 15 (2001), 88. In dialect, Haag's grandfather said, "D Sozi sin Lotzi!"

20. Though the utility was not formally subject to direct government control, Premier Hans-Filbinger chaired its board while Minister of Economics Rudolf Eberle served as vice chair.

21. On early difficulties recruiting antinuclear activists in the Upper Rhine Valley, see Michael Doelfs, "Erst beim Wein sprang der Funke über," *Badische Zeitung,* 26 January 1977; and "Wie gefährlich können Kernkraftwerke sein?," *Badische Zeitung,* 3 May 1971.

22. Interessengemeinschaft der Kaiserstuhl- und Tuniberggemeinden to Das Wirtschaftsministerium Baden-Württemberg, 28 September 1972. StA-EN III. A 842, 1971–74.

23. "500 Kaiserstühler Bauern demonstrieren gegen Kernkraftwerk," *Klassenkampf. Extra Blatt,* 19 September 1972. ASB "Wyhl—Die Anfänge," 3581.

24. In fact, turnout was slightly lower on the Kaiserstuhl in the federal election than it had been in the state election, but it still increased by ten percentage points over the 1968 federal election. There is, therefore, little evidence that vintners made good on their threat to abstain from the November 1972 election.

25. "Meinungen zur Landespolitik: Umweltschutz oder Energiedarbietung?," *Staatsanzeiger für Baden-Württemberg* 76 (23 September 1972), reprinted in Auer and Reich, "Gebrannte Kinder."

26. Ida Tittmann, quoted in Auer and Reich, "Gebrannte Kinder," 96.

27. Memories of the evacuation were coupled, of course, with memories of returning to bombed-out villages after the war. Weisweil was 90 percent destroyed. Heinz Ehrler (director, *Museum der Geschichte von Weisweil*), interview with the author, Weisweil 23 February, 2010. See also "'Wir protestieren mit Nachdruck' Offener Brief der Weisweiler Frauen an Filbinger," *Badische Zeitung,* 19 July 1974.

28. Ida Tittmann, quoted in Auer and Reich, "Gebrannte Kinder," 101.

29. Ibid., 96.

30. Ernst Schillinger, "Breisach—der Kampf beginnt," in *Wyhl. Kein Kernkraftwerk in Wyhl und auch sonst nirgends. Betroffene Bürger berichten,* ed. Bernd Nössler and Margret de Witt (Freiburg, 1976), 29–33.

31. "Atomkraftwerk Breisach in der Diskussion," *Freiburger Wochenbericht,* 9 November 1972, 5.

32. In fact, Baden-Württemberg's Minister of the Interior had taken a strong stance against Breisach as a potential reactor site at a cabinet meeting months before the hearing. At that time, Eberle had agreed with his colleague that the "possible negative effects of the cooling towers on agriculture and viticulture" were reason enough to abandon Breisach. Instead of "formally repudiating the Breisach site," and thereby appearing to acquiesce to the protesters' will, however, Eberle continued to promote the project in public. His conscious efforts to downplay popular concerns evidenced a carefully devised strategy of ignoring and misinforming his constituents: behavior that reinforced doubts about government officials' intentions and even the democratic order itself. Sibylle Morstadt, "Die Landesregierung von Baden-Württemberg und der Konflikt um das geplante Kernkraftwerk in Wyhl" (Freiburg, 2002), 21–22.

33. Aktionsgemeinschaft gegen Umweltgefährdung durch Atomkraftwerke, "Atomkraftwerk Breisach. An die Verantwortlichen unserer Demokratie." ASB "Wyhl—die Anfänge," 17577.

34. Balthasar Ehret, quoted in Freia Hoffmann and Walter Mossmann, "Bürger werden Initiativ—Vier Beispiele," transcript (Broadcast 7 October 1973), 24. ASB "Wyhl—Die Anfänge," 17517.

35. "Atomkraftwerk jetzt in Wyhl," (July 1973). HSAS EA 1 / 107 Bü 763; ASB "Wyhl—Die Anfänge," 18171.

36. Balthasar Ehret, quoted in Hoffmann and Mossmann, "Bürger werden Initiativ."

37. "Ein Internes Papier der Kraftwerk-Union," Erlangen, 15 July 1974. ASB "Wyhl—Die Anfänge," 2968.

38. Dieter Berstecher and Günter Sacherer, interview with the author, Oberrotweil, 18 February 2010.

39. Walter Mossmann, "Die Bevölkerung ist hellwach!," *Kursbuch* 39 (April 1975). Reprinted in *Die Störung. Tonstück und Texte zur Anti-AKW-Bewegung,* ed. Walter Mossmann and Cornelius Schwehr (Emmendingen, 2000), 12. All page references here are to the reprinted edition.

40. Mossman and Schwer, *Die Störung.*

41. "Weil die Wyhler kein Atomkraftwerk wollen," *Lahrer Zeitung,* 12 July 1974.

42. "Nicht gegen den Willen der Bevölkerung durchsetzen. Brief von Pfarrer Peter Bloch an Bundesminister Maihofer," *Badische Zeitung,* 14 August 1974.

43. "Weil die Wyhler," *Lahrer Zeitung.*

44. Bernd Nössler, "Das Genehmigungsverfahren," in *Wyhl. Kein Kernkraftwerk in Wyhl und auch sonst nirgends. Betroffene Bürger berichten,* ed. Bernd Nössler and Margret de Witt (Freiburg, 1976).

45. Ibid. See also Hans-Helmut Wüstenhagen, *Bürger gegen Kernkraftwerke. Wyhl, der Anfang?* (Hamburg, 1975), 51; and "Weil die Wyhler," *Lahrer Zeitung.* The *Kommunistische Volkszeitung* estimated that 150 protesters took part. See: PA, OG Freiburg and HB, OAG Emmendingen, "Der Widerstand der Wyhler wächst. Die Anhörungstermin wurde zu einer Niederlage für die Landesregierung," *Kommunistische Volkszeitung,* 24 July 1974.

46. Andre Weckmann, "Marckelse," in *Wyhl. Der Widerstand geht weiter. Der Bürgerprotest gegen das Kernkraftwerk von 1976 bis zum Mannheimer Prozeß,* ed. Christoph Büchele, Irmgard Schneider, and Bernd Nössler (Freiburg, 1982), 8.

47. On protest camps as meeting spots, and the role of the infrastructure that protesters build in this process, see Anna Feigenbaum, Fabian Frenzel, and Patrick McCurdy, *Protest Camps* (London, 2013), Chapter 5. For firsthand accounts of life on the Wyhl site, see Nössler and de Witt, *Wyhl.*

48. Die Bürgerinitiativen, "KKW Wyhl" (12 May 1975). ABEBI 2HL2.

49. Die 30 Bürgerinitiativen, "Aufruf!," ASB "Wyhl—Die Anfänge," 3691.

50. "Geschichten aus dem Wyhler Wald," *Was Wir Wollen* 5 [n.d. likely May 1975].

51. Filbinger's commitment to order emerged already during the Third Reich, when he sentenced four sailors to death for desertion in April and May 1945. He famously defended himself by proclaiming "What was done legally then cannot be illegal now!"

52. "Signal Wyhl," *Der stille Weg* 27, no. 5–6 (1975): 20.

53. "CDU-Gemeinderatslisten sind gefährdet," *Badische Zeitung,* 25 February 1975.

54. "CDU Ortsverband wegen Wyhl aufgelöst," *Badische Zeitung,* 25 February 1975.

55. "Nit allem sich neige," *S'Eige zeige!, Badische Zeitung* (paid advertisement), 25 February 1975.

56. Annemarie Sacherer, "Zehn Jahre danach," in *Wyhl. Der Widerstand geht weiter. Der Bürgerprotest gegen das Kernkraftwerk von 1976 bis zum Mannheimer Prozeß,* ed. Christoph Büchele, Irmgard Schneider, and Bernd Nössler (Freiburg, 1982), 38. Sacherer won election to the village council. Walter Mossmann saw her as one of the most important antinuclear activists of his generation (i.e. around thirty years old in the mid 1970s). Walter Mossmann, *Realistisch sein: das unmögliche verlangen. Wahrheitsgetreu gefälschte Erinnerungen* (Berlin, 2009), 186.

57. "Endgültige Ergebnisse der Wahl zum Landtag von Baden-Württemberg am 4. April 1976," *Statistische Berichte* B VII 2—76, 28 April 76.

58. Ortsverein Wyhl, *10 Jahre SPD-Ortsverein Wyhl.*

59. Kreisverband Emmendingen, "Meldebogen M1," 1960—1982. ACDP, KV Emmendingen, 02-163-025/1.

60. Bösch, "Die Krise als Chance," 307. Bösch further describes the CDU's transformation—especially as a result of the emergence of Helmut Kohl—during the 1970s in this essay.

61. Siegfried Göpper and Albert Helbing, "Fahrt nach Hannover Ende März 1979," in *Wyhl. Der Widerstand geht weiter. Der Bürgerprotest gegen das Kernkraftwerk von 1976 bis zum Mannheimer Prozeß,* ed. Christoph Büchele, Irmgard Schneider, and Bernd Nössler (Freiburg, 1982), 133–35.

62. Uli Beller, "Sonderzüge nach Hannover und Bonn," in *Wyhl. Der Widerstand geht weiter. Der Bürgerprotest gegen das Kernkraftwerk von 1976 bis zum Mannheimer Prozeß,* ed. Christoph Büchele, Irmgard Schneider, and Bernd Nössler (Freiburg, 1982), 136–38.

Bibliography

"Alle blicken wie gebannt auf dem 23." *Der Spiegel,* 17 April 1972.

Aly, Götz. *Unser Kampf: 1968—ein irritierter Blick Zurück.* Frankfurt: Fischer, 2008.

Auer, Gerhard A., and Jochen Reich. "Gebrannte Kinder. Vorgeschichten vom Kampf gegen das Atomkraftwerk Wyhl." *S'Eige zeige* 15 (2001): 87–112.

Beller, Uli. "Sonderzüge nach Hannover und Bonn." In *Wyhl. Der Widerstand geht weiter. Der Bürgerprotest gegen das Kernkraftwerk von 1976 bis zum Mannheimer Prozeß,* edited by Christoph Büchele, Irmgard Schneider, and Bernd Nössler: 136–38. Freiburg: Dreisam Verlag, 1982.

Berstecher, Dieter, and Günter Sacherer. Interview with the author. Oberrotweil, 18 February 2010.

Bösch, Frank. "Die Krise als Chance." In *Das Ende der Zuversicht. Die siebziger Jahre als Geschichte,* edited by Konrad H. Jarausch: 296–310. Göttingen: Vandenhoeck & Ruprecht, 2008.

———. *Macht und Machterverlust. Die Geschichte der CDU.* Stuttgart: Deutsche Verlags-Anstalt, 2002.

Diehl-Thiele, Peter. "Die Hoffnung auf einen Erdrutsch bleibt unerfüllt." *Frankfurter Allgemeine Zeitung,* 25 April 1972.

Michael Doelfs. "Erst beim Wein sprang der Funke über." *Badische Zeitung,* 26 January 1977.

Feigenbaum, Anna, Fabian Frenzel, and Patrick McCurdy. *Protest Camps.* London: Zed Books, 2013.

Filbinger, Hans. "Geleitwort des Landesvorsitzenden der CDU." In *Die CDU in Baden-Württemberg und ihre Geschichte,* edited by Paul-Ludwig Weinacht: 5–7. Stuttgart: Kohlhammer, 1978.

"Ganze Wahrheit." *Der Spiegel,* 17 April 1972.

Göpper, Siegfried, and Albert Helbing. "Fahrt nach Hannover Ende März 1979." In *Wyhl. Der Widerstand geht weiter. Der Bürgerprotest gegen das Kernkraftwerk von 1976 bis zum Mannheimer Prozeß,* edited by Christoph Büchele, Irmgard Schneider, and Bernd Nössler: 133–35. Freiburg: Dreisam-Verlag, 1982.

Herbert, Ulrich. *Geschichte Deutschlands im 20. Jahrhundert.* Munich: Beck, 2014.

Hockenos, Paul. *Joschka Fischer and the Making of the Berlin Republic.* Oxford: Oxford University Press, 2007.

Hoffmann, Freia and Walter Mossmann. "Bürger werden Initiativ—Vier Beispiele." Transcript. Broadcast 7 October 1973.

"Im Südwesten ein achtes Weltwunder." *Der Spiegel,* 17 April 1972.

Jarausch, Konrad H. *After Hitler: Recivilizing Germans 1945–1995.* Oxford: Oxford University Press, 2006.

Judt, Tony, and Timothy Snyder. *Thinking the Twentieth Century.* New York: Penguin, 2012.

Michelsen, Danny, and Franz Walter. *Unpolitische Demokratie. Zur Krise der Repräsentation.* Berlin: Suhrkamp, 2013.

Morstadt, Sibylle. "Die Landesregierung von Baden-Württemberg und der Konflikt um das geplante Kernkraftwerk in Wyhl." Diploma Thesis, Freiburg, 2002.

Mossmann, Walter. *Realistisch sein: das unmögliche verlangen. Wahrheitsgetreu gefälschte Erinnerungen.* Berlin: der Freitag, 2009.

Mossmann, Walter, and Cornelius Schwehr, editors. *Die Störung. Tonstück und Texte zur Anti-AKW Bewegung.* Emmendingen: verlag die brotsuppe, 2000. Nössler, Bernd. "Das Genehmigungsverfahren." In *Wyhl. Kein Kernkraftwerk in Wyhl und auch sonst nirgends. Betroffene Bürger berichten,* edited by Bernd Nössler and Margret de Witt: 45–55. Freiburg: Dreisam-Verlag, 1976.

Mossmann, Walter, and Margret de Witt, editors. *Wyhl. Kein Kernkraftwerk in Wyhl und auch sonst nirgends. Betroffene Bürger berichten.* Freiburg: Dreisam-Verlag, 1976

"Nicht gegen den Willen der Bevölkerung durchsetzen. Brief von Pfarrer Peter Bloch an Bundesminister Maihofer." *Badische Zeitung,* 14 August 1974.

P. A., O. G. Freiburg and H. B., O. A. G. Emmendingen. "Der Widerstand der Wyhler wächst. Die Anhörungstermin wurde zu einer Niederlage für die Landesregierung." *Kommunistische Volkszeitung,* 24 July 1974.

Rodgers, Daniel. *Age of Fracture.* Cambridge, MA: Harvard University Press, 2011.

Rudolph, Hermann. "Kein Vergleich mit 1968." *Frankfurter Allgemeine Zeitung,* 26 April 1972.

Sacherer, Annemarie. "Zehn Jahre danach." In *Wyhl. Der Widerstand geht weiter. Der Bürgerprotest gegen das Kernkraftwerk von 1976 bis zum Mannheimer Prozeß,* edited by Christoph Büchele, Irmgard Schneider, and Bernd Nössler: 3839. Freiburg: Dreisam-Verlag, 1982.

Schillinger, Ernst. "Breisach—der Kampf beginnt." In *Wyhl. Kein Kernkraftwerk in Wyhl und auch sonst nirgends. Betroffene Bürger berichten,* edited by Bernd Nössler and Margret de Witt: 29–33. Freiburg: Dreisam-Verlag, 1976.

"Signal Wyhl." *Der stille Weg* 27, no. 5–6 (1975): 20.

"Der Sündenfall." *Der Spiegel,* 10 April 1972.

Vullhorst, Udo. "Strukturwandel und Wirtschaftsentwicklung." *Statistisches Monatsheft Baden-Württemberg* 65, no. 4 (2012): 49–54.

Weckmann, Andre. "Marckelse." In *Wyhl. Der Widerstand geht weiter. Der Bürgerprotest gegen das Kernkraftwerk von 1976 bis zum Mannheimer Prozeß,* edited by Christoph Büchele, Irmgard Schneider, and Bernd Nössler: 8. Freiburg: Dreisam-Verlag, 1982.

"Weil die Wyhler kein Atomkraftwerk wollen." *Lahrer Zeitung.* 12 July 1974.

Weinacht, Paul-Ludwig. "BCSV und CDU in Baden." In *Die CDU in Baden-Württemberg und ihre Geschichte,* edited by Paul-Ludwig Weinacht: 83–112. Stuttgart: Kohlhammer, 1978.

———. "Die Badische CDU in Südbaden." In *Die CDU in Baden-Württemberg und ihre Geschichte*, edited by Paul-Ludwig Weinacht: 195–211. Stuttgart: Kohlhammer, 1978.

———. "Einführung Südwestdeutsche CDU." In *Die CDU in Baden-Württemberg und ihre Geschichte*, edited by Paul-Ludwig Weinacht: 13–30. Stuttgart: Kohlhammer, 1978.

"Wie gefährlich können Kernkraftwerke sein?" *Badische Zeitung*, 3 May 1971.

Winkler, Heinrich August. *Der Lange Weg nach Westen*. Vol. II. Munich: Beck, 2000.

Wolfrum, Edgar. *Die geglückte Demokratie: Geschichte der Bundesrepublik Deutschland von ihren Anfängen bis zur Gegenwart*. Stuttgart: Klett-Cotta, 2006.

Wüstenhagen, Hans-Helmut. *Bürger gegen Kernkraftwerke. Wyhl, der Anfang?* Hamburg: Rowohlt, 1975.

Wyhl, Ortsverein. *10 Jahre SPD-Ortsverein Wyhl*. 1985.

Part IV

Family Histories

Chapter 10

Die Bratus
Sketch for a Minor German History

Michael Geyer

The German history I introduce here is the history of the Bratu family—
Artur and Ruth Bratu and their children Dorothea and Robert. The
story is distinctly German, although the family name suggests a Romanian background, and according to family lore, there is a "gypsy violinist" involved. Moreover, one of the protagonists of my story, Ruth, was
born in the British Mandate for Palestine, Tel Aviv to be exact, and another
one—known in academic circles as Miriam Bratu Hansen—lived most of
her adult life in the United States. It is only Robert, known as Micha, who
lived all his life in Germany, though he would much rather have spent his
time in Crete.

Sadly, the four Bratus are all dead. Artur and Ruth, born in 1910 and
1923, respectively, died in 1993 and 2000; the children, born in 1949 and
1955, both succumbed to cancers, Miriam in the spring and Micha in the
late summer of 2011. It was a pretty tight family, even though they all
protected their individuality in relation to each other and to their spouses,
Micha's wife Monika W. and me, husband of Miriam Hansen (née Bratu).
They ultimately demonstrated their togetherness with their choice of being buried in Prague, which had been Ruth's wish.

Ruth was the only one in the family who had some deep roots, even
though her varied life had led her, thanks to circumstance and not inconsiderable pluck, from Tel Aviv to Berlin and Königsberg and on to
Prague and London and finally to Darmstadt, where she settled for some
forty years. Ruth's paternal grandmother, Mathilde, Vienna-educated and

Notes for this chapter begin on page 275.

proud owner of a goose farm dating back to the late eighteenth century in Votice, halfway between Prague and Tabor in the Bohemian countryside, had died in Prague in 1938 and was buried there. The five of them can be found in the Nový židovský hřbitov in Prague-Žižkov, but under the name of Theiner. Theiner was Ruth's maiden name, a common German-Czech family name that identified her more clearly than Bratu ever would. On the same gravestone, you will also find the names of Ruth's parents, Thea and Hugo Theiner, as well as Leo, Antonia, and Rudolf Theiner (Ruth's uncle and his family). In contrast to many stones nearby, their places of death (Auschwitz and Maly Trostenets) are not named. The one member of the family who was actually born in Prague, Ruth's younger sister Esther, died and was buried in England.

"It's complicated," as they say. But for all its variegations, the history of the Bratus is an unmistakably German story.

Major and Minor Histories

But is it German History? This is a question that would have concerned me some thirty years ago, when history had not yet become the sprawling enterprise it is today. The German history debates were notoriously contentious, but they were also unselfconsciously national. Whether you opted for *Primat der Innenpolitik* or *Primat der Außenpolitik,* the more social scientific *Gesellschaftsgeschichte,* the more culturally inflected general history, or the more universally inclined *Begriffsgeschichte,* the nation was the main subject—and if not the subject, at least the frame of reference within which to tell your story. Indeed, the nation was self-evidently central to the many historians' debates, from the Fischer controversy on German culpability for World War I in the 1960s, to the storm over the Wehrmacht and its involvement in the Holocaust in the 1990s.[1] *Alltagsgeschichte* seemed to provide an alternative to these combustible national histories, shifting the perspective from the national to the local and from the history of elites, "Great Men," or collective subjects, such as the proletariat or bourgeoisie, to everyday people. But the emphasis on the "local" had always, even in the nineteenth century, carried with it the time-honored recognition of the nation and continued to do, perhaps less explicitly than before, but still quite obviously in the early histories of everyday life.[2] The nation established the "relevance" of the assembled stories and their narrative, or an explanatory "fit," in regard to how representative they were. Quite magically, the nation made stories into history.

The scene of history has changed quite dramatically over the past thirty years. The great debate over the meaning of German history in the 1980s, the *Historikerstreit,* has given way to a crazy quilt of stories. Mostly this has to do with the ever more expansive reach of history, whether national or transnational, which has discovered the rich field of lifeworlds beyond the categorical imperatives of *Gesellschaftsgeschichte, Politikgeschichte,* or *Begriffsgeschichte.* As a result, these grand opposite tendencies of the1970s have transformed themselves beyond recognition. But more to the point, the quite lowly everyday life histories and, perhaps even more so, the post-1990s boom in twentieth-century memoirs and autobiographies, have amply demonstrated that life is far more inventive than art. The poor historians attempting to put the cacophony of voices into a sensible composition are hard pressed.[3] There is no ready "small form" for this kind of history writing, with the effect that the most well-received microhistories, like *The Cheese and the Worms,* are written as macro-narratives. Yet stories and experiences have a way of flitting in and out of such macro-narratives. It seems that this happens especially with uncomfortable stories in a "gray zone" (Primo Levi) that are freighted with impossible choices, but it occurs quite as frequently with vagrant stories that run counter to narrative expectations.[4] The Bratu stories are among the latter, and even their gray zones are unsuspected.

Even in the 1970s, though, the theory behind these unruly histories was quite well developed. It just took some curious detours for this thought to be recognized and to be connected to actual stories. Thus, a French author, rather unknown at the time, Jean-François Lyotard, propagated what he (or rather his translators) called "herrenlose Politik."[5] Lyotard's notions of what constituted minor narratives appears quite counterintuitive. The idea seemed to garble the (German) language, which is not untypical for this kind of 1970s thought. (The original French was not much clearer.)[6]

> Man ... entdeckt ... eine ganz neue Einsicht: daß die Geschichte aus Wolken von Erzählungen besteht, Erzählungen, die man berichtet, die man erfindet, die man hört und spielt; daß das Volk nicht als Subjekt existiert, daß es ein Haufen von Milliarden unbedeutender oder folgenschwerer kleiner Geschichte ist, die sich bald anziehen und sich zu Riesenerzählungen verdichten, bald sich in umherschweifende Elemente zerstreuen, im allgemeinen jedoch mehr oder weniger aneinanderhängen und bilden, was man gemeinhin die Kultur einer zivilen Gesellschaft nennt.[7]

It took the foremost practitioners of Alltagsgeschichte, like Alf Lüdtke, decades to work with these wild and woolly ideas and turn them into history.[8] It was Eve Rosenhaft's history, born from the willingness to live with unresolvable puzzles, and Alfred Frei's effort to reinvent history as play that made histories out of the *petits récits.*[9]

Like most other historians, I stopped at the critique of the *grands récits* or master narratives. Miriam Bratu Hansen was in a similar bind. She was enthralled by another liberator of stories, Alexander Kluge. But she was also an upright professional in a still uncertain discipline, Film Studies. Although she appeared occasionally in Kluge's shorts for TV, Miriam's intellect, life, and art did not flow together without difficulty. Desire pointed in one direction—the effervescent stories of Alexander Kluge or the surrealist early films of Ulrike Ottinger—while the reasoning strictures of "Critical Theory" pushed her the opposite way. Her breakthrough came in the lengthy foreword to *Public Sphere and Experience* and the celebration of the delirious movements in Max Ophuls's films.[10] In a posthumous essay she embraced, what she had known in principle for a long time, "the accidental collisions and opportunities … [the] unpredictable conjunctures and aleatory developments—conditions under which alternative formations [of publicity], collective interests, may gain momentum of their own."[11]

It is the small stories that matter, and according to the Dutch literary and scholarly vagabond, André Jolles, it is the "einfache Formen," memorabilia among them, by which they are captured.[12] The idea, the experience, and the narrative forms have been available all along (and not just since the 1970s), but it is only in the new century that they have gained a new lease on life. And who knows, some poet-historian may even forge a history from this storytelling. There are certainly enough efforts of this kind to suggest that something may come of it.[13]

The Compulsion to Collect

Still, it needs an "archive," even if often unconventional ones, to build stories. Thus, it takes some chutzpah, which Irene Dische certainly has—spoiler alert!—in order to allow one's grandmother and matriarch to tell her own and her family's outrageous stories, Irene's among them, from beyond the grave.[14] The archive in this case is ethereal, one might say. In contrast, Peter Schneider bases his writerly recollections on his mother's letters to her lovers.[15] In other instances, a trove of interviews, personal recollections, or other memorabilia like photo albums, even individual photos, become sources of sometimes more literary and sometimes more historical contemplation.[16]

The range of "the archive" used by historians, which for so long remained predictable and state- and institution-centered, has thus expanded dramatically, to include all kinds of records, from state-generated records (such as birth certificates) to private letters, photographs, diaries, memorabilia, material objects, and so on and so forth. Since this expansion of the archive came just at the moment of yet another transition—the shift to digital records—it would seem entirely possible for a thoughtful historian to complete the work of Alf Lüdtke and others and explore the peculiar nature of the twentieth-century archive (in the Western world).

However, this essay does not deal with the question of archives in general, but rather with the peculiar need or desire (and the capacity) of people to hang on to memorabilia. Without "every(wo)man" collecting traces of his or her own past (having the volition and time, money and space to accommodate them), the modern-day Herodotus would strike out in vain. Perhaps there is now less of an oral tradition (stories passed on from one generation to the next) and more of a material tradition (letters and photographs). But what is striking is this compulsion to collect one's own past. One might think that people would not keep those embarrassing letters or those revealing photographs of lynchings and mass killings. Obviously, this is not the case, for otherwise there would not be this surfeit of collections, especially if we assume, as we must, that a vast majority of unwanted memorabilia end up in the trash bin. In the Bratu case, Artur stipulated that some letters he had kept be burned—nobody had known they existed in the first place—and Micha and Miriam made sure they were.

Being the historian in the family, I have been sorting through the assembled records of Artur and Ruth since their deaths. More recently, I have had the widower's task of sorting through Miriam's possessions. Monika W did the same for Micha only months later. All four of them had kept voluminous memorabilia over the years and stuffed them away in desks, cabinets, and boxes upon boxes. Unsurprisingly, in the course of this cleanup, one or another family secret was revealed. It is also not surprising that quite a bit of this material, beside what Monika W and I kept as personal keepsakes, got deposited in public archives. Artur and Ruth's papers and a smaller depository for Micha sit side by side, as minor holdings, with the papers of Willy Brandt and Helmut Schmidt in the Archiv der sozialen Demokratie. Miriam's voluminous papers are deposited in Special Collections of the University of Chicago, where they share space with Nobel Prize winners and poet laureates.[17] Thematically, this is where they belong. But while these functional collections tell us a great deal about what is considered archive-worthy (at least for the time being), they reveal little about the compulsion to collect. And it is this compulsion to collect that gives us a first glimpse of who the Bratus were.

It was Micha who became the keeper of the family record, the sprawling collection of photographs, paintings, and objects, which he blended with his own more lighthearted memorabilia. His home in Griesheim became the home of the Bratu family, although he had spent a young, tense life battling the grip of the past, his parent's past, on the present. This was not yet-another Nazi past, quite the opposite; and yet, like so many adolescents in the 1970s and 1980s, he found it utterly and completely suffocating. He did everything he possibly could to get away while staying in place. He confronted his parents, rebelled against the treadmill of employment, and fought the full-scale industrialization of the environment; he developed for himself a very personal, individual "alternative" way of life—really rather a *joie de vivre* in the spirit of Nouvelle Vague French films (that his older sister Miriam studied), and thus lived a life that his father, fluent French speaker but born into a different age, might have lived and, as some photos from the 1930s suggest, even tried to live, until the Nazis put an end to it. In fact, the more "alternative" Micha became in his lifetime, the more he lived a future that his father never had and never could have had. Thus his taking on the role of keeping the archive was more than simply a chore, though it was that too. It was a choice. Nonetheless, the archive was just that, records of a time that could not end fast enough. Much to the disapproval of his sister Miriam, he educated his two children with no religion, no national identity, no political conviction, so as to liberate them from the hold of the past over their lives, although he himself became ever more deeply convinced that his life-destroying illness proved the futility of his own escape. Even as he built his alternative world, the past had taken root in his body, and this poison destroyed him.[18]

Older and more responsible than Micha, Miriam was engaged in quite different battles. Her studies in the nearby University of Frankfurt could still be seen as tribute to her father, who had studied there in the early 1930s, though he had no truck with his daughter studying or in any case felt she would have to do it pretty much with her own money. (The malicious story is— we are here among Social Democrats of the first postwar generation—that Miriam applied for a fellowship from the Social Democratic Party (SPD)-oriented Friedrich Ebert Stiftung, whereupon the treasurer of the SPD contacted her father and fellow party member to admonish him not to be so stingy with his daughter.) She persisted nevertheless, but she also did what good daughters had done for a long time; she married early. And while it was pure love, the sting was that her long-haired, Frankfurt-style revolutionary husband came from a family with impeccable Nazi credentials. It was the last time that she took another man's name, but the name stuck. Miriam came to own it.

None of these family squabbles kept her from getting deeply involved in preserving her family's stories. She initiated and conducted interviews with both her parents and would have interviewed her brother if he had let her. She brought her mother to the attention of Deborah Dwork, who subsequently interviewed her as well. This thorough and professional interview was just one among others at the time, because Ruth's life story was in demand.[19] Miriam's interest was in part personal. Her parents' life stories had that vagrant quality Lyotard alluded to, which both fascinated and irritated her. But Miriam's family labors also became the consuming interest of her academic pursuits. She was possessed by the task of preserving and presenting in its pristine form the tradition of German-Jewish thought—foremost, Siegfried Kracauer and Walter Benjamin—to the point of becoming a philological shrew in the minds of some of her colleagues.[20] But this also entailed a mischaracterization. She was not a *Vergangenheitsbewältigerin* and not concerned with philological accuracy as such. Rather her commitment to the past—the destroyed past of German–Jewish (intellectual) life—served the end of moving on with this legacy and beyond it. She felt their thought was the treasure, her treasure, which needed recovery in order to think about the future. Alexander Kluge made this solicitude for the *futur antérieur* into Miriam's persona on TV.[21] Reinhart Koselleck's *Future's Past* parallels Miriam's actualization of the past, although Koselleck took a different and treacherous route.[22] Recollecting the past in order to set free the future became "the" German enterprise of the last quarter of the twentieth century.

Then again, you cannot easily historicize the Bratus. Xinyu Dong, one of Miriam's younger colleagues in the Department of Cinema and Media Studies, captured this fact in a telling, if roundabout way. She was struck by the foreword to *Cinema and Experience,* which revealed a German Miriam Bratu Hansen that was a shock to her American friends who had known her as a consummate academic, though her existence as a rebellious student, as Hausfrau and radical feminist, as Critical Theorist, as well as Ezra Pound expert, came as less of a surprise for her German contemporaries. Like her brother and an entire generation of young Germans, she had to explode the world she lived in in order to breathe. She chose to leave an academic career in Germany. And yet, Miriam did what her parents had done before. Through the various stations of her life, she carried box upon box of letters, photographs, and objects—no real secrets there, but lives unknown that she had lived at some point. She preserved the traces of these lives, one must presume, for fear she might forget or because she needed memorabilia to remember what she had been and could have become. She carefully preserved the archive of her vagrant lives, while making the transition from a dutiful German daughter into a formidable transatlantic presence.

We know nothing yet about her parents, Artur and Ruth, except that there is a hidden story beneath their existence in Darmstadt, where they lived for half their lives, between 1949 and 1993/2000. Their life journeys were far more dramatic and existential than anything the children experienced. Above all, they were more accidental, dependent on luck and circumstance, and more cruel. Not least, the stations along the way and the outcomes were far more ironic than even fiction might allow—though their respective stories were not more unusual in their absurdity than other such stories that have been coming to light.

But how do we know? Well, Artur left behind a suitcase of memorabilia, with photos and even exam papers, when he fled before the onslaught of the Third Reich, and Ruth carried along in her suitcase some memorabilia from the childhood she left behind in 1939. The content of these suitcases ended up stored in boxes in the basement in Darmstadt after the war, many of them never opened again until I got involved in the suitably professional role of sorting through the material upon Artur and Ruth's deaths. I did what many other Germans did at about the same time and what historians came to pursue as a new way of doing history.[23] But for Artur and Ruth, and Miriam and Micha, their memorabilia were not records, they were the traces that gave them the chance to preserve unity and identity in fractured existences, broken genealogies, and vagrant memories. As situations and circumstances changed, they lived through it all, and they needed their own archive as memory palace.[24] Much as with the original memory palace, the objects of the archive always referred to a fully lived reality. The historian cannot possibly reconstruct the fullness of this reality. But they can capture stories and see how they might stack up on a storyboard, while they flit in and out of old and new *grands récits* of German history.

Bratu: What's in a Name?

Ruth met Artur in Offenbach in 1946. At the time, she was in American uniform, working for the Civil Censorship Detachment of the U.S. Army in Frankfurt. She had just recently married Ernst(l) P., whom she tended to introduce (entirely truthfully, but not quite to the point) as the younger brother of a friend from back in Prague. She swept Artur off his feet—or so we must presume, because Artur's collection of lovingly inscribed photo portraits of young women from Germany, Belgium, and England suggests that he was quite the lady's man. In 1945, Artur was a Warrant Officer in British Intelligence, stationed in Bad Oeynhausen, with the opportunity to become a British citizen. He went by the name of Arthur Edgar Bennett and had returned to his native city of Offenbach to visit his family. However, his family name was assuredly not Bennett, but neither was it Bratu.[25]

Artur was a man of many names—and what initially had been dint of circumstance eventually became a choice and in the end something of a joke. The story is simple enough. Artur was born in 1910, the son of an unwed mother, who worked as a maid in the home of one of the many leather-goods factory owners in Offenbach. He got his first name from his father, except that there were two Arturs, Sr and Jr, and later in life Artur, the son, led everyone to think it remained unclear who his father was. In actual fact, Artur knew who his father was and made every effort to find him, but when he finally discovered the whereabouts of his father, Artur Jr, in Paris in the 1970s, the latter refused to see him or even respond to his inquiries. Then again, at least his father's first name was Artur. But he was not a Bratu either.

His unwed mother had given away her son, much as she gave away a second, younger child, Lene, Artur's half-sister, whom she had with a man whom everyone described as a good-for-nothing, working-class dandy. Artur was fostered by a loving working-class family, who needed the money that came with foster care. Thus, Artur acquired his first last name, only to be rudely reminded when he entered elementary school that legally he still carried the name of his mother (or so Artur told the story). The teacher had called up a certain Artur K, who did not promptly respond, because he knew himself as Artur E, and instantly got a first reprimand. He stuck with K as a last name for the time being.

Artur came to acquire the name Bratu, when his mother finally married, and his stepfather, a Bratu, formally adopted him. But that was not a straightforward affair either. The story Artur told was that there were actually two brothers Bratu and—Wendy Doniger would be tickled to know[26]—it was unclear, which of the two the actual stepfather was. One or both of them played the violin and posed as gypsy violinists, and they were, photos testify to the fact, upstanding coffeehouse owners in Bochum, one of the hard-scrabble working-class cities of the industrial Ruhr Valley. On surviving photos, father Bratu looks like a proper proprietor with a fine bourgeois establishment, except that we do not quite know whether it is him or his brother and who is the proprietor and who is not. Artur in any case preferred his stepfather on the wild side of life and cherished the gypsy act, of which there are enough photos to suggest that there is some truth to this loopy story. Curiously, Bratu became Artur's last last name, firmly and permanently, only in Darmstadt after the war. That is, as he settled in postwar Germany for good, Artur thus took on a distinctly "foreign" last name; it is Romanian and commonly identified as a Jewish last name. For Artur "Bratu" was the identity he held on to. It was a German identity, but not too much of one.

It was Miriam who was most enthralled by the idea that her grandfather was a gypsy and coffeehouse violinist (and later on in the spirit of Doniger's Bedtrick that there was not one but two of them). Her exoticism was less a prejudice than a reflection of her own early sense of estrangement. The foreign name was the least of the Bratus' problems in Darmstadt in the 1950s. After all, they had arrived from England in a town that was destroyed by the British. On top of it, Miriam happened to be a redhead and liked to play with the other redheads—gypsy children who lived in public housing next door to where she and Micha grew up on the outskirts of the town, on the top floor of the local school. The accommodation was a privilege of the newly minted school inspector Artur Bratu, because the town had been firebombed, and housing was exceedingly scarce. Needless to say, their neighbors, the gypsies, lived in rundown former barracks.

Artur stuck to the name, but the history and memory attached to the name turned out to be bittersweet. He had acquired a (step)father. But he could not have known him very well, because his birth mother and stepfather moved on to Rotterdam in the early 1930s. This is where the three met in the mid-1930s under once more changed circumstances. According to Artur, his mother had at that point become an avid Nazi sympathizer. After sitting through a radio speech by Goebbels or Göring during his visit, Artur decided to shun her. His mother eventually returned to Frankfurt after the (apparently natural) death of her husband in 1941, about a year after the German bombing of the city, where she proceeded to marry a policeman and settled nearby. Artur never again visited his mother until his sister Lene begged him to see her on her death bed. His mother's double betrayal, personal and political, haunted him for life. Much as he acquired a patronym without a father, he had lost his mother to the Nazis—if not in Offenbach, then surely in Rotterdam.

I cannot help but think that class also played a role in the disenchantment of a son with a mother who had developed Nazi sympathies. It would be hard to prove, because due to Artur's boycott we know next to nothing about his mother. But Lene's recollections, both oral and unrecorded, fill some of the void. Nazi sympathies could not have been quite the whole story, even as one would wish they were. Artur could be quite forgiving insofar as Nazis were concerned. Most egregiously, in the 1930s, his beloved half-sister had married a fellow worker who joined the *Ordnungspolizei* (ORPO or the "Green Police") to escape the military and promptly ended up in Eastern Poland, where police forces played a central role in terrorizing the local population and carrying out the Holocaust. As Lene told this story, on a warm afternoon in her small working-class apartment in Offenbach after Artur's death, she clearly intimated her awareness of the mass murder and recollected one of the more egregious atrocities she knew. Artur was aware of this history, she said, but he embraced his sister though he never forgave his mother. His sister was old-fashioned Offenbach working class. On that sunny day in Offenbach, her memory of the Nazis revolted her, but this was what life had served up to her, like so much else.

Artur saw himself in a similar light, though his life's servings were rad-ically different. But that difference did not exculpate him as we shall see. As to his mother, who had moved from a poor rural background in Hes-sen to the big city of Offenbach, like so many young girls before World War I, and had found good employment, it was her dream of respect and, as Artur explained (and Lene confirmed), her pursuit of righteousness that made reconciliation extra difficult. She was anything but the way-ward woman with two illegitimate children with two different fathers — or, rather, she was, but that was not what she wanted to be and not the way she saw herself. She wanted respect, and she found it with the Nazis, as Lene explained. Artur was dead, when Lene told the story. It was one of those moments when an ethereal communication would have helped. What on earth did Artur think? Miriam had a sensible psychological inter-pretation, while I would have preferred an Arendtian one. But those are typical second-generation efforts to make sense of (and to escape from) a moral dilemma that in one way or the other all Germans faced. Miriam and Micha were sheltered by the choices Ruth and Artur, their parents, made, but they lived in Germany and among Germans and were Ger-mans, and that was, for a seemingly endless time, to live with not just any Nazi past, but your own traces of a Nazi inheritance.

We have seen how Micha and Miriam came up for air and developed a lifestyle. We also know or, in any case, can interpret Artur's behavior. He liked and loudly proclaimed his working-class credentials — and a racket he made in every way. He was not polite in a society that was walking on egg shells, and while it could be said that he was truth-saying, he was often enough just letting off steam. It was neither his taste nor his political creed that led him to play the *Internationale* to Sunday churchgoers in the early 1950s, but it was the attitude of a proletarian *Bürgerschreck* — even though he had turned into a paragon of upward mobility in the postwar Federal Republic, and in the end even got a street named after him in Darmstadt, although the street is very short.

But then there is a history to be reckoned with. Artur's achievements were substantial and in many ways quite extraordinary, but postwar suc-cess came on the ruins of his previous existence. You could say the same for many, if not most Germans, because so many lives and life projects got destroyed — physically, morally, politically, and culturally. His brother-in-law and his sister carried with themselves the memory of their part in Nazi terror and mass murder. His foster-brother Otto was a good work-ing man in Offenbach and lay low. He is the one who noticed his broth-er's books, when they ended up in the pile of books to be burned to heat the Offenbach swimming pool. He also left a chilling report of himself as member of his factory's fire brigade coping with British bombing, though he was less forthcoming about forced labor. Artur had asked Otto to write down the experience of the bombing, we must presume in order to understand what shaped and moved ordinary, working Germans. Otto, Lene, and the rest of his foster family were participants in and witnesses to a history he escaped. Artur had been in England fighting the Nazis and the Third Reich. His history of escape and anti-fascist action was to be celebrated in the late Federal Republic, but Artur always knew—or in any case, he arranged his archive as if he knew—that this late triumph was the result of his utter and complete failure as a young man. He had failed to stop the Nazis, and because of his failure, his German family was caught in the Third Reich. He was less concerned with their deeds and for that matter with the criminality of the Nazis, which were self-evident to him. However, he was keenly and painfully aware of the failure of Weimar democracy and especially of his own Social Democrats to stop them—and he took this defeat personally and his return to Germany was motivated by the effort to undo it.

The failure of Weimar was personal! Despite the contortions with names and identities and despite his working-class background, he had a most auspicious adolescence. The Weimar Republic gave Artur a future that he proudly and happily preserved, image by image. He rose from working-class poverty all the way to university thanks to his precocious intelligence as well as the steadfast support of his foster mother. Neither would have been enough, if it had not been for the Weimar welfare state and the progressive school system in Hessen, which had instituted a kind of magnet school, an *Aufbaugymnasium,* a boarding school for talented, poor kids. After successful completion of the gymnasium in nearby Bensheim, he took up studies in 1929 in Darmstadt in order to become a special education teacher, before moving on to Frankfurt to continue his studies.

The early curriculum vitae captures the persona of young Artur well. He neither ventured very far from home nor aimed very high in terms of his studies (choosing a vocationally oriented training). Still, he was broadly interested, artistically inclined (as his paintings of the time suggest), and more than eager to educate himself. He also had a strong social conscience. When he moved on from Darmstadt to Offenbach as aspiring teacher and to Frankfurt as part-time student, he was deeply impressed by Paul Tillich, the Lutheran theologian and Christian existentialist, though he had no discernible religious affiliation. It was Tillich's anti-Nazism that attracted him. Inasmuch as this reflected what Tillich summarized later on in the United States in his *Ontology of Courage*—courage as an act of self-affirmation in the face of death, guilt, and the meaninglessness of existence—it gets at Artur's self-fashioning.[27]

Artur had an abundance of talents. While excelling in school and at university, he painted quite a few paintings in his late teens that for the most part fit nicely the local modernist style prevailing in Darmstadt with its sizeable artistic community. He would befriend artists throughout his life. He turned from a proletarian kid into a modern, young man of the Weimar Republic without ever losing touch with his home in Offenbach. Throughout his time as a pupil and student, he worked as a laborer in factories in Offenbach, and it is no surprise at all that he joined the SPD early and became a founding member and chairman of the Socialist Student Group at Darmstadt University and a Social Democratic activist—and all this while he was just nineteen years old and painting late expressionist rural scenes in his spare time.[28]

There were two Socialists who would shape his destiny far beyond molding his personal and political outlook. Of the two, Carlo Mierendorff was most important. Artur's admiration for him was boundless.[29] There is a precious little photograph that shows him with Mierendorff in the early 1930s, both of them exuding self-confidence and determination and not a little insouciance. Mierendorff's slogan, "von jetzt an geht es nur noch aufwärts: entweder an die Macht oder an den Galgen," captures the not inconsiderable swagger of the two.[30] But there was more to Mierendorff's influence than a certain posture. He made Artur into an anti-fascist fighter. Long before he became Arthur Edgar Bennett, he was—yet another name— Gustav Kämpfer (Fighter), Artur's *nom de guerre* as anti-fascist. And after 1945, it was Artur who held up the memory of Mierendorff as a member of the resistance group Kreisauer Kreis and martyr of anti-fascism.[31]

His dedication to Mierendorff's memory was unfailing, and if Darmstadt commemorates the resistance against Nazism it is very much Artur Bratu's doing. Then again, it is not just Mierendorff whom he admired. Artur was also deeply fascinated by the Belgian socialist Hendrik de Man, who was a leading socialist theorist when he taught at Frankfurt University and had Artur among his students. There is a deep link between the socialism of Mierendorff and de Man, which Artur made explicit with his edition of de Man's *Zur Psychologie des Sozialismus*.[32] But whatever link there is, the comparison is also odious. De Man became chairman of the Belgian Workers Party (BWP/POB) after the death of Emile Vandervelde in 1938, argued vigorously for appeasement and turned into a Nazi collaborator in 1940, becoming the de facto prime minister after the Belgian defeat in 1940. Hendrik de Man continued drifting to the Right even after he ran afoul of Flemish Nazi collaborators and exiled himself to Nazi-occupied Paris. He ended up being convicted in absentia for treason. Artur's relationship to the de Mans, father and son, who had found refuge in Switzerland, was inconspicuous after the war, but he kept up with both of them, though he was not at all pleased, when in the 1980s, Miriam, then at Yale, introduced him to Paul de Man, Hendrik's nephew.[33]

Mierendorff was the more decisive influence. Artur was too young and too insignificant to be even a footnote in the prevailing histories,[34] but what links the two is a peculiar Weimar sensibility and an awareness of the need for a mass-democratic, anti-fascist politics. The most famous example of this is the logo — three white arrows in a black circle — for the *Eiserne Front*, the militant frontline SPD organization against the radical Right and the radical Left. Designed by Sergei Chakhotin together with Mierendorff, as an alternative to the Nazi swastika, it is based on Chakhotin's theory of mass-psychology, but more generally, it recognized the need for a more emotional politics, if the Social Democrats wanted to prevail.[35] The symbolism is also a reminder of Mierendorff's *Wandervogel* past, his literary ambitions, and his career as a journalist. This career included the journal *Die Dachstube,* edited by the teenagers Joseph Würth and Mierendorff in Darmstadt, Mierendorff's postwar political journal *Das Tribunal: Hessische Radikale Blätter,* and his role as editor-in-chief of the feuilleton of the *Hessische Volksbote.* This profile was Artur's dream as a young man, and it became so much part of Artur's recollections of the prewar years that one might mistake it for his own past. What appealed to Artur was the fusion of literary and political careers (Mierendorff also started a Socialist student group together with the writer Carl Zuckmayer, became Secretary in the Transport Workers Union, and so on) in a movement-type, Socialist organization and the dynamic force it was meant to unleash.[36]

Artur got himself involved head over heels. Fact and fiction are difficult to separate. Artur joined Mierendorff, becoming a member of the *Eiserne Front*. He also threw himself into the melee, and it is in that context that he began to write under the name Gustav Kämpfer. Deeds followed words. In one of Artur's most treasured photographs, he could be seen standing honor guard over the dead body of a comrade murdered by Nazi thugs in Offenbach.[37] The photograph turns out to be staged. Artur later on could not remember the names of his fellow honor guards, though the Offenbach SPD did. But he was present, if awkwardly, in the uniform of the *Eiserne Front* that he barely filled out. Anti-fascism was his cause, and he left no doubt about it. The photograph circulated widely in the press in conjunction with articles that denounced the Nazis in no uncertain words as murderers and thugs. Artur put himself visibly right into the middle of the anti-fascist struggle. While he was not a street fighter, he testified which side he was on.

It is less clear if and how he was involved in Carlo Mierendorff's major coup of the early 1930s. At issue was the revelation of documents, emerging from the Hessian NSDAP under Werner Best, that indicated Nazi plans for a coup d'état, the so-called *Boxheimer Dokumente*. These were plans of dubious import, drawn up by an overly ambitious Nazi lieutenant who later on had an eminent career during the Third Reich.[38] Politically, the revelation was a triumph quite in the spirit of Mierendorff's (and Artur's) militancy, because for the time being they cut short efforts to bring the Nazis into local government in Hessen, where they had become the strongest party by 1931. But this was a political issue far above the head of Artur. It involved ultimately the Hessian Interior Minister Wilhelm Leuschner and his Prussian colleague Severing (together with the indispensable Mierendorff) and the Reich's Cabinet. Artur was but a working-class student, a Social-Democratic activist, and a militant front man. Still, he was a known Social-Democratic militant, and he was a marked man.

Artur's goal was to become an educator with an interest in pedagogy and special education. He also was just twenty-one, and while politics was all-consuming in these final years of the Weimar Republic, Artur had a life, he had ambitions and dreams—and not least he had a beautiful girlfriend in Darmstadt. Militant politics was his choice, but there was a life to live and a future to be had. This future never happened—or rather it arrived twelve long years after the Weimar Republic was destroyed; Artur had become a grown man with the name of Arthur Edgar Bennett, and his former girlfriend had married. Artur's Weimar existence, so full of promise at the time, was a future that was cut short—only to be lived under quite radically different circumstances, emulated by Micha (who was among the more militant pupils and students in Darmstadt and prepared for a career in social work), and revivified as memory by Miriam.

All this, the personal and the political investment in the future of a democratic German society, came to naught with the Nazi seizure of power. Carlo Mierendorff fled briefly to Switzerland, only to return in order to vote as member of the SPD Reichstag faction against the *Ermächtigungsgesetz*, to be seized upon and beaten up by the SA, and arrested in June 1933. He disappeared into various concentration camps until 1938, when he was released, still enough of a fighter to join the Kreisauer Kreis resistance group in 1941. He died in 1943 in a bombing attack on the Leipzig main train station.[39] Meanwhile, Artur happened to be attending a teacher's congress in Belgium upon the invitation of Hendrik de Man in early February 1933. When the SA and the political police came to look for young Artur in Offenbach, his foster parents knew how to respond. They sent him a suitcase with his clothes. When the Nazis attempted to use his girlfriend in Darmstadt as a honey trap, she refused.

Artur did not return. He was a less valuable target than Mierendorff, but that could well have made the situation worse for him. What kept him abroad was his youth and his many named past. It may well have been the case that in a life full of separations since birth, this was just another one. We do not know. We do know, though, that Artur continued to wage war against the Nazis. In Belgium, where he remained in exile until 1940, he was involved in the Matteotti Fund, in the International Teachers' Union, and other anti-fascist causes, while studying pedagogy at the Free University of Brussels, teaching part-time at the Belgian Workers College, and moving in the penumbra of the BWP. After completing his studies and after a year in Harlech in North Wales, in 1939, he found a job as a teacher at a vocational school in Eksaarde, Belgium, for young Jewish refugees from Germany to be trained for emigration to Palestine. It remains unexplained why he ended up there, though we have plenty of photos of him and his boys. He built up a new life with its ups and downs, career-wise and personal. Judging from the photographs of this period, he might well have built a new life in Belgium. But again it was not to be.

Despite some anxious moments, the Belgian state protected him against deportation. In 1938, the Nazis expatriated him. His name appeared on the same page of the *Reichsgesetzblatt* as that of Erich Maria Remarque. However, the reason the Nazis gave for his expatriation stung. All his life Artur wanted to be recognizable as an anti-fascist, but the Nazis expatriated him as a *Mischling*—not gypsy, but Jewish. Artur *was* Jewish, at least according to Nazi law. This was an identity Artur refused until the end, though he became something of an "honorary member" of the Darmstadt Jewish community. His resistance is puzzling and surely has not to do with the rules of (Jewish) Halakha. It may simply have been that he considered himself to be an anti-fascist in the spirit of Carlo Mierendorff. But there are also indications that he thought he had to refuse the attribution if he wanted to live among Germans again and if he wanted to fulfill his life's mission—to create a democratic Germany through pedagogy. He was keenly aware—experientially and intellectually—of the appeal of Nazi anti-Semitism, and he knew that this appeal would not disappear with defeat. He came back, deliberately as German anti-fascist, in order to continue the fight and, evidence suggests, did not want to compromise his position with being Jewish.

More immediately, in 1940 he was just barely thirty years old and was fleeing yet again, this time before the advancing Wehrmacht units. Artur tried to evacuate his group of students in the direction of France, lost most of them to the rapid German advance, but managed to flee with one of them, ending up in the Dunkirk pocket where he was—quite implausibly, but verifiably —evacuated with the British expeditionary forces. Finally, he ended up in Pentonville Prison in London, where he survived the Blitz.[40] The next four years were not his greatest, even if he did come out of the war as Warrant Officer or, as he liked to tell the story, as Sergeant Major.[41]

Like other German refugees, he went from prison to internment camp on the Isle of Man, from there to the Pioneer Corps, and ultimately joined the army, where he had a desk job in military intelligence, not a very glamorous assignment. Artur was a fighter, but he was never a warrior. War made him deeply, viscerally unhappy. In photographs, he appears as a strapping soldier, but even in the official mug shots he looks unmistakably civilian. The most cherished one shows him à l'*anglaise,* sitting behind a desk in uniform with a pipe in his hand.

His most heroic moment was also his most unfortunate one. At the time he met Ruth, he was part of a British Nazi-hunter outfit, but if there was anything to brag about, it has not surfaced. He was even less happy in his first nonmilitary job. He had become a public prosecutor in the denazification trials in Darmstadt between 1947–49. He had the ideal typical biography of an anti-fascist German, but he felt uneasy in his prosecutorial role.[42] He loathed the job of classifying various grades of Nazis and Mitläufer. He did not believe in accidental Nazis and would have liked to have seen the lot behind bars. He hated the obfuscation of good society and had no sympathy for claims of victimhood, even in a town that was firebombed. And yet he also knew from his own family—and if he did not know at the time, he learned soon enough—that people made all sorts of choices, some dumb and some criminal. It seems, based on hearsay but entirely plausible, that he thought that an entire generation of Germans, those who went through the Nazi system and the war, was lost anyway. Denazification could not be anything but a fiasco. His solution—this is mostly guesswork, because he left little evidence for the immediate postwar years— had much to do with his sense that the Germans had forsaken democracy. This fact largely explained the helplessness of Weimar democrats, including his own, in the face of the Nazi onslaught. Hence, the solution was to make German democracy strong and sustainable. Perhaps, his position is best summarized by saying that he thought of himself as part of a small, anti-fascist elite that came back in order to use the total defeat of Nazi Germany to work on democratizing the Germans. Darmstadt, it turns out, was an exceptionally good place to be for this kind of endeavor.

It was a great relief when in 1949 he could dedicate his energy to the rebuilding of the school system, as superintendent of schools for Darmstadt, as a combative councilman, and subsequently as a member of the city government, as a dedicated state-level politician in Hessen, and as chair of the national and international Social-Democratic teachers organization. Artur became a fixture in postwar public life in Darmstadt, a public figure admired for his drive as a forward-looking and undogmatic school inspector and alert councilman. In the same vein, he put his heart into the popular sister-city program, designed to link city governments across Europe in order to foster friendship and understanding. His friends referred to him somewhat coyly as *Monsieur Jumelage*. It helped that he was one of the few in the city government to speak English, French, and Flemish fluently and that he had the credentials of a good German behind which others could hide a more toxic past. Last but not least, he became the local voice for the two members of the German resistance against the Nazi regime associated with Darmstadt, Wilhelm Leuschner and Carlo Mierendorff. Artur's life became one of the redeeming stories of the Federal Republic, and since German memorial culture knew how to celebrate its successes, he was celebrated as an exemplary Darmstädter for quite some time.

Ruth's Story

For most of their lives, 1949–1993/2000, Ruth and Artur lived in Darmstadt in West Germany. In the course of these forty years, they moved from the margins very much into the mainstream of Darmstadt life, leaving behind unsteady and uncertain lives. Artur became a highly respected public figure, and while Ruth was less in the public limelight, she not only held her own, but gained publicity in her own right. She even began to outshine her husband in later life, and those who met her invariably admired the cultured, silver-haired grande dame with her enthusiasms and her surfeit of stories. They both were quintessential success stories of the Federal Republic.

And for the most part, this is the way it was. My generation of historians has grown up to doubt such stories and to act as investigative magistrates. Such investigative historians were needed to cut through the thicket of lies and deceptions that had grown quickly over the Third Reich. And, no doubt, a fair dose of doubt is in order, if we want to capture the subterranean disorders in a settled life.

But maybe it is time to reconsider the role of the historian as magistrate. In any case, the magistrate may not be the right historian for minor and minoritarian histories. Miriam, for example, was a historian of a quite different kind—and not only because she was deeply concerned with literary, philosophical, and visual "texts" (a slightly different kind of archive than I typically use). She rather took on the role of the historian as conversationalist. Her goal was to put her protagonists (Siegfried Kracauer, Walter Benjamin, Theodor Adorno) "in a conversation—conversations that actually took place, virtual conversations that could have occurred, and in the case of Adorno and Kracauer, conversations that had become ritualized exercises in talking past each other." These conversations could only happen, as she wrote in November 2010, because of the conversations she had with the dead authors, much as she hoped in her posthumously published book "that *my* conversations with these writers will inspire readers to engage *them* in their own."[43] This is one of the surprises of her archive, though it is plain to see. What she asks for is a robust intimacy in the conversation with the dead and in the reimagination of their conversation among themselves. I think what she is telling me is that the millions upon millions of dead I have been typically writing about may have numbed my historical senses, although I have been arguing for a long time that each one of these millions died their own individual death.[44]

Conversations, though, pose their own problems. On the surface, it was simply the fact that I got to know Artur and Ruth when Artur was already quite feeble due to a stroke, and Ruth had reached the apogee of her storytelling prowess and of her public presence as witness in a pervasive German memorial culture. What was left is the reflection of Artur's life stories in the recollection of others, above all of his daughter, who (perhaps because she had separated early on in her marriage caper) kept the flame of Artur's exploits alive. By contrast, a conversation with Ruth was simply a matter of getting a word in, while it was a matter of getting Artur out of his late-in-life silence and reimagining him as the charming, urbane, and cosmopolitan raconteur that everybody who knew him says he was or, as may be, he became. Ruth talking and Artur being quiet even seemed to me a fair trade, in the sense that their respective roles late in life reset a gender balance that had given all the power—including the power of speech—to the man who very much thought that this was his due. But it did not make conversation any easier.

The real problems were (and are) to put the two into conversation and to have them both converse with us. Ruth and Artur were two different people with two different life stories, Artur's story being the more public and Ruth's the more private one. The conversational historian is challenged, moreover, over long stretches of their Darmstadt life to get a conversation going among them where there was none. However, the altogether weightier problem is that Ruth's stories conjured up quite a different German history than Artur's did and that Ruth's stories prevailed. Artur's story of the rise from working-class poverty to middle-class respectability and of an exemplary anti-fascist career that was vindicated despite setbacks in the Federal Republic and not least his memory of German resistance—all this became not simply less attractive than Ruth's story. It actually became quite unintelligible—and I am certain Artur knew it, because he early on developed a keen eye for such slights. "Monsieur Jumelage"—how to communicate the underlying concept without a smirk? Then again, it is even harder to fathom that a life story that began in Tel Aviv—it is a quintessentially Jewish story—should become so distinctly a

German story — a German history as *einfache Form*. I could easily imagine it as a *Kalendergeschichte* in the manner of Johann Peter Hebel.

In the end, the story of the Bratus became the story of a (German-)Jewish family, which it had not been so long as Artur dominated family life and public appearance. His was a history of anti-Nazi resistance as the wellspring for German renewal. Artur yielded, and it is therefore entirely appropriate that the story of the Bratus should end where I began it — not in Offenbach or Darmstadt, but in Tel Aviv and Prague. The Bratu story became the no less vagrant and shifty-eyed story of a Theiner daughter, who made her way, counter to all sensible expectations, from 1920s Tel Aviv in the British Mandate for Palestine to postwar Darmstadt/West Germany by way of Prague and London. It is a story about what it means to be a Jew and a German in the heartland of Europe, and although this story evolved parallel to Artur's story in real time and even shared a place, London, as the prime site of their wartime experience, it is inseparable from conversations that only became communicable in the 1980s and 1990s — and then became German memory and more tentatively German history in a minor key.

Ruth in the 1990s had become what friends called a "grande dame," an inspiring and striking figure with strong opinions she was ready to share with and, if need be, impose on most everyone. She was extraordinarily gregarious, drawing in far-flung friends, acquaintances and friends, friends of friends, and many more. She spoke German, English, and Czech with ease, but no doubt she had heart-to-heart conversations even with Hebrew speakers, whose language she did not share. There was a steady and dizzying stream of guests from everywhere, a long-time lodger who was an opera singer (and daughter of a Hungarian musician, who had made a career with the Prague Symphony Orchestra, before leaving for Switzerland) and became a close friend of the family, and there were her grown-up children and their spouses and her grandchildren. Some of us were a bit quieter, but the charm of this life was that Ruth's gregariousness was shared by her friends, whether in the local *Kaffeekränzchen* or across the ocean. It was one earth-girdling, chattering scene.

She had recently become a board member of the Darmstadt Jewish community. I learned only later that, while she had been a presence in the small Jewish community from the beginning, she had actively joined the community only rather late in life, in the late 1960s or early 1970s, just at about the time when the small community of survivors had begun to sink more permanent roots. Many of them never abandoned their packed suitcases, not metaphorical but real ones, but the small community had come to settle despite itself. All but a handful of the community members had come from elsewhere, mostly Eastern Europe, though there was also a Persian family, a French family, and the occasional Israeli and American. Each of them had his or her own story of survival, which everyone knew. Some of the outspoken members, above all Moritz Neumann, did go public, but he had been a leading (national) journalist and activist in the first place.[45] They had survived, but their families had not; they had gotten stuck in Germany, but never thought they would have children—and they did. It remained a community of exiles with an orthodox rabbi, a wise, learned, and patient man, who had come from Romania by way of Israel.

The capstone of this slow accommodation to their German environment was the building of a new synagogue, with the political and financial backing of the city of Darmstadt.[46] It was an expression of the growing public presence of the community and a reflection of the city's wish to make amends. It came in the context of similar activities, such as the invitation extended by many cities in Germany to their former Jewish residents to visit, and was part of a growing, but still hotly contested memory culture. The opening of the new synagogue in Darmstadt was a major public event, a moment to reflect on the destruction of the interwar communities and their synagogues and a gesture on the part of city and state officials, meaning to officially welcome the Jewish community in Darmstadt. A police car stationed in front of the synagogue was less a reminder that this welcome might not be shared by all Darmstädters (which undoubtedly was the case, because Darmstadt like the entire Weinstrasse had been notoriously "brown"), than a reflection of typical anxieties of the German state and the Darmstadt community after the Holocaust. The anxieties were mutual. Even if the Jewish community had been safe, it never quite felt that way. That is, it felt safe for Artur and the kids (though they had their own panics to be sure), but it did not for Ruth even though she had become fully part of Darmstadt life.

The feelings of the Jewish community members (quite apart from what friends in Israel or the United States might have thought) about their German root-taking were ambivalent. They were and are proud of their beautiful synagogue. But building it and accepting it also entailed the recognition that the place where they had gotten stuck after the war for one reason or another had become a permanent home. The new Darmstadt synagogue was a token of this homecoming in a strange and for many still a cursed land. The response to this situation differed greatly, but it engendered in each case a reckoning with the past. Not that the destruction of Jewish life had ever not been present, even for the Persian and French families, because they still had to deal with the fact that they lived in Germany. But these personal and community memories were one thing. The great sedimentation of stories in the 1980s and 1990s that made up the memory of the Holocaust was a quite different phenomenon.[47] For better and worse, it forced community memories into public life. Whatever it was for gentiles, it open old wounds in front of everybody else that were hard enough to deal with at home.

You could not escape the memorialization of the Holocaust in the public media if you lived in Germany. Ruth and Artur's closest friends, for example, did not reveal their own enduring sorrows, except in their circle of family and friends. They had experienced far too much to ever render their experience into readily presentable stories, and memory for them was less a thing or tale than an ever harrowing presence. Their daughter escaped to Jamaica and only upon her return found her medium of expressing their parents' experience in art. Some refused to talk. Others in the community were more fortified and, even considered it their duty to speak out in order to testify. The *Gesellschaft für Christlich-jüdische Zusammenarbeit* became an important forum for this kind of encounter, and for some twenty to thirty years, left a deep impression on all those, who were drawn to it. But quite apart from what individuals and associational life in Darmstadt did or did not do, the experience, memory, and history of the Holocaust and of Jewish survival had become an obsession for German gentiles and an inescapable media presence.

Ruth participated and thrived in this effervescent memory culture, as it took shape around her and so did Moritz Neumann who had become chairman of the Jewish community. They spoke as (German) Jews to (gentile) Germans, while most members of the community spoke mostly among themselves, insofar as they did at all. Memories did flow more easily than in the old days, or so I was told. The community members knew each other and when not in relation to gentile company it did not need much to convey "experience." It was different for those who had come from England (apart from Ruth and Artur, there was another person who had come back in British uniform), but they were assimilated into the quiet discourse of survivors. In all of this, Ruth had a unique place. She inhabited both the gentile and the Jewish worlds as well as the world of the Holocaust and the world of a refugee who was saved.

Ruth's role in the community had always been that of a bridge between the small Jewish community and gentile town. Some might say she wanted to have her cake and eat it too, but this would miss what is crucial about Ruth's position and why it matters in all its beautiful strangeness. Ruth was born in Tel Aviv, but raised as a secular German-Jewish girl, who lived for most of her childhood among Czechs in Prague—and what she wanted was to live her secular German Jewish life.[48] Darmstadt gave her the opportunity late in life (and Prague did the same in death). Darmstadt in the 1980s and 1990s allowed her to be a German Jewish woman from Prague who had found a German home in Darmstadt. And since she was also a gregarious person, she made sure to tell everyone about it. What makes Ruth's story so difficult to decipher is the difference between substance and tone. It is the hard story of an unsuccessful beginning in Palestine and of a child refugee that was effusively and, yes, happily told, because right or wrong she felt on safe ground and had been able to make peace with herself. There were enough gaps and cracks, her parents were murdered in Auschwitz, and there were private moments of utter sadness and despair, but her stories enchanted.

The 1990s are the moment when the Bratu story metamorphosed into a Theiner story. Prague is its cornerstone, though it is not where it originated. If Artur came into the world without a certain name and no recognizable history, Ruth's Jewish genealogy reached deep into the past. In recorded history, it goes back in time on her paternal side into the Bohemian countryside and its well-off farmers and on her maternal side to the Rhineland to Wiesbaden, Rheydt, Essen, and also, in a different branch of the family, to Königsberg, where relatives raised Ruth's mother Dorothea Sophar (known as Thea). More recently, some two generations of emancipated Jews had made good as professionals, lawyers, and journalists. The two branches came together in a Zionist agricultural camp in World War I somewhere near Dresden, where Hugo Theiner met Thea Mirjam Sophar, then an aspiring journalist. After marriage, they followed the footsteps of Hugo's older brother, who had already emigrated to Palestine. This is where their daughter Ruth was born in 1923. One of the most treasured family photographs shows mother and daughter in the bright Mediterranean light against the background of the dunes near Jaffa. But the photograph is deceiving. The three of them did not catch on, and when Thea needed urgent surgery, they returned to Europe. While Ruth initially stayed with relatives in Berlin and Königsberg, they eventually settled down in Prague, where Hugo opened a not very successful delicatessen and fish store.

The decline of Hugo's fortunes is an unhappy reminder of the difficulties of making a living in the 1930s. Hugo was not a very good businessman, though this was certainly not for lack of wanting to provide for the family. We know about this in loving detail, because many of the letters that Thea would send after the German occupation detailed how Hugo went out of his way to take on all kinds of odd jobs—he proved most successful in coloring postcards—and made long forays into nearby woods (before this was forbidden) to collect berries and mushrooms. The consequences of this decline, however, proved fatal. When it came to deciding about emigration in 1939, the family was unable to settle tax debts and thus was stuck in Prague. Hugo's younger brother, a successful engineer, was similarly unlucky. When he finally was convinced to leave and got the papers, he fractured his leg. His family was deported to Maly Troste-nets. Thea's letters about these years of ever-growing misery only ceased when Hugo and Thea were deported to Terezin—and even then there were faint signs, by way of Red Cross postcards and through a family connection provided by the Austrian sculptor Fritz Wotruba and his wife, a Theiner relative. Silence descended when Thea and Hugo were deported to Auschwitz.

Bratu/Theiner family lore held that Thea was part of Hugo's misfor-tune. As the very German wife of a Czech delicatessen owner in the Vynohrady district in Prague, she did not exactly advance his business. There are, however, some details about what she was like. A Theiner maid called Resi remembers Thea's generosity.[49] Resi, from a German village adjacent to Karlovy Vary, is likely the same person, who, as Thea reported in a letter, made a point of greeting her in the street in 1940. It turns out she was involved with the Czech resistance. We next glimpse her visiting Ruth in Darmstadt as German expellee. Similar glowing reports have ac-cumulated over time from many sources. Thea may have brought misfor-tune to business, but she held her family together with determination and was an inspiring force for Ruth's young friends. Her letters to Ruth are a testimony to courage and endurance—and contain carefully measured doses of truth about the ever-worsening restrictions, the impoverishment of Jewish life, and, though only indirectly, persecution in Prague.[50] Thea remained the propulsive power in the Theiner family.

A small collection of documents from the 1930s that Ruth had kept, apart from telling us something about what mattered to Ruth as a teenage girl, reinforces this view.[51] Ruth had kept vacation camp diaries, programs, songs, and skits (in Czech and German) of the *Rote Falken* (Red Falcons, the youth organization of the German Social Democrats in Czechoslovakia). Ruth's mother, Thea, was an inspirational leader of her group of young-sters. She was also deeply involved in rescuing comrades, initially those who had fled from Nazi Germany and later those from the Czech Suden-tenland after the devastating collapse of the German Social Democratic Workers Party (DSAP) in the election of 1935 and again after the takeover by Nazi Germany. Thea was good at humanitarian rescue, and as a result of her activities, her daughter Ruth was aware beyond her age of the po-litical situation. Ruth's participation in the socialist youth group as a teen-ager in Prague put her distinctly on the German end of things. Undoubt-edly, the large number of German Social Democratic exiles in Prague only heightened her sense of Germanness. One of her best friends later in life, Marianka (Marianne), was one of these exiles. Back in the 1930s and 1940s, Marianka was among the girls who did not get out, but she survived in Terezin and toward the end of the war in one of the associated labor camps.

Marianka counts among her treasures from Terezin a *Poesie-Album* (with the typically romantic or wise entries, as the one by Leo Baeck—often of acquaintances to be deported).[52] Miriam facilitated its publication.

Thea had grown up with orthodox relatives in Königsberg. She had become an avid Zionist in her (prewar) youth. She turned into a secular Jewish Socialist sometime after the family moved to Prague, although she apparently maintained a kosher household, and Hugo and Thea were members of a synagogue. The names of her children, Ruth and Esther, left no doubt who she was and what female role model she wanted for her children. Thea insisted that her children learn proper Czech and put Ruth in a Czech school, but in the city of synagogues, Hebrew did not figure at all. Judaism or even the Jewish sites had no place in Ruth's recollections of her life in the Czech capital.

In the end, their German-Czech upbringing counted for nothing. Being Jews became their destiny. Ruth and Esther escaped in the second to last *Kindertransport* from Prague in 1939 with a small contingent with a similar social democratic background. Her *Kindertransport* friends, at the very least, had membership in the Red Falcons in common. Their British sponsors were the Woodcraft Folk.[53] Ruth and Esther survived as refugees in England. Ruth was the much older one; she was fifteen turning on sixteen. Esther had just turned ten. Ruth was designated to maintain contact with their Prague parents. Although none of Ruth's letters survive, most of Thea's letters do. (Typically, Thea wrote, and Hugo added a coda.) The collection ends with Ruth's frantic efforts to make contact when the parents had been transferred to Auschwitz.[54]

It is not at all exceptional, either, that one of the sisters, Ruth, toughed out the transition, whereas Esther was deeply shaken and remained at edge throughout her short life.[55] We do not know much about them in wartime England, but it seems clear that while Esther remained superbly needy, Ruth developed the hard skin of survivordom. She turned into a tough and calculating young woman in love and war—not an altogether pleasant figure even in her own recollection. She found shelter with maternal relatives—this part of the family came from Essen, where they had owned an old-age home that had been taken over by the German Labor Front. They had left for Italy, hoping for an authoritarian refuge to their taste, but moved on with their possessions to England, returning to their old business running an old-age home for German refugees in Blackheath in Southeast London. They employed Ruth as the maid from Eastern Europe, and Ruth got along with them like an Eastern European maid would with her employer.[56]

Among the coterie of *Kindertransport* and *Falken* friends from Prague, Ruth was easily the most unruly, as more than one of them recalled even in old age. When the Blitz smashed the old-age home to pieces, Ruth used the occasion to move away, took up work, and ended as a manual worker in a factory that produced rubber tubes for the war and as seamstress mass-producing uniforms. She hated these jobs and everything that came with them, but the wages kept her relatives at bay. Her Prague dream had been to become a fashion designer and dressmaker for which she had apprenticed after finishing school, and there are a few sketches scattered among her papers as tokens of her *futur antérieur,* which proved as elusive in her life as it is in the German language.[57]

Had Ruth met Artur at this point, they might well have stayed in England. But although both were in London, were refugees and German Social Democrats, they traveled in quite different circles. While Artur had quite a few affairs with English girls, Ruth was different. She strung along a few would-be boyfriends and eventually married one of them, but they all were from the same German-Czech environment she had come from. They were also part of the network of émigrés with ties to the (Czech-) German DSAP. However, they opted for the Czechoslovak Legion when it came to joining the war. It is one of the curiosities that Artur, the Social Democratic activist of the 1930s, made no inroads whatsoever with fellow socialist émigrés in London, but Ruth did. Ever since her wartime days in England, she maintained a lifelong friendship with the Ollenhauers among others. Given the Bratu family dynamics, it takes a while to recognize that she, not her husband, befriended some of the leading postwar Social Democrats—except that they came from a minor, if quite vociferous corner of the Czech-German faction in the West German SPD. This connection was also the reason she decided to join the U.S. Civic Censorship Detachment in late 1944 or early in 1945. Partly she was fed up with the drudgery of factory work in wartime England, but partly she took the job in order to facilitate communications among Social Democrats and other left-wing friends whose letters made it through the censorship division thanks to her—or so she said.

Whether the departure to England was the best solution for her sister is another matter. Ruth came to resent that she had to take care of her sister, who deeply loved her older sibling and clung to her tightly, as a moving photograph of the two from ca. 1945 suggests. But at that point, Ruth was on her way out with the U.S. Army and the sixteen-year-old Esther was by then (or soon thereafter) pregnant. She gave away the baby boy, who was raised in an orthodox Jewish family to become a woodworker. He cut his ties to his mother and her English family completely.[58] In the extensive literature on the trauma of *Kindertransport* children, there is rather little on sibling conflicts, though even in Esther's and Ruth's cohort there is at least one other case of similar tensions.

Ruth's initial idea likely was to use the privileges of the American uniform to explore the possibility of returning to Prague with her husband and search for her parents. But her parents had disappeared in Auschwitz, and Prague was forbidding for Germans and less than welcoming for Jews in 1945. Ruth's uniform protected, but it also afforded her an unvarnished glimpse of Prague realities. She concluded that she would have to abandon her home in order to have a life. That Artur appeared on the horizon at this moment was serendipitous. It was of far more consequence that her past—her parents, her home—had evaporated before her very eyes. She had come back to Prague as a Jewish-German Czech, but left as apatride. She was only twenty-two, but war does strange things to people. For Ruth an entire history imploded, and all that was left of the moment is an eerie photo album of buildings in an empty Prague. It took some twenty years and more until her life before the *Kindertransport* returned, and Prague came back as a future that never was. One of the more endearing gestures of this return occurred in the early 2000s when she joined Miriam and me in a cafeteria at the University of Chicago, saw a portrait on the wall of what everyone considered to be some dean, and cried out "My President!" The portrait showed Tomáš Masaryk.

The Devil's Gap

Darmstadt it was and an exemplary German life in the Federal Republic it would become. Masaryk's Prague was a fond memory that Ruth could live with at last.[59] Artur found comfort and a final home in his story as well. He even found pleasure in the supreme irony that the Darmstädters often spoke of him as the Jew and of his silver-haired wife as the gentile. All's well that ends well, one might say.

But not quite. The predictability of the story line smoothens out the vagrancy of the stories. We have the stories of two main protagonists (Artur and Ruth), which reach an apex in the 1930s and 1940s and conclude in postwar lives that recover, under painfully changed circumstances a future both Artur and Ruth once might have had. Artur becomes a successful pedagogue, and Ruth recovers her childhood Prague in a thriving memory culture. Both stories pivot around points of decision (Artur's choice to stay in Belgium in 1933; Thea and Hugo's decision to have their children join the *Kindertransport* in 1939) that shaped the rest of their lives, but come to rest in the miraculous stabilization of the Federal Republic. In this kind of history, the role reversal of Artur and Ruth in their late lives— manifestly one of the stories gains (Ruth's Jewish past) and the other one loses (Artur's anti-fascist past)—could be seen as part of a deeper German *Umkehr* in the context of a growing Holocaust awareness.[60]

So what's wrong with an altogether "right" narrative? More critical historians might want to make more of the fact that Artur and Ruth's stories are really (anti-fascist and Jewish) counternarratives in an altogether less than successful overcoming of racism and anti-Semitism in postwar Germany. In this view, Artur and Ruth's stories form not just a minor, but a minoritarian German history. But this neither conforms with Artur and Ruth's experience nor with their own, always alert view of the society around them. They were safe around friends and well-wishers—and there were many of them, and they controlled Darmstadt politics and, at crucial moments in Artur's career, the state of Hesse and the Federal Republic. But then Nazi success had been based on local and national mass political mobilization. The latter not only altered indelibly the course of German history (and the lives of the Bratus) but everyday life, which includes the way people made sense of the world. Artur and Ruth reentered this history after the defeat of Nazism, but the edge of *Weltanschauung* remained as everyday meaning-making, even if it was polished off in their later years. Ruth repeatedly told the story of a kindly official at a reception, who, when he understood that she was Jewish, asked with great sympathy and understanding when she would return to Israel. There were crude anti-Semites as well, but by the 1980s, they had been pushed to the margins of Darmstadt and West German society.

Still, this entire debate about the "Good German" and the bad Germans manages to miss what disturbed Artur and Ruth, and in more subterraneous ways Darmstadt and German society. It makes short shrift of *die Lücke, die der Teufel läßt* (the gap that the devil leaves behind), to quote Alexander Kluge once more.[61] This is the gap left by Artur and Ruth escaping destruction, but paying the price of losing home, family, and futures that seemed so bright for both of them. "The Holocaust" came to stand in for this loss in history and memory, but even though Ruth lost her family, her loss encompassed so much more, because her challenge was to live—and life proved immensely difficult ever after. Artur returned to his defeat—the "failure of Weimar democracy"—time and again in his wartime diaries and all of his politics was shaped by it. Kluge, of course, wrote about Halberstadt and the devastating bombing attack that destroyed it; how far back you would have to go in order to avert this future; and what effort it took—emotionally, politically, and intellectually—to recognize the trap the devil set in making everybody, murderers and their victims, face loss and devastation.

The past opened a devilish gap, a void of destruction and loss, and amid this mayhem, a surfeit of moral gray zones (think of Ruth and Esther, Artur and Lene, and yet untold stories about Miriam and Micha) never quite resolved. For Holocaust survivors, this gap remained the source of nightmares held at bay only with extraordinary fortitude.[62] The gap never closed, though all our protagonists learned to live with it most of the time and told their stories accordingly. What we get as our story board is the smoothing effect of making a life notwithstanding the devil lurking within it. Artur and Ruth's lives "took place" in Darmstadt, a town in which affective connections to British royals ran deep and yet a small city that was destroyed calamitously by British bombers. Moritz Neumann has told this history well, because he knew the stakes.[63] The resulting drama of rebuilding a community and a society is breathtaking for the stupefying, truly devilish struggles that it engendered, and Artur was in the middle of it, building schools, revising curricula, as well as forbidding his wife to return to dressmaking. The turbulences of personhood and identity, of finding (a) home rather grew with prosperity and grew once again, when the children, Micha and Miriam, got into the act. The turbulences exploded in the long 1960s, and it is doubtful that they were ever resolved. Our narratives cheat, inasmuch as narratives aim for resolution and closure, when life and its wayward stories continue. Suffice it to say that by the late 1970s and surely by the early 1980s, Artur was celebrated as one of the founders of postwar, democratic Darmstadt, while the balance of storytelling shifted to his wife. Meanwhile their son was in a mood of total rejection ("Wer hat uns verraten: Sozialdemokraten!"), while their daughter had left her marriage and her career and started over in the United States.

Alas, lifetimes and historical time are not the same. Lives and their stories can become history even in one's lifetime—not really because of historians like me appropriating them, but because they are surpassed by changing reality. Some twenty-odd years after the building of the new synagogue, the ruins of the old liberal synagogue were unearthed, when the city of Darmstadt built a new hospital. The city council decided to turn the ruins into a memorial site. Ritula Fränkel, who had returned to Darmstadt—where her parents had been stranded as holocaust survivors—with her Jamaican husband Nicholas Morris, completed the artistic and pedagogic design for what became the Erinnerungsort Liberale Synagoge. The latter is one of several memorials, which are now part of yearly guided tours for Darmstadt students in the context of a city-sponsored project *Schüler gegen das Vergessen*.[64] In the more intimate environment of the new synagogue and subsequently in the Jewish Museum in Berlin, Ritula Fränkel and Nicholas Morris had previously, in 2001, exhibited an installation of a quite different kind that looked forward rather than back and that gives us a clue of how the Bratu story became history.

When the Darmstadt Jewish Synagogue was consecrated, the Jewish community in Darmstadt, which always had been small, was at the verge of extinction. As the memorialization of the Holocaust expanded, the communities of survivors shrunk. They were getting old; the children were moving away either physically like Miriam or spiritually like Micha; and the proud act of restoration could well have been seen as a deed that, not unlike so many Jewish memory sites all over Europe, commemorated a people disappearing from Europe and thus effectively completing a project the Nazis had started.[65] Anyone visiting Prague or Krakow must be painfully aware of this gray zone of memorialization. Ruth never saw it this way. Much as she happily participated in the culture of memorialization, which included the memorialization of her own life, the Jewish community for her was about life and made only sense when it had a future. This future arrived without much notice and rattled everyone. Starting in 1990/91 and then rapidly growing in the mid 1990s, the size of the Jewish community in Darmstadt grew beyond anything imagined and imaginable. If there were barely forty to fifty members in the 1980s, there are now, in the year 2015, some 700.

Ritula Fränkel and Nicholas Morris's installation of 2001, X-odus, knits together the memory of those who got stuck in Germany — "Josef's Mantel," for example — and of those who newly arrived — a table and a chair decked out with Russian cooking recipes.[66] The main pillars of the congregation are now former Soviet school teachers, engineers, and other professionals, whose memories were shaped by the Great Patriotic War that they fought against the Germans and who busied themselves with mixed success becoming Germans and Jews and Russians in Darmstadt. Some hundred years earlier, another, much more exalted Darmstädter, Princess Alix of Hesse and by Rhine, favorite granddaughter of Queen Victoria, had tried the reverse journey, becoming the spouse of Nicholas II. She was executed as the "German" Tsaritsa Alexandra Feodorovna together with her family in Yekaterinburg, which was renamed Sverdlovsk and regained its old name in 1991. This is history in a major key. It asks what are the origins and consequences of life-changing events? Minor histories, by contrast, pick up on the stories that make life livable and survivable in the mid of these events. They would not be "whole," if they did not reflect on the many futures that were cut short or remained unlived. And they would be immoral, if they dissolved murderers and their victims into hapless elements in a maelstrom of violence, much as it would be misleading to think that just because some stories end well all is well.

Ruth and Artur's as well as Miriam and Micha's journeys end peacefully in Prague in the New Jewish Cemetery. They live on in a multitude of stories, some small and some large, some consequential, and some not that at times coagulate and at times disaggregate, but in a general way stick together and thus form the bonds that constitute civil life. It is a happy coincidence that Kafka's grave is just around the corner.

Michael Geyer is the Samuel N. Harper Professor Emeritus of History at the University of Chicago.

Notes

1. Klaus Grosse Kracht, *Die zankende Zunft: historische Kontroversen in Deutschland nach 1945* (Göttingen, 2005); Gerrit Dworok, *"Historikerstreit" und Nationswerdung. Ursprünge und Deutung eines bundesrepublikanischen Konflikts* (Cologne, 2015).
2. The two exemplary studies on the subject are Celia Applegate, *A Nation of Provincials: The German Idea of Heimat* (Berkeley, CA, 1990); Alon Confino, *The Nation as a Local Metaphor: Württemberg, Imperial Germany, and National Memory* (Chapel Hill, NC, 1996).
3. Mark Roseman, *A Past in Hiding: Memory and Survival in Nazi Germany* (New York, 2000); Nicholas Stargardt, *The German War: A Nation under Arms, 1939–45* (New York, 2015).
4. Primo Levi, *The Drowned and the Saved* (New York, 1988). See also among others Jonathan Petropoulos and John K Roth, eds, *Gray Zones: Ambiguity and Compromise in the Holocaust and Its Aftermath* (New York, 2005). An example for the latter is Erica Fischer, *Aimée & Jaguar: eine Liebesgeschichte Berlin 1943* (Cologne, 1994).
5. Jean François Lyotard, *Das Patchwork der Minderheiten: Für eine herrenlose Politik*, trans. Clemens-Carl Haerle (Berlin, 1977). As sobering and exhilarating context, Philipp Felsch, *Der lange Sommer der Theorie: Geschichte einer Revolte; 1960–1990* (Munich, 2015).
6. The Merve blurb for the short text of desires and aspirations, ca. 1977: "Lyotard folgt den Minderheiten, ihren Listen und Finten, die die monotonen und zentralisierten Räume verdrehen, ihre Bewegungen in der verzwickten Zeit des Begehrens, und schleicht sich mit ihnen in ökonomische, politische Diskurse ein, um Paradoxa zu installieren, die deren Ordnung und Logik platzen lassen."
7. Jean François Lyotard, "Heidnische Unterweisungen," in *Apathie der Theorie*, ed. Jean François Lyotard (Berlin, 1979), 7–71, here 29.
8. Alf Lüdtke, *Eigen-Sinn: Fabrikalltag, Arbeitererfahrungen und Politik vom Kaiserreich bis in den Faschismus* (Hamburg, 1993).
9. Eve Rosenhaft, "One Man, Two Men, a Girl, a Car, a Flag: A Test for the Emeriti," in *Alltag, Erfahrung, Eigensinn: historisch-anthropologische Erkundungen*, ed. Belinda Davis, Lindenberger Thomas, and Michael Wildt (Frankfurt, 2008); Alfred Georg Frei and Susanne Asche, *Friedrich Hecker in den USA: eine deutsch-amerikanische Spurensicherung* (Konstanz, 1993).

10. Oskar Negt and Alexander Kluge, *Public Sphere and Experience: Toward an Analysis of the Bourgeois and Proletarian Public Sphere*, trans. Peter Labanyi, Jamie Daniel, and Assenka Oksiloff (Minneapolis, MN, 1993).

11. Miriam Hansen, "Foreword"; Negt and Kluge, *Public Sphere and Experience*, XI; Miriam Hansen, "Max Ophuls and Instant Messaging: Reframing Cinema and Publicness," in *Screen Dynamics: Mapping the Borders of Cinema*, ed. Gertrud Koch (Vienna, 2012), 22–29.

12. André Jolles, *Einfache Formen: Legende, Sage, Mythe, Rätsel, Spruch, Kasus, Memorabile, Märchen, Witz* Halle, Saale, 1930); André Jolles, *Andre Jolles (1874–1946): "gebildeter Vagant"; brieven en documenten*, ed. Walter Thys (Amsterdam, 2000).

13. See for example the machinima, "Eine deutsche Geschichte, Kapitel 1" Glanz und Gloria Filmproduktion 1929, https://www.youtube.com/watch?v=p7oR4g8BRHQ and "Eine deutsche Geschichte, Kapitel 2" Glanz und Gloria Filmproduktion 1929, https://www.youtube.com/watch?v=lv60NtMOaHU.

14. As if to prove my case about the difficulties of shifty-eyed stories in the United States, the tremendously successful translation of Dische's Book into German was published before the American original. Irene Dische, *Großmama packt aus: Roman*, trans. Reinhard Kaiser (Hamburg, 2005); Irene Dische, *The Empress of Weehawken* (New York, 2007).

15. Peter Schneider, *Die Lieben meiner Mutter* (Cologne, 2013).

16. A good example for a novelist, who cannot help being a historian: Per Leo, *Flut und Boden: Roman einer Familie* (Stuttgart, 2014). One of the earliest examples of this genre is Marianne Hirsch, *Family Frames: Photography, Narrative, and Postmemory* (Cambridge, MA, 1997).

17. Friedrich Ebert Stiftung, Archiv der sozialen Demokratie (AdsD), Bonn-Bad Godesberg, Nachlässe Artur E. Bratu, Ruth Bratu und Deposit Micha Bratu; University of Chicago Library, Special Collections Research Center, Miriam Hansen Papers, 1902–2011.

18. Monika W. shared some intimate notes, written during Micha's illness with me that lend themselves to this interpretation, which is entirely my own.

19. Deborah Dwork and R. J. van Pelt, *Flight from the Reich: Refugee Jews, 1933–1946* (New York, 2009). Transcripts of the interviews are in my possession. See the recent essay by Godehard Lehwark, "Ruth Bratu: Ein exemplarisches jüdisches Leben," in *"Geh nicht den alten Weg zurück!" Festschrift zum sechzigjährigen Bestehen der Gesellschaft für Christ-lich-Jüdische Zusammenarbeit Darmstadt 1954–2014*, ed. Thomas Lange and Lothar Triebel (Darmstadt, 2014), 96–105.

20. The result, though, was spectacular: Miriam Hansen, *Cinema and Experience: Siegfried Kracauer, Walter Benjamin, and Theodor W. Adorno* (Berkeley, CA, 2012).

21. Alexander Kluge, *Die Lücke, die der Teufel lässt: im Umfeld des neuen Jahrhunderts* (Frankfurt, 2003), 221–22. Some of these short films are available at https://kluge.library.cornell.edu/conversations/hansen.

22. Reinhart Koselleck, *Futures Past: On the Semantics of Historical Time*, trans. Keith Tribe (Cambridge, MA, 1985).

23. Sebastian Jobs and Alf Lüdtke, eds, *Unsettling History: Archiving and Narrating in Historiography* (Frankfurt, 2010); Elisabeth Domansky, "A Lost War: World War II in Postwar German Memory," in *Thinking about the Holocaust after Half a Century*, ed. Alvin H Rosenfeld (Bloomington, IN, 1997), 233–72.

24. Jonathan D. Spence, *The Memory Palace of Matteo Ricci* (New York, 1984). Useful for this essay: Jo Alyson Parker, Michael Crawford, and Paul Harris, eds, *Time and Memory, Study of Time* (Boston, 2006).

25. This section is based on interviews and a first sifting of the holdings of the AdsD as well as on papers in my and photographs in Monika W.'s possession.

26. Wendy Doniger, *The Bedtrick: Tales of Sex and Masquerade* (Chicago, 2000).

27. Paul Tillich, *The Courage to Be* (London, 1952). Artur's adolescent existential ruminations are evidenced among other things in an otherwise not very successful painting, a still life with a skull.

28. There are some eight paintings surviving. It is unclear who held on to them during the Third Reich.

29. Carlo Mierendorff, *In Memoriam Carlo Mierendorff: literarische Schriften; [1897–1943]*, ed. Artur E. Bratu (Darmstadt, 1980).

30. Ullrich Amlung, Richter Gudrun, and Helge Thied, eds, *"—von jetzt an geht es nur noch aufwärts: entweder an die Macht oder an den Galgen!": Carlo Mierendorff (1897–1943), Schriftsteller, Politiker, Widerstandskämpfer* (Marburg, 1997).

31. Karl Otmar Freiherr von Aretin, ed. *Darmstadt und der 20. Juli 1944: [10 Beitr.], Darmstädter Schriften, vol. 35* (Darmstadt, 1974); Günter Brakelmann, *Die Kreisauer: folgenreiche Begegnungen: biographische Skizzen zu Helmuth James von Moltke, Peter Yorck von Wartenburg, Carlo Mierendorff und Theodor Haubach. Schriftenreihe der Forschungsgemeinschaft 20. Juli.* (Münster, 2004).

32. Hendrik de Man, *Zur Psychologie des Sozialismus,* ed. Artur Egon Bratu (Bonn-Bad Godesberg, 1976).

33. Artur Egon Bratu, "Hendrik de Man und die deutsche Sozialdemokratie," *Bulletin de l'association pour l'étude de l'oeuvre d'Henri de Man* 4 (1976): 1–5.

34. However, he was very much involved in advising Richard Albrecht, *Der militante Sozialdemokrat Carlo Mierendorff, 1897–1943: eine Biographie* (Berlin, 1987).

35. Sergeï Chakhotin, *The Rape of the Masses: The Psychology of Totalitarian Political Propaganda* (London, 1940).

36. See the remarkably clear-eyed analysis of the attractions of Nazism Carlo Mierendorff, "Gesicht und Charakter der Nationalsozialistischen Bewegung," *Die Gesellschaft; Internationale Revue für Sozialismus und Politik* 7 (June 1930): 489–504. On this essay, see Martin Broszat, "Zur Struktur der NS-Massenbewegung," *Vierteljahrshefte für Zeitschichte* 31, no. 1 (1983): 52–76.

37. Jürgen W. Fritz, *Die beginnende Nazi-Diktatur und der Mord and Christian Pleß in Offenbach am Main* (Offenbach, 1984).

38. Ulrich Herbert, *Best: biographische Studien über Radikalismus, Weltanschauung und Vernunft, 1903–1989* (Bonn, 1996).

39. Jakob Reitz, *Carlo Mierendorff 1897–1943: Stationen seines Lebens und Wirkens* (Darmstadt, 1983).

40. This tall and quite unbelievable story is well documented and can be reconstructed on the basis of Artur's calendar, which became a very condensed diary, as well as from the correspondence with one of his Exaerde students who had settled in Australia.

41. We know about the period between 1942–46 in more detail than any other period in his life, because Artur left a carefully crafted, reflexive diary, written in French, in addition to his calendar entries.

42. The somewhat mystifying records the Darmstadt Spruchkammer are in the Hessische Hauptstaatsarchiv, Wiesbaden. See as background Clemens Vollnhals, ed., *Entnazifizierung: politische Säuberung und Rehabilitierung in den vier Besatzungszonen 1945–1949* (Munich, 1991); Armin Schuster, *Die Entnazifizierung in Hessen 1945–1954* (Wiesbaden, 1999).

43. Hansen, *Cinema and Experience,* XVIII.

44. Michael Geyer, "Eine Kriegsgeschichte, die vom Tode spricht," in *Physische Gewalt: Studien zur Geschichte der Neuzeit,* ed. Thomas Lindenberger and Alf Lüdtke (Frankfurt, 1995), 136–61.

45. Moritz Neumann, *Im Zweifel nach Deutschland* (Springe, 2005); Moritz Neumann and Eva Reinhold-Postina, eds, *Das zweite Leben: Darmstädter Juden in der Emigration: ein Lesebuch* (Darmstadt, 1993).

46. Eva Reinhold-Postina and Moritz Neumann, *Das Darmstädter Synagogenbuch: eine Dokumentation zur Synagogen-Einweihung am 9. November 1988: im Auftrag des Magistrats der Stadt Darmstadt und der Jüdischen Gemeinde Darmstadt* (Darmstadt, 1988).

47. While there is a huge literature on the subject, it may suffice to cite a short essay that Miriam and I wrote as we started our conversation. Michael Geyer and Miriam Hansen, "German-Jewish Memory and National Consciousness," in *Holocaust Remembrance: The Shapes of Memory,* ed. Geoffrey H Hartman (Cambridge, MA, 1994), 175–90.

48. Ruth Bratu, "Ruth Bratu," in *"Wir waren ja eigentlich Deutsche": Juden berichten von Emigration und Rückkehr,* ed. Franz J Jürgens (Berlin, 1997), 227–48.

49. It is another story in the Bratu spirit. Resi had taken in an orphan, Elisabeth, in 1940. The daughter of Elisabeth (with a Scottish last name) just recently sent me an e-mail from Holland with photographs. She is writing a history of her family.

50. The letters are in the AdsD and are partially transcribed. I used them for Michael Geyer, "Virtue in Despair: A Family History from the Days of the Kindertransport," *History & Memory* 17, no. 1/2 (2005): 323–65.

51. As comparison: Wilma Iggers and Georg G. Iggers, *Zwei Seiten einer Geschichte: Lebensbericht aus unruhigen Zeiten* (Göttingen, 2002); Madeleine Korbel Albright and William Woodward, *Prague Winter: A Personal Story of Remembrance and War, 1937–1948,* 1st ed. (New York, 2012).

52. Marianne Zadikow May, *The Terezín Album of Mariánka Zadikow,* ed. Deborah Dwork (Chicago, 2008).

53. See the recollections of Zusanna Medusova and Susan Pearson on the website of the Woodcraft Folk: https://www.woodcraft.org.uk/history/kindertransport%20memories. The literature on the Kindertransports and the role of Nicholas Winton as the instigator of the Czech Kindertransports is now extensively remembered and explored – as well as controversially discussed. See among many others Claudia Curio, *Verfolgung, Flucht, Rettung: die Kindertransporte 1938/39 nach Grossbritannien* (Berlin, 2006); Jeremy Seabrook, *The Refuge and the Fortress: Britain and the Persecuted 1933–2013* (New York, 2013); Magdalena Wagnerová, *Winton Train: po sedmdesáti letech znovu do Londýna* (Praha, 2009); Barbara Winton, *If It's Not Impossible: The Life of Sir Nicholas Winton* (Kibworth Beauchamp, 2014). Brade, Laura E., and Rose Holmes. "Troublesome Sainthood: Nicholas Winton and the Contested History of Child Rescue in Prague, 1938–1940." *History & Memory* 29, no. 1 (2017): 3–40. See also Winfried Georg Sebald, *Austerlitz,* 1st ed. (New York, 2001); Sara Paretsky, *Critical Mass: A VI Warshawski novel* (New York, 2013).

54. Geyer, "Virtue in Despair."

55. Among others: Federica K. Clementi, *Holocaust Mothers & Daughters: Family, History, and Trauma* (Waltham, MA, 2013); Andrea Hammel and Anthony Grenville, eds, *Exile and Everyday Life* (Leiden, 2015).

56. The relationship changed when Ruth had married Artur and settled in Germany (though it must remain unclear if that is the reason). Ruth and Miriam visited England

regularly throughout the 1950s. Miriam in particular became fond of her great aunt, and the sentiment seems to have been returned.

57. Futur antérieur: "Das, was sich in meiner Geschichte, der Geschichte eines lebendigen Menschen, darstellt, ist nicht die ABGESCHLOSSENE VERGANGENHEIT (das war, weil es nicht mehr ist), auch nicht das Perfekt dessen, was gewesen ist in dem, was ich bin, sondern das ANDERE dessen, was gewesen sein werde für das, was ich zu werden im Begriff bin.—Das ist nicht leicht zu verstehen.—Es steht bei Lacan." Ruth never ceased to dream of being a tailor of fashionable women's cloths. The quote is from Kluge, *Die Lücke, die der Teufel lässt*, 221.

58. We know of his existence due to an e-mail inquiry by his daughter who wanted to hear more about her grandmother, which caused great excitement. However, she did not want to maintain the conversation.

59. Günter Schindler and Juergen Seuss, *Prag: Ein Bildband mit einem Textbeitrag von Andreas Razumovsky* (Frankfurt, 1967). This collection of photos emerged from visits in Prague with Ruth and Miriam.

60. Konrad H. Jarausch, *Die Umkehr: deutsche Wandlungen 1945–1995* (Munich, 2004); Konrad H Jarausch, *After Hitler: Recivilizing Germans, 1945–1995* (Oxford, 2006).

61. Kluge, *Die Lücke, die der Teufel lässt*.

62. Johanna Fränkel, *Die Reise nach Krakau: Tagebuch Mai 1999* (Darmstadt, 2014).

63. Moritz Neumann, *1945 nachgetragen: in den Trümmern von Darmstadt: das Ende der Diktatur und die Monate nach dem Krieg* (Darmstadt, 1995); Fritz Deppert and Peter Engels, *Feuersturm und Widerstand: Darmstadt 1944* (Darmstadt, 2004); United States Strategic Bombing Survey, *A Detailed Study of the Effects of Area Bombing on Darmstadt. Area Studies Division report*, 2nd ed. (Washington, DC, 1947).

64. https://www.darmstadt.de/standort/stadtportraet/gedenkstaetten/erinnerungsort-lib erale-synagoge/; https://www.darmstadt.de/standort/stadtportraet/gedenkstaetten/.

65. On disappearance see Bernard Wasserstein, *Vanishing Diaspora: The Jews in Europe since 1945* (London, 1997). The German title is more provocative: *Europa ohne Juden: das europäische Judentum seit 1945*, trans. Bernd Rullkötter (Cologne, 1999). Wittingly or unwittingly, the title makes the connection to the Nazi notion of a "disappearing people" that leads us back to Prague. Dirk Rupnow, *Täter, Gedächtnis, Opfer: das "Jüdische Zentralmuseum" in Prag 1942–1945* (Vienna, 2000); Dirk Rupnow, *Vernichten und Erinnern: Spuren nationalistischer Gedächnispolitik* (Göttingen, 2005).

66. Ritula Fränkel and Nicholas Morris, *X-Odus: Installation im Jüdischen Gemeindezentrum Darmstadt* (Darmstadt, 2001).

Bibliography

Albrecht, Richard. *Der militante Sozialdemokrat Carlo Mierendorff, 1897–1943: eine Biographie*. Berlin: Dietz, 1987.

Albright, Madeleine Korbel, and William Woodward. *Prague Winter: A Personal Story of Remembrance and War, 1937–1948*. 1st ed. New York: Harper, 2012.

Amlung, Ullrich, Richter Gudrun, and Helge Thied, eds. *"—von jetzt an geht es nur noch aufwärts: entweder an die Macht oder an den Galgen!": Carlo Mierendorff (1897–1943), Schriftsteller, Politiker, Widerstandskämpfer*. Marburg: Schüren, 1997.

Applegate, Celia. *A Nation of Provincials: The German Idea of Heimat.* Berkeley: University of California Press, 1990.

Aretin, Karl Otmar Freiherr von, ed. *Darmstadt und der 20. Juli 1944: [10 Beitr.], Darmstädter Schriften, vol. 35.* Darmstadt: Justus-von-Liebig-Verlat, 1974.

Brade, Laura E., and Rose Holmes. "Troublesome Sainthood: Nicholas Winton and the Contested History of Child Rescue in Prague, 1938-1940." *History & Memory* 29, no. 1 (2017): 3-40.

Brakelmann, Günter. *Die Kreisauer: folgenreiche Begegnungen: biographische Skizzen zu Helmuth James von Moltke, Peter Yorck von Wartenburg, Carlo Mierendorff und Theodor Haubach. Schriftenreihe der Forschungsgemeinschaft 20. Juli. 2.* Münster: Lit, 2004.

Bratu, Artur Egon. "Hendrik de Man und die deutsche Sozialdemokratie." *Bulletin de l'association pour l'étude de l'oeuvre d'Henri de Man* 4 (1976): 1–5.

Bratu, Ruth. "Ruth Bratu." In *"Wir waren ja eigentlich Deutsche": Juden berichten von Emigration und Rückkehr,* edited by Franz J Jürgens, 227–48. Berlin: Aufbau Taschenbuch Verlag, 1997.

Broszat, Martin. "Zur Struktur der NS-Massenbewegung." *Vierteljahrshefte für Zeitschichte* 31, no. 1 (1983): 52–76.

Chakhotin, Sergeĭ. *The Rape of the Masses: The Psychology of Totalitarian Political Propaganda.* London: G Routledge, 1940.

Clementi, Federica K. *Holocaust Mothers & Daughters: Family, History, and Trauma.* Waltham, MA: Brandeis University Press, 2013.

Confino, Alon. *The Nation as a Local Metaphor: Württemberg, Imperial Germany, and National Memory.* Chapel Hill: University of North Carolina Press, 1996.

Curio, Claudia. *Verfolgung, Flucht, Rettung: die Kindertransporte 1938/39 nach Grossbritannien.* Berlin: Metropol, 2006.

Deppert, Fritz, and Peter Engels. *Feuersturm und Widerstand: Darmstadt 1944.* Darmstadt: Schlapp, 2004.

Dische, Irene. *The Empress of Weehawken.* New York: Farrar, Straus and Giroux, 2007.

———. *Großmama packt aus: Roman.* Translated by Reinhard Kaiser. Hamburg: Hoffmann und Campe, 2005.

Domansky, Elisabeth. "A Lost War: World War II in Postwar German Memory." In *Thinking about the Holocaust after Half a Century,* edited by Alvin H Rosenfeld, 233–72. Bloomington: Indiana University Press, 1997.

Doniger, Wendy. *The Bedtrick: Tales of Sex and Masquerade. Worlds of Desire.* Chicago: University of Chicago Press, 2000.

Dwork, Deborah, and R. J. van Pelt. *Flight from the Reich: Refugee Jews, 1933–1946.* New York: Norton, 2009.

Dworok, Gerrit. *"Historikerstreit" und Nationswerdung. Ursprünge und Deutung eines bundesrepublikanischen Konflikts.* Cologne: Böhlau Verlag, 2015.

Felsch, Philipp. *Der lange Sommer der Theorie: Geschichte einer Revolte; 1960–1990.* Munich: Beck, 2015.

Fischer, Erica. *Aimée & Jaguar: eine Liebesgeschichte Berlin 1943.* Cologne: Kiepenheuer & Witsch, 1994.

Fränkel, Johanna. *Die Reise nach Krakau: Tagebuch Mai 1999.* Darmstadt: Privatdruck Justus von Liebig Verlag, 2014.

Fränkel, Ritula, and Nicholas Morris. *X-Odus: Installation im Jüdischen Gemeindezentrum Darmstadt.* Darmstadt: Jüdisches Gemeindezentrum Darmstadt, 2001.

Frei, Alfred Georg, and Susanne Asche. *Friedrich Hecker in den USA: eine deutsch-amerikanische Spurensicherung.* Konstanz: Stadler Verlagsgesellschaft, 1993.

Fritz, Jürgen W. *Die beginnende Nazi-Diktatur und der Mord and Christian Pleß in Offenbach am Main.* Offenbach: SPD Offenbach Mitte, Druckerei Wendorff, 1984.

Geyer, Michael. "Eine Kriegsgeschichte, die vom Tode spricht." In *Physische Gewalt: Studien zur Geschichte der Neuzeit,* edited by Thomas Lindenberger and Alf Lüdtke, 136–61. Frankfurt: Suhrkamp Verlag, 1995.

———. "Virtue in Despair: A Family History from the Days of the Kindertransport." *History & Memory* 17, no. 1/2 (2005): 323–65.

Geyer, Michael, and Miriam Hansen. "German-Jewish Memory and National Consciousness." In *Holocaust Remembrance: The Shapes of Memory,* edited by Geoffrey H Hartman, 175–90. Cambridge, MA: Blackwell, 1994.

Grosse Kracht, Klaus. *Die zankende Zunft: historische Kontroversen in Deutschland nach 1945.* Göttingen: Vandenhoeck & Ruprecht, 2005.

Hammel, Andrea, and Anthony Grenville, eds. *Exile and Everyday Life.* Leiden: Brill Rodopi, 2015.

Hansen, Miriam. *Cinema and Experience: Siegfried Kracauer, Walter Benjamin, and Theodor W. Adorno.* Berkeley: University of California Press, 2012.

———. "Max Ophuls and Instant Messaging: Reframing Cinema and Publicness." In *Screen Dynamics: Mapping the Borders of Cinema,* edited by Gertrud Koch, 22–29. Vienna: Synema—Gesellschaft für Film und Medien, 2012.

Herbert, Ulrich. *Best: biographische Studien über Radikalismus, Weltanschauung und Vernunft, 1903–1989.* Bonn: JHW Dietz, 1996.

Hirsch, Marianne. *Family Frames: Photography, Narrative, and Postmemory.* Cambridge, MA: Harvard University Press, 1997.

Iggers, Wilma, and Georg G. Iggers. *Zwei Seiten einer Geschichte: Lebensbericht aus unruhigen Zeiten.* Göttingen: Vandenhoeck & Ruprecht, 2002.

Jarausch, Konrad H. *After Hitler: Recivilizing Germans, 1945–1995.* Oxford: Oxford University Press, 2006.

———. *Die Umkehr: deutsche Wandlungen 1945–1995.* Munich: Deutsche Verlags-Anstalt, 2004.

Jobs, Sebastian, and Alf Lüdtke, eds. *Unsettling History: Archiving and Narrating in Historiography.* Frankfurt: Campus, 2010.

Jolles, André. *Andre Jolles (1874–1946): "gebildeter Vagant"; brieven en documenten,* edited by Walter Thys. Amsterdam: Amsterdam University Press, 2000.

———. *Einfache Formen: Legende, Sage, Mythe, Rätsel, Spruch, Kasus, Memorabile, Märchen, Witz.* Halle (Saale): M Niemeyer, 1930.

Kluge, Alexander. *Die Lücke, die der Teufel lässt: im Umfeld des neuen Jahrhunderts.* Frankfurt: Suhrkamp, 2003.

Koselleck, Reinhart. *Futures Past: On the Semantics of Historical Time.* Translated by Keith Tribe. Cambridge, MA: MIT Press, 1985.

Lehwark, Godehard. "Ruth Bratu: Ein exemplarisches jüdisches Leben." In *"Geh nicht den alten Weg zurück!" Festschrift zum sechzigjährigen Bestehen der Gesellschaft für Christlich-Jüdische Zusammenarbeit Darmstadt 1954–2014,* edited by Thomas Lange and Lothar Triebel, 96–105. Darmstadt: Justus von Liebig Verlag, 2014.

Leo, Per. *Flut und Boden: Roman einer Familie.* Stuttgart: Klett-Cotta, 2014.

Levi, Primo. *The Drowned and the Saved.* New York: Summit Books, 1988.

Lüdtke, Alf. *Eigen-Sinn: Fabrikalltag, Arbeitererfahrungen und Politik vom Kaiserreich bis in den Faschismus.* Hamburg: Ergebnisse Verlag, 1993.

Lyotard, Jean François. *Das Patchwork der Minderheiten: Für eine herrenlose Politik.* Translated by Clemens-Carl Haerle. Berlin: Merve, 1977.

———. "Heidnische Unterweisungen." In *Apathie der Theorie,* edited by Jean François Lyotard, 7–71. Berlin: Merve, 1979.

Man, Hendrik de. *Zur Psychologie des Sozialismus,* edited by Artur Egon Bratu. Bonn-Bad Godesberg: Hohwacht, 1976.

May, Marianne Zadikow. *The Terezín Album of Mariánka Zadikow,* edited by Deborah Dwork. Chicago: University of Chicago Press, 2008.

Mierendorff, Carlo. "Gesicht und Charakter der Nationalsozialistischen Bewegung." *Die Gesellschaft; Internationale Revue für Sozialismus und Politik* 7 (June 1930): 489–504.

———. *In Memoriam Carlo Mierendorff: literarische Schriften; [1897–1943],* edited by Artur E Bratu. Darmstadt: Darmstädter Verlag, 1980.

Negt, Oskar, and Alexander Kluge. *Public Sphere and Experience: Toward an Analysis of the Bourgeois and Proletarian Public Sphere.* Translated by Peter Labanyi, Jamie Daniel, and Assenka Oksiloff. Minneapolis: University of Minnesota Press, 1993.

Neumann, Moritz. *1945 nachgetragen: in den Trümmern von Darmstadt: das Ende der Diktatur und die Monate nach dem Krieg.* Darmstadt: Roether, 1995.

———. *Im Zweifel nach Deutschland.* Springe: zu Klampen Verlag, 2005.

Neumann, Moritz, and Eva Reinhold-Postina, eds. *Das zweite Leben: Darmstädter Juden in der Emigration: ein Lesebuch.* Darmstadt: E Roether, 1993.

Paretsky, Sara. *Critical Mass: A VI Warshawski novel.* New York: Putnam Adult, 2013.

Parker, Jo Alyson, Michael Crawford, and Paul Harris, eds. *Time and Memory, Study of Time.* Boston: Brill, 2006.

Petropoulos, Jonathan, and John K Roth, eds. *Gray Zones: Ambiguity and Compromise in the Holocaust and Its Aftermath.* New York: Berghahn Books, 2005.

Reinhold-Postina, Eva, and Moritz Neumann. *Das Darmstädter Synagogenbuch: eine Dokumentation zur Synagogen-Einweihung am 9. November 1988: im Auftrag des Magistrats der Stadt Darmstadt und der Jüdischen Gemeinde Darmstadt.* Darmstadt: E Roether Verlag, 1988.

Reitz, Jakob. *Carlo Mierendorff 1897–1943: Stationen seines Lebens und Wirkens.* Darmstadt: Liebig, 1983.

Roseman, Mark. *A Past in Hiding: Memory and Survival in Nazi Germany.* New York: Picador USA, 2000.

Rosenhaft, Eve. "One Man, Two Men, a Girl, a Car, a Flag: A Test for the Emeriti." In *Alltag, Erfahrung, Eigensinn: historisch-anthropologische Erkundungen,* edited by Belinda Davis, Lindenberger Thomas, and Michael Wildt. Frankfurt: Verlag, 2008.

Rupnow, Dirk. *Täter, Gedächtnis, Opfer: das "Jüdische Zentralmuseum" in Prag 1942–1945.* Vienna: Picus, 2000.

———. *Vernichten und Erinnern: Spuren nationalistischer Gedächnispolitik.* Göttingen: Wallstein, 2005.

Schindler, Günter, and Juergen Seuss. *Prag: Ein Bildband mit einem Textbeitrag von Andreas Razumovsky.* Frankfurt: Büchergilde Gutenberg, 1967.

Schneider, Peter. *Die Lieben meiner Mutter.* Cologne: Kiepenheuer & Witsch, 2013.

Schuster, Armin. *Die Entnazifizierung in Hessen 1945–1954.* Wiesbaden: Historische Kommission für Nassau, 1999.

Seabrook, Jeremy. *The Refuge and the Fortress: Britain and the Persecuted 1933–2013.* New York: Palgrave Macmillan, 2013.

Sebald, Winfried Georg. *Austerlitz.* New York: Random House, 2001.

Spence, Jonathan D. *The Memory Palace of Matteo Ricci.* New York: Viking Penguin, 1984.

Stargardt, Nicholas. *The German War: A Nation under Arms, 1939–45.* New York: Basic Books, 2015.

Tillich, Paul. *The Courage to Be.* London: Nisbet & Co, 1952.

United States Strategic Bombing Survey. *A Detailed Study of the Effects of Area Bombing on Darmstadt. Area Studies Division report.* 2nd ed. Washington, DC: Area Studies Division, 1947.

Vollnhals, Clemens, ed. *Entnazifizierung: politische Säuberung und Rehabilitierung in den vier Besatzungzonen 1945–1949.* Munich: Deutscher Taschenbuch Verlag, 1991.

Wagnerová, Magdalena. *Winton Train: po sedmdesáti letech znovu do Londýna.* Praha: Havran, 2009.

Wasserstein, Bernard. *Europa ohne Juden: das europäische Judentum seit 1945.* Translated by Bernd Rullkötter. Cologne: Kiepenheuer & Witsch, 1999.

———. *Vanishing Diaspora: The Jews in Europe since 1945.* London: Penguin, 1997.

Winton, Barbara. *If It's Not Impossible: The Life of Sir Nicholas Winton.* Kibworth Beauchamp: Matador, 2014.

Chapter 11

On Losing One's Children Twice
An Intimate *Vergangenheitsaufarbeitung*

Elizabeth Heineman

Correspondence, Family Ties, and History

On 18 June 1945, a social worker with the Jewish Refugees' Commission (JRC) typed an entry into the case file of one of her charges, a fourteen-year-old boy named Herbert. Almost exactly six years earlier, Herbert had arrived in the United Kingdom with the Refugee Children's Movement, known colloquially among German-speaking Jews as the Kindertransport to England. Two items occupied the social worker's five-line entry. First, the JRC had received word that the child's parents were alive. They had been liberated in Theresienstadt, and the news was being communicated to Herbert and his older brother, Eric. Second, the boy needed gym shorts. B'nai B'rith should be asked to provide funds, and the organization should be instructed to see whether Herbert had any other pressing needs.[1]

This interweaving of banal business with questions about the survival of one's parents characterized the experience of Kindertransport children. Contemporary and retrospective accounts alike make clear that separation from one's parents was traumatic, and many refugee children suffered through abusive, emotionally cold, or frequently changing placements.[2] Yet compared with Jewish children who survived the war in occupied Europe, those who made it to the United Kingdom were enormously privileged; some genuinely flourished there. Herbert was one of them. And so before we write off the second half of the social worker's entry as a

---

trivial side bar to the sensational news of his parents' survival, we might entertain the possibility that the social worker was responding to Herbert's articulation of his own needs. For an adolescent boy, anxieties about ill-fitting gym shorts might have felt more important—or at least more time-sensitive—than the fate of his parents. Herbert had been without his parents since he was eight. He had to face his peers in the locker room several times a week. But if gym shorts were near the top of Herbert's concerns, we might imagine difficulties when he and his survivor parents were finally reunited.

In his first letter to his parents following their liberation, Herbert—or "Herbi," as he signed his letters—expressed his joy at their survival and reassured them that he and his brother had been well cared for in England. Yet his words pointed to a common challenge of parents and children reunited after several years' separation: "Wir sind ganz gross geworden, und Ihr wird [sic] uns kaum erkennen können."[3] ["We've grown a lot (lit: We've become very big), and you will barely be able to recognize us." "You will" is incorrectly conjugated.] Herbi's suggestion of unrecognizability was a casual expression of pride at his growth, not a prediction of problems, and Lisette and Max might have been reassured that he still wrote well in German, despite the occasional grammatical error: some parents survived the war only to discover that they and their refugee children could no longer communicate. Thirty years later, however, Herb's sense that his parents failed to recognize his maturation was much more consequential: "I am, and always will be, your son," he wrote in a letter of 1974. "But I am no longer your child. This distinction—or rather, failure to make the distinction—is at the root of a good part of the problem."[4] "The problem," as he put it, was the dismal relationship between him and the rest of the family.

If it were not for the fact that families have frequently been separated, historians would know much less about their internal dynamics: the correspondence prompted by separation is often our only window into this intimate sphere. To be sure, families usually experienced separation as an exceptional state, linked to external circumstances that were threatening, such as war; or at least temporary, such as staggered migration or work-related travel. (Permanent migration of grown children has historically been a significant exception.) Correspondents thus not only discussed and enacted their relations with each other: they also reflected on the reasons for their separation. And so historians have mined family letters not only to understand the texture of intimate life, but also for their authors' private reflections about the larger circumstances in which they found themselves, albeit within limits posed by such factors as censorship, the cost of postage, and the effort of writing at length.[5]

This has certainly been the case for the upheavals of Germany's early and mid twentieth century.[6] Thanks to widespread literacy, an efficient postal system, and the vast scale of conscription and emigration, family correspondence within the context of historical crisis became a nearly universal practice. Shorthand phrases captured people's sense that these were shared experiences. German authorities in World War I worried about "Jammerbriefe" — letters of complaint from home that might diminish morale among fighting men.[7] Jewish parents who sent their children abroad to escape Nazi persecution lamented that "aus Kindern werden Briefe" ("children are transformed into letters").[8] Such correspondence usually ended with reunion or the death of one of the correspondents. For this reason, it offers insight into family members' interpretation of their circumstances during their separation, but it does not help us to understand the longer-term impact of their time apart.

The Heineman family correspondence constitutes an exception for two reasons. First, the family's reunion was an exceptional event. Although some 40 percent of children sent to England with the Kindertransport were reunited with at least one parent, few such reunions involved parents who had survived the war in occupied Europe.[9] Rather, the overwhelming majority involved parents who had found their own routes of escape — a task ironically made easier once they were unencumbered by children. In many cases, parents followed their children to the United Kingdom within a few weeks or months. Some escaped elsewhere and then sent for their children to join them in after a relatively short period of separation. Yet others spent the war years in far-flung locations and saw their children again only after the war. Reunions between refugee children and survivor parents were the rare exception.

As historian Vera Fast notes, though, reunion "was not necessarily a happy time for the Kinder, parents, or assisting agencies," especially when the separation had been lengthy and the parents had experienced years of hiding or internment in occupied Europe.[10] We have many testimonies from the children about difficult reunions, few about happy ones.[11] From the children's testimony, it becomes clear that parents' survival was often followed by the bitter realization that they could no longer reestablish meaningful ties to their children, or worse, that their children experienced their parents' sudden reappearance as yet another disruption.[12]

Yet direct evidence regarding parents' experience of reunion is hard to come by.[13] In this regard, too, the Heineman family correspondence constitutes an exception. After Max and Lisette sent their sons, Eric (b. 1927) and Herb (b. 1930), to England in June 1939, the family corresponded extensively until the war made it impossible. They began writing again after the liberation of Theresienstadt, where Max and Lisette were interned from July 1942 to May 1945, and continued through the parents' nineteen months as displaced persons. Once the parents made it to London in December 1946, correspondence ceased—but only temporarily. In 1957, Herb moved out of his family's Bronx apartment to take a medical internship in Durham, North Carolina; subsequent moves took him to Pittsburgh and Philadelphia. Eric remained with his parents through Max's death in 1967 and Lisette's in 1982; Eric died in 1985. Phone calls and personal visits helped Herb to stay in touch with his family of origin, but written correspondence remained very important. Not only were letters more economical than phone calls or visits, but the family had long-established habits of letter-writing. Furthermore, letters offered a measure of distance and control that made it easier to discuss contentious issues.

And there were contentious issues aplenty. Herb's family saw his move away from New York as a betrayal; four years later, his marriage to a gentile woman was even less well received. Preceding and following these major ruptures was a constant thrum of lesser irritants: arguments over an adolescent romance, birthdays come and gone without a call, perceived verbal slights during visits, and so on. Of course, many families fight, and in some ways the Heinemans faced a common challenge: a grown child's desire to plot a life course that diverges from his or her parents' wishes. Yet in their correspondence, the Heinemans interpreted their conflicts in light of their history, and they deployed the past in their efforts to influence the outcome of ongoing conflicts. In so doing, they revisited larger issues such as Nazi persecution, forced migration, and divisions within the Jewish community. Significantly, they contended with family tensions that predated the rise of Nazism; their history gives lie to the comforting but overgeneralized claim that close Jewish family ties constituted a partial refuge from persecution.[14] In other words, the correspondence bears witness to a *Vergangenheitsaufarbeitung*—a working through of the past—that referred both to the intimate sphere and to history writ large.

The surviving correspondence came to me via Herb, who is my father. Not surprisingly, he mainly possessed letters he had received. Only rarely did letters he had posted find their way back into his hands. On a couple of occasions, he made copies of his own letters before mailing them. Frequently, his words were quoted in subsequent letters back to him, usually with a demand for explanation. Thus the collection includes some evidence of Herb's epistolary activity, even if the rest of the family is much better represented.

The collection consists of four major clusters. The first, with fifty-seven letters, postcards, or fragments of letters, consists largely of letters from Max and Lisette to Eric and Herb in the summer and fall of 1939 with a few dating from 1940 to 1942. There are a smaller number of letters from other relatives and friends to Eric and Herb, and from Eric and Herb to Max and Lisette and other family in Germany and elsewhere during those same years. The second cluster, with sixty-seven items, covers Max and Lisette's period as displaced persons, from June 1945 to December 1946. Most are letters or postcards from Max and Lisette to their sons jointly or separately. Additional items include correspondence by other family members and friends as well as telegrams, including a small number of letters from Eric and Herb to Max and Lisette. The correspondence between the parents and their children from 1939 to 1946 is in German. In general, the letters Max and Lisette sent directly to their sons appear to have survived nearly in their entirety for the years 1939–46, although other types of correspondence from these two clusters is quite sporadic.

The correspondence from Herb's adulthood survives in much more fragmentary form. After departing his parents' home in 1957, Herb did not save what he regarded as routine correspondence: health updates, vacation greetings, reports on the antics of children and pets. Rather, with few exceptions, he saved only letters documenting conflict. The majority of these fall into two clusters: a few weeks in spring 1961, as Lisette, Max, and Eric tried to dissuade Herb from marrying his gentile fiancée, Maggie (fifteen letters); and December 1982 to July 1985, when Eric's grief at Lisette's death and contemplation of his own declining health found expression in an outpouring of grievances against Herb (forty-six letters and ephemera). The remaining twenty-two letters from Herb's adulthood are chronologically scattered but likewise mainly record conflict.[15] Almost all of the post-1957 correspondence is in English, with Eric occasionally switching to German toward the end of his life.

A correspondence spanning so many decades invites two kinds of analysis: close inspection of key moments, and a longer view of correspondents' interpretation of their present circumstances and their shared history. This essay focuses on a key moment: the spring of 1961, when Herb announced his engagement to Maggie. Since knowledge of the longer story shapes our reading of shorter moments, however, a few words about the longer story as well as the larger body of correspondence are in order. Certain dynamics appear consistent throughout the many decades of correspondence, most notably Lisette's dominant role in family matters. Letters cosigned by her and Max, for example, usually include several paragraphs in her handwriting followed by a few lines in Max's. But other family dynamics, particularly those involving the growth of pre-adolescent brothers into men of middle age, involved significant change.

Writing about one's own family has certain advantages beyond the accident of inheriting correspondence. In pursuing my research, I enjoyed the trust of family members and friends who provided oral histories, access to archival records that are open only to those who can demonstrate a family connection, and my own memories. Yet even in a post-Rankean age that denies the possibility of perfect objectivity, writing about one's own family raises special questions about the historian's relationship to her subject, especially in a family marked by deep divisions.

The next Heineman generation—mine—was largely spared both the weight of history and the weight of family quarrels. Despite their many differences, members of Lisette and Herb's generations seem to have tacitly agreed not to drag the grandchildren into their rows. My memories of our frequent visits to Lisette and Eric's Flushing apartment are not of fights, but rather of the strangely chewy Toblerone chocolate Lisette spoiled us with and the African violet leaves she wrapped in dampened paper towels for me to transplant from her collection to my own. And they are of the framed, colored-pencil sketches of scenes of Theresienstadt, gifts from friends in the ghetto, which shared wall space with Lisette's needlework. My siblings and I understood the intimate presence of atrocity without being overwhelmed by it.

I did not become a historian because my paternal family history weighed unbearably upon me. For that I am grateful to those who spared my generation that weight. But presented with the type of evidence about my family history that historians find irresistible—a stack of letters from multiple members of a single family spanning decades—I felt both a scholarly and a personal impulse to dig further. The fact that I felt personally *competent* to explore this history with empathy toward all parties likewise resounds to the credit of both the Philadelphia and the New York branches of my family. For that, too, I am grateful.[16]

The Kaufmann-Heinemann Family

Neither Lisette nor Max came from particularly elevated circumstances.[17] Lisette Kaufmann, born in 1900, was the youngest of six surviving children of a butcher's family in the tiny Rhineland village of Irlich, adjacent to the town of Neuwied. (Three siblings died in infancy.) The Kaufmanns were the only Jews in Irlich, but Neuwied had a substantial enough Jewish community that it could support a one-room primary Jewish school. Like all of her siblings except her brother Max, Lisette had a primary education only. Lisette's resentment at Max's privilege—she felt she was as bright as he, and dreamed of becoming a doctor—was a factor in the siblings' lifelong hostility toward each other. In 1926 Lisette married another Max— Max Heinemann, an only child born in 1891—whose right arm had been paralyzed in World War I. Together with his widowed father, Max Heinemann ran a small business selling supplies to Krefeld bakeries. (In the following pages, "Max" refers to Max Heinemann; "Max K" refers to Max Kaufmann.) The couple's two surviving children were Eric, born 1927, and Herb, born 1930; a daughter born in 1928 died shortly after birth. After Hitler's rise to power, all but one of Lisette's siblings immigrated to scattered destinations, but Lisette and her family did not find a way out. After the pogrom of November 1938, in which their apartment was destroyed, the family was moved to a "Jew house." Lisette and Max's experience during the first half of the war is hard to reconstruct but appears to have included at least one more move within Krefeld and Lisette's task of assisting elderly Jews in nearby Bonn, a job Lisette described in her restitution claims as forced labor. Together with Lisette's widowed sister and widowed mother, Lisette and Max were deported to Theresienstadt in July 1942. Lisette's mother was deported further and murdered in Treblinka; her sister met the same violent end in Auschwitz.

In June 1939, Lisette and Max sent their sons on the Kindertransport to England. Over the next years, Eric and Herb moved frequently but, unlike many siblings on the Kindertransport, they remained together almost until the end of the war. Their most consequential move was to an orthodox hostel in 1942, which turned the boys, whose parents' practice had been liberal, to orthodoxy. Aside from their common religious turn, Eric and Herb experienced England very differently. Herb, not quite nine when he arrived, adapted easily. He quickly picked up English, had friends and eventually a serious girlfriend, and excelled academically, winning a scholarship to an exclusive grammar school. All this was facilitated by the fact that, by his own later admission, he did not particularly miss his parents or worry about them. Eric, who had just turned twelve, had a much harder time. He struggled with the new language, with school, with a facial paralysis that may have left him vulnerable to taunts, and no doubt with his emerging homosexuality. And he missed his parents terribly and worried constantly about their fate. The brothers' different responses to separation from their parents signaled the beginning of their lifelong rift. Eric considered Herb shockingly uncaring about their parents, while Herb considered Eric a nag and resented his older brother's claim to the moral high ground.[18]

The parents survived three years in Theresienstadt, then waited over a year and a half as displaced persons until they were able to obtain a visa to travel to England. After a year in England, the family immigrated to New York. There they again encountered Lisette's brother, Max K, now a successful accountant to the orthodox community in the heavily German-Jewish neighborhood of Washington Heights, where the penniless Heinemans initially settled. (They dropped the final "n" of their last name upon immigration.) Max K himself had become orthodox, although Lisette was skeptical about the sincerity of his belief, convinced that economic motives were at play: Max K's professed orthodoxy gave him access to a valued clientele. Eric and Herb retained their orthodoxy for a few years, but starting in the mid 1950s, they both drifted from strict religious practice. Eric settled into the liberal Judaism of his parents and his own childhood, while Herb eventually left Jewish practice and affiliation entirely.

Following their move to New York, the two sons worked full-time to support the family while first completing coursework required for American high school diplomas, then attending college. Max, who was fifty-six upon his arrival in New York, with a paralyzed right arm and halting English, never found work above the level of an office gopher. Lisette kept house for the three men.

Eric had trained as an electrician in England and found work in New York, eventually earning a bachelor's degree and becoming technical director for a local TV news station. Herb put himself through college and medical school before leaving New York against the wishes of his family in 1957 to take a medical internship in Durham. He moved again to Pittsburgh for his residency, where he met and married Maggie. The couple moved to Philadelphia and raised three children, of whom I am the oldest. Eric remained with his parents, and after Max's death in 1967, he and Lisette had a close relationship that lasted until her death in 1982. Along the way were a few awkward attempts to find a wife and at least one serious relationship with a man, about whom nothing is known. Eric died less than three years after his mother, at age fifty-eight, in 1985.

There were two fault lines upon the family's reunion after the war. The first was religious. Neither the orthodox sons nor the liberal parents were inclined to change their practice, but given the strict rules of orthodoxy, it was incumbent on the parents to adapt if orthodox and liberal were to share a household. Eric and Herb not only required a kosher kitchen but also called on their parents to perform tasks forbidden to them on the Sabbath, such as switching lights on or off and carrying parcels. This was traditionally the role of "Sabbath goyim": non-Jews who helped their Jewish neighbors or employers by performing minor tasks forbidden to Jews on the Sabbath. To ask less observant Jews to perform these tasks came perilously close to suggesting that they were not Jewish at all. Yet Lisette and Max indulged Eric and Herb for roughly a decade, until the sons relaxed their practice. Abetting their sons' orthodoxy did not just minimize conflict. It also prolonged the sons' dependence on their parents, enabling Lisette in particular to make up for lost time, as she did most of the work required to facilitate her sons' orthodoxy.

The religious fault line thus bound the sons to the parents even as it (temporarily) divided them. Observance also created two factions of equal numeric strength: two liberal parents, two orthodox sons. The second fault line differed in both respects: it pitted Herb, with his vision of independence and self-determination, against the other three members of the family, who embraced interdependence and deference to parental authority.[19] Already during the war, the fact that Eric had suffered while Herb had flourished while separated from their parents had caused tension. Once the family was reunited, Herb, like Eric, took his parents' authority for granted—but there were early warnings that Max and Lisette's reappearance would prove more constraining for Herb than for Eric. Lisette, for example, did not welcome the news that Herb had a girlfriend: another Kindertransport refugee named Irene. Eric's lack of interest in women meant that his parents did not face similar competition for his affections. (It is not clear when Eric became aware of his homosexuality. As a young orthodox Jew in the homophobic environment of wartime and early postwar Britain, he may well have been deeply closeted to himself as well as to others. It is possible that fealty to his parents provided an emotionally and socially acceptable reason for declining to develop relationships with women.)

Irene and Herb's romance ended with Herb's immigration to New York and Irene's to Chile, where her mother had spent the war. Once in New York, the family reestablished itself as an interdependent unit: the three men worked, the two sons attended school, and the mother kept house. Yet Irene's brief reappearance early in the 1950s (the precise date is unclear) helped to solidify the deepening fault line between Herb and the other three. After they had been out of touch for years, Irene wrote to Herb announcing an upcoming visit to New York and inviting him to a party that some of her old girlfriends from England—now also in New York—planned to throw for her. Lisette not only demanded that Herb write a letter to Irene requesting that she never contact him again, but also sent Eric to the party to convey the message in person. Eric had adopted the role of enforcer and defender of Lisette's position in conflicts with Herb.

Against this background, the decision to take a medical internship in Durham rather than in New York was personal as well as professional for Herb: at the age of twenty-seven, he could finally establish an independent existence. For the rest of the family, Herb's decision was a betrayal. A scant ten years after their reunion, he was now breaking up the household again.

Thus, the main drama of the family, from its reunification until Eric's death, was the deepening schism between Herb and the others. This schism was foreshadowed—or perhaps it really began—with the sons' early separation from their parents and Herb and Eric's wartime tensions with each other. Given the extent to which that history had been shaped by Nazi persecution, it was perhaps inevitable that telling family history would entail telling Nazi history. But the point for family narrators was not to understand the Nazi past. The point was to understand the family's past, as well as its present—and to shape its future by convincing an antagonist to change his or her behavior.

The family correspondence reflects changing relationships as a unit comprised of parents and their young children evolved into a unit comprised of adult sons, elderly parents, in-laws, and grandchildren. But letters did not simply record changes that had occurred elsewhere, such as in face-to-face contact. Rather, they were in their own right a site for negotiating relationships.

The earliest letters, immediately following the boys' departure from Krefeld, display efforts to maintain the familiar parent–child relationship. In letters addressed to both Eric and Herb and occasionally employing an epistolary version of baby talk, Lisette and Max shared news of family and friends, used pet names, repeated running jokes, and asserted parental authority, for example by critiquing the children's letters.[20] With the second cluster of letters, from 1945 to 1946, family members worked to become reacquainted by exchanging photos, news of the intervening years, and ongoing developments. Letters also, however, helped to establish new hierarchies and alliances, as they were the main vehicle through which Eric and his parents collaborated on the task of bringing Max and Lisette to England. Herb's passivity in these efforts may have appeared natural to Max and Lisette—after all, Eric had completed school and lived in London, close to administrative offices, while Herb was still busy with school in Manchester. Herb and Eric, however, probably recognized the division of labor as continuing the familiar pattern of Eric's greater concern for their parents.

The post–1957 correspondence is rich with references to all these stages of the family history, as well as chapters that had preceded and followed them: from Lisette's lifelong conflict with Max K through Eric and Herb's responses to Lisette's death. Yet these letters, too, do not simply record existing tensions: rather, they were a vehicle for their intensification and attempts at amelioration. It was in the 1961 correspondence that Herb took his most definitive step away from the family by insisting on his plans to marry a gentile woman, while the rest of the family formed a unified front in seeking to dissuade him. In the early 1980s, with little face-to-face or telephone contact between the estranged brothers, Eric and Herb's letters determined whether the brothers would reconcile before Eric's death.

History and Coming to Terms with the Present

By 1961, Herb was living in Pittsburgh, where he had taken up his medical residency. On 10 February, Herb wrote to Eric that he hoped to bring a young woman, Maggie, to meet the family.[21] Herb had mentioned Maggie in a letter to Eric of 24 January, but had noted that she wasn't Jewish and that the relationship thus probably would not go very far. Even in that letter, however, Herb had appeared to hedge his bets by noting that he himself "[hadn't] been much of a Jew these last few years."[22] Eric shared the letters with his parents. Herb's plans to bring Maggie to New York caused alarm: the rest of the family concluded, correctly, that this meant Herb and Maggie were discussing marriage. What ensued was a three-month flurry of correspondence in which Lisette, Max, and Eric tried to dissuade Herb from following through with his plans. Their ways of drawing on history evolved as the dispute deepened.

In the first stage of the correspondence, the points of reference were close: immediate family, events of the last few months, and—very occasionally—the extended family and broader Jewish community. Descriptions of physical distance between Herb and the rest of the family often blurred into metaphors of emotional distance. On 14 February, Eric wrote: "You left home in 1957 and since then you have become more of a stranger." On the same day Lisette wrote: "It seems to me you are further away from your family than the mileage from NY to Pittsburgh." Three days later, she elaborated on the theme: "I cannot get over it, that a man with your brain (nothing to say, my son), could drift so far away from himself and his family … if you had been a little closer to us, maybe it would have been different."[23]

Herb's geographic and emotional distance from his family, however, was not an urgent matter: it had been the state of affairs for some time. The emergency was Herb's plan to intermarry. This would amount to a permanent break with Judaism (no branch of Judaism condoned intermarriage at the time) and gentile status for his children (Judaism traces belonging through the maternal line). Orthodox parents performed rituals of mourning for children who intermarried: such children were as good as dead. But not only were Lisette and Max not orthodox: their response to Herb's plans made clear that their disdain for the orthodox—and orthodox family members' disdain for them—were among their reasons for objecting. "We built up here a nice liberal Jewish life and gained a bit of respect despite our own enemies in the meshpoche [extended family]," Max wrote on 14 February. "When you look back all this [*sic*] years just starting with England, so I'm telling you clearly that I hope this people wouldn't point their fingers on us when [if] this terrible thing becomes true." "The meshpoche" — characterized here as "enemies" — boiled down to Lisette's brother, Max K., and those within his circuit.

This first stage of the correspondence is overwhelmingly focused on the present and the very recent past. Max's words about "all this years just starting with England" is one of only two passages that goes back that far, but it is not entirely clear in his passage *what* started with England. Lisette's sole reference to those years is more precise: "You are willing to bring a gentile girl in our house," Lisette wrote, "you the one who couldn't get over it, that his parents weren't religious enough when we met in England?"[24] The history of Herb's shifting observance and tensions within the extended family mattered, but what is most notable in the initial stage of the correspondence is how little space is devoted to *any* history prior to the last few months — and the complete silence about the years before 1946.

In these earliest letters, Lisette and Max did not seem to realize the extent of their challenge. (After his initial letter of 14 February, Eric remained silent until 6 April.) Although they made clear their disapproval of Herb's relationship with Maggie, Lisette and Max's letters also included friendly chitchat ("I lost six pounds"[25]), reminders of shared jokes, and discussion of other serious matters such as medical news and the progress of restitution claims against the West German government.

Herb brought Maggie for the much-anticipated visit on the weekend of 25–26 February. But Lisette turned Maggie away at the door. Herb accompanied Maggie to her hotel, stayed with her for a lengthy conversation, then returned to his parents' apartment late at night for what he recalls as a heated argument. The next day, he picked up Maggie for the drive back to Pittsburgh.

Curiously, Lisette and Max initially seemed optimistic after this visit. Their letters from that Monday opened with formulaic lines expressing their hope that he had arrived safely back home, then proceeded to questions about their restitution claims. Max wrote not a word about the visit; Lisette interpreted their argument as productive. "I feel sorry that your visit this time was not the same it used to be, but I'm still glad we talked about this situation. I did not like it, that we had to use some harsh words and had to hurt each other, but you may know, it is sometimes necessary to put your foot down, even if you hurt somebody you love. It is to be done, because you love him, and you do not want him to get in trouble and get hurt by his own decision." Most remarkably, Lisette acknowledged a possible earlier misstep, albeit with a quick qualification: "And thinking of yesterday's discussion, I must say, I feel terribly about my interference in your affair (or better romance) with the girl from Chile [Irene] years back. But didn't I make you write this letter after she was engaged to somebody else, and still wrote you letters with love and lipstick?" This is the only moment in the surviving correspondence in which any of the protagonists acknowledge their own role in the worsening family relations. But in keeping with her sense that their argument had cleared the air, Lisette then turned to "the lighter side"—thanks for a recent gift—before signing off.[26]

Only with the receipt of Herb's subsequent letter did Lisette, Max, and Eric understand that Herb's position had hardened, not softened, as a result of his visit. From this point on, letters rarely strayed from the central themes of Herb's marriage plans and his alienation from the family, and there were few efforts to lighten the tone. Rather, the realization of just how high the stakes had become prompted the family to its deepest reflection, and harshest accusations, regarding family dynamics and their historical context. In the second stage of the correspondence, from 8 March to 17 April, a struggle for the future set into motion a struggle for the past.

Herb apparently made the first reference to Germany in his response to the letters of 27 February (which does not survive). In her letter of 8 March, Lisette paraphrased him: "What does it mean, that your environment has changed so much, and that you have grown up in places so far from home ... Who sent you to Durham and later to Pittsburgh? ... Now ... I hear you talking about after Pittsburgh going to California. More and more away from us ... does it mean you're giving up going to what you called 'home'?" Lisette's words draw our attention to the multiplicity of reference points, the many possible points of origin from which departure meant trouble. Was "home" Germany, the childhood home far from which Herb had grown up, for reasons none of them could control? Or was it New York, which—Lisette pointedly reminds him—Herb had departed voluntarily? The designation of guilt depended on the point at which the telling of history began.

Herb was the first to refer (if obliquely) to their years of separation, but the heightened stakes brought Lisette to the theme as well. Her initial recourse to Nazi-era history was a line that was packed with meaning—even if it also happened to be the ultimate rhetorical weapon in survivor families: "Is that the price we have to pay for surviving the concentration camp?"[27] But the Nazi past did not just underscore the seriousness of Herb's betrayal. Rather, it provided a set of lessons against intermarriage. In her longest letter of the series, penned on 8 March, Lisette wrote: "Herb, there is an invisible wall between Jews and goyim, even more when they are Protestant." (Lisette had fond memories of Catholic neighbors in Germany; Maggie's family was Protestant.) "They were it in principle who brought all the miseries upon us for long years, and for you too. First we had to go through this hell, because we are Jews, when we came to the

USA we were kicked around, because we were not enough Jewish, and now you are coming and make us pay the big price for it." Two weeks later, she drew on history to make dire predictions: "Your children—nebbich [poor things]—they will be pushed from synagogue to church forth and back—they never will know where they belong to, and when after generations some kind of Hitler comes to power they'll have to suffer even more than the 100% Jews!"[28] Even as she acknowledged Herb's seriousness, Lisette claimed greater wisdom based on her experience. "You are fighting for something and I'm—we the rest of the family—are doing the same against it ... I have more reasons 'against' than you have 'for.' My reasons are based on a life of experience while all what counts for your point of view is how you feel toward *this* girl, and it is not an opinion in general."

But Lisette's reflections on history were also deeply personal. "O Herbi,"—the use of an interjection, "O," is completely uncharacteristic of her writing style—"what are you doing? For nearly eight long and horrible years we were praying to see our children again, and after a few years of being together you wanted to go your own way. ... Herbi, what I wanted for the rest of my life, was peace of mind, that is gone. I'll always have to think what did I wrong, what for am I losing my son to a Christian girl?"[29]

Lisette's words are heartfelt, but also conspicuous for what they omit. "*First* [in Germany, emphasis added] we had to go through this hell because we are Jews," *then* "when we came to the USA we were kicked around because we were not enough Jewish." "For eight years we prayed to see our children again; after a few years together you wanted to go your own way." But Herb had lived in England from age eight to seventeen, and when he wrote about growing up in places far from home, he surely referred as much to England as to New York. Yet nowhere in Lisette's correspondence is there any indication that she understands that England was a significant chapter in her son's life—a chapter that informed *his* "life of experience."

In the last week of March, Herb wrote a letter that appears to have heightened tensions yet more. Although the letter does not survive, Lisette and Max's responses of 29 March give some hints of its tone and content, as well as their bitter acknowledgment that their persuasive efforts had been futile. "How did you get the idea to write to *your parents* in such a nasty manner," Max wrote. "Your letter is a document for us as long as we are alive." Both parents quoted Herb's line—"*we'll* make the decision"—as a shocking deviation from filial deference. Lisette, who had formerly called Maggie a "goyte" (a female "goy" or non-Jew—the term can be but is not necessarily pejorative), now switched to the highly insulting "chickse":

technically any non-Jewish woman, but in vernacular usage one who uses her sexual allure to tempt a Jewish man from the fold. "She is a clever one," Lisette wrote. "She hooked herself a wonderful boy with an excellent future, and time will tell you how big a fool you are, to fall for it."

In this third stage of the correspondence, following Herb's declaration that *"we'll* make the decision," the futility of further argument appears to have rendered the past irrelevant. The letters of 29 March were tightly focused on the present. Gone were the references to Nazi persecution and to tensions between liberal and orthodox Jewry; gone were the attempts to convince Herb by warning him that their religiously confused descendants might suffer when the next Hitler came along. Instead, Herb and Maggie were the offending parties. "It does not even enter your mind what you're doing to us," Lisette wrote. "I know now perfectly how little you care for us."[30]

And then: silence, at least on Lisette and Max's part. On 6 April, Eric wrote a letter underscoring Lisette and Max's distress over Herb's plans and urging him to change his mind. Eric's next two letters, dated 12 April and 17 April, indicated that plans were moving forward, to Eric's displeasure, as he expressed his anger at having been Herb's second choice as best man. Rather than comply with this insulting request, Eric declared, he would probably boycott the wedding. (Herb's first choice, his best friend from medical school and now family physician to Lisette and Max, had declined—a decision Herb interpreted as taking his parents' side in the familial schism, particularly hurtful since Herb had served as best man at *his* wedding.) By this time, the date for the wedding had been set: 7 May.

The breakthrough came on 22 April. In separate letters to Maggie and Herb, Lisette welcomed Maggie to the family. Lisette referred to letters that had arrived in the interim from both Herb and Maggie, but wrote that it was Maggie's letter "that made us change our minds and that took the pressure of the last few months from us." What was it about Maggie's letter that required that Lisette "read it over and over to believe what is in it"? We do not know; the letter does not survive. Perhaps in that letter Maggie announced her eleventh-hour conversion to Judaism: in Lisette's letter to Herb, she asked for details about what would clearly be a Jewish ceremony. Both of Lisette's letters were unconditionally warm; both expressed the hope to look forward rather than dwell on the past.

Max's two-line postscript to Lisette's letter to Maggie was as clear an introduction to family dynamics as a new daughter-in-law could hope for: "As usual my boss wrote the letter and I have to give, with pleasure, the O.K." In a different way, Max's contribution to Lisette's letter to Herb was also a good reminder of family dynamics. Max listed twelve addresses of family and friends who might be invited to the wedding. "Those mentioned above to whom you may like to write is O.K. with us." And he continued: "How you feel about 177th St. is up to you." "177th St." did not appear on Max's list. That was where Max K. lived.

On 4 May, Eric wrote that Herb should not be fooled by Lisette and Max's efforts to put a good face on things; they were still distraught. The family traveled to Pittsburgh for the wedding and, the night before the ceremony, tried again to talk Herb out of his plans. They failed; Herb and Maggie married; and twenty-plus years of subsequent correspondence bear witness to the family's continued disappointment at Herb's distance as well as his choice of wife.

What does this well-documented and critical moment in one family's history tell us about private efforts to come to terms simultaneously with a difficult past and a difficult present? There are two chronological frames to this correspondence. The first is the literal time span of the exchange, three months in spring 1961. These three months have a clear arc. The earliest letters suggests a sort of bewilderment about the state of family relations. Correspondents express this bewilderment with language about drifting away from Judaism and lost closeness to family. In the second stage, the family is jolted into greater urgency as Herb clearly is not easily swayed from his plans. This urgency is expressed both by more poignant expressions of loss ("O Herbi") and by citing the enormity of history in the hope that historical argument might do the trick. It is in this phase that members of the family refer to anti-Semitic persecution, past and projected. Once it becomes clear that the argument is lost, the stage narrows sharply to the scale of the nuclear family, but now shorn of bewilderment or questioning, and instead with a sense of definitive break: "I know … how little you care for us." In the temporary armistice that constitutes the coda to this correspondence, the scope broadens ever so slightly, as decisions about whom to invite inevitably require discussion of the extended family. The reference to extended family, however, is practical and brief: it does not explicitly extend to the overlap of religious and familial fault lines.

The longer arc extends from Herb's childhood (when he grew up far from home) to generations into the future (when another Hitler may come). Flashbacks and flash-forwards appear scattered throughout the first two stages of the correspondence, but the clearest effort to order them—to create a historical narrative—appears in Lisette's lengthy letter of 8 March. "*First* we had to go through this hell, because we are Jews, [*then*] when we came to the USA we were kicked around, because we were not enough Jewish, and *now* you are coming and make us pay the big price for it" (emphasis added). Each step of the way has a different antagonist: first the Nazis, then the orthodox, then Herb. Although later correspondence is beyond the scope of this essay, it is notable that the same progression reappears in Eric's letters to Herb in the early 1980s.

How can we understand this narrowing of the stage: from the Nazis' deadly persecution of Jews, to aggravating but hardly lethal conflicts within the Jewish community and extended family, to the actions of a wayward son, whose main offences were leaving town for a medical career and marrying the (highly-educated, beautiful) woman of his choice? One possible explanation is literal: this sequence is, quite simply, the chronology of the greatest challenges Lisette (and by extension the family) faced. Yet the recounting of history is so closely intertwined with the immediate crisis that we must also consider its strategic value (in efforts to sway Herb) and the ways in which it was an expression of emotion (at a moment of anger and perceived loss). In the context of the family crisis of 1961, it is the evident equation of the antagonists rather than their chronological sequence that is most striking. Herb is now causing the family misery, just as Max K. and his orthodox circles have done since the family's arrival in New York—and just as the National Socialists had done even earlier.

The equation suggests a desperate argumentative strategy: if Herb could be made to understand that he was causing suffering just as the Nazis had, perhaps he would come around. It also, however, offers a way to interpret Lisette's manner of bringing past and present into dialogue with each other in order to emotionally manage both. To roughly equate Herb's marriage plans with Nazi persecution exaggerated Herb's offenses—but it also tamed National Socialism. More precisely, it reflected a taming of National Socialism that was already underway. This was not a household in which a hushed silence surrounded the subject of the Holocaust. Nor was it a household in which the survivor parents obsessively relived their experiences. Rather, Max and Lisette told stories of Theresienstadt matter-of-factly, giving the impression of neither repressing nor being overwhelmed by their memories of persecution.

For Max and Lisette, the Holocaust was not an event-outside-history; it was integrable into ordinary secular frameworks for understanding their lives. Lisette had witnessed her sister and mother's sufferings in Theresienstadt and further deportation. Yet the fact that most of her siblings had survived, and especially the reconstitution of the nuclear family she had created as a young adult, surely helped to make such an integration possible. Max's status as an only child of parents who had died of natural causes before the war made the continuity within Lisette's family into his key touchstone as well. For both Max and Lisette, the Holocaust was embedded in personal relationships that had preceded the war, persisted through it, and continued afterward. Behind any utterance of Lisette's regarding Max K. were memories of their childhood arguments, his postwar wealth—and his failure to try hard enough (in Lisette's opinion) to facilitate the emigration of members of the family left behind in Germany in the 1930s. Behind any utterance regarding Herb were memories of his cleverness as a young child, his decision to move to Durham for his medical residency—and Lisette and Max's wartime hopes of reconstituting family life with him and Eric.

It is impossible to know whether this integrable Holocaust was the result of a difficult but in some way successful struggle with episodes that had once caused unbearable pain—or whether this integration had itself been a strategy (even if unconsciously adopted) for surviving the persecution in the first place. If the former, it is impossible to reconstruct the path that led Lisette and Max to the emotional state in which they found themselves by 1961. We can, however, partially reconstruct the interplay of past and present in the imaginations of members of the Heineman family—and particularly Lisette—in 1961. Her words speak to deep tensions, but also to a way of making a troubled past manageable.

Still, it is hard to miss the melancholy in these letters. How had Herb come to be so estranged from the family? Had the estrangement started during the period of separation, as Herb had grown up "far from home"? Or perhaps during the early years of their reunion, when religious observance had caused tension and Lisette had interfered with Herb's renewed contact with Irene? Was the real turning point a few years after that, when Herb had decided to move to Durham? Or had the fundamental estrangement been much more recent—could all involved look to a time, just the previous fall, when Herb had been attracted to another woman but had recognized the relationship as futile because she was a Unitarian—showing, as Max wrote, "on this time you were closer to us & you still felt where you belong."[31] As historians, we might conclude that the process of estrangement was cumulative—but what is interesting here is the way family members themselves, at a moment of enormous stress, struggled to locate the origin of their troubles.

In her longest and most searching letter of the 1961 series, on 8 March, Lisette grieved that she could not rewrite the past. "Why didn't you talk to us in the beginning?" she plaintively asked. If only he had brought up the relationship with Maggie earlier, she implied, she could have talked him out of it before he had become too emotionally involved. But then, Lisette moved on to a formulation that suggests a slippage between the recent and more distant past. "Why didn't you talk to us in the beginning, or step back in time?" What she meant was: why had Herb not *stepped back* from his relationship with Maggie *in time* to salvage the situation? It is easy, however, to hear another meaning in Lisette's colloquial English: a wish that Herb might *step back in time*—to the year 1960, perhaps, before he had become involved with Maggie; or maybe 1956, before he had moved away from home; or 1946, before their reunion made the boys' orthodoxy a point of contention. Or perhaps, Lisette might have fantasized, they might turn back the clock to 1938—before she and Max had lost their son for the first time.

Elizabeth Heineman is a professor in the departments of History and Gender, Women's, and Sexuality Studies at the University of Iowa.

Notes

1. ACC/2793 Kindertransport file of Herbert Heinemann, London Metropolitan Archives, City of London. File accessed by the express permission of World Jewish Relief.
2. Mark Jonathan Harris and Deborah Oppenheimer, *Into the Arms of Strangers: Stories of the Kindertransport* (London, 2000); Gideon Behrendt and Claudia Curio, *Mit dem Kindertransport in die Freiheit: Vom jüdischen Flüchtling zum Corporal O'Brian* (Frankfurt, 2001).
3. 21 June 1945 Herb to Max and Lisette, Folder 3, Box 1, Herbert Heineman Collection, Leo Baeck Archive.
4. 31 May 1974 Herb to Lisette, author's personal collection.
5. Rebecca Earle, *Epistolary Selves: Letters and Letter-Writers, 1600–1945* (Aldershot, 1999).
6. Konrad H. Jarausch and Klaus Jochen Arnold, *Das Stille Sterben …: Feldpostbriefe von Konrad Jarausch aus Polen und Russland, 1939–1942* (Paderborn, 2008); Rebecca L. Boehling and Uta Larkey, *Life and Loss in the Shadow of the Holocaust: A Jewish Family's Untold Story* (Cambridge, 2011); Dorothee Wierling, *Eine Familie im Krieg: Leben, Sterben und Schreiben 1914–1918* (Hamburg, 2013).
7. Christa Hämmerle and Edith Saurer, "Frauenbriefe—Männerbriefe? Überlegungen zu einer Briefgeschichte jenseits von Geschlechterdichotomien," in *Briefkulturen und ihr Geschlecht: Zur Geschichte der privaten Korrespondenz vom 16. Jahrhundert bis Heute*, ed. Christa Hämmerle and Edith Saurer (Vienna, 2003).
8. Gudrun Maierhof et al., *Aus Kindern wurden Briefe: Die Rettung jüdscher Kinder aus Nazi-Deutschland* (Berlin, 2004).
9. Most of our information on the experience of the "Kinder" comes from oral histories and memoirs. The sole effort at large-scale data collection is the survey of the Association of Jewish Refugees, "Making New Lives in Britain," http://www.ajr.org.uk/kinder survey. The Association of Jewish Refugees sent out some 1,500 surveys to Kinder with known addresses and received in response 1,025 "main questionnaires" filled out by living Kinder and 343 "supplementary questionnaires" filled out by friends or relatives

of deceased Kinder. Long-lived Kinder and those who remained in Britain were over-represented in this census.

10. Vera Fast, *Children's Exodus: A History of the Kindertransport* (London, 2011), 166.

11. Karen Gershon, ed., *We Came as Children: A Collective Autobiography* (London, 1966); Bertha Leverton and Shmuel Lowensohn, *I Came Alone: The Stories of the Kindertransports* (Lewes, 1990); Edith Milton, *The Tiger in the Attic: Memories of the Kindertransport and Growing up English* (Chicago, 2005). For a differentiated telling of a complex reunion, see Gerd Korman, *Nightmare's Fairy Tale: A Young Refugee's Home Fronts, 1938–1948* (Madison, WI, 2005).

12. Judith Tydor Baumel-Schwartz, *Never Look Back: The Jewish Refugee Children in Great Britain, 1938–1945* (West Lafayette, IN, 2012).

13. For testimony of two mothers who made it to the United Kingdom before the war: Charlotte Levy and Franzi Groszmann, both in Harris and Oppenheimer, *Into the Arms of Strangers, passim.*

14. Mary J. Gallant, "The *Kindertransport*: Gender and the Rescue of Jewish Children 1938–39," in *Different Horrors, Same Hell: Gender and the Holocaust,* ed. Myrna Goldenberg and Amy H Shapiro (Seattle, 2013), 198–217.

15. The correspondence of 1939–46 is held in the Leo Baeck Institute in New York. Subsequent correspondence is in my possession, as are recordings of oral histories.

16. Perceptive discussions by scholars reflecting on their experience writing about their own families include Sheila Fitzpatrick, "Getting Personal: On Subjectivity in Historical Practice," in *Unsettling History: Archiving and Narrating in Historiography,* ed. Sebastian Jobs and Alf Lüdtke (Frankfurt, 2010), 183–98; Irene Kacandes, *Daddy's War: Greek American Stories* (Lincoln, NE, 2009); Marianne Hirsch and Leo Spitzer, *Ghosts of Home: The Afterlife of Czernowitz in Jewish Memory* (Berkeley, CA, 2010).

17. This summary draws heavily on oral histories with Herb Heineman, Maggie Heineman, Irene Ruschin, Miriam Rosen, and George Kronenberg.

18. On the significance of cognitive and emotional development on the experience of children of different ages, see Susan Rubin Suleiman, "The 1.5 Generation: Thinking about Child Survivors and the Holocaust," *American Imago* 59, no. 3 (2002): 277–95.

19. Helen Epstein, *Children of the Holocaust: Conversations with Sons and Daughters of Survivors* (New York, 1988); Anne Karpf, *The War After: Living with the Holocaust* (London, 1996).

20. On such efforts to maintain "normalcy," Michael Geyer, "Virtue in Despair," *History & Memory* 17, no. 1/2 (2005): 323–65.

21. Eric to Herb, 14 February 1961; Max to Herb, 17 February 1961, author's personal collection.

22. As quoted in Lisette to Herb, 14 February 1961; Max to Herb, 17 February 1961.

23. Lisette to Herb, 17 February 1961.

24. Lisette to Herb, 14 February 1961.

25. Ibid.

26. Lisette to Herb, 27 February 1961.

27. Lisette to Herb, 8 March 1961.

28. Lisette to Herb, 22 March 1961.

29. Lisette to Herb, 8 March 1961.

30. Lisette to Herb, 29 March 1961.

31. Max to Herb, 14 February 1961.

Bibliography

ACC/2793 (Records of the Refugee Children's Movement), London Metropolitan Archives, City of London.

The Association of Jewish Refugees. "Making New Lives in Britain." Retrieved from http://www.ajr.org.uk/kindersurvey.

Baumel-Schwartz, Judith Tydor. *Never Look Back: The Jewish Refugee Children in Great Britain, 1938–1945.* West Lafayette, IN: Purdue University Press, 2012.

Behrendt, Gideon, and Claudia Curio. *Mit dem Kindertransport in die Freiheit: Vom jüdischen Flüchtling zum Corporal O'Brian.* Frankfurt: Fischer Taschenbuch Verlag, 2001.

Boehling, Rebecca L., and Uta Larkey. *Life and Loss in the Shadow of the Holocaust: A Jewish Family's Untold Story.* Cambridge: Cambridge University Press, 2011.

Earle, Rebecca. *Epistolary Selves: Letters and Letter-Writers, 1600–1945.* Aldershot: Ashgate, 1999.

Epstein, Helen. *Children of the Holocaust: Conversations with Sons and Daughters of Survivors.* New York: Penguin Books, 1988.

Fast, Vera. *Children's Exodus: A History of the Kindertransport.* London: IB Tauris, 2011.

Fitzpatrick, Sheila. "Getting Personal: On Subjectivity in Historical Practice." In *Unsettling History: Archiving and Narrating in Historiography,* edited by Sebastian Jobs and Alf Lüdtke, 183–98. Frankfurt: Campus Verlag, 2010.

Gallant, Mary J. "The *Kindertransport*: Gender and the Rescue of Jewish Children 1938–39." In *Different Horrors, Same Hell: Gender and the Holocaust,* edited by Myrna Goldenberg and Amy H. Shapiro, 198–217. Seattle: University of Washington Press, 2013.

Gershon, Karen, ed. *We Came as Children: A Collective Autobiography.* London: Gollancz, 1966.

Geyer, Michael. "Virtue in Despair." *History & Memory* 17, no. 1/2 (2005): 323–65.

Hämmerle, Christa, and Edith Saurer. "Frauenbriefe—Männerbriefe? Überlegungen zu Eener Briefgeschichte jenseits von Geschlechterdichotomien." In *Briefkulturen und ihr Geschlecht: Zur Geschichte der privaten Korrespondenz vom 16. Jahrhundert bis Heute,* edited by Christa Hämmerle and Edith Saurer. Vienna: Böhlau, 2003.

Harris, Mark Jonathan, and Deborah Oppenheimer. *Into the Arms of Strangers: Stories of the Kindertransport.* London: Bloomsbury, 2000.

Hirsch, Marianne, and Leo Spitzer. *Ghosts of Home: The Afterlife of Czernowitz in Jewish Memory.* Berkeley: University of California Press, 2010.

Jarausch, Konrad H., and Klaus Jochen Arnold. *Das Stille Sterben …: Feldpostbriefe von Konrad Jarausch aus Polen und Russland, 1939–1942.* Paderborn: Schöningh, 2008.

Kacandes, Irene. *Daddy's War: Greek American Stories.* Lincoln: University of Nebraska Press, 2009.

Karpf, Anne. *The War After: Living with the Holocaust.* London: Minerva, 1996.

Korman, Gerd. *Nightmare's Fairy Tale: A Young Refugee's Home Fronts, 1938–1948.* Madison, WI: University of Wisconsin Press, 2005.

Leverton, Bertha, and Shmuel Lowensohn. *I Came Alone: The Stories of the Kindertransports.* Lewes: Book Guild, 1990.

Hermann, Simon, Gudrun Maierhof, and Chana Schütz, *Aus Kindern wurden Briefe: Die Rettung jüdscher Kinder aus Nazi Deutschland.* Berlin: Edition Berlin im Metropol Verlag, 2004.

Milton, Edith. *The Tiger in the Attic: Memories of the Kindertransport and Growing up English.* Chicago: University of Chicago Press, 2005.

Suleiman, Susan Rubin. "The 1.5 Generation: Thinking about Child Survivors and the Holocaust." *American Imago* 59, no. 3 (2002): 277–95.

Wierling, Dorothee. *Eine Familie im Krieg: Leben, Sterben und Schreiben 1914–1918.* Hamburg: Wallstein, 2013.

Index